John Strange Winter

Cavalry Life

Sketches and stories in barracks and out

John Strange Winter

Cavalry Life
Sketches and stories in barracks and out

ISBN/EAN: 9783337815509

Printed in Europe, USA, Canada, Australia, Japan

Cover: Foto ©ninafisch / pixelio.de

More available books at **www.hansebooks.com**

CAVALRY LIFE

OR

SKETCHES AND STORIES

IN BARRACKS AND OUT

By J. S. WINTER

A NEW EDITION

London

CHATTO AND WINDUS, PICCADILLY

1885

LONDON :

KELLY AND CO., PRINTERS,

GATE STREET, LINCOLN'S INN FIELDS, W.C. ;

AND MIDDLE MILL, KINGSTON.

PREFACE.

I HAVE received orders from my publishers to write a Preface to the collection of sketches now to be offered to the public.

A Preface! What an order! I would as soon write another volume; it certainly would be the easier task of the twain. It has to be done, of course; but how, I don't know. I never wrote a Preface in my life. I have not the least idea how to set about it; though I am in an utter agony of apprehension, lest defects in this absolute necessity should "mull" the effect of the whole.

I have consulted a friend on the subject, who says: "Pooh! if you can write a book full of sketches, you can write a Preface;" and he says it as glibly as if it is nothing more difficult than an acceptance of a dinner invitation, and can be dashed off at a moment's notice.

I explain to him that a book full of "sketches" is an easy matter. I simply take a real soldier out of a real regiment, and give him somebody else's real name; I put real jokes into his mouth, and relate real incidents which happened to him or to somebody else. But I cannot do that with a Preface; where shall I find a Preface in real life?

My friend assumes a serious aspect; and, leaving the question of the Preface altogether, remarks that, in his opinion, I am playing a dangerous game.

"Supposing," says he, wisely, "supposing any fellow recognizes his own portrait."

I know that "any fellow" is much more likely to recognize some "other fellow's" portrait than his own: though, goodness knows, they are nearly all unvarnished enough for the most obtuse self-blindness to see clearly through the thin disguise cast over them.

Mais revenons à nos moutons—otherwise our Preface! I fear all this is terribly out of order; yet there are one or two things I should like to say, whether they are out of order or not.

I wish the sketches to be taken strictly for what they are—*portraits from life* of our British-born sons of Mars. I own frankly that characters and incidents are, for the most part, real characters and incidents, slightly shuffled and embroidered; and that *all* have a foundation of truth.

The old letters introduced into "His Princess" (date 1759-1761) are simply copies of the originals. I certainly did mend up the spelling and the punctuation a bit—both were vile: for, finding it such a nuisance to wade through them myself, I feared my readers would never trouble to look at them, unless I *translated* them into plainer English.

And thus I launch my military children (not quite of fancy) upon the world; dedicating the portraits to the originals—to all the gentlemen who have been unconsciously my models, I make my bow, and sign myself the thereby greatly obliged

AUTHOR!

CONTENTS.

CAVALRY LIFE.

REGIMENTAL LIFE.

Very few people have any conception of how severe a school the Army is. I speak more especially of the mounted branch of the service, because popular writers of fiction are more fond of "writing up" cavalry officers than any other.

One has grown intimately acquainted with life in the mess-room, as so many authors depict it. One has learned all the names officers are popularly supposed to bestow upon one another. There is always a colonel, old, white-haired, and singularly amiable, who is a sort of protecting father to all his officers. He looks after their love-affairs, of which, by-the-bye, in real life, a chief is supposed to remain in blissful ignorance. He sees they are not "put upon" by their seniors; is frequently spoken to as "old fellow," and very often falls in love with the young lady who has gained the affections of one of his "subs." of, say, six weeks' standing.

Then comes the major; generally a woman-hater this. Why a major should invariably hold the fair sex in detestation is not often explained; but there the truth is, stern and unvarnished, and the reader has to make the best of it. Sometimes this woman-hater falls in love, and is transformed into a husband of the most exemplary description, but more often he remains in his unpleasant character to the end of the chapter.

I wonder does it never occur to the writer that, in the natural course of events, a man fond of soldiering, who sticks to it, must get promotion? In that case, does the major take up his

B

predecessor's paternal line of action, and was the typical chief a woman-hater also, before he obtained his regiment?

Amongst the captains there are various characters; there is one who can do anything or everything. He can sing, hunt, fish, ride—he can win a steeple-chase on the veriest screw, by virtue of his brilliant riding; he can shoot, draw, and paint, act, dance, and do everything under the sun with equal perfection. He is one of those whom the gods love, and he does not die young. He is like the princess in the fairy tale, who was fortunate enough to have three fairy godmothers, for every luxury and blessing seems to have been showered down upon him. He is singularly handsome, too—generally of the type which, but for the moustaches, might serve for the face of a young duchess; he has more money than he can spend, which, as he is in a cavalry regiment, must be considerable. He has a wonderful constitution too, for he can drink all night—brandy-and-sodas, save the mark!—and yet he is up with the lark in the morning, at some innocent and healthy pursuit, which, though you might find occupying a schoolboy, never, in this world, induced an officer, after a night of unlimited brandy-and-soda, to turn out of his comfortable bed until the very last moment. And the most wonderful of all is that, in spite of these excesses, our hero's eyes never lose their brightness or their clearness; his hand and aim are invariably as steady as a rock.

To finish the list of this gentleman's charms, he is an accomplished flirt; his very name is a terror to mothers and husbands, and yet he usually ends by marrying some insipid unformed child just out of the schoolroom, and, like the married major, settles down into a steady-going country squire, without a wish or an idea beyond his childish wife, his hunting, and his short-horns; in fact, he sinks into a state of bucolic stupidity, and altogether forgets the days when he was the boast—very frequently the toast—of "ours," and was known far and wide as "Beauty" so-and-so.

Then there is another captain who smokes. Of him we do not see very much; his life, his thoughts, his conversation, and his character may be summed up in the single word *smoke ;* and so very properly his existence, for us, is but hazy.

The senior subaltern and his duties are utterly ignored ; and most prominent of all these military children of fancy is the young cornet. He is very young, this wonderful boy, and he has a decided tendency to go wrong ; but every one pets him and makes much of him, and he is popularly known as " Baby " or " Prettyface," sometimes as " the Cherub " or " the Seraph." For this youth the protecting friendliness of the fatherly colonel comes into play, and it is wonderful how many duties and infringements he is excused. He, like our friend the popular captain, is fair to look upon, being of the duchess type, graceful in bearing, and dainty in coloring.

Lastly, we have the regimental surgeon, whom we must one and all own a perfect monstrosity. He is lanky, ugly, ill-dressed, speaks with a strong brogue, or maybe a Tyne-side twang or Northumbrian burr, and altogether excites the curiosity of the reader as to how such a man attained his position.

Sometimes we are admitted into the troop-rooms, and the chief feature we find there is the blind devotion of the men to the officers, or *one* officer in particular ; not only blind devotion, but passionate admiration and keen interest in all their proceedings.

How very, very different is real life in a barrack ! How respectful the " sir " with which the colonel and the major are addressed ! How very different is the behaviour of the junior officers, and how mercilessly severe are the manner and judgments of " the senior sub." !

The very slightest infringement of regimental rules is visited with an ante-room court-martial ; and the punishments awarded are no mere child's play ; they are often corporal, and in all cases severe.

In one regiment, which for convenience' sake we will call the Cuirassiers, two subs., lately joined, omitted to rise for early stables, when it was their turn for duty as orderly-officer. The result was, not that these two only were reprimanded, but that the whole of the subalterns were called into the orderly room, and, to use their own language, were "jolly well slated." The two delinquents were not especially mentioned, and thought to hear no more of the matter. Not so. The others simply bided their time until midnight, when, the senior officer having retired, an ante-room court-martial was called, and the defaulters were brought up for trial, and, being convicted, sentenced to punishment. And in what did that punishment consist? Not in a "slating," but each was sentenced to receive three strokes of a birch rod from every member of the court-martial; that is, about thirty strokes each, and *well laid on !*

As soon as a subaltern joins his regiment, he is submitted to a course of practical jokes, ill-treatment, and bullying all round, to which he must offer no resistance, or his career will be a short one. For instance, a few years ago a man named Royd joined this same regiment, and on his first evening amongst his new comrades was "drawn." That is to say, he was visited in his room during the small hours of the morning and ordered to go down into the ante-room for court-martial, the charge against him being that he had risen from the dinner-table whilst an officer senior to him remained sitting. Royd, being of huge stature and gigantic strength, stoutly resisted, and eventually picked up the largest man in the room, carried him out on to the landing, and dropped him over the baluster on to the flagged passage below. The effect was magical; in an instant all the hubbub was hushed, and the injured man was raised. Fortunately the result was nothing worse than a sprained ankle and a severely-bruised hip. He took it very quietly, and merely looked up at Royd, who was standing near, and said coolly, " I'll have you out for this."

Very possibly the new-comer did not think much of the threat, but his career was virtually over; at every hour of the day and night did he have cause to repent that hasty action, and during the autumn manœuvres of that year the climax came. It was in this wise; on a pouring wet day, or rather night, he had to visit the pickets, and as, for some reason, he had no horse, was compelled to do the rounds on foot. On coming in after a tramp of some miles thoroughly soaked and tired out, he was ordered to visit yet another outlying picket six or seven miles away. Then was his tormentor's opportunity; he would not permit him to take a troop horse, though he himself was riding. Tired, cold, and wet, this young subaltern reached the picket; something went wrong, as did his temper, and he swore at one of the men. His fate was sealed. His senior immediately put him under arrest, and he was told by the colonel that he must send in his papers or undergo trial by court-martial. Of course he left the regiment.

A young officer is not even permittted to dress himself as he pleases. It was reported in the ante-room of the Cuirassiers that one of the junior officers had been seen in Piccadilly wearing an inverness cloak. On his return from town he was ordered by the senior captain to produce the article in question, and it was burnt before his eyes.

" Whilst you are an officer of the Cuirassiers, sir," said the senior captain, " you will dress like a gentleman, and not as if you had bought your clothes out of a slop-shop in Bloomsbury."

Sometimes a newly-joined officer attempts the hail-fellow-well-met style of intercourse with his seniors, but his intentions are nipped in the bud with marvellous celerity. Such an one joined the Cuirassiers during the leave season, and tried his system upon the major.

" Ah, Houghton," said he, one day after lunch, while several officers, including the major, were standing about the ante-room fire, " will you go down to the rink with me this afternoon ?"

The cool audacity of this proposal stopped every tongue in the room, and all listened breathlessly for the major's reply.

" I don't mind," he said quietly, much more quietly than they had expected, but probably he wished to see how far this young gentleman's assurance would take him.

" Ah, very well. I'll be ready about four o'clock, so come round to my rooms and look me up."

This was a matter for the senior sub.'s notice, and although he was not in the room at the time, the conversation was quickly reported to him, and he as quickly sent for the delinquent.

"Now look here, young chap," he began, " this sort of thing won't do at all. If the major asks you to go anywhere with him, you will tell him whether you'll go or you won't, but you'll not propose going to the rink or anywhere else with him. And another thing, when you address him you will say ' major' or ' sir.' I am very much astonished that the major did not speak to you himself about it."

Then life in a barrack is by no means such an existence of ease, luxury, and time-killing as novelists would fain make us believe. Take, for example, the duties of the orderly officer for the day. He must rise at six o'clock for early stables, or the whole of the subalterns suffer in consequence; then he has to go round the breakfasts, see that they are all right, and hear any complaints ; then if it is not a field day he must ride with the troops to watering order ; he must visit the hospital ; then come morning stables, and as likely as not, if he be stationed at Aldershot or Colchester, he will be on court-martial, for which he has all the nuisance of getting into full dress, and may think himself very lucky if he miss the orderly-room business and the round of the dinners. In the afternoon he must again visit the hospital, and probably there will be a parade ; certainly he will have the picket to mount, and as likely as not he will have to walk a mile or so to do it. Then he has the first hour's rest of the day, and at half-past five he must turn out again for afternoon stables and " teas;" then hospital once more. He does eat his dinner in peace, but he must receive the watch-setting reports and mount the guard ere bedtime. Nor should mention be omitted of the number of times the orderly officer has to sign his name and to change his uniform. If his turn fall upon Sunday, he must accompany the commanding officer round the married quarters, but as some compensation for that he escapes church parade, and so is spared the trouble of getting into full dress—no light matter, more especially in the item of the boots.

The imposition of fines is another method of punishing infringements of regimental rules. If an officer is not properly shaven, if he puts on any part of his uniform wrongly, he must pay for the champagne drunk at dinner that evening. This fine is also enforced for swearing or using bad language in the presence of the chaplain or any senior officer, and also for dropping the sword. On certain occasions an officer must pay when it is not a case of fining. If he gets promotion, if he brings home the regiment from the drill field for the first time as commanding officer, if he wins a race, or is going to be married, at all such times he has to " stand " champagne.

Our novelists do well to give their military heroes an inexhaustible rent-roll. There are very few such out of the Guards, and soldier servants have to be very well up in methods of getting rid of duns and such other unwelcome visitors as their masters do not care to be at home to.

Another terrible mistake made by novelists is the magnificence with which they surround their heroes in quarters. If such could but once peep into the room (for an officer has seldom but one room, even if he is no longer a subaltern, excepting at Colchester, where each cavalry officer has a room about 12 feet by 14 and a tiny dressing-room, just half that size) of any ordinary hussar, dragoon, or lancer, he or she—I suspect it is most often the women who are so fond of soldier heroes—would never again depict him in rooms resembling a very fine lady's boudoir. Oh, the patched walls, the bare paint, the marks on the door where the lock gave way the last time the owner was " drawn " by his comrades, the blackened ceiling, the almost invariable absence of window-blinds, the miserable regulation fender fastened to the floor, the more miserable regulation coal-scuttle, and, most miserable of all, the regulation barrack chairs! It is all so wonderfully unlike the barrack-room of fiction. There is the very rickety crib of a bed, made to take in pieces upon occasion, and which by daytime the servant, with the aid of cretonne covers for the pillows and a fur carriage rug, converts into a sofa; and there is the dressing-table, likewise hung all round with cretonne, and which strikes one as being remarkably high for its purpose. Just pull the cretonne curtain a little, and half the front will open, showing you that it is but a make-believe table after all, and, stripped of its hangings, would stand forth a packing-case! Well, it is both a toilette-table and a wardrobe now, for piled upon the shelves, which have been put in temporarily, are the various suits of clothes belonging to the owner of the room.

Then over there, on the other side of the room, is the inevitable chest of drawers, which, when travelling, just fit nicely inside the dressing-table. They are exactly like the drawers in every room in the barracks; are of mahogany, have brass handles, and a despatch box and writing desk combined in the middle drawer at the top. Then the lid of our friend's bath, being fitted with three legs which screw in and out at pleasure, makes a very convenient writing table if covered with a cloth, and into the bath itself, for travelling, the legs go, together with the tripod, washing-stand, and the tin basin and ewer. Some officers have pianos, but they are always hired; and most officers have a few pictures and little trifles to scatter about their room. For instance, a couple of fur rugs thrown across the huge barrack armchairs take off from their ugliness much; and if a soldier is fortunate enough to know a lady who will work him a cover for his cot, his room will look much more presentable. And yet at best a soldier's room is but a " shake-down;" and if he be rich or poor, he seldom attempts to make it otherwise. The handsomest room I ever saw in barracks was that of a captain of dragoons; in fact, he had been fortunate enough to secure two large rooms, those which, if he had required them, would have been allotted to the major. This man was very rich, and had certainly taken a good deal of trouble to make his rooms habitable, and yet—well, they were only barrack-rooms. There were the usual make-shifts; and when the fur rug slipped off the great easy chair in which I sat, I saw the broad straps which served for arms, and which told me it was just the same as I had seen in barrack-rooms so many times before.

The rooms of a well-known colonel of cavalry, a man who now possesses a title and thirty thousand a year, were simply beggarly, not nearly so handsome as was the one little room of his Vet., of which I had just a glimpse. And why? Because one room was the man's hobby; the other was not.

One more word and I have done ; it concerns the fancy names bestowed upon soldiers in novels. They are all fancy names, and in real life do not exist. In no case have I ever known a name given in recognition of a man's personal comeliness, such as Cherub, Beauty, Adonis, Apollo, Prettyface, and the like. One of the handsomest men I ever knew was commonly known as The Spider. Why, I cannot tell—not because he was like one. In closing, I will give a few names I have actually known : The Infant (weighing twenty-one stone), The Cob, David, The Winter Apple, King Kobo, Old Muzzie, The Spider, Landy-fandy-Widden, Sprouts, Bole, The Admiral, Paddy K——, Tin Whistle, Illigant John of Bath, The Lady-Killer, Mother Hubbard, Billy Buttons, Piggie, Alphabet. Most frequently men's own names are abbreviated; thus at one time in a distinguished lancer regiment there were any amount of Bills and Billys. In another of hussars, the name of David prevailed ; nearly all were Davids, even a racehorse belonging to one of the officers.

When the personal appearance of an officer is not prepossessing, a name is quickly found for him. Any remark on the subject of " looks " meets with a rejoinder sharp and to the point. Said one Cuirassier to another,

" Why, your nose is so stuck up, one might hang one's hat on it."

" Well, my dear chap," was the ready reply, " one certainly couldn't on yours."

And it was true enough.

A REGIMENTAL MARTYR;

OR, HOW GERARD ST. HILARY WAS DRIVEN INTO MATRIMONY.

CHAPTER I.

"MAKE hay in St. Hilary's room to night."

Lieutenant Gerard St. Hilary came leisurely down the broad corridor and staircase of the officers' quarters in the cavalry barracks at Milchester, and crossed the passage leading to the ante-room. As he turned the handle of the door, a fragment of the conversation within fell upon his ear—"*Make hay in St. Hilary's room to-night.*"

"The deuce!" ejaculated that young gentleman.

"Sentry-box him first," cried a voice, which he recognised as Captain Gurney's, a man well up the list of captains, who was old enough to have known better, "and if that doesn't fetch him, hammer the door in."

"Ha, ha, ha!" laughed a chorus of voices, under cover of which the intended victim beat a retreat.

"Sentry-box me! Ah, thank you, Captain Gurney," he exclaimed, when he had reached the shelter of his own room; "forewarned is forearmed, and I'm on my guard, this time."

Hastily changing his undress for mufti, Mr. St. Hilary made the best of his way out of barracks, going in the direction of Milchester.

The regiment of which he was butt-in-chief for practical jokes, was the 52nd Dragoons of famous Peninsular memory. Perhaps his unfailing good temper made him more subject to this form of wit than would have been the case if he had borne malice and sulked.

An outsider would, perhaps, say, Why did not he report the

offenders, and so secure peace? But anyone with the least knowledge of regimental life could answer, that for a subaltern to adopt such a course would simply be to limit his career in the army to a very short period. Of course during the process he blustered a good deal, and frequently threatened to tell the chief all about it the very first thing in the morning; but, fortunately for his brother officers, Gerard St. Hilary had a peculiarity. After two a.m. he could not keep his eyes open, and was glad to make any bargain which would leave him in peace.

It was invariably the same; Lieutenant St. Hilary, lightly clad, as likely as not soaked with water, standing in the centre of a group of excited comrades in mess-dress, expressing his determination " to have no more of this foolery, by Jove !"

" Go it, Jerry; pile it up, my boy !" one would cry, amidst the jeers of the bystanders.

" I'm surprised at you, D'Albert," poor Jerry would cry in disgust. " I'll report you in the morning, upon my soul I will, though you are a captain."

Small heed did the 52nd take of these awful threats. Was not the end unchanging? Presently St. Hilary would begin to shiver; then Sleep would come dropping her grains of sand into Gerard's blue eyes, and his comrades knew that then was their time.

" Now, Jerry, old man, if you forgive us, you shall go to bed."

" Well, let me be quiet," was poor Jerry's answer (it was always the same), " and I'll say no more about it."

The gratitude of the rioters was generally shown on these occasions by the careful way in which they tucked Gerard up in bed and reduced his room to something like order. Alas ! only something. Order generally took days and a visit to the upholsterer's to effect, with much groaning from Jerry's man on the subject of what he called " them idjiots."

Poor Gerard had undergone every possible form of practical joking, and he was become a little tired of it; the trodden worm will turn, and he was thoroughly determined to put a stop to it once for all, though it must be owned he didn't quite know how to set about it.

However, enough on that head. I will just explain what is meant by "sentry-boxing" and "making hay," and then go on with my story.

The doors of an officer's rooms are usually made of strong material, the hammering in of which is a long process; in order therefore, to draw the victim from his lair without his suspecting mischief they knock at his door, and tell him the colonel or the major wants him at once, or cry "Fire!" at the other end of the corridor. If this succeeds, well and good; but on gala nights the sentry-box is brought into play. It is placed close against the victim's door, after the manner of a trap, so that when he comes out he may go crash against the back of the box. I need not add that the more bruised and angry he is the better pleased his comrades are.

Making hay is simply breaking or turning topsy-turvy everything the intruders can lay their hands upon.

The cavalry barracks at Milchester are about a mile from the town, which is a cathedral city, chiefly noted for the beauty of its young ladies and the good tone of its society.

In common with most cathedral towns Milchester was just a little dull. In summer the Botanical Gardens, and in winter the Winter Palace, were the principal places of amusement. To the latter Mr. St. Hilary made his way, it being, when my story opens, the dreary month of November. It was an "off" day. Had the bonny dappled hounds been after their little red-coated friend, Captain Gurney would probably have come in too tired and stiff to think of anything beyond his dinner and his bed; but there was no meet that day, and thus we have a striking instance of what Satan finds for idle hands, which is not, I trust, too severe a reflection on the gentlemen of her Majesty's army.

It was three o'clock; the Palace was full, and a crowd of well-dressed people were promenading to the strains of "Ger-leibt und Verloren" waltz.

Gerard passed in with all speed, and quickly made his way

up and down the gay throng, as though seeking for some particular individual. He was evidently a great favourite with the fair sex, for wherever he went he was greeted with smiles and other little pleasantries. Tall, short, fair, or dark, all seemed equally pleased to see him. There were girls in blue and girls in green, in sealskin and sable, in spoon bonnets and pork-pie hats; and for each and all he had a bright word or compliment, but he lingered with none.

He did not find the object of his search very readily, for he was a trifle short-sighted, and, as I know from experience, the wearing of an eyeglass confines one's sight to the space immediately in front.

At last his patience was rewarded; walking slowly with several gentlemen came a young lady, who attracted the attention and admiration of all. She was not very tall, rather under than over the middle height, with a graceful figure and carriage, delicate little hands and feet, and a small mignon face, of which the nose was just a wee bit up-turned, and the eyes were brilliant gleaming hazel. Her hair, which was extremely abundant, was twisted round her small shapely head in massive coils, and was of the deepest auburn hue. She was dressed in a tight-fitting costume of prune-coloured serge, and her hat was of the same material. Her waist and throat were clasped by heavy silver belt and necklet.

The name of this young lady was Elinor Warwick. Her father held the appointment of deputy-assistant commissary-general. She lived on the same side of the town as the barracks were situated, and was, as was natural from her father's position, on very intimate terms with both the cavalry and infantry officers stationed in Milchester.

The preference was, however, given to the former, and Mr. St. Hilary enjoyed the distinction of being Miss Warwick's slave-in-chief. Poor Gerard, slave-in-chief and butt-in-chief! Not an enviable fate; but the former office he would not have delegated for any consideration, while words will not express Mr. St. Hilary's feelings on the subject of the latter.

It was a remarkable fact that, although ladies never could

see anything in Miss Warwick, " a little pert snub-nosed thing," she always had three or four men " in tow." On that afternoon she had a cavalier either side, while one or two others made up the rear. As she said herself, " The clumsy fellows could never get out of the way; it was just like walking with outriders."

Gerard went up, his blue eyes ablaze, and sauntered alongside of her for some distance, to the intense disgust of the man he had supplanted. Miss Elinor had, however, no intention of allowing him to remain there. Her way of showing him favour was by ill-using him, yet giving him certain small liberties which she did not accord to the men she took the most pains to please. One man would say to another when she was ordering Gerard about, " I would not stand that; what a big duffer the fellow is !"

But Gerard would not have exchanged the sweet familiarity of his intercourse with Elinor for all the civil speeches in the world; in fact, it was a case of " Betty know'd her man."

" You're coming to our ball, Miss Warwick ?" asked he.

" Oh, yes, of course !" she answered, in a quick clear voice.

" How many am I to have ?" pleadingly.

" I really don't know. How many do you want ?"

" Every one."

" Well, but you can't have them. I'll give you one quadrille if you like, the third."

" And four waltzes besides ?"

" No," very decisively. " I'll give you three, if you will make yourself generally useful and agreeable this afternoon; do your duty like a man, you know."

" May I walk home with you ?"

" Well—yes."

" I won't do it for three," announced he, leaning forward with a dangerous look in his blue eyes.

" Four, then," said Elinor, in rather a frightened tone.

" *And* supper."

" Now, Mr. St. Hilary, you're asking too much. It's not in season,"

" And supper," repeated our hero firmly, " or I'll not stir an inch."

" Well, go away."

Away he went, having learned a soldier's first lesson thoroughly. He managed to keep Miss Warwick in sight, and when she disappeared from the gay throng, he followed in time to help her into a huge fawn-coloured paletot, which, as the inhabitants of Milchester remarked, "no one but Miss Warwick would have the courage to wear."

As the two walked home together through the dreary November fog, Elinor became aware that something was amiss with her companion. More than once he sighed dolefully, and was altogether so different from the Gerard St. Hilary whose jolly laugh was heard every two minutes, that she was completely puzzled.

" Whatever is the matter, Mr. St. Hilary ?" she said at last.

" Oh !" moaned Gerard, with another long sigh, " I've got such a dose before me to-night."

" A dose ?"

" Yes; the fellows are going to make hay in my room to-night."

" Make hay !" repeated Elinor, in a tone of real surprise. " What, in November ?"

Then Gerard told her what he had heard, and described the process.

" I assure you, Miss Warwick," he said, shaking his head solemnly, " that by this time to-morrow everything in my room will be smashed to bits."

" What a shame !" cried Elinor, warmly. " If I were you I'd try——"

" What ?"

She reached up to her companion's ear, and whispered a few words to him ; he burst into a roar of laughter.

" By Jove, what a brick you are !" he cried, forgetting his manners. "I never heard such a splendid idea in my life. Gad, what a clever girl you must be !"

" It's quite original," she responded, saucily.

" It's absolutely perfect," replied Gerard, "and worthy of you in every way.   How they will hop to-night !"

Elinor's musical treble joined his deeper laugh ; and as she parted from him at the gate of her father's house, she turned back, and said impressively,

" Mind it's white, and don't stint the quantity."

" All right," answered Gerard ; " I'll get plenty."

He did not go into the barracks, but walked past them straight into Milchester, meeting on his way several of the officers returning to dinner.   He evaded all their enquiries and offers to go back with him, and went on his way alone.   He stopped at the first tinner's shop he came to, and purchased the largest flour-dredger they had.   This he took with him, in spite of the shopman's entreaties to be allowed to send it.   He next went to a general dealer's, and made another purchase, which he put into his pocket with much care, and as though he were very much afraid the paper might burst.   What could it be?

Lieutenant St. Hilary went to mess that night with a face as innocent as that of a little child.

" Well, Jerry, my boy," quoth Captain Gurney, " what have you been doing to-day ?"

Gerard looked at his superior sideways.   He would have known what this display of affectionate interest meant without any previous warning.

" Palace," answered he, with laconic laziness.

" Was the lovely Elinor there ?"

" Yes."

" Did you see her home ?"

" Of course."

" Have tea there ?"

" No ; I had some shopping to do," with a little grin at the remembrance of that same shopping, " I'm downright done up. Trailing up and down that Palace is fifty times harder work than hunting.   I shall turn in early to-night, to be fit for to-morrow," with another small grin at the look of intelligence which passed round the room.   " Are any of you fellows going to the theatre to-night?   They're having *The Rivals.*"

"Yes," answered Gurney; "but I can't go. I've promised to go in and see old Patterson to-night; so I'm on duty."

"On duty," thought Gerard; "on duty with a sentry-box."

After this the conversation was on general topics; and soon after eleven o'clock Gerard, with many yawns, departed, ostensibly to bed. To that haven of rest, however, he did not go, but, piling up his fire, threw himself into an easy chair, and quietly bided his time.

He had not long to wait; for presently he heard the sound of men treading lightly in their stockings. Thereupon he carefully snored, so as to make them believe he was safe in the arms of Morpheus.

"He's fast asleep," he heard Middleton say.

"Then fetch it, and be quick," was the answer.

As noiselessly as possible the heavy sentry-box was brought up and placed against his door. Then the officers, retreating, went laughing, and with much joking and bear-fighting, to their different rooms, shutting the doors with good hearty bangs, which seemed to indicate retirement for the night.

In a few moments a sharp knocking began at Gerard's door.

"Hallo!" bawled he, in a sleepy voice; "who's there?"

"Please, sir, the colonel wants you at once. There's something wrong with B troop, sir."

B troop was Gerard's.

"Tell the colonel to go and be hanged," was Gerard's unceremonious answer.

"I daren't, sir," was the reply.

"You daren't! Then go and be hanged yourself! This fish don't bite."

"He twigs it!" shouted Middleton. "Come out, you beggar, or we'll stove the door in!"

"Stove away, old man!" laughed Gerard, rising, and taking his flour-dredger to within a yard of the door.

"Come on!" yelled Gurney's voice. "Yeave ho, push with a will, boys; nothing like haymaking!"

Gerard waited till they were all exerting their strength to the uttermost; then flung open the door, showering the

C

contents of the flour-dredger upon them as they tumbled head-long into the room.

"Ah !" (sneeze.)

"Ugh !" (sneeze.)

"Brute !" (sneeze, sneeze.)

"I'll pay you out for this !" gasped Gurney, shaking his fist at Gerard, while the tears ran down his face.

"Will you !" laughed Gerard, sending another shower .full into his face ; "then take that, and that, and that, and make hay elsewhere, confound you ! I'm about sick of this game ;" as he spoke keeping up a continual shower upon the intruders.

Raving, swearing, spitting, sneezing, choking, and stamping, the crestfallen officers made the best of their way down the corridor in all the ignominy of utter defeat. From head to feet they were covered with the strongest white pepper, the embroidery on their mess-jackets forming grand receptacles for the frightful powder. Their hair, eyes, noses, mouths, and moustaches were all filled with it, and it was hours before the terrible sneezing and choking subsided. So thoroughly was it scattered over each practical joker, that for several days the opening of a door or window would send a fresh waft of it across the ante-room or dinner table, to the intense disgust of the more peaceably-disposed members, who were loud in their demands that for the future St. Hilary should be left in peace.

In peace, however, Gerard St. Hilary was not allowed to remain. On making his appearance in the mess-room on the morning following the *feu du poivre*, he was greeted with a volley of forage caps, newspapers, and other small missiles of a similar character.

He came into the room with a jolly laugh, his blue eyes shining with merriment, and looking, in his well-got-up hunting costume, as he always did look, "thoroughbred."

"Expect a good run this morning, Gurney ?" he began, as he sat down, "or is your cold too bad !"

"My cold ?" said that gentleman interrogatively.

"Yes. I heard a good deal of sneezing in my vicinity last night."

" Ah, you rascal," cried Gurney, laughing in spite of himself ; " we are going to pay you out for that fine trick."

" By Jove, how you did sneeze !" cried Gerard, with shrieks of laughter. " This was it, major : ' Ugh !' (sneeze) ; ' Ah '' (sneeze) ; ' Brute !' (choke), ' I'll pay you out for this !' (sneeze, choke, choke, sneeze.)   Gad, it was fine !"

" Serve them right," growled the major ; " they'll let you alone now, St. Hilary."

" Will we !" cried a chorus of voices ; " don't flatter yourself, Jerry."

At this moment another officer in " pink " entered the room, and seated himself next to St. Hilary.

" 'Pon my soul, Jerry," he began, " but that was a scurvy trick you played us last night.   I can't get your confounded pepper out of my moustaches."

" That's awkward for you, Jack," laughed Gerard.   " It's my idea that when fellows get engaged to be married they should leave their neighbours in peace."

" Perhaps you're right," answered Jack Hilton.   " Anyhow, I left my man cursing you after the fashion of Rheims ; but, unlike the little Jackdaw, you seem to flourish under it amazingly."

" I had an uncommonly good night ; and you'd better tell your man that ' curses, like chickens, come home to roost.' "

" I think his come home to him with every shake of my clothes or movement of his brush," cried Hilton, laughing.

" Ha, ha, ha !" screamed Gerard, in high glee.   " Well, I must be off.   Are you coming, Jack ?"

At the door he turned back to fire a parting shot.

" I hope on my return, my dear fellows, to find that the influenza is somewhat improved."

" You were a big fool too, Jerry," said Jack Hilton gravely, as the two rode through the soft November fog   " I never saw any fellow in such a rage as Gurney was in last night—never in all my life.   He swore he would be revenged on you ; take my word for it he will.   They're going to fill your bed with beetles to-night."

2

" That's pleasant," said Gerard grimly. " However, you are a good fellow to tell me. And now let us talk of something else ; what's done cannot be undone, and I suppose I must grin and bear it."

They found the meet that day but very poorly attended. There was only one lady present. Of course that one was Elinor Warwick.

" Well," she inquired eagerly, as Gerard rode up, "how did it answer?"

" Oh, if you'd only been there !" cried Gerard, giving her a graphic description of the stampede ; but ending with, " I hear from Hilton that I am to suffer a perfect martyrdom of retaliation."

" Poor thing !" said Elinor softly ; whereupon Gerard forgot all his troubles, and only remembered that, whatever happened, he would be sure of Elinor's loving pity and commiseration.

The word which he had used to Elinor Warwick in jest was realised by him in all its stern hideousness. A martyr he in very truth became. It seemed as if his tormentors could neither forget nor forgive the *feu du poivre*. They no longer dared disturb him at night—their fear of his pepper-pot was too wholesome, but by every other means in their power did they worry and annoy him. His bed was, as Jack Hilton had predicted, filled with cockroaches ; and this course was followed up by frogs, dead mice, fender and fire-irons, plentiful administration of lard and wet sponges. His boots were filled with burrs or cobbler's wax, and, in fact, his life was made a burden to him. On the day of the ball, however, matters came to a climax.

CHAPTER II.

It was a fortnight after the *feu du poivre*. The officers had tried their best to get Gerard made " orderly " on that day, but failed ; and while he was down at the Palace with Miss Warwick set their wits to work to devise some new form of torture. They went to the colonel, and asked as a great favour that dressing for mess might be excused, on the plea that it would be a great nuisance to dress twice, and their full dress was very inconvenient to dine in on account of the heat.

" You see, colonel," said they, " we shall be obliged to dance all night, and we want to begin as cool as possible."

With a slight demur the colonel consented, and then they knew that their trick was safe.

Gerard went in rather late, and on hearing that dressing was excused, sat down to dinner without going near his room. At nine o'clock one of the mess waiters came behind his chair, and whispered that his man wanted him at once.

From the sudden " hush " in the room poor Gerard suspected mischief. His man was awaiting him at the door with an anxious face.

" What's the matter ?" demanded Gerard.

" Oh, sir," exclaimed he, " I hardly dare tell you."

Gerard dashed up to his room, and there on the bed lay his tunics and mess jackets, with every seam neatly ripped up. Going to the ball was out of the question ; etiquette would not permit him to go in ordinary evening attire.

" Don't look like that, sir," said Jones, in an imploring tone —for Gerard had never uttered one word, but stood gazing on the wreck of his property, growing whiter and whiter every moment—" don't look like that ; I've sent for the master tailor. I should think he will be able to get them sewn up in something like time."

In a few minutes that functionary arrived, but could not promise that the work should be complete before midnight. For three weary hours did Gerard pace his room, giving no answer to the various knocks from the men who wanted to know how their trick had succeeded.

Soon after midnight Gerard was in a cab, driving as fast as possible to the assembly rooms, where the ball was given Colonel Lifford with whom he was a great favourite was standing near the door when he passed in.

" Well, my boy," he said kindly, " you are very late."

" Yes, sir, I am rather," answered Gerard, his voice shaking still.

"Why, what's the matter, St Hilary?—you are very white. Are you not well?"

"Yes, thanks, colonel;" and Gerard passed on

Now Gerard was engaged to Miss Warwick for the first, fifth, tenth, and sixteenth dances. The tenth, he very well knew, was the supper waltz. He found that the ninth was then being danced; so, after all, though he had missed two dances with her he was not so very badly off.

He hung about looking for her, and at last saw her bright chesnut hair in very close proximity to Captain Gurney's scarlet-clad shoulder. Gerard's blue eyes flashed at the sight, for Gurney was not a favourite of Elinor's; yet here she was sitting in an out-of-the-way corner, flirting desperately with the man who had done his best to prevent his coming to the ball.

He waited impatiently for the dance to end, that he might claim Miss Warwick for the waltz, and meanwhile amused himself by studying her face and dress, which was of white silk, unrelieved by any colour. Her hair was plaited in a long braid and hung far below her waist; and nestling in it were two white roses, placed just at the top of the braid behind the left ear. She wore no ornaments whatever; and the only speck of colour she had about her was a large bouquet of crimson and white flowers which Gerard had sent her. His foolish heart throbbed at the sight of it; but it sank to zero when she raised her face, and he saw that it was as white as her dress, and that she had, what he had never seen there before, a hard glittering look in her gleaming hazel eyes.

At last the dance was ended, and the instant the signal sounded for the next one Gerard crossed the room, and bending his arm to Elinor, said—

"My dance, I believe."

"I have given your dance away," said Miss Warwick, coolly. "I sat out the two best waltzes of the evening waiting for you, and you really must forgive me if I did not care to waste any more." And taking Captain Gurney's arm she swept away.

Gerard was thunderstruck. He stood for a moment speechless with rage and astonishment. This was a catastrophe he had never bargained for. No, poor fellow; he had expected to receive at Elinor's hands sweetest pity and commiseration. He determined not to leave the room without an attempt at an explanation; so he followed them, and began gently.

"Will you not let me explain?"

But Elinor was too thoroughly angry to listen to reason, and she faced him haughtily.

"Thank you, Mr. St. Hilary, that is quite unnecessary. I assure you, it is not of the slightest consequence."

With a frigid little bow she passed away, leaving Gerard with anything but a pleasant expression on his usually pleasant fac . He stood and watched them go down the room; he saw Captain Gurney bend towards her, as though he were saying something especially tender; and the sight of that, and the sound of the light laugh with which Elinor answered it were more than he could bear. He rushed out of the room, and entering the first cab, ordered the man to drive as quickly as possible back to barracks.

"Tell you what, George," said one of his tormentors to another, "I wish I was well out of this joke: that fellow will go mad."

"Umph! Gurney is such a beggar for running an idea to death."

Gerard reached his room in a state of misery too intense for words. He felt sick and dizzy, and was thankful that for once his bed had been left in decent order. Sleep, however, he could not. He tossed about to and fro; his bed was hot and uncomfortable; and first one and then another of his comrades disturbed him by coming along the corridor with clanking of spurred boots.

At last he sank into a troubled fretful doze, which lasted until Jones came to wake him at six o'clock, for he was orderly officer that day. When the candles were lighted, what Gerard in his agony called the "fiendishness of the plot" was revealed: from head to foot he was as white as any miller.

His man begged him not to have his usual bath, but be rubbed down with coarse towels as quickly as possible.

"If you get into water, sir," he entreated, "it will all turn to paste. I'll rub it off in a few minutes."

"You'll have to be uncommonly quick," said St. Hilary, grimly; "for I must be out in ten minutes."

Jones rubbed and scrubbed with a will, until Gerard was quite clean and presentable, except on one point. That point showed itself with painful obtrusiveness: it was his hair. That, and his particularly long yellow moustache were as white as the driven snow. Jones got a couple of big brushes, and worked hard; but though a tremendous cloud of the treacherous white powder came off, no perceptible difference was made in Lieutenant St. Hilary's appearance.

"I don't know what to do, sir," said he at length, with a great sigh.

At this moment a knock was heard at the door.

"Come in," roared Gerard.

"Stables, sir," announced an orderly; "the adjutant's out, sir, already."

This was the last ounce on the camel's back.

"Good heavens!" gasped Gerard. "Ask him to come up here."

Presently the adjutant came up, amazed at the unusual request.

"Just look here, Harrington," said Gerard, displaying his whitened hair; "see what those brutes have done. I can't come into sight like this."

"Certainly not," answered he, promptly. "I'll tell Hilton to do your duty."

"And I say, Harrington, don't peach, there's a good chap."

But Harrington, "a gentleman adjutant," was a married man, and did not approve of the pranks which were carried to such excess amongst the officers of the 52nd Dragoons. So he departed without vouchsafing any reply to Gerard's continued entreaties.

He breakfasted alone, and soon after ten o'clock the colonel sent for him to the orderly room.

" What's the meaning of this, St. Hilary ?" began the chief, sternly.

" I couldn't go on duty like this, sir," said poor Gerard, deprecatingly.

" What in the world—" began the colonel, suddenly breaking off into roars of laughter, as his eyes fell upon Gerard in all the freshness of a hoary old age. Then, recovering himself, said stiffly, " This should have been reported to me at once."

" Please, sir," said Gerard, " I've been trying to get it out."

Again the colonel was afflicted with a sudden convulsive choking, something between a cough and a sneeze.

" Well, you had better report it now."

" I don't know who did it, sir," was the reply.

" My good fellow," said his chief, " I admire your principles immensely, but you don't expect me to believe that you could be covered with flour from head to foot without knowing who did it ?"

" Yes, sir," answered Gerard, laughing, " for they filled my bed."

" With flour ?" said the colonel incredulously.

" I don't think it is flour, colonel ; it's scented, and I think it's complexion stuff, and that, you know, is made to stick on."

" Umph ! Well, you are excused duty to-day ; go away." And Gerard went.

After another brushing by Jones he went to luncheon with as unconcerned a face as he could put on, and for a few moments no one took any notice of him.

Presently, however, Captain Gurney left his seat, and, coming behind him, took a leisurely survey of his still whitened locks.

" What have you been doing with yourself, my boy ? Have you been acting in private theatricals, or are you going to a *bal masqué* at the Palace to-night ?"

Gerard answered never a word; and with another attempt at chaff, Captain Gurney retired to his seat.

"I should advise you to let that fellow alone, Gurney," said the surgeon-major, next to whom he was sitting; "the chief's awfully keen about it and St. Hilary had some difficulty to prevent peaching."

"Oh, Jerry'd never peach," said he carelessly.

"I don't know; but apart from that you are knocking the poor lad's health up."

"The poor lad's four-and-twenty," laughed Gurney, with a sneer.

"He cannot stand having his rest broken, and you must stop it," said the surgeon decisively. "If anything more of this kind occurs I shall report it immediately. I won't stand by and see any fellow's health tampered with, and this persecution has gone on beyond all bounds."

Gerard St. Hilary sat throughout the meal in dignified silence, and presently his dog-cart with his high-stepping roan mare was brought round, and he drove away in the direction of Colonel Warwick's house.

The young lady's anger had cooled down during the night, and she was repenting very bitterly her unkindness of the previous evening. She told herself that she ought to have listened to his excuses. If, as Captain Gurney had hinted, he had purposely avoided dancing the two first dances with her, why had he come for the supper waltz of all others? He would never ask her to make friends again, and she had thrown away her life's happiness at the instigation of a man she thoroughly disliked and despised. Poor Elinor! She did not realise, till she thought she had lost him, how very dear the yellow-haired, blue-eyed dragoon had grown to her!

She sat alone in her pretty drawing-room—alas, that she had no mother to share it with her!—and wondered, with a dull aching at her heart, whether all those happy days were past and gone, never to return.

She heard a carriage drive up to the door, but so little did she expect Gerard that, when he was ushered into the room, she uttered a low cry of surprise and joy, and went with outstretched hands to greet him.

"So you have forgiven me?" said Gerard, forgetting all his sorrows at the sight of her tender hazel eyes.

Elinor hung her head, the painful blushes coming thick and fast.

"I was very rude last night, and unkind, but I thought—" she stammered.

"You thought what?" said Gerard, eagerly.

"I—I thought you did not care to dance so many times with me, for Captain Gurney said you were lounging about your rooms doing nothing."

"Curse him!" muttered Gerard under his breath. "So you thought I had forgotten you, did you, darling? And if I had would you have minded much?"

Elinor did not speak; and, strange to say, Gerard did not notice the omission, for he established her in a low chair in front of the blazing fire, and bending over her, said, in a dangerously gentle voice—

"My child, you were very cruel to me last night; nothing else than the cause which kept me away could have held me from your side."

Then he told her all his troubles, and showed her his still whitened hair, which, in her agitation, she had not noticed. Poor Elinor was in an agony of confusion and regret.

"Can you ever forgive me?" she murmured.

"Yes, my love, on one condition—that, as a penance for your sins, you give me your darling self."

"That will be a curious penance," said Elinor, looking upwards lovingly. "No penance at all."

"Don't be too sure. I shall be horribly jealous, and exacting to a degree. I shall not allow any flirting, and shall probably make your life a burden to you."

"I shall not want to flirt," whispered Elinor.

"Won't you, my darling? Will your great, stupid, lumbering husband content you?"

Elinor thought he would—she thinks so still.

* * * *

Amongst the regimental plate of the 52nd is a large golden pepper-pot, encrusted with jewels, and the date engraved thereon is that of Gerard St. Hilary's wedding. It was given by Elinor's wish in remembrance of the regimental martyrdom which had gained for her the truest heart that ever beat, though her husband frequently assures her that he had made up his mind ages before, so that it only hastened matters by a few weeks.

A REGIMENTAL VALENTINE;

OR, HOW PATRICK O'SHAUGHNASSY WAS HELPED INTO MATRIMONY.

CHAPTER I.

" RUN?" said Patrick O'Shaughnassy, in answer to a question put to him, as he slipped into his chair at the early mess-dinner, just as the soup was being served; "run? B-y Jove! I should think I did run, as hard as ever I could lay legs to ground!"

" What made you so late, Pat?" inquired George de Lyle, the "senior sub.," next to whom he sat.

" Up at the colonel's. Mrs. Lifford had a lot of girls in to tea, and I couldn't get away," he answered. " Just had seven minutes to get here and dress in."

" Sharp thing, that. Why didn't you wait for the late dinner?"

" Concert down town; can't get off going."

" Did you try?" said De Lyle slyly.

" Well, no," said the other honestly, " I didn't"

Mr. De Lyle laughed, and, when after a very hurried meal Pat O'Shaughnassy rose from the table, remarked to his neighbour on his other hand that " it really is an awful pity, but Pat, poor devil, is going the way of all the others."

" What way's that?" said the man in question, who, being brother to one of the officers, and only a visitor in barracks, did not understand the allusion; " I don't see anything amiss with him."

" I'll tell you," answered De Lyle. " You must know that the colonel is guardian to a niece, who is immensely rich and very pretty, but the most terrible flirt in creation. Well, whenever a young fellow joins, it is part of the programme that he shall go through a course of instruction at Miss Lifford's hands. They all do, just as children have the measles and the whooping-cough."

"And how old is Miss Lifford?"

"Oh, perhaps two-and-twenty; and really the very nicest girl you ever met. She takes them all in hand, and, somehow, contrives to keep good friends with them, even after they've got their dismissal. Now the joke is, that Pat O'Shaughnassy has known her ever since she left school; and as he stands second on the list of subs., he might reasonably be expected to know better. Within the last few weeks he has literally lived to the tune of Alys Lifford. The days he is on duty he is an absolute nuisance to every one; indeed, I am obliged to lock my door against him. And yet, do you know, I'm sorry for him, for he's a downright good sort of chap."

An hour later the regular mess-dinner was in full swing, when suddenly Captain Gurney asked "what had got Pat O'Shaughnassy?"

"The old game," answered a voice from the other end of the table.

"Silly fool!" remarked the senior captain, with great contempt.

"He's not been polished off quite so soon as they usually are," observed Jack Hilton. "I should have thought Miss Lifford would have got sick of him by this time."

"Don't know," laughed another. "Pat's very amusing sometimes. I heard a lady ask him, at St. Hilary's wedding, whether his name was pronounced O'Shanassy or O'Shaucknassy, as she knew both families. Pat told her, with the most barefaced coolness, that he wasn't an Irishman at all; he came from Kent."

"Awfully good!" cried a chorus of laughing voices.

"Ah, but he said a neater thing than that," put in Jack Hilton. "One day last week Miss Lifford asked us to go in to tea on Sunday afternoon; and Pat said, gravely, 'I think I will be on duty, but I'll come if I can; but if I don't come, you won't expect me.'"

This raised another laugh. Most of my readers are probably aware that it does not take much to provoke mirth and hilarity at a military dinner-table.

"Stop a bit, stop a bit," cried Jack; "you haven't heard the cream of the joke yet. On Sunday, you know, young Drew was on duty; so Pat and I went up to the chief's together.

"'So you managed to get off,' said **Alys**, as we went in.

"'Well, no I didn't,' answered Pat.

"'Then how is it you're not in barracks?' she asked, evidently thinking he had been fool enough to sneak out unawares.

"'Because I told Micky Drew's man to call him early this morning; and faith, the poor chap got up, in all the cold, and did my work, without being any the wiser.'"

"And the beauty of the joke is," continued Hilton, "that Pat, in his innocence, really thinks he has stolen a march upon Drew, and hasn't a ghost of an idea that his name was changed for Drew's in the order-book late on Saturday night."

"How was it his man did not tell him?" said some one.

"Because, to make all complete, Pat told him that Mr. Drew was going to take his duty to-morrow; and, of course, the man having seen the order-book, thought nothing about it. It was pure good luck his pitching upon Drew, though."

"By George!" exclaimed Captain Gurney, "this is the 12th, surely. We must send Pat a valentine!"

"So we must!" cried the others.

"I wonder if Miss Lifford will send him one?" said Fred Gordon.

"Not she. Suppose we send him one from her."

"So we will. What shall it be? Hollo, Gurney! what have you got in your head now?"

For the senior captain was leaning with both elbows on the table, his face buried in his hands. Presently he raised it.

"Wait a minute, you fellows," he said, slowly. "Pat's on duty to-morrow, isn't he?"

"Yes."

"Then we'll write a proposal from him to Miss Lifford, and

send the note by an orderly; her answer, which is safe to be a refusal, will be a grand surprise for him on St. Valentine's day."

This daring proposition was received in silence; the officers of the 52nd Dragoons looked from one to another in speechless amazement, mingled with admiration for the master-mind which had conceived this brilliant plot.

At length Fred Gordon relieved his feelings by a prolonged "B—y Jove!" and then the whole assembly broke out into a torrent of eager questions.

" Will it be safe?"

" You'll tell us exactly what to say to Pat?"

" You'll write as if from him?"

" I suppose she is quite sure to refuse him?" said Jack Hilton, doubtfully.

" Safe to," replied Captain Gurney, confidently, "it will be the best joke we have had since St. Hilary got spliced."

" Who will write it?" said George Wintringham; " because it must be done carefully, and made spoony enough."

" I'll write the rough copy," replied Captain Gurney, " and then we must get hold of some of Pat's writing to imitate."

" You need not do that," announced Fred Gordon; " Billy Childers writes exactly the same fist as Pat."

" Are you sure?"

" Perfectly certain; I don't think even Pat himself could tell the difference; and Miss Lifford will not be so familiar with his hand as all that."

By the united efforts of the officers the following letter was produced:

Cavalry Barracks, Milchester,
February 13th.

My dear Miss Lifford,—I have been trying for some time to speak to you on a subject which lies very near my heart; but, somehow, I have never had an opportunity. I am not much of a hand at letter-writing, but I think you must know what I mean. Will you marry me, darling? That I love you with all my heart and soul you must have known for some time, and faith! I can't help thinking you do care a little for me.

I am fast all day in this dreary barrack-square, so won't you send me one little word to say you will be my valentine to-morrow? and make the very happiest man in the world into

PATRICK O'SHAUGHNASSY.

Captain Gurney read this brilliant production aloud.

"There!" he exclaimed, in a self-satisfied tone, "I think that reads like Pat, particularly the wind up. Can any of you suggest an improvement?"

There was a general reply in the negative; they all considered it beyond improving.

"One of you run up to Pat's room and get some of his own paper; it will be in the blotting-book on the writing-table— don't bring that with the regimental crest on; bring his own."

Fred Gordon said he would go. He very soon returned with the spoils, and the letter was copied and ready for sending in no time.

CHAPTER II.

THE following day Captain Gurney sent an orderly to Colonel Lifford's house with the letter, and after some little time the man returned, with a note directed in Alys Lifford's bold hand-writing to P. O'Shaughnassy, Esq. According to orders, he took it to Captain Gurney's room, where several of the conspirators were waiting to receive it. Their senior, however, locked it up, out of harm's way, saying,

"I suppose a lot of young fools like you would be tearing it open, because your curiosity could not wait till another day; but I'll have none of that nonsense. No; here it stays until I post it, and you will see it opened with the others to morrow at luncheon."

"Are you going to post it?" said Billy Childers, in amazement.

"Why, of course, you young duffer; you don't suppose I'm going to give it to Pat, do you? Lord bless the child, he's as innocent as a serpent! If it were not posted Pat would smell a rat directly, and never believe it came from Miss Lifford at all."

The answer was accordingly posted; and on the following day, as usual on the feast of St. Valentine, all the letters were saved until luncheon, at which meal the officers were assembled to enjoy the fun.

" Here's one for you, Chim," said Patrick O'Shaughnassy, taking a packet from the heap; " come, open it out, man, and let us see."

The packet contained a lady's long fur ruff, and a very official-looking note, purporting to have come from the commanding officer of the 90th Hussars (for Mr. Drew had only a few months before exchanged into the 52nd from that regiment), to the effect that the caudal appendage had been found in Sub-Lieutenant Drew's quarters, and was therefore forwarded, with a request that any other such property which Mr. Drew might have left behind should be at once removed, otherwise his late quarters in —— Barracks would be seriously incommoded.

Mr. Drew might certainly have passed for the missing link we hear so much about, and his regimental cognomen of Chimpanzee, more often shortened into Chim, suited his personal appearance to a nicety. As usual, he had to laugh off his chagrin with the best grace he could muster, when, happily for him, the general attention was diverted from him, as Patrick O'Shaughnassy carelessly picked up from the heap on the table the delicately perfumed crested note, which was to convey such startling news to him. He did not dream that it came from Miss Lifford, and turned it over with infinite contempt.

" Ugh !" said he, " an afternoon tea, I suppose. ' My dear *Captain* O'Shaughnassy '—Ah, I know their little ways."

" For the love of Heaven, don't sit drivelling there, man !" cried an impatient voice.

" Oh, it isn't a valentine," remarked another, in a disappointed tone, when O'Shaughnassy took out a note and began reading it.

" Go on with the others," said Gurney, in order to avert suspicion ; a command which no one obeyed, all being too busy watching Pat, amid a silence which had become quite oppressive.

" What the d—" began he, then checked himself, and turning the paper over, read it again ; changing colour the while from scarlet to white, then from white to scarlet, as though he could not make up his mind which was most becoming to his complexion, finally compromising the matter by remaining the colour of a mangel-wurzel. He picked up the envelope and examined it; then he took up the letter again carefully

" Well," he said at last, surveying the eager faces crowding round him, " you chaps have got yourselves into a fine shindy this time, and no mistake about it."

" What is it? what does she say?" they cried, as with one voice.

" Upon my—," he began.

" Here, give it me," said Gurney, who began to suspect Pat was right, and they had got into a " shindy," as he said—" give it to me;" at the same time snatching it out of his hands, and reading it quickly.

It was not a very long epistle, but its contents elicited an oath, not loud, but deep, from between the reader's closed teeth.

" I told you so," said Pat, reassuringly.

" What is it?" cried the others, " She has not, surely, accepted you?"

O'Shaughnassy nodded.

" Oh, well, it's all right, then," said Gordon, in a relieved tone. " Pat's got all he wants, and she need never know anything at all about it : a very good thing for Pat, I say."

" Perhaps Pat says the contrary," interposed that young gentleman. " I've not asked Miss Lifford to marry me, and, what is more, I am not going to do so. I don't intend to marry a woman simply to get you fellows out of a scrape. No, no ; Pat O'Shaughnassy may be a thundering fool, but he's not quite such an idiot as to do that."

" Why, Pat," exclaimed Jack Hilton, " we all thought that you were ' dead nuts ' on Miss Lifford."

" Did you, really? Well, all I have to say is, that you've got yourselves into a pretty shindy this time, and won't there be old Harry to pay when the chief comes home ! By Jove ! I wouldn't stand in your shoes for a good sum. Perhaps, after this, you will be leaving your neighbour's private affairs alone."

" Dash it all !" snapped Gurney, " why can't you marry Miss Lifford, and have done with it ? You've been dangling after her morning, noon, and night, for weeks."

"To tell you the honest truth, my dear fellows," said Mr. O'Shaughnassy, with slow deliberation of utterance, "to tell you the honest truth—*I am already engaged to be married!*"

CHAPTER III.

IF the hero of this little history had suddenly emptied a pail of iced water over the group of officers assembled in the mess-room of the Milchester Barracks, a more perceptible shiver could not have run through them. Not a word was spoken. The brave men who would have cheered their troops on against an enemy, or faced grim death without a sign of flinching, looked in one another's faces blankly, each asking a tacit question—"What are we to do?" receiving for answer—"I'm dashed if I know!"

In their midst stood Patrick O'Shaughnassy, taller, by some inches, than any of them; his arms carelessly crossed upon his broad chest; his good-humoured face wearing a pleasant smile, and his gray eyes—real Irish eyes they were—shining with mirth. At last the smile deepened into a laugh, which displayed strong white filbert-shaped teeth.

"Well, as I said before, gentlemen, you've got yourselves into a pretty shindy."

"No one can compliment you on the pleasing variety of your remarks," sneered Captain Gurney; "that's the fourth time you've made that brilliant observation."

"So it is. Well, Gurney, you've a very good opportunity of showing your wonderful cleverness," said Pat, who could afford to be civil, "and letting the world see if you are as clever at getting out of scrapes yourself as you are of getting other fellows in. When you've got the thing settled, I'll change the ' into ' into ' out,' and say it as many times again. I'm going now. I shouldn't like my presence to be any hindrance to the general conversation. Good-bye."

With a gay laugh, O'Shaughnassy went noisily out of the room, and ran quickly up the echoing corridor to his own domain. Safely there, he immediately locked the door, and flinging himself on his bed, indulged in the luxury of a hearty laugh, rolling over and over—burying his face in the pillows to smother the sound of his hilarity. At last he calmed down a little, and, smoothing out Miss Lifford's letter, which he had recaptured from Captain Gurney, read it again with care. I mentioned before that it was not lengthy; indeed, it ran thus:

You have made me happy—very happy indeed. Of course I will be your valentine to-morrow. Whose should I be, if not yours?—Always your own,

ALYS.

Mr. Patrick O'Shaughnassy kissed the crumpled paper rapturously.

"My darling, my sweet Alys!" he murmured, blissfully. Then his more natural mode of expressing his satisfaction came in the words, "By Jove! what a lucky chap I am!"

Could Mr. O'Shaughnassy be alluding to the young lady about whom there had been so much discussion below?

His next movement was to change his uniform for plain clothes, and, after locking Miss Lifford's note in a secure place, to light a cigar, and proceed to search amongst the chaos on the table for a pair of gloves. Whilst he was thus employed, some one tried to open the door.

"Come in!" roared Pat. "Come in, you fool, can't you? Oh, the door's locked, is it? Well, old man," as Jack Hilton came in, "what's up now?"

"'Pon my word," began Jack, dolefully, "how the deuce we are to get out of this business I don't know; I've a good mind to send my papers in at once."

"About the best thing you can do," said Pat, consolingly, and still continuing his search; "and as you are going to be married, it won't make much odds to you."

"By George! but Gurney is in a funk."

"And so should I be," said Pat, "if I were in his shoes—a confounded fool! It's to be hoped this will cure him. Well now," having found his gloves, "I must be off; ta-ta!"

"Stop, stop!" cried Hilton; "where are you going? To the colonel's?"

" Now, my good fellow, do you expect me to go and patch up your damages just by being asked ? "

" O Lord ! I didn't know ; you always do go there."

" If it's any satisfaction to you to know it, I'm going into Milchester."

" To meet Miss Lifford ?" said Hilton, eagerly, like a drowning man ready to catch at the weakest straw.

" I am not going to meet Miss Lifford," said Pat, looking back at the door, and closing it just in time to escape a missile, in the shape of a boot, which Mr. Hilton flung at his head. Ah, it is only in a university or a barrack that one man can go into another man's room and fling his own boots at his head without provoking offence ! Truly there is something of Arcadia in both places !

When Patrick O'Shaughnassy told Jack Hilton he was going into Milchester, he was speaking sober truth ; for into that most dreary of dreary towns he really did go. At the first stand, however, he took a cab, and pulling up the blind windows, ordered the man to drive to Colonel Lifford's. The chief's house was in the centre of a village about a mile and a half from Milchester, on the road which led past the barracks.

Having satisfied himself by a peep from the little window at the back that none of the officers were in sight, he slipped out, telling the driver to come back in an hour, and answer no questions.

He found Alys Lifford sitting alone in the drawing-room, and, as she sprang up with pretty eagerness to meet him, took her bodily into his arms.

" My darling ! My best and dearest ! "

For some time their conversation was not rational, nor indeed was it fluent. Then Patrick, feeling that " life is short and time is fleeting," set about broaching to Miss Lifford the subject which was just then occupying the attention of the gentlemen in the Milchester Barracks.

" My darling," he began, with a cough, " you got a note from me yesterday ?"

Miss Lifford raised her head from his shoulder and regarded him with blank amazement.

"Of course I did, and answered it. You didn't write to me again, did you?"

"I didn't write at all," blurted out Pat.

"Did not write at all? What do you mean? Are you mad, Mr. O'Shaughnassy?"

"Well, it was 'them.' I knew nothing at all about it till I got your letter this morning."

"*Them?*" repeated Alys, slowly, unconsciously using Pat's ungrammatical form of speech. "Did they write the letter I got yesterday?"

"Yes, confound them!"

"And did they see my answer?"

"I could not help it," said Pat, humbly. "What was one against so many? You won't be angry with me, will you, my darling?"

"Captain Gurney and Mr. Hilton," said a servant, opening the door.

Alys Lifford came forward as the two men walked into the room.

"I never, in all my life, heard of such an ungentlemanly, disgraceful action, never. I could not have believed it possible. Unmanly, cowardly!" she cried, passionately, though the sound of tears was in her voice. "I do not know which of you is the worst or the most to be blamed; but as surely as I am Alys Lifford, I will never speak to any of you again."

She vanished into an inner room, and the three men stood as if turned to stone. All the colour faded from Patrick O'Shaughnassy's ruddy face, leaving it as white as death. He crossed the room to where his senior was standing, and gripped his shoulder with trembling fingers.

"As I live, I'll pay you out for this fine trick," he said, in a low voice, shaking with suppressed passion. "You shall live to repent it, confound you!"

Then he stalked out of the room without another word.

"I shall send in my papers at once," said Jack Hilton, in the tone of a martyr. "As for you, Gurney, you had better shoot yourself."

"Umph!" said Captain Gurney, doubtfully.

CHAPTER IV.

A WEEK passed away, and still Colonel Lifford did not return from his leave. The officers of the 52nd, during that time, went through various stages of misery.

Occasionally they displayed symptoms of swaggering bravado, but they neither deceived themselves nor each other; and the general tone of society in the mess-room might be fairly described as "hang-dog." Colonel Lifford was a martinet of the very fiercest calibre, and the dread with which his return was anticipated was simply pitiable.

The state of Mr. O'Shaughnassy's temper did not add to the general hilarity of the community. As George De Lyle expressed it, "Pat was for all the world like a bear with a sore head."

None of them ventured into his room, nor indeed said a word to him on any subject whatever, except one or two who were not involved in the scrape.

Jack Hilton kept his word and sent in his papers, so consequently felt a little more at his ease than his comrades; and Miss Lifford kept her word and "cut" the whole of them, which was, as Thorald told her, an awful shame, on the strength of which she made an exception in his favour, and flirted with him in a disgraceful manner. For poor Patrick O'Shaughnassy she had no mercy. At the Cathedral, Palace, or theatre, and at all other places where they met, she did not deign to notice him in the least, though he, poor fellow, as all his comrades knew, tried again and again to soften her wrath.

At the end of a week the news came that Colonel Lifford had fallen in the hunting-field and broken his arm. I'm afraid his officers were not so sorry as they should have been; but the accident meant to them a respite, and when Mrs. and Miss

Lifford departed to join the sick man, they fell back into their old ways and breathed freely once more.

Patrick O'Shaughnassy's ill-temper, however, increased visibly, and, after a fortnight not very pleasantly passed, he announced that he had got a month's leave and was going to be married.

"Going to be married!" cried the officers in chorus. "Why, Pat, we all thought——"

"What business had you to think, then?" retorted Pat, it must be owned somewhat uncourteously. "I can't stand this any longer; so I'm going to get married, and see if that will mend it."

At the door he fired a parting shot.

"And I hope you'll find it pretty warm when the chief comes back."

"Selfish brute!" remarked Captain Gurney, when he had gone.

"Poor devil!" commented De Lyle. "I never thought Pat would have taken it so much to heart. Anyway, I do pity the girl."

The weeks slipped away and still Colonel Lifford was absent; his broken arm proved very troublesome, and he had received such a shaking from his fall that his medical advisers forbade his returning to duty for some time. At length he was able to do so, and the major announced that he might be expected on the 7th of the month, during the week that the Yeomanry Cavalry were assembled in Milchester for their annual training. This news filled the gallant officers of the 52nd anew with dismay and consternation. They were in "no end of a funk, by Jove." And when it was reported that he had arrived in the town, and did not make his appearance in the barracks, it was considered a very bad sign, from which they inferred that his wrath was indeed terrible.

Whilst this black state of affairs was being discussed in the ante-room, Patrick O'Shaughnassy walked in, looking as bright and jolly as if he had never had a trouble in his life.

"I hear the chief's back to-day," he said, with a hearty laugh. "I suppose you men are all quaking in your shoes!"

No one answered, and there was silence until Gordon said that they understood he had gone away to be married.

"So I did," he answered.

"And didn't it come off? We never saw any announcement."

"Come off? Of course it did. The missis is down at the 'Royal Swan.'"

"Who is she?" asked Billy Childers.

"Who is she? Why Mrs. O'Shaughnassy, of course."

"Shall we see her at the ball those yeomanry fellows give to-night?"

"Oh, yes. Good-bye. Wish you good luck for to-morrow."

A few hours later, the officers of the dragoons went into the brilliantly lighted ball-room.

"Do you think the O'Shaughnassys have come?" said De Lyle to one of the hosts.

"Yes, half an hour ago at least. What a pretty girl she is! You'll see them somewhere about," said he, and moved away.

"There's Pat," said Gurney; "and, by the Lord Harry, he's dancing with Alys Lifford! What does that mean?"

"She looks happy enough, and better friends than Pat's wife will like if she hears the story."

"Oh, she never will hear it. Pat isn't such a fool as to tell her himself. I wonder which is she?"

"There's Pat. I say, Pat, aren't you going to introduce us to your wife?"

"Oh, yes, to be sure. Come along."

He led them across the room to where a lady, dressed in the richest bridal costume, was talking with other ladies.

"My darling, here are some of my brother-officers come to make your acquaintance," he said. "Captain Gurney and Mr. Gordon—Mrs. O'Shaughnassy."

To their unspeakable astonishment, Mrs. O'Shaughnassy had the dark eyes, the pure profile, and the smiling mouth of Alys Lifford.

" Why—Miss Lifford!" gasped young Gordon. " I—I—you—at least—"

" Ah," she laughed, " you are thinking of the tragic vow I made the day I found you out. Well, I have kept it. I am not Alys Lifford now, you know."

" And I think I kept mine," laughed her husband joyously. " I think I paid you all out. Oh, did we not steal a march upon you! I can tell you, though, it was precious hard work keeping up the sulks."

Although everything came to such a happy and orthodox ending, Colonel Lifford said a few words the next day, which brought the tingling blood into the cheeks and ears of his listeners; and, since that time, Captain Gurney finds it as well to leave his friends' private affairs in their own hands. He has learnt from experience that there is a Nemesis which repays even such apparently insignificant unkindness as he took so much pleasure in inflicting upon others, for into two of the most pleasant houses amongst the married officers of the 52nd he is never asked; and although Gerard St. Hilary and Patrick O'Shaughnassy, having obtained their hearts' desire, would willingly forget and forgive past offences, their wives imperatively decline to give Captain Gurney the chance of making more mischief, on the very sensible ground that " prevention is better than cure."

A REGIMENTAL POET;

OR, BORROWED PLUMES.

CHAPTER I.

It was just eleven o'clock when Stephen Thorold went up the dreary stone staircase to his rooms on the second floor of the block, known as G, in Colchester Barracks. He was very tired for he had been orderly officer for the day, with the delight of a court-martial thrown in. The colonel had been particularly disagreeable all day, and he had after dinner, worse luck, as he told himself, somehow got into conversation with the major, who had talked the prosiest and driest of " redbook " for two long hours. It was, therefore, with a sense of intense relief that he found himself free to go to bed, with no fear of being orderly officer again for at least a week.

He went slowly up the empty, echoing stairs, his sword clanking after him noisily, and entered his room, banging the door to, as if he wanted to try the strength of its panels and the reliance to be placed on its lock. Everything looked very comfortable and inviting; the fire blazed brightly in the grate and cast a pleasant, mellow glow over the whole apartment; the crimson curtains, drawn closely over the windows—there were no blinds —if a little faded and shabby by daylight, looked well and cosy enough in the fire-light's fitful glow, which danced and gleamed over everything—now on the broad frames of the pictures, then on the ivory keys of the open piano. It flickered across Stephen's crisp, curly, yellow hair, and for a moment dazzled his tired grey eyes, so that he had to put up his hand to shade them. Then he slipped off his belts, hung his forage cap on one of the pegs behind the door, and sank lazily into the huge arm-chair, with a sigh of the deepest content that the worries of the

day were over. And it certainly had been a tiresome day; he
didn't know what had possessed the chief lately but he was very
different to what he used to be: perhaps it was with getting
married! And then a vision of a bright face, with ruddy
brown hair and laughing blue eyes, came before him and he
decided that matrimony could not surely be the cause of the
lamentable alteration in the commanding officer of his regiment.
But, all the same, the bright face and the ruddy brown hair
and laughing blue eyes did not belong to Mrs. Lifford, but to
Judith Scrope, the fifth daughter of the brigade-major's
father-in-law; that is to say, she was Mrs. Winton's only
unmarried sister. Stephen wondered wistfully what she had
been doing all day? He had passed her house, or rather the
brigade-major's house, that morning, when he rode with the
troops to watering order, but not a glimpse of her had he seen,
either in going or returning. There had been a garden party
up at Lexden, he believed; he wondered had Judith been there?
He hardly thought so: she had said a few days before that it
was getting too cold for garden-parties, particularly as she did
not care much for them. Having arrived at this important conclusion, Stephen thought he would go to bed; he
upheaved himself therefore out of his chair, locked his door,
kicked his boots off, not without an anathema upon their
tightness, and, after a careful survey of himself in the glass,
went into the little inner room where his bed was, and in less
than two minutes was sound asleep. But in that sleep—at
least, it seemed so to him, it was not like the half-moment
between sleeping and waking, but must have been drawn out
over hours—Stephen had a dream, a truly awful one, for he
dreamed that Judith Scrope had married the Devil, and that
they had come to take him away to the infernal regions, that
they might there amuse themselves and the numberless
legions of the imps and fiends, by putting him to death by
torture of the most cruel and lingering description.

As might reasonably be expected, Stephen Thorold awoke
with a start, trembling in every limb, and with great beads of
agony standing out upon his forehead. There was a great noise

going on, and for a moment he hardly realised that he had just then no fiends to encounter worse than his brother-officers and comrades-in-arms. As soon as the truth of the situation flashed across his brain, he jumped out of bed and opened the door into his sitting room. Pouf! It was all filled with smoke! Then those confounded idiots were trying to blow his door in. Ugh! the rooms would smell of gunpowder for a week. He went back to bed and laid listening to them. He could hear hushed voices just outside the door, then a dead silence, save for a faint sound as of one metallic substance tapping against another! He knew what that meant well enough; they were filling the lock with powder. Then there was a breathless pause, followed by a scramble across the landing, and a fouf—f —f—fizz—*bang!* Stephen leaned out of bed, and, as the smoke gradually cleared away, saw, with a thrill of intense satisfaction, that the door had not given way. Of course he did not doubt for a moment that they would ultimately succeed in effecting an entrance—he had been there too often for that—but still it was some satisfaction to know that they had had a good deal of trouble in doing it. He lay peeping round the corner between the two rooms, so that he might hear what went on, and yet be ready to jump under the bedclothes and feign slumber when the crisis did come. They were wonderfully quiet; whatever could they be at now? He had not the smallest hope that they had gone away and left him in peace; he knew them all too well!

"Scatter a good lot under the door," he heard a voice say; Chantry's he thought it was.

"All right," was answered with a laugh.

Quick as thought Stephen sprang out of bed. "Confound them; the whole place will be on fire," he muttered, then ran and flung the door open. "What the devil do you want?" he asked fretfully. "Hang it, I do think you might choose a night when a poor devil hasn't been on duty."

He might as well have talked to the winds! There were eight or ten of them, all flushed with champagne and full of mischief, exasperated by the two tedious hours they had to remain, whilst the major was prosing to Stephen. Amongst the babel of voices, Stephen's was lost entirely, and they shoved him in with scant ceremony, and began ' hay-making !''

Poor Stephen was so thoroughly tired and sleepy that he almost dozed off as he stood, notwithstanding the general havoc which was being made of his furniture. He half hoped they were going to leave him in peace and quietness, when they had turned everything thoroughly topsy-turvy, and he wished they would be quick and get their task done.

Unfortunately, he had left the despatch box drawer in his chest open, and one of them perceiving it, half-a-dozen hands plunged into it instantly ; that roused him quickly enough.

" Oh ! confound it," he exclaimed, energetically, and rushed into the midst of the excited group, " leave that alone will you ?"

But the harder he fought, the more they persisted in ransacking the contents of the drawer. He raved, he cursed, he swore, to no more purpose than making them laugh.

He was a fine strong young fellow, nearly six feet in his stockings ; but what was the strength of one man—in his night shirt too, and with bare feet, which every now and then got a prick from his tormentors' spurred heels—against so many.

" Hold him fast, can't you ?" said Captain Gurney, in an authoritative voice, as Stephen almost succeeded in wrenching a handful of papers out of his grasp. " Oh, by jove, they're poems !"

A shriek of laughter greeted this announcement, and Stephen struggled yet more fiercely to shake off his captors grip.

" They're poems," said Captain Gurney complacently, crossing the room leisurely, and proceeding to light the two tall candles on the mantel-shelf. " Ye-es, they're poetical effusions. Now if you'll keep the young cub quiet, I'll read them aloud."

A cheer of applause greeted his proposal, followed by renewed but ineffectual efforts from Stephen to free himself. At length, however, order was sufficiently restored for the senior captain to make himself heard.

" To an old glove !" he began amid loud cheers and an authoritative order for " Silence !"

Crumpled and buttonless,
　Tarnished and torn ;
You're to be pitied, but--
　You she has worn.

Pressing her little hand,
　Happy you were ;
You toyed with her earring,
　Played with her hair.

Fortunate more than all,
　Blessed finger tips ;
You kissed her dainty cheek
　Even her lips.

" Rather strong that," said the reader, by way of comment.

Constant companion,
　But for a day ;
Truly your happiness
　Fleeted away !

Why all this rhapsody ?
　You're but a glove,
Bringing before me
　The ghost of a love.

Like you, love faded, and
　Lightly was worn,
Lightly was thrown away,
　Tarnished and torn !

" So she tossed you over, did she, Stephen ?" said Hugh Chillingly, more commonly known as the " Cabbage."

But Stephen, finding his efforts unavailing, had relapsed into sulky silence, and did not reply.

" Old Stephen looks as black as a double-distilled thunder-cloud," laughed Jennyns, sending a pellet of paper at Stephen's head.

" Here's another," said Gurney at that moment.

" Oh, let's have it by all means !" cried Hunt. " Don't be shy, Stephen; never mind chaff, old chap. Tell them to do better if they can."

" Devil take you ;" growled Stephen, civilly.

" By no means," his comrade returned sweetly; " I always like to encourage juvenile efforts."

"Shut up!" Stephen cried, trying once 'more to get away from his warders.

"Do you want to hear any more?" Gurney asked.

"Yes, yes," they all cried; "let's have them all."

"All right; then here goes."

THE PRISONER AND THE FLOWER.

A prisoner had a flow'ret,
　That grew within the niche
Of his window, barred with iron—
　In his flow'ret he was rich!

It was his sole possession,
　His garden and his park;
It made his cell less dreary,
　And his gloomy life less dark.

A ray of sunshine used to come,
　For one hour of the day;
The flow'ret drank its radiance,
　And flourished bright and gay.

A wall was built beyond the cell,
　It blocked the sunbeam bright;
The flow'ret drooped and faded, for
　It missed the cheerful light.

The prisoner mourned for the ray,
　That each day stayed an hour,
And cheered his life and kept in bloom,
　His paltry little flower.

The flower was Hope, that flourished in
　The ray, your presence dear;
Fate was the wall that grew beyond;
　My life the prison drear.

The flower is dead, and dark and dull
　Is now the prison wall:
No sunshine of your presence casts
　A glory over all.

"Old Stephen seems to have given it up as a bad business," laughed Gurney, sneeringly.

"I've heard it before," put in Hunt, thoughtfully, "the idea, at all events. Wasn't there some Italian chap, who—"

"Yes, his name was Pic—dash it, what was it? Pic—Pic - well, something like that," said Standish.

"By gad, but it's pretty, Stephen," remarked a tall man, who had hardly spoken as yet, by name Cosmo Lawson.

"Dam," returned Stephen, politely, at which the screams of laughter rang out anew, "I say, are you fellows going to let me get into bed? It's beastly cold here."

"Bring him nearer the fire," commanded the senior, "and listen to this."

TO AN OLD CLAY PIPE.

'Tis but a cutty,
    A copper it cost ;
Yet I feel somehow
    A friend I have lost.

Clayey companion,
    Faithful and true,
I was proud of the blackness
    I'd given to you.

I've smoked you while skating,
    Sharpest the breeze ;
Returning from drilling.
    Marching at ease.

"Most defective line," put in a laughing voice; "why, hang it, it sounds like a dragoon at the manœuvres.'

"Keep quiet," was the unceremonious reply from the reader, who continued —

Oft on the river, too,
    Laid in a skiff,
I basked in the sunlight
    Enjoying a whiff.

Stretched on the sand, too,
    Watching the sea,
Thinking of nothing.
    I puffed at thee.

Plans I projected,
    In council with you,
Dreams I indulged in
    That never came true.

Calming all fretfulness
    Out of my soul ;
Placid forgetfulness
    Came from your bowl.

All things must finish,
    And pipes have an end;
Your ebon bowl's broken
    Too badly to mend.

Yes! Lastly I broke you,
    Companion of clay;
No more shall I smoke you,
    But—throw you away.

They had all remained quite silent to hear the last poem, but as Gurney's voice died away a torrent of comments broke forth.

"Old Stephen will be Poet Laureate yet," quoth one.

"By gad, but they are clever," said a second.

"Don't look so black, old man," cried a third; "there's nothing to be ashamed of in them.'

"I think," put in Hunt, "that after that we ought to let old Stephen go to bed, poor chap. After all, he got the worst of the major's infliction."

"I think so, too."

"And I."

"And I. I say shake hands, Stephen, and don't bear malice. They're deuced good verses"

Half-a-dozen hands were stretched out to grasp Stephen's, and, by the time he was free, Captain Gurney had gone.

He did not stay out of bed very long; he snatched up the loose slips of paper off the mantel-shelf, and gathered up those scattered about the floor, tumbling them all into his drawer and locking it securely. Then he went to bed as before, and slept, not dreaming this time that Judith Scrope had married the Devil. His visions were even worse than that, for he dreamed that she had married Captain Gurney; and when he awoke he was not sure that, of the two, the latter would not be the greatest and most dire calamity. He absolutely hated the senior captain.

CHAPTER II.

THERE was no doubt whatever that Stephen Thorold, lieutenant of the 52nd dragoons, was very much in love with the brigade-major's sister-in-law. That the senior captain of that regiment was in the same boat with him was a fact not generally so well known; nevertheless it was perfectly true. At last Captain Gurney had fallen in love! not, mind you, in the " lightly-come-lightly-go " fashion, in which nine men out of ten are perpetually paying court to the sightless god, but in real, genuine, downright earnest. He had, two or three years earlier, been attracted by Mrs. St. Hilary—then Elinor Warwick—and later, he had admired Alys Lifford, sufficiently to do everything he could to prevent Patrick O'Shaughnassy from marrying her; but for neither of these ladies had he ever felt as he did for Judith Scrope. He used to wonder sometimes what there was in the girl to make him care for her so much ? She was hardly a beauty—indeed, her beauty was chiefly of the kind known across the Channel as *du diable.* She was young and bright, had clear, laughing blue eyes and ruddy brown hair, but she really was not a beauty. Captain Gurney admitted that, and yet—and yet—those laughing eyes disturbed his slumbers quite as often as Stephen Thorold's ; and since he had known her, he had grown *almost* tired of practical joking. After all, he thought, when he left Stephen's room that night and sought his own—after all, it was but poor fun ; and he didn't know if it was not rather beneath him to indulge in it. He would, most likely, be major before very long, and then, of course, that sort of thing would be utterly out of the question—as impossible almost as for the commander-in-chief himself. And so, he thought, as, with a great sigh, he flung himself into a chair and stared moodily into the fire, he didn't know if it would not be as well to give it up at once. It certainly was but stupid work, and lately he had found it but poor sport—that was since he had known Judith. And then Captain Gurney leaned back in his chair, and, closing his eyes, gave himself up to delicious waking dreams, dreams of the bright chestnut-haired girl that he had learned to care for, even so much that he wanted to amend his ways for her sweet sake—dreams of her, Judith Scrope no longer, but his wife—dreams of her, together with him, in foreign lands on their wedding-tour—at home in the old house, where he had scarcely ever cared to go since his mother died, because the memories, which pervaded the whole place, seemed out of harmony with the life he was accustomed to lead : quiet, happy, *respectable* dreams they were, in which Judith Scrope was the leading figure.

The little travelling clock above his head rang out two sharp strokes, ere Captain Gurney roused himself. Then, unlike Stephen, he divested himself of his clothes very deliberately, and stayed to read several much-crushed papers ere he, at length, sought his couch—and the papers were some of Stephen's poems of which he had taken possession !

When Stephen Thorold turned out of his bed the following morning, his man had set his room in something like order. Therefore, to his master's eyes, the " hay " which had been made the previous night was of a very trifling description. He looked round with an air of satisfaction, and muttered : " Not so bad ; they've torn that chair-cover, though. I say, Simpson—Simp —*son !* "

" Yes, sir," Simpson answered, bustling in with two large cans filled with water.

" See Mrs. Saunders mends that chair-cover," he said ; " I think that's all the damage."

"This 'ere glass vase smashed, sir," Simpson returned, pointing to an empty space on the top of the drawers, " and the piano's scratched a good deal."

" Umph ! Well, there'll be the deuce to pay when Aggie sees that. Ah ! well, I suppose it can't be helped."

There was no doubt of that ; and Stephen Thorold was a young man of as fairly a philosophical turn of mind as may be met with now-a-days—ergo, he said no more about the mischief done in his room but set about dressing.

Five minutes later the outer door opened, and Hunt entered.

" Are you here, Stephen ? " he asked, as he pushed the door

open. He glanced round the empty room, and hearing the splashing of much water in the adjoining apartment, seated himself leisurely in the largest of the three easy chairs to await Stephen's appearance. At last he came—fresh, rosy smiling.

"Oh, it's you, is it?" he remarked.

"Yes. I say, old man, you're in for it, and no mistake."

"In for what?" turning sharply round, and looking enquiringly at his comrade, with his comb suspended in the air above his head, and his curly hair all over his eyes.

"For a three weeks' march."

Stephen groaned aloud, and banged his comb down, with an ugly naughty word upon his lips.

"No use making a row," laughed his friend.

"No, hang it; I only wish there was," returned poor Stephen, in great disgust. "How do you know? Where is it to?"

"It's to Dublin, with that draft of horses for the 4th," he answered. "And I know, because I've just been down to the mess, and the major told me."

"Why on earth, I wonder, couldn't the colonel have sent Osborne?" Stephen grumbled, taking up his brush again and proceeding with his toilet.

"Oh!" with a laugh, "he has got out of it nicely. Told the colonel he has a boil under his knee, and got the doctor to back him up."

"Brute," said Stephen, with a sigh. "By Jove, but I will pay him out for this."

"Can't you get up an ailment?" Hunt laughed.

"Why, look at me," he returned dolefully; "a miserable, pasty-faced duffer like Osborne can always be ill on occasion; but I—why, the chief would only laugh at me."

"Well, you must make the best you can of it," his friend said, rising and taking a leisurely survey of the numerous little knick-knacks on the mantel-shelf. "I say, Stephen."

"Well."

"Has it ever occurred to you how Gurney is altered?"

" Altered! No."

" Ah! I thought you'd have seen it. I can't make out whether he's getting old, or fallen in love, or what; but if you just think of it a moment, he is very much tamer and quieter than he used to be."

" Yes, perhaps he is," Stephen answered. " He doesn't care so much about 'drawing' fellows as he used to do. Getting past it, I should think."

But no suspicion of the truth crossed his mind. He found, when he went down to the mess, that Hunt's news was but too true. His orders were to start at nine the following morning in charge of a draft of forty-four horses and thirty-four men—the horses for the 4th at Dublin, and to return with the men by sea from Dublin to Portsmouth, and back to Colchester by rail. " It will take at least three weeks," muttered Stephen, blankly, when he had learned these details and given up a forlorn hope which had, until that moment, flourished in his breast, that, after all, Hunt's information might be but a joke.

" Cost you a pound a day," said one officer.

" Wish I was going," cried another.

" Horrid bore; the responsibility and all that," quoth a third.

" I shouldn't mind it but for the beastly sea part of it," remarked a fourth.

But Stephen took no heed of their comments; he hurried through his breakfast, and was already outside the mess when officers' call sounded. He was one of the first into the office, and, as soon as he had received his orders, asked for leave from morning stables. It was granted, as a matter of course, and Stephen rushed up to his rooms, hurrying off his uniform and dragging on plain clothes with double-quick speed.

" Hollo, Stephen, where are you off to?" cried one or two comrades who were dawdling about outside.

" Bye, bye," Stephen shouted in reply and was off like the wind.

His way took him to the brigade-major's house on the Lexden Road, which he reached in an incredibly short time, ringing a peal loud enough to awaken the seven sleepers, and supplementing his efforts by a prolonged hammering at the door. He was performing in the last respect when the man flung the door open.

"Miss Scrope at home, or Mrs. Winton?" he asked, mentioning Mrs. Winton as an afterthought, just for the sake of appearances.

"The ladies have gone up to town, sir," the man replied.

"For the day?"

"Yes, sir. They are to return by the last train."

"Oh !—thanks."

He left a card, though it was so early in the day, and turned away feeling dazed and queer, for upon such a calamity as this he had not for a moment counted. And yet, that two ladies should go up to town for the day was not an unusual occurrence; it was only particularly unlucky. For a moment, as he went slowly along the pretty road, he wondered whether it would be much use to go up to town after them? No; it would be like looking for a needle in a bottle of hay, or a pearl amongst a peck of barley. No, that was out of the question; but there was one thing he could do. He might be at the station—by accident, of course—when the last train came in, and there would be no chance of missing them. Having decided upon this plan, he went more hopefully into town, to do a moderate amount of shopping, necessarily of a very moderate description in Colchester, and found his way back to barracks in time for lunch. Most of the officers were already at the meal, and the moment he showed himself in the mess-room he was greeted by a volley of chaff.

"Hallo! here's D.C.L.," one laughed.

Stephen looked very blank indeed. "What the deuce is the joke of that?" he asked.

"I say, Stephen," cried another, "you won't forget me when you get to the top of the tree?"

'What tree?"

"Stephen Thorold, D.C.L., Poet Laureate," he laughed.

"Oh! shut up," Stephen cried, with great good temper, all things duly considered.

"Are you good at impromptus, Stephen?" asked a bald-headed captain, who, having been in the ranks, was much older than any officer at the table.

"Pretty fair," said Stephen, and forthwith put up a long arm and emptied the contents of the mustard-pot over the ancient captain's hairless pate. "Of that kind at least, my friend."

Stephen was like Betty, of world-wide renown; "he knowed his man," and he disposed of Captain McKey's chaff in a more summary manner than he would otherwise probably have dared to do. For a moment the laugh turned against the Scotchman, but it surged back to its original butt immediately.

"Well," remarked the captain next in seniority to Gurney, "I've been in this regiment a good many years, and I've seen a good many changes. We've had fellows who could sketch and paint; fellows who could sing and play, or shoot and ride; but I'll be shot if we ever turned out a poet before."

"By-the-bye," exclaimed another, "how did the chief get to hear anything about it?"

Stephen looked up, the very picture of dismay. "The chief," he gasped.

"Yes, man, the chief!" I heard him laughing with the major about it this morning."

"Where?"

"Oh! I was lying on the sofa in the ante-room, and they were outside."

"What did they say, Standish?" Hunt asked.

"The colonel said he understood they were very clever, and then the major—confound him—croaked out that he thought Thorold would be better employed learning his duty instead of occupying his time in trashy sentimental verses."

"What did the chief say?"

"Oh! he laughed outright and said, 'Well, I dare say you will never waste your time that way.'"

The tide was quite turned from Stephen then, and the absent major took up every one's attention."

" I should think not, ugly brute," muttered one officer. " I never could understand how he kept civil long enough for that nice little wife of his to marry him."

" Nor I," Stephen answered. "How miserable she does look always."

" Oh ! they say he thrashes her," put in the man on Stephen's right.

" Nonsense," said one or two incredulous voices.

" Fact ! I've seen her wrist all finger-marks myself, though of course they mightn't be his doing ; but, from the way I've seen her watching him when I've been calling or dining there, I should be inclined to believe the worst."

" I wonder she doesn't leave him."

" Nowhere to go. Don't you know who she was ?"

" Not an idea."

" Her father was major of the —rd Foot, and she hasn't a relation in the world—she told me so herself."

" Poor little soul," said Stephen, tenderly. " Oh ; but upon my word, the women have hard times very often ;" and then he wondered, would the time ever come when he would leave black tokens of his fingers upon Judith Scrope's little slender white wrists ? Stephen felt very sure he would not; but, then, doubtless, no man—not even the objectionable major —starts with the fixed intention of leading his wife a life of terror and wretchedness.

Colchester is not a particularly amusing place, and the day seemed almost as long as the previous one had done. Stephen dawdled through the dull afternoon as best he could, and hailed the dinner-hour with unusual gladness; generally he did not care much about it—one way or another. The colonel was dining that night, so he was spared any very marked chaff, and the little that went on, in a subdued tone, in his neighbourhood he did not mind. He could not help reddening a little, though, when Colonel Lifford addressed him once or twice, but since he said nothing on the subject he did not care for that very much either, and so the evening slipped over quickly and pleasantly enough—rather too quickly for Stephen, for it was nearly

eleven when the colonel rose, and he was free to betake himself
to the station.

He did not, naturally, spend much time in changing his
clothes, and, being a good walker, was at the station long
before the arrival of the train. Well, that was a comfort!
He lounged about the platform, looking at the placards posted
up on the walls, consulting his watch, and thinking it not a
little strange that Major Winton had not come to meet his wife
and sister-in-law. Perhaps he was away; at all events, it
would be all the better for him, for he would be able to see them
safely home, and thus have a chance of saying what he wanted
to say to Judith. He had not to wait very long, for presently
the appearance of a light in the distance told him that the train
was coming. The light gleamed larger, and clearer, and nearer,
through the darkness and the night-gloom, and then, the train,
like an insinuating monster, glided almost noiselessly up to the
platform, and the passengers for Colchester streamed out.
Stephen stood still and watched eagerly. There was Bernard
of the Artillery, Lucy of the 200th and his wife, a few soldiers,
the quartermaster of his own regiment, and a dozen or so
of shabby civilians and women—*and there was no Judith Scrope.*

Poor Stephen was utterly dismayed. He waited until the
train had taken its departure, and then he walked slowly out of
the station like a man in a dream, refusing an offer of a seat in
Captain Bernard's cab without thinking of what he was doing.
What could he do? They must have returned by the five
o'clock train! What a fool he had been not to come up and
meet that one on the chance of their having come by it. Well,
he had never thought of it, and it was no use crying over that
now; nor could he very well make any excuse to go to Major
Winton's house at that time of night. Therefore he could do
nothing but submit himself to Fate; that was what was
against him. When he reached his rooms he opened his blot-
ting book and took therefrom a sheet of paper, on which was
written a little poem which had escaped the eyes of his
tormentors on the previous night.

KISMIT.

Alla il illa,
Wah Mahmoud rasool ila !
Fellow mortals, why complain !
When you suffer grief or pain !
Or why triumph when you gain
  Kismit ! It is destiny !

Surely as the minutes climb,
Round the mighty clock of Time,
And the hour's succeeding chime,
  You fulfil your destiny.

See a man crowned with success,
Fortune ever seems to bless,
And he knows no bitterness :
  He fulfils his destiny.

See a man, who, for no sin,
Ev'ry effort beaten in,
Ever fated not to win :
  He fulfils his destiny.

Grievèd be not then or gay,
Whether rough or smooth your way,
Take things as they come, and say,
  "Kismit ! It is destiny."

What is joy or sorrow worth ?
Valueless both grief and mirth ;
We are puppets on this earth !
  "Kismit ! It is destiny."

"I believe there's something in it," Stephen said aloud, as he laid the paper back in its hiding-place; "at all events, I've done my best to see her, and failed, so Fate must have had something to do with it. If it's for the best 'Kismit' will keep her true until I come back. I'll run the risk of trusting her."

And so it happened that Stephen Thorold went away from Colchester without seeing Judith Scrope again, though, if he had known what a very determined rival he had in the person of Captain Gurney, it is probable that he would not so readily have left his future so trustfully to Fate ! And thus also it was that he never missed the verses, which had been purloined during the scramble on the previous evening ; he had thrust those left on the chimney-shelf back into his drawer, and never thought of examining them closely to see if any were gone.

Chapter III.

Stephen Thorold had gone, and then Captain Gurney had, he felt, a fair field; for, what was best of all, there was no probable, or, indeed, possible, chance of his return for at least three weeks. And what might he not be able to do in three weeks? He sauntered up to the brigade-major's house that afternoon, and, more lucky than poor Stephen had been on the previous day, found Mrs. Winton and her sister at home. He was just in time to join them at their afternoon cup of tea, and contrived to make himself so agreeable that Mrs. Winton asked him to dine on the following evening.

And he had a good deal of chat with Judith, too, for several other people came in, and so engrossed Mrs. Winton's attention. He was very glad of that, of course, and thought Judith's blue eyes looked more irresistible than ever; he caught himself thinking wistfully, yet with great happiness, that, if only he could win them for his own, if only he could teach the bright face to brighten at his return, the soft eyes to sadden when he left them,—he thought his future would have much more real placid, lasting joy than he had ever had in the past. His past had not been happy! He was ashamed, now that he contrasted himself with this ruddy-haired, blue-eyed girl, wearing in all her looks and words, and surely he could trust his life upon it, in her thoughts, too, "the white flower of a blameless life:" he was ashamed of his past; it was so widely apart from hers. The last fifteen of his five-and-thirty years, he had spent to worse than no purpose. If he could have gone to sleep at twenty and never wakened up to the present d y, he felt even such oblivion would have been better than his worse than wasted years.

"What are you thinking of?" Judith asked suddenly. "I am sure of something unpleasant."

"The past," he answered, briefly.

"Dear me," with a laugh. "Has that been so very disagreeable?"

"It has been regretful," said he, gravely, "and I regret it, though I never did until—*now*."

"Oh!" she cried, lightly, "it is never any use looking back; and between you and me, Captain Gurney, I always thought it a little—a little—what shall I say? well, spiritless."

"Your past and mine have been different."

"How do you know?" she asked coquettishly.

Captain Gurney smiled. "I know what mine has been," he answered, the smile about his lips deepening, "and I look at you and—*voila!*"

Some swift, subtle instinct told Judith that he was right. She knew nothing of the wild orgies, the reckless dissipation, the mad follies and sins in which his life had been spent, but she looked in his face and she saw the traces of those years' work but too plainly visible. Perhaps Captain Gurney saw that she perceived it, for he changed the subject abruptly, and they drifted away into other topics of a less personal nature, and presently Miss Scrope showed him a well-drawn caricature of the commanding officer of the 200th, which Major Winton had brought home from their mess-table the previous evening.

"I say it is incomplete," she said, brightly; "it should have a few words or verses of explanation at the foot; but Mr. Osmond, who drew it, says he has no gift that way."

"Let me add the foot-note," he suggested.

"Very well. Here is a pencil, or do you care for ink?"

"This will do, thanks." He wrote a few lines hastily beneath the sketch, and handed it to Judith for perusal. She looked half puzzled for a moment, then began reading, in a low voice, "*Speaks short and sharp, eyes unsettled, face flushed. Alas! poor Roland. That bout last even, must have been too much e'en for thy seasoned head, or perchance the dice were unpropitious, or perchance some fair dame—but no, methinks you would not fret yourself for that, my philosophical Roland. But cheer up: care, thou knowest, brought a cat to an untimely end.*"

"Where did you get that?" the girl asked; "what is it out of?"

"Oh, it is part of a scene I wrote some years ago," the

soldier answered, carelessly. "I thought I had mistaken my vocation, and ought to have been poet instead of dragoon."

"Oh, you write poetry?"

"Certainly not," with a laugh. "But in my schoolboy days I strung a few lines together, and thought them verses."

"You have not any with you, I suppose?"

"My dear young lady, most assuredly not," he returned.

"I am so fond of poetry," Judith said, dreamily; "I wish you would bring some of your verses to-morrow evening?"

"If you really insist upon it," in a deprecating tone; "but really, Miss Scrope, my poor attempts are—are not worth the trouble of reading."

"Bring them," said she, imperatively; "I shall be dreadfully disappointed if you do not."

"Then you leave me no choice," he replied, gallantly.

He betook himself back to barracks a few minutes later as sorely puzzled as ever any man was in this world. What he should do he didn't know. He knew perfectly well that the verses he had spoken of would only make Miss Scrope laugh —being the merest doggrel, of this type—

> Oh! my heart is very sore,
>   For I shall never see her more,
> And very often I could roar
>   For Mary Jane!
>
> Oh! I loved her very much,
>   And my love for her was such,
> I could bear no one to touch
>   My Mary Jane!
>
> My love had eyes of liquid blue,
>   She vowed she would to me be true,
> She said it, with her head askew,
>   My Mary Jane!

He felt it would not do to take such an "attempt" as that for Miss Scrope's inspection. He was completely hedged, for he dared not go without them; and where to get any fairly good original poems he did not know. Then suddenly an idea occurred to him. Ah! why should he not copy out those verses he had taken from Stephen Thorold the other night? Happy thought! He would act upon it.

Act upon it he certainly did, and found his way to the Winton's house the following evening, fully prepared to undergo a searching examination from Miss Scrope on the subject of verse writing.

"I hope you have not forgotten the verses," she said, confidentially, when he gave her his arm into dinner.

"I could not forget anything you wished," he responded.

"Oh," remarked Miss Scrope, a little blankly : she had not bargained for that tone of devotion. But after dinner, all the same, she demanded the poems, and, with a little show of unwillingness, Captain Gurney produced them. She took them from him and began reading, in the way she had done on the previous day, almost to herself.

CHARGE OF CHASSEURS.

The smoke cleared away as the foe was advancing,
Their massy battalions loomed darkling and large ;
The sun on their bayonets was fitfully glancing,
As the notes of our trumpets rang out for the charge.

And Fortune, alas ! ever fickle, had left us,
And hurled us from victory into defeat ;
Of our best and our bravest black death had bereft us,
The rest of the army was beating retreat.

The Moblôts were routed, the fellows who spouted,
In terms so heroic—the ci-devant braves ;
Save the wounded and dying, the rabble were flying,
Mixed up with the line and the tawny Zouaves.

An aide-de-camp, panting, our orders had brought us,
With bloody foam flecked was his gay sabretache !
He reeled, ere our lesson he fully had taught us,
The blood welling under his yellow moustache.

Our colonel's stern face, as he turned to address us,
Lit up with the battle-glow, lurid though wan,
" The foe must be checked ; you perceive how they press us,
My lads : we must stop them, or die to a man."

Miss Scrope laid the paper down with a long, long sigh.

"I think it is perfectly lovely," she said, at last.

"Oh ! hardly that !" Captain Gurney answered, with much humility. "Mere doggrel."

"I don't see why it is always necessary for people to

noise, and most of my readers will know that it takes a good deal to astonish officers of dragoons.

In spite of their efforts to discover who the author was, Stephen refused to tell them; but presently, when Captain Gurney came up and asked him the question plainly, he gave him a plain, straightforward reply.

" Who wrote those poems, Thorold?" he asked curtly.

" Miss Scrope," said Stephen, quietly.

Captain Gurney stood quite still for a moment, and Stephen, being like Duncan Grey of old " a lad o' Grace," forebore to look at him at all, but confined his attention strictly to the pictures on the opposite wall.

The older man tried for a moment to think ! The events of the past month surged into his brain with painful distinctness ; how Judith had praised the poems and lifted her blue eyes with such innocent sweetness to his—how she had held him at arm's length, yet each day drawn him on a little further and a little farther—how she had—bah ! he couldn't think of it any longer, but he rapped out two short words, which nearly sent Stephen's gravity off the balance, and they were—" Little Devil !"

THE HERO OF THE REGIMENT

Chapter I.

Captain Gurney was utterly tired of his old regiment, and had made up his mind to leave it. So long as his comfort depended upon the behaviour of his brother officers he was very well content, for all soldiers are willing to overlook practical jokes, and subalterns are compelled to do so. But sometimes the juniors have wives, and when those wives are very beautiful and very popular women, they have it in their power to make matters particularly unpleasant for any officer to whom they may have taken a dislike. However greatly an officer may be offended and annoyed by so-called jokes, even though they have been carried beyond all bounds of reason, three words will generally set everything straight and make him forget all about it; but with his wife reconciliation is not always so easily effected; if she resolutely declines to forget what is past, and cannot forgive " fun "—at the worst only intended to relieve the tedium of dull country quarters—the unlucky offender may find his life much less pleasant than it might otherwise have been to him. Now this was precisely the box in which Captain Gurney found himself, and he did not relish the position at all. When, after dinner or ball, the men were, one and all, raving of the beauty, and the wit, and the charms of Mrs. Gerard St. Hilary or Mrs. Patrick O'Shaughnassy, not forgetting Mrs. Stephen Thorold, it was galling in the extreme to this gallant gay Lothario to be obliged to own that he had no acquaintance with any of them. When all his comrades went on Sunday afternoon to the house of one or other of those ladies, for an early cup of tea, he could not do likewise, because he had not been asked. When he met the two first in the street (Judith was more merciful), they

looked him full in the eyes without the slightest inclination of
either handsome head; he felt all his temper—and it was a
passionately fierce one—surging up tumultuously within him,
and he vowed bitter vengeance against the pair of them, and
looked forward with intense eagerness to the day when he should
have brought one or both of them to his feet, when they should
acknowledge his power and atone for by-gone scorn with
pleading humiliation; when those eyes which looked so straightly
into his own, should drop before his in supplicating fear.   Nay,
I must confess, he looked eagerly forward to the time when
Gerard St. Hilary and Patrick O'Shaughnassy should find their
hearts desolate; but

> There's a divinity that shapes our ends,
> Rough-hew them how we will.

The day which Greville Gurney anticipated never came.   Without doubt, he was handsome enough and fascinating withal, but,
bless you, the man never got a chance.   Elinor St. Hilary and
Alys O'Shaughnassy wouldn't have him at any price . . . they
agreed that their safest plan would be to keep on the firm ground
of non-acquaintance, and not trust themselves upon the perilous
and extremely uncertain ocean of Captain Gurney's friendship.
At last he felt he could endure life in the old regiment no longer :
he was too fond of his profession to dream of leaving the army,
but he made up his mind that he must exchange, when, to his
unspeakable joy and satisfaction, he obtained the majority, and
immediately exchanged with Major Ford of the 7th Lancers,
then in India. So he turned his back upon the old set, followed
only, I fear, by the regrets of his commanding officer, for he was
a smart soldier, whom Colonel Lifford was sorry to lose, and
Colonel Cornwallis was glad to gain.   He gave a handsome
piece of silver to the mess-plate, and had a grand farewell
dinner given to him, at which, if my reader had been present,
he might reasonably have supposed that the officers were, one
and all, convinced that the hope and prestige of the regiment
were departing from them in the person of Greville Gurney, and
yet they knew—and what was worse, he knew—that they were
all very glad to be rid of him.   But his advent into the 7th was

eagerly expected, more especially by the chief, for smart officers, like good-looking curates, are at a premium, so he felt that the change was all for the best.

He had never thought, or indeed intended, to go to India; but, after all, he rather liked the idea. The 7th had only some three years to remain in India, and, by the time he returned, he could set about finding a wife in downright good earnest.

However, before the good ship sighted the Rock, the idea had entered his brain and taken very firm root there, for, curiously enough, he found amongst the passengers Mrs. Cornwallis, the wife of his new colonel, and her sister, Miss Bannister.

Violet and Dorothea Bannister were co-heiresses, and had been left orphans at a very early age. In appearance they were not much alike, for Violet, the elder by two years, was fair, with a gentle, saint-like expression of countenance, and large limpid eyes, of so deep a blue that her fanciful young mother had insisted upon her being called—Violet.

"You know, Jack," she had said to her husband, when he demurred a little, wishing himself to call the child after her, "we can give the next one my great mouthful of a name," and so the child was christened Violet, later shortened into Vi; but when the next one came there was no question of dispute about her name, for the young mother lay in a darkened chamber above, while a grave-faced clergyman performed the ceremony of baptism in haste, fearing that the morsel of humanity, whose tiny life had cost so dear a price, would die in his arms ere it was concluded.

But the child did not die: the elder Dorothea, with all her strong affections and her bright hopes of life, passed away; but the younger one, with her few hours' hold upon existence, struggled on and lived.

About her name there had been no question, but by it she was never called. Mr. Bannister could not bear the sound of it, and was eagerly glad when, somehow, the tiny, dark-haired, dusky-eyed child came to be known in the household as Floss. So Floss she was called, and Floss she remained, long after her father had followed his young wife across the dark river, and after Vi had been three years married to Colonel Cornwallis of the 7th Lancers.

When Vi had married, at twenty, to go to India immediately —for she had met Colonel Cornwallis whilst on leave—Floss had not been in very robust health, and the doctors had advised her not accompanying her sister just then. She therefore went to live with the aunt, with whom they had spent all their holidays, and who divided her time equally between Paris, London, and Scarborough. The three years had passed in a perfect whirl of pleasure for Floss, but she had not followed her sister's example and entered upon the holy state of matrimony. Mrs. Garth was in no hurry to lose the girl who made her life so daily, hourly bright, whose fascinating ways made her house the most sought after domicile in whatever town they happened to be living ; and so it happened that when, after a few hours' illness, Mrs. Garth was taken away from the pleasures she loved so dearly, Floss was completely left alone. She had no relatives but the Cornwallises, and she telegraphed to Vi to come, if possible, to settle their aunt's affairs, and take her back to India with her.

Thus it happened that, after a three months' sojourn in England, Mrs. Cornwallis was returning to her husband, taking Floss with her. And then everything seemed *couleur de rose* to Greville Gurney's eyes. Surely no man ever went that voyage with a more contented heart than his ! He had nothing to do, nothing to worry him, no disagreeable, handsome subalterns' wives to annoy him with their airs and graces ; he had no temptations to indulge in his old favourite pursuit of practical joking, and he had at all hours of the day Floss Bannister to watch and talk to. And, of course, it was pleasant for the sisters to have the major of their own regiment travelling with them : they made pleasant little excursions wherever they stopped ; they had a dozen little innocent jokes of their own— that is to say, strictly among themselves—which they did not share with the other passengers, and the trio enjoyed life immensely. It was *couleur de rose* for all of them. Vi, who was

going back to her husband, and to seeing whom she counted
the days and almost the hours, used to idle under a huge white
umbrella, thinking of little else save the stern, bronzed face,
with its well-waxed dark moustaches, which was to her as no
other on the whole earth ; and Floss, always restless, always
with some employment, flirting with Greville Gurney, who, for
his part, was so supremely, calmly happy, that he almost wished
the voyage would last for ever.

But it did not : in time it came to an end, and they reached
Bombay, where they found Colonel Cornwallis waiting for them.
It may readily be imagined that during the days which followed
Captain Gurney's opportunities of seeing Floss Bannister were
not lessened : he opened his eyes in astonishment at the marvellous way in which the chief's little wife bloomed out and
expanded after they landed ; he could hardly believe it was the
same woman. He had wondered during the voyage if she could
really be Miss Bannister's sister ; they seemed so different : the
one all fire and vivacity, the other so languidly indifferent to
all subjects save that of reaching Bombay. But now that he
saw her under what Floss called " favourable circumstances,"
he was fairly dumb with amazement. It was as if a little
sickly bud, with seemingly not sufficient strength to bloom, had
suddenly been transformed into a gorgeous rose, with all her
velvet-like petals, her fragrance and her many graces set forth
for the benefit of all beholders : he wondered if Floss would
ever love him like that? He did not know ; he was not sure.
He thought she seemed brighter and more sparkling when he
was near her ; he fancied her great dark eyes lighted up with
more than their usual radiance when he approached her ; he
tried hard to persuade himself that he was *quite* sure she loved
him, but he could not altogether succeed. He had made several
mistakes upon that subject lately, and, somehow, he had not
heart enough to put it to the test and have done with it. He
haunted the colonel's bungalow until the chief suggested to his
wife that Gurney had better take lodgings with them altogether,
but he got no further with Floss. Try as he would, he could
not induce her to look at anything in a serious light : if ever

he approached, no matter how cautiously, the topics of loneliness or marriage, Floss immediately opened out upon what she called her " views."

" I don't think I quite believe in marriage, Major Gurney," she said one day, when he had expressed his envy of a fellow-officer, who was just entering the holy state. " It's all very well for *men*, but for us poor women !—why, it is neither more nor less than giving up a kingdom to become a slave. Now, just take me for an example ! I have now between twenty and thirty adorers—humble, abject adorers."

" Yes, I know," muttered Major Gurney between his teeth. There were just seven and twenty, without counting himself.

" Not that I consider them very delightful," Floss continued, with gravely pursed-up mouth. " In fact, strictly between you and me, they are rather a nuisance, so many of them. But then, supposing I was to marry one of them—why, he might turn out like the husband of a friend of mine. What do you think he does ?"

" Beats her perhaps," suggested the major.

" *Much* worse," Floss cried, energetically—she had not been in India long enough to become languid. " She is five and twenty, a gentlewoman by birth and education, the mother of two children, and he *never gives her a penny !*"

" By Jove !" muttered the major, in astonishment ; " but perhaps she has money of her own ?"

" Not a farthing."

" But how does she dress herself ?"

" Oh, when she cannot do without a dress any longer, he goes and buys her one, and he pays her dress-maker's bill himself. I have seen him buy six pair of gloves for himself and *one* for her ; and once, when I was staying there, he went himself to pay a woman who had been helping in the kitchen," she ended, indignantly.

" What a mean hound !" ejaculated Major Gurney, in very real tones of condemnation.

The mischievous laughter in Floss Bannister's dusky eyes

deepened, and the indignant ring in her voice grew more pro-nounced.

"Ah! but I told that story once to a man who wanted to marry me," she laughed, "and he used those very words, 'What a mean hound!' I must admit that they sounded so real that he completely took me in, but I heard not long after-wards that during the nine years he was married—for he was a widower—he never once bought *his* wife a gown, and the only decent dresses she had, her mother gave her!"

Within himself Major Gurney groaned. It was no use arguing with Floss any further, he knew; she had triumphed. Yet he laughed! He had, he was perfectly aware of it, many objectionable (points, but meanness was not one of them. He laughed half a dozen times that day at the idea of his paying Floss's bills, and doling out a pair of gloves at a time. He thought it would be rather nice than otherwise to have those coaxing eyes up-lifted to his, that coaxing mouth teazing for a new dress or a set of furs, to hear her winning tones saying persuasively, "Greville, *do* buy me that bonnet."

And yet to him there was something absolutely appalling in the idea of a pretty woman not being able to have as many gowns and bonnets as she required. He should like the coaxing eyes, the coaxing mouth, and the winning tones dearly enough, but he would prefer to hear them say, "Greville, *do* take me for a drive," or, "Darling, *please* don't stay away a moment longer than you can help," to "Greville, *do* buy me that bonnet."

When a man is in love it does not take much to put him into a perfect paradise of bliss—only about as much as is required to throw him into a fever of unrest and misery. Major Gurney that evening was happy—very happy. He went to bed and slept soundly; he did not often do that. He was not bitten once by *anything* during the whole night, and he dreamt that Floss Bannister had come and put her soft arms round his neck and said, "Love me, Greville. Poor fellow, it was like falling from Heaven into the nethermost torment, when he woke to find his bearer's black face peeping through the curtains, and

"Four o'clock, Sahib," sounding in his ears. Why it was an absolute insult to Floss that a wretched Hindoo should recall her to his mind.

As usual, during his morning ride, he fell in with the Cornwallises and Miss Bannister, and, for a wonder, the latter was unattended.

"How grave you look," she remarked, when they were riding quietly abreast, "Had a bad night?"

"Quite the contrary—an unusually good one," he replied.

"Then what is the matter?" she persisted.

"Oh! I've been thinking of what you said yesterday," he returned gravely.

"What about?"

"About getting married."

An expression of intense amusement came into her eyes, as quickly followed by a certain tenderness, which, if Major Gurney had noticed, would have set everything straight between them; but unfortunately he did not, for Floss's face was bent almost to her saddle.

"And what have you been thinking about?" she asked at length.

"Well, of course, what you told me was very bad, very despicable," he answered, "and a fellow who behaves like that to his wife, ought to be sent to Coventry; but, still, there's something to be said on our side. Now, I know a lady, Miss Bannister, who never speaks to her husband, if she can possibly help it."

"Perhaps he deserves it," Floss suggested.

"Very likely, only that is hardly the way to help him to grow better, is it?"

Floss pulled her horse up sharply. "Don't speak to me in that way," she cried; "I'm not anyone's wife, thank goodness —if I were, I should behave myself properly; but don't bully me for some one else's misdoings." And then, like two silly children they burst out laughing, and rode on again. The major, however, had something to say, and he meant to say it.

"And I once knew a lady who spent just five times as much

as her husband could afford. He was a barrister; and to see
the poor chap toiling and slaving and working to provide things
for her, without thanks even. Oh! by George! but it did
make my blood boil. She used to do all sorts of things, too,
that he didn't like; and once, she proposed a mad freak, which
I said I was certain her husband would never permit.

"'Permit,' she laughed. 'Pooh!—I have a hold over that
man.'"

"Hateful wretch!" cried Floss, passionately. "I should
like to marry her to Winny's husband—he would let her see!
Hateful wretch!"

But, still, although he had gained a victory over Floss, it
cannot be said t'at Major Gurney's wooing throve apace. As
if to make up for the serious conversations they had indulged
in, Floss, for a few weeks, gave Major Gurney but little of her
society. Of the seven and twenty adorers, each had a turn—
such a turn, too, that with every one a match was predicted;
and then one or two new ones arrived on the scene. Floss
polished them all off. She was very particular, too, to carry on
her warmest flirtations just under the major's nose, driving him
thereby to the very verge of desperation.

And then the Cornwallises obtained leave, and went to Simla,
from whence he heard plentiful accounts of Floss's doings, and,
shall I dare to say it, misdoings? Poor Major Gurney, he
railed at the fate which would not give him leave; at the
utterly unjust and unequal way in which the little blind god
distributes his favours; and thus March and April slipped
away; and then he had fresh cause for grumbling, for just as
the Cornwallises returned, an attack of fever laid him on the
sick-list, and another fortnight passed before he saw her.

And, when at length he was able to crawl over to the
colonel's bungalow, there were rumours afloat, which put such
thoughts as favour and marriage out of his head, rumours
which gave the officers grave faces and the wives fearful hearts,
for the chiefest of them was—MUTINY.

Chapter II.

All English people know the history of that fearful struggle by heart—some by the brotherhood of nationality, others by bitter heartaches and weary blanks in the family circle, which may be filled up never more. And there are not a few who can look back to those weary months, when they stood cheek by jowl with grim death, with famine, torture, and even dishonour in his ghastly train. The words "Cawnpore," "Delhi," and "Lucknow," are sufficient to bring to our minds scenes and details which sickened us to read, and which sickens us now to recall to our remembrance. How gently-born, delicately-nurtured women and little children went through fearful privations and hardships during that awful time, only to end by finding themselves widowed or orphans. How thousands won for themselves a glorious crown of martyrdom, cruelly as did ever saints of old. How parents saw their little innocent babes murdered before their eyes while waiting for their own turn to come. Husbands shot their wives to save their honour—the tender wives whom they had brought from the safe shelter of their English homes. How, even after that, we are told, they died praying to the end—died, seeing resistance useless as only the English aristocrat can die—and are not the English of the truest aristocracy, inasmuch as they can fight like tigers and die without a murmur?

Colonel Cornwallis's first anxiety was to get his wife and sister as much out of harm's way as possible, and to the comparative safety of Simla he decided to send them, but, when the arrangements were all completed, an obstacle, unthought of before, presented itself in the shape of Mrs. Cornwallis's consent. He had taken that for granted. The idea of gentle, obedient Vi dreaming for one moment of setting up her will in opposition to his had never occurred to him. Vi, who lived and breathed and had her very being in him! Vi, who drooped and faded like a flower torn from the parent stem, if parted from him even for a day. That Vi should flatly refuse to go he had never anticipated, yet that was what she did.

" I won't go," she said, decidedly.

" Neither will I," announced her sister.

Colonel Cornwallis fairly groaned. That Floss should show her will was nothing new, or that she should follow her sister's lead, once in a way. If Vi had stormed and cried, had begged him, with sobs and tears, not to send her away, he would, he knew, have prevailed, but Vi did nothing of the sort. She lifted her great violet eyes boldly to his, she folded her hands placidly, and she said, " I won't go."

" Neither will I," said Floss.

" But my dearest," the colonel replied, " God only knows to what this may lead. In Simla you will be fairly safe. Think of my anxiety, if I see you here suffering and am unable to help you, think of my sorrow, if—if you are wounded, if—Oh, Vi, my darling, you must go! I shall at least have the comfort of knowing that you are safe. I insist upon your going."

" No," she replied, firmly, " I will not go. I have never once crossed your will since our marriage day. I cross it now by refusing to obey you. It is of no use insisting, I refuse to obey. I took you," she continued, with a sob in her voice, " for better for worse, for richer for poorer, till death us do part! This is my place, and here I remain."

" But, great heavens!" cried the major, who was present, " you may be killed! We cannot tell what the consequences may be. Floss"—stepping forward and taking her hand— " Floss, persuade her to do as we wish."

But Floss turned upon him with an indignant flash in her dark eyes, and flung the hand from her. " Do you think we Bannisters are cowards?" she cried, passionately. " If there is danger, we can share it; privation, we can try to lighten it; death, we can die like christians." And so they gave in, and the two brave girls won the day, but not before Colonel Cornwallis tried once again.

" Supposing I am killed, Vi," he said gravely, " I shall die with the agony of knowing that you are left at the mercy of these savages. Will you add that misery to my difficulties?"

" No, Bruce," she answered, "if we should be taken, I shall find death come sweetest from your hand, out of the pistols which I have loaded and polished for you so often! Yes, in that case, to save me greater torture, you will shoot me—it will be over in a moment! If you are killed, I can trust your officers to protect me, and, failing them," with a smile, " I shall have quite sufficient courage to send the bullet home myself." And so the day was won!

The story went from mouth to mouth, bringing tears to the eyes of the rough stalwart troopers, courage to the drooping hearts of their wives, who had not had the chance of escape, and comfort to the souls of the two men, who knew now what was the depth of those brave, loving, faithful hearts. They were glad then that their entreaties had not prevailed, for the two gentle girls had not stayed to become a burden and a hindrance. Their time was fully occupied, tending the sick and wounded, cheering the brave little band—which grew daily smaller and smaller—going fearlessly amid shot and shell on their rounds of hope and mercy, the sisters won the passionate love and admiration of every man, woman and child in the garrison. It was Vi, who gave her last tin of milk for the sick child of a private's wife ; it was Vi, whose breast pillowed the dying head of trooper and officer alike ; Vi, who wrote down loving messages of farewell, to be given if she should live through the rebellion ; it was to please Vi, that wounded men hushed their groans and terrified women tried to be brave. And Floss, what of her? Of the nursing and the cooking and the washing she did her share, but there was one duty she took upon herself and never failed in. The chaplain had enough upon his hands in burying the dead and helping Vi to comfort the dying, more than twice in the day, he could not visit the out-posts. Floss went almost every hour! How the men looked for her coming. With her pale, pale face, and her dark eyes, with her dark silky hair cut close to her head, partly on account of the terrible heat, partly to save time and trouble ; with her gown, which had once been white, but alas! was now all stained and yellow, and with her brave heart, open to all!

alike now, she seemed to them like some glorious angel, for surely it was the light of Heaven, which shone upon her face. Sometimes she brought her Bible and read a few verses, sometimes she sang a hymn, but more often she knelt simply down and repeated " Our Father" in her clear ringing tones, ending " The Lord bless us and keep us."

She would bring to one man news of his sick wife, to another tidings of his wounded comrade, to all courage and comfort, and still she did not shirk her woman's work.

And then the labour which fell upon her grew heavier, for Colonel Cornwallis was grievously wounded. Vi, who had worked like a very slave, left much of her work in the hospital to Floss ; she could scarcely be torn from her husband's side, and so Floss worked harder than ever. Her face grew paler and more wan, her eyes more haggard, her gown more torn and yellow, and upon the little hands, which had once been so white and soft, the traces of work became more apparent, and the enemy crept closer and closer. As her work in the garrison grew heavier, so did her self-imposed labour of love at the outposts and fortifications diminish, for, with almost every day, she had fewer to visit. Every day brave, bronzed, bearded faces were missing—faces that had brightened at her coming ; eyes that had lifted up with tenderest love for her were now closed in the sleep of death ; lips that had kissed the little work-worn hands gratefully were silenced for ever. She missed them, with a bitter heartache, and dared not trust herself to think which face might be gone when she came again ; but she bore up bravely through it all.

In what the defenders of the garrison were pleased to term safety, the misery was greater. No one had time for grief ; widows saw their dear ones carried away, but they might not sit down and weep ; there was more work than could be done waiting for their hands. Even Vi, having managed to get her husband a room alone in the little bungalow which stood in the compound of the one they had occupied, but which now formed the hospital, left him a good deal, that she might lighten her sister's load ; and so the time went on. Amongst others, the chaplain was killed, so then Floss was the only comforter of the defenders. They watched, anxiously enough, the pale face growing paler, the circles round the dark eyes deepening; they noted the least falter in the gentle voice, which had not much ring left in it, which had neither time nor strength for reading or for hymns, which now only gave utterance to those two short prayers,

Thy Kingdom come,
Thy will be done.

Only that and "the Lord bless us and keep us."

CHAPTER III.

At last Greville Gurney had given in, not from wounds, not sunstroke, not malady of any kind—only from sheer fatigue, from overpowering sleep.

Some of the men lifted him on to a mattress and carried him to the first room of the hospital. Just as they turned away Floss came out of an inner apartment with scared eyes and a single word upon her lips—" Wounded?"

" No, no, Miss, darlin'," answered one of them; " only dead beat he is; an hour of sleep'll do him all the good in the world."

" Ah!" with a great sigh of relief, then leant her head against the wall and closed her eyes. The big Irishman looked at her in silence for a moment.

" I'd just go an' lie down me-self, if I was you, Miss, dear," he said : " at last you'll be wearin' yerself out, and we'll have never a soul to say a word of comfort to us."

" I'm afraid I must," she answered; " I'd go and lie down by the colonel, only I'm so tired."

The big lancer picked her up like a baby, and ran across the compound with her, taking her right into the chief's room, not a little to Vi's dismay, who feared she was hurt.

" Miss Floss is just tired out, mem," he announced, " and we've frightened her to death by carrying in the major, who's dead beat."

" I thought he would have to give in," Mrs. Cornwallis said,

G

as the man retired. " Lie down here, Floss, and I will go and see after things."

" Could you go round the posts ?" Floss asked, imploringly. " They will be expecting me, and it wouldn't take you long : just the ' Our Father' and the blessing, Vi."

" Yes, I'll do it," and then she went away.

And so the brave souls slept heavily. Floss within sight of the wounded colonel, and Greville Gurney on the floor of the hospital ; and while they slept, the enemy crept a little nearer, forced the defenders back, and covered the space between the two bungalows with their fire. At the very first shot Vi Cornwallis sped back to her husband's side, just as Floss, with dazed eyes and scattered senses, sat up on her bed, wondering what the noise meant.

" What is it, Vivi ?" she asked.

"I think the end has come," she said calmly ; "let me have your hand, Bruce, darling." All her bravery, all her courage rose to the surface then. She sat down quietly beside her husband, with one hand in his, a revolver in her right hand, and a second lying ready loaded on the bed.

" What's that ?" Floss cried, clasping her hands together.

There was no answer : a shell came through the roof with a crash, while from the opposite building rose a wild shriek of " Fire !"

" What's that ?" Major Gurney asked, starting up from his hardly-earned repose.

A young officer, just entering the room, answered him hastily, " A shell has sent the colonel's room to smash, and they're all there !"

Greville Gurney sprang from his couch without a moment's delay, and ran as fast as possible round to the side of the hospital, opposite to which the Cornwallises' room was. A little group of soldiers and ladies were standing within the shelter, one of the women sobbing unrestrainedly.

" Good heavens ! are you going to leave them there?" Greville cried passionately: " a wounded man and two helpless women in a burning house!"

" The roof has fallen, major," one of the men replied, " and there is a sharp fire between us."

So there was : they could watch the bullets whistling and whirling through the air between them and the Cornwallises' hut. As the man spoke several officers came running to the spot : " The colonel's room ?" one asked.

" Yes, I'm going," the major answered.

" So am I," and " So am I," cried the others.

" No, no ; I'll have no married men," Greville cried decidedly. " Maude, you may come."

As he spoke he caught up a mattress, and dashed straight across the open space, followed by young Maude, both of them reaching the verandah of the opposite bungalow in safety. There, under the verandah's scanty shelter, they found the two women, who, between them, had managed to drag Colonel Cornwallis out of the rapidly-burning building. Floss uttered a glad cry, as the two men ran round the corner; little Mrs. Cornwallis breaking into a passionate torrent of tears.

" Maude, you are less than I," Major Gurney said, hurriedly, when they found the ladies were still unhurt; " take Mrs. Cornwallis ; she is the least. Put your arm round Maude's throat, Mrs. Cornwallis, and try your best to keep behind the shelter of the mattress."

" I won't leave Bruce," the little woman announced : " you must take him first."

" Nonsense : do as we tell you," imperatively.

" I won't," sitting down by her husband and taking his hand.

" You must," said the major firmly. " Colonel, will you use your influence ?" bending over him tenderly. " Mrs. Cornwallis objects to leaving you, but we will come back for you, when they are in safety."

" Go, my darling," said the colonel faintly, " but kiss me first."

Vi bent over to do his bidding, and did what was, perhaps, the best thing she could possibly do under the circumstances—fainted away.

" That's better," muttered Greville. " Pick her up, Maude,

and run off with her; stay, have your mattress so," tearing a long hole in the cover for the young man to pass his arm through.

"Now, Floss, trust yourself perfectly to me."

"No, no; I'm heavy," she answered, "I can run, you've no idea how fast; and I'll slip this long skirt off, and surely between us we can carry Bruce across."

"Nonsense; I must take you myself," he answered.

"Well, then, here is the mattress Bruce was on when we dragged him out; let me take that and go by myself; I'm not afraid. Oh, Major Gurney, what is the matter with Bruce—is he dead?"

"Fainted," he returned briefly, "all the better for my purpose. If you're not going to take that skirt, I will use it as a sling, and regularly hang him round my neck, so;" then, having slipped the long muslin skirt under the colonel's knees, and tied a knot ready to slip over his head, he turned to Floss: "I must see you off first, darling."

"I am ready when you tell me."

Major Gurney arranged the mattress to the best advantage, and led her to the corner. "Floss," he said, hoarsely, taking her by the hand and bending his face down to hers, "will you kiss me before you go? and if I get hurt—for I shall have a good weight to carry," looking doubtfully at the unconscious form beside them, "I shall know if you cared or not."

"Yes, dear," Floss answered, simply, holding up her face to his.

"Now go," he said, quietly, "go at once."

Floss Bannister turned her soft dark eyes upon his in silence, and, with that one look, ran boldly round the corner, and was lost to view.

"Alone!" cried a dozen eager voices as she gained the opposite verandah. "Why, where's Gurney?"

"Bringing the colonel," Floss replied, at which poor Vi's tears broke out anew—tears of gratitude those.

"Where's Mr. Maude?" Floss asked, looking round.

"Shot in the shoulder; Dr. Moss is attending to him."

" All my fault," Vi sobbed.

" Hush ! here he is," as Greville Gurney left the shelter of the opposite building, staggering under the heavy weight of the still unconscious colonel, yet keeping to his task bravely, and holding his slender cover as best he could between them and the enemy's fire.

" He'll do it !" cried one.

" Somebody run out and help him," said another; " let me go."

" No, no, Jack," cried an anxious wife, holding him back.

" Let him alone," put in another, with his arm in a sling ; " he'll manage it best alone."

" He's shot !" Floss screamed ; " I saw it. Oh ! I tell you, I saw it. I saw him stagger."

" No, no, it was the chief's weight."

" I don't know ; he's very shaky—now—put your hand out ; I've only one. Ah ! here he is. Bravo ! well done !" as the major reached the shelter, and a dozen hands were ready to relieve him of his burden. " Hold up a moment, man, till we get it off," trying, with his left hand, to free the major's throat from the muslin sling.

" I can't," he gasped, sinking on his knees.

" Hollo !" forgetting his shattered arm in his effort to hold him up. " You're not hurt surely ?"

" I'm done for," Greville said, faintly ; " did she get in safe ?"

Mrs. Cornwallis, with an ingratitude for which she may surely be forgiven, had flown to her husband's side, and left his deliverer unheeded ; but Floss, with a face so white and eyes so filled with pain, that the little group stood aside to let her pass, came swiftly beside him, and lifted his head upon her arm.

" I am here," she said, softly ; " the doctor will be with us in a moment."

" No use, dear ; it's all up," he gasped: " got a bullet through my lungs."

" Don't talk," she said, imperatively.

" Make—no difference, and there are some things I must say.

Floss, if all this trouble had never been, would my love have been of any good? Would you ever have loved me?"

For one moment she raised her eyes to the sorrowful sympathetic faces round them, then she answered clearly,

"If it pleases God to take you from me, I will come to you in heaven—Floss Bannister still."

"Thank you, dearest. No, don't touch me, doctor; no use."

"My dear fellow, we cannot tell that till I have looked at you," the surgeon said, kindly.

"No use; it will be over in a minute or two now. Floss, if ever you come across any of the old 52nd tell them I am sorry now I did not make myself more to them; that I thought of them all kindly at the last."

"Yes, I'll tell them," Floss answered, in a strangely far-off sounding voice.

"I dare say they've forgotten all the old quarrels now," he said, faintly; then, after a long silence, "Still there, Floss?"

"Still here, darling."

He smiled at her words, and felt blindly for her hand. His breathing grew more laboured, his face more deadly pale. Then a sudden glad light flooded into his blue eyes, the smile on his lips deepened, and he tried to speak again. But the effort only ended in a crimson stain upon the kerchief Floss held to his lips, followed by a sigh and a shiver, and Greville Gurney lay dead, with his face turned up to the brilliant Indian sky, surely one of the grandest heroes that ever Queen or regiment boasted of. And beside him lay Floss Bannister, in the blessed unconsciousness, which sometimes comes to lull our keenest agonies, for a little while, to rest.

* * * * *

It was months later that Geoffry Maude, writing to Stephen Thorold, gave, at Floss Bannister's desire, Greville Gurney's last message to his old comrades, and Mrs. Stephen, with tears in her soft eyes, read the letter to such of the regiment as had assembled in her drawing-room that Sunday afternoon for tea and chat. It was received in silence, more than one hardy soldier turning away to hide the emotion he was ashamed to show. Alys O'Shaughnassy had hidden her face against her husband's arm, but little Mrs. St. Hilary looked up bravely, though there was an ominous glitter of tears in her large eyes, and a piteous quivering about her mouth.

"I always liked him," she said, trying hard to steady her voice, "I *always* liked him, and I'm sorry I bore malice so long. So are you, Alys, I know; but he was a gentleman and a brave soldier, and he will have forgiven us. He has come out in his true character—that of a chivalrous hero, and now that he has gone where mistakes and resentment have no place, he will surely know how deeply we regret him, how any ill-feeling there may have been between him and us is blotted out by the glorious way in which he has shown us all how duty may be done!" And then the little woman broke into a passionate torrent of tears.

THE ORDEAL BY PAINT;

OR, MY FIRST DAY IN THE REGIMENT.

" HERE he comes !"

" By gad, so he does ! Hurrah ! Some sport to-night."

" Looks rather pale, doesn't he ?"

" Yes, and will want a good deal of setting up, too."

" Poor devil ! I pity him."

As I was not at all afflicted—in that instance I might have said blessed—with deafness, these were a few of the remarks I could not help hearing, as I drove up to the officers' mess of the cavalry barracks at Colchester, where I had come to join the regiment, to which I had been gazetted a couple of months before.

Quite unwittingly, I had chosen a very poor time for presenting myself. " Mid-day stables " were just over, and almost all the officers of the regiment were waiting about the verandah till luncheon should be ready. They were none of them in very amiable tempers; for they had just heard in the office that a letter had come down for them to hold themselves in readiness to march to the autumn manœuvres at Aldershot, and Aldershot is, as most people know, a spot no cavalry officer rejoices to find himself near, even when there are no manœuvres going on.

Anything more uncomfortable than were my feelings that morning could not be easily imagined. I had never met my regiment before. I knew none of the men, and I was quite at a loss to know to whom I must address myself. However, I was compelled to act; and stumbling out of the cab, with my heart in my throat and great beads of perspiration breaking out upon my forehead, I stood for a moment while my future comrades inspected me, as if I were a polo pony for sale.

My hesitation lasted but an instant. I chose my man, an elderly, rather good-looking officer, with a bald head and well-waxed moustache; so, with a ghastly grin, I blurted out,

" I've come to join."

" Oh, have you ?" said he, carelessly, and with an expression of intense amusement on his face ? " Your name's Winter, I suppose ? Oh, all right. Come along with me, and I'll introduce you to the colonel. I think you have not met him yet ? "

" No," I answered, beginning to feel a little more at my ease.

" Wait a moment ; I'll just make you acquainted with these fellows first."

This terrible ordeal over, I was hustled off by my elderly friend to be presented to the colonel, whom we found sitting in the office with his adjutant making arrangements for the coming manœuvres.

" I've brought Mr. Winter to see you, sir. He's come to join," said my guide.

" Ah, how are you?" said the colonel. " I'm very glad to see you ; for we're rather short of subalterns, and every addition is a great help. Have you got your uniform and that sort of thing ? I hope you'll like your work. Are you fond of riding ? "

I answered modestly that I was, but I was afraid my experience in that line was rather limited. As I spoke, a few riding-school anecdotes began to crop up in my mind ; for, during the two last months, every man I had met seemed to consider it his duty to impress upon me the fact, that a riding-school is neither more nor less than a second *inferno.*

" Brought any hunters down with you ?"

" No, sir."

" Umph ! A pity ! This is a fair hunting district. However, those are little additions easily made, and I've no doubt you'll soon fall into the ways of the regiment. You'll find your brother-officers quite ready to help you in anything so far as sport is concerned."

Of a truth I did ; for as soon as it became known that I was anxious to buy a hunter, there was scarcely an officer in the regiment who was not anxious to sell me one, " perfectly sound, and quite good enough to win a steeplechase."

My interview with the colonel over, I was taken by my elderly friend to have lunch. On the way to the mess-room we met an officer, who seemed to me very old to be still in the army.

" Here's old Muggins, the riding-master," said my guide, whom I afterwards found was called " the Fossil," on account of his antique appearance. " Well, Muggins, this is Mr. Winter, just joined."

" Ho !" said Mr. Muggins. " Glad to see you. Fond of riding ? Hey ?"

I returned the same answer that I had given to the colonel on that subject, and Mr. Muggins grinned—a grin which somehow reminded me of a cat playing with a mouse.

" Ho, my boy," said he ; " don't know much about it, don't you? Well, we'll soon tickle you hup a bit. Hey, Moore ?"

" Yes, I daresay," in rather a bored tone. " Come along, Winter. Beastly old cad, Muggins !" he burst out, as soon as we were out of earshot. " Always sneaking about and getting the young chaps into trouble, except they happen to be willing to bribe him."

At lunch I was posted next to a young subaltern of about six months' service, who, having himself just got over the rough part of joining, thought it his bounden duty to " swagger " over me. He was a babyish-looking, flaxen-haired cornet, with about as much hair on his upper lip as you might find upon that of a boy of twelve. He went—as I very soon heard, in spite of my fright—by the name of " the Boy," occasionally varied by that of " the Brat."

" Ah ! which is your county ?" drawled this youngster, quite affecting the old soldier.

" Devon," said I, trying in vain to swallow a lump of cutlet which had found its way into my mouth ; how, I was really too much excited to know, for I was painfully aware every eye in the room was upon me.

" Ah! any hounds down there?"

" Oh yes, I think so," I stammered, being in too much of a "funk" to know, or rather remember, whether there were or not.

" Ah!" said my young cornet; and there our conversation ended, and I was thus enabled to hear a little of what was going on at the other end of the room; for two or three fellows, who had finished their lunch, had left the table and were standing in a group on the hearthrug.

" I should like to buy that chap at my valuation, and sell him at his own," said one. " I'm rather hard up, and a profit might help me a bit."

" What a rum way the young beggar pronounces his *h*'s!" said a second, taking no notice whatever of the previous remark.

" Ah!" put in a third, "yes, poor devil! Probably he's only just learned them."

" Not much to look at, is he?" said the first one, following up his own train of thought.

It may easily be imagined that these remarks did not tend to cure my extreme nervousness, which was evidently taken for " swagger."

After I had finished, or pretended to finish, some lunch, during which I managed to capsize a tumbler of beer half into my plate and half over the table, I was shown my room by the boy of tender years, who, being junior, was told off to look after me and set me straight a bit.

My room proved to be about thirteen feet square by eleven high, and there I found two men busily engaged in unpacking my furniture, which had been sent down from town the day before.

Amongst a great number of deficiencies I found I had forgotten to buy sheets for my bed ; but, luckily, one of the men, who was servant to another officer, managed to borrow a pair for me until I could get some sent up from the town.

In course of an hour or two my room was put into something

like order; and, just as the men were leaving, I asked how my luggage had got there, and who had paid for my cab. They told me that they had done so, having rescued my boxes from a lot of young officers, anxious, I daresay, to discover where I had bought my uniform, belts, boots, and, indeed, everything I possessed.

In my gratitude for their thoughtfulness I inquired how much they had paid the cabman, magnanimously intending to double it when I repaid them. The price they named, however, entirely precluded the possibility of this; in fact, it was so large that it would, I thought, have been sufficient to buy the cab itself, horse, man and all, out and out. One of the men informed me that he had been ordered to look after me, until I had got a servant of my own, and that he would return at half-past seven to dress me for dinner. As there was only about an hour to spare I got out some writing materials and wrote a letter to my father. Then I lay down upon my new bed until half-past seven should arrive.

I think I must have fallen asleep, for I remember nothing until I heard a loud "jar-r-r-at" at my door.

"Come in!" I cried.

"It's half-past seven, sir, and I've brought you some hot water and your uniform; but I can't find no mess-waistcoat, sir."

"The devil!" I ejaculated, remembering suddenly that my tailor had told me the day before that it still required a little pressing, but should be sent down that night without fail; a promise he had, of course, taken infinite pains not to keep.

"Perhaps I can borrow one for you, sir," suggested Robinson.

"For goodness' sake, go and try," I said, eagerly.

He left on the table a letter, which I immediately opened and found it was an invitation from the colonel and officers of the regiment to dine. Not knowing the custom of the service, I at once set that down as "chaff," and the idea of answering it never once entered my head.

In about five minutes Robinson returned, with a dilapidated

article, which I almost failed to recognise as a cavalry mess-waistcoat.

"I am not going to put that thing on!" I said, with much indignation.

Robinson, however, assured me that, even if I had it, it would be useless to wear anything better; for the 400th Foot, who were quartered on the opposite side of the town, were to dine with the 52nd Dragoons that night, and there was sure to be some extra rough work going on.

When my dressing was complete, I found, as every one does on joining, that my uniform did not fit as it seemed to do in the tailor's shop. My overalls were too loose and baggy, and not high enough in the waist. Indeed, it was only by strapping them up till I thought they would crack that I managed to make the top of the overalls and the bottom of the waistcoat meet at all. The borrowed waistcoat, too, was so tight and uncomfortable about the neck that I thought if I could persuade anything more solid than soup or champagne to pass down my throat that night, I should be extremely lucky.

At last I was ready, and compelled to betake myself off in spite of the utter discomfort I was in. It was wonderful how I missed the tails of my ordinary evening coat; and I went down the steps—one could hardly call them stairs—and along the verandah into the ante-room, feeling as if I had suddenly been transformed into an exceedingly long-legged Manx cat.

Here I found a couple of waiters busily handing sherry-and-bitters to a room full of officers, some of whom, from the difference in their uniform, must, I knew, belong to the 400th. I approached one of the latter, in a very deferential spirit, and had certainly not said a dozen words before he remarked, "Ah, I suppose you've just joined!"

This was a fact which I was most anxious to conceal, and the same sort of feeling crept over me which I should fancy comes over a man suddenly convicted of theft. I thought further parley with him would be useless, as he would be sure to laugh at everything I said, so I left him and sat down in a corner by myself until dinner was announced.

Being a guest, I was allowed to pass in amongst the first few, and had the pleasure of sitting next Major Silver, a man devoted to hunting, and never happy except in the pursuit of that sport or when talking of long runs, hunters, and hounds. Now, as I wasn't very well versed in that line, we bored each other terribly, and I was glad when he transferred his conversation from me to his right-hand neighbour, and I was left alone. I was very tired with unpacking; the dinner was so long, and the ready banter and chaff so bewildering, that once or twice it was as much as I could do to keep myself from falling asleep—an achievement which, if I had indulged in it, would have probably been attended by very serious consequences, and of which, so long as I remained in the army, I should never have heard the end.

Happily, however, dinner could not last all night, and at eleven o'clock the colonel and major, with some of the senior 400th guests, rose and went into the ante-room. I was following them, at a very respectful distance, when—whirr, squash!—against the back of my head came an over-ripe orange, which sent me flying, as I thought for a moment, into another world. I turned as quickly as I could to see who had thrown it, but not a man was out of his place, there was not a smile upon a single lip. One of them, however, asked me to come back and have another glass of champagne before I went to bed. So I returned, and had the pleasure of a glass of wine with a man called Burroughes, the senior subaltern, and a wild harum-scarum sort of fellow, as I afterwards found to my cost.

This glass was followed by another and another and another, with first this and then that member of the mess, and, as the order of the night was no "heel-taps," I began to think that the best thing I could do would be to slip away and be off to bed. So five minutes afterwards, little thinking how eagerly my brother officers were awaiting this event, and fondly imagining they were all too much occupied to take any notice of me or my exit, I quietly went to bed. In ten minutes I was sound asleep; but how long that sleep lasted I cannot say. I only know that I had a terrible dream, for I thought I had fallen into the hyena's den at the Zoological Gardens, and then I awoke. There was such a yelling and shouting and holloaing at the foot of my stairs that at first I feared there must be a fire or something of that sort. I soon discovered that the sounds were approaching my door with startling rapidity; and then, catching the sound of my own name, I knew instinctively that they were seeking me and meant me no good.

My first idea was that the best thing I could do would be to jump out of bed and slip on a smoking-suit or dressing-gown, and pretend I hadn't been to bed at all; but, on consideration, I thought I would stick to my bed and feign sound sleep. I was fool enough to imagine that perhaps, if they found me asleep, they might go away. Poor deluded Cornet Winter!

My heart had given a tremendous jump when I first heard them; and as they came nearer and nearer, so it got higher and higher, until by the time they reached my door it was fairly in my mouth.

"Has he locked the door?" I heard a voice say.

"Yes, rather."

"Oh, capital!"

What could that mean?

"Go on, somebody."

In two minutes my door gave way, and about a dozen officers came rolling and tumbling over each other into the room. Then a voice, which I recognised as Burroughes's, called out,

"Winter!"

No reply.

"Winter!"

This time a little louder.

Still no answer.

"Young devil's shamming! pull him out."

Thereupon one or two seized the bar at the head of my bed, while as many others took hold of that at the foot, and they completely overturned me on to the floor, where I lay quite helpless with fright. Two young fellows immediately lifted me up, and, in spite of my urgent protests, conducted me downstairs to the ante-room, a prisoner of war, and dressed exactly as I had tumbled out of bed, with the addition of a pouch-belt and girdle, which they put on over my night-shirt to give me a martial bearing, as they termed it. I found that the ante-room table had been completely cleared of the newspapers, which were usually scattered upon it, and five chairs had been placed round it. In front of each were put blue paper, pens, and ink. I grew more and more frightened when I found I was to be tried by court-martial for a great and heinous offence committed against her Majesty.

Burroughes did not waste a moment in taking his seat at the table as president of the court-martial, and the other four were quickly filled in by junior officers. A sixth was appointed prosecutor; two were announced as witnesses, and three were told off as a guard, one of them being promoted to the rank of corporal of the guard in charge of the prisoner.

The charges were then read as follows: 1. Conduct prejudicial to the maintenance of good order and discipline on the part of John Strange Winter, cornet of the 52nd Dragoons, in having, at Colchester, on the night of the 10th of July, 18—, gone to bed, whilst several guests, officers of another regiment, remained in the ante-room—it being the duty of John Strange Winter, cornet, to entertain them. 2. Conduct unbecoming a subaltern in going to bed whilst senior officers remained in the ante-room.

I was then placed at the foot of the table between my escort, one of whom shouldered a pair of tongs and the other a shovel, whilst the corporal of the guard was armed with a poker, wherewith he every now and then gave me a dig behind, if I did not stand bolt upright at "attention."

I was asked if I objected to be tried by any of the officers whom I saw at the table, and on receiving my answer in the negative, the oath was read.

" You shall well and truly try and determine the case according to the evidence in the matter new before you, so help you Jorrocks, &c."

This was taken in due form, and with the utmost gravity, *Handley Cross* being, I believe, the book used ; and the trial proceeded.

Lieutenant Bates, on being duly sworn, stated :

"Sir, at Colchester Barracks, on the night of the 10th of July 18—, I saw the prisoner now before the court-martial sneak off to bed about half-past eleven. There were several guests, officers of another regiment, still remaining in the ante-room. I was also present when the prisoner was arrested in his own room."

Lieutenant Cavasson, being duly sworn, stated :

"Sir, I was in the mess-room when the prisoner went to bed. There were several captains and other senior officers still in the room."

This closed the evidence for the prosecution, and the question was put to me,

"Have you anything to urge in your defence?"

I told them in a tremulous voice that I really was very tired, that I did not dream that I was committing an outrageous offence, and that I wouldn't do it again.

Then I was conducted out of the room whilst the court considered its sentence.

Whilst we were waiting outside, my guards, with the witnesses and junior officers, amused themselves and terrified me by relating previous sentences, and wondering what I should get. It was awfully cold waiting about, for, although it was midsummer and very hot in the day, yet, in the small hours of the night, to wait ten minutes in a draughty hall, with no more clothing than a night-shirt and a pouch-belt, is a very different matter. At last we were summoned within, and I was led to my place at the foot of the table. Lieutenant Burronghes broke the silence,

"John Strange Winter, you have been found guilty of two very glaring and very heinous offences, and this court has adjudged that you receive two strokes from a birch-rod from every member of the mess now present, I hope it may be a warning to you for the future."

11

This announcement was received by my tormentors with a ringing cheer. I was ready to sink with fright when I saw the birch produced, and rough hands were laid upon me. My guard with the tongs, although apparently the roughest of the lot, whispered to me to "hold my jaw, and neither struggle nor cry out;" and something in the kindly voice told me his advice was good, so I took it.

The castigation was mere child's play, except when it came to Burroughes's turn.

"Ah, this won't do," I heard him say; "we shall have the young beggar laughing in his sleeve at us. We really must show him that there is something like discipline in the regiment." And he certainly did.

"Well, come now," said that stern gentleman, when my punishment was over, "the young one's plucky, at all events."

If my brother officers had administered necessary strictness, I certainly could not complain of the way in which I was treated afterwards; for they carried me off into the mess-room, where we found a supper of grilled bones and devilled kidneys, and so forth, spread upon the table.

When we had eaten and drunken I was ordered to mount the brass and sing a song. The "brass" was a square piece of that metal formed by the meeting of the leaves of the table; and a queer figure I must have cut in my scanty attire. They seemed to think so, for they all laughed and cheered heartily.

I had the sense to know that a moment's hesitation would be fatal to my popularity, and I dashed at once into the first comic song that came into my head. It was the story of a sailor who got cast away upon an island, taken prisoner by savages, who appropriated his clothes to themselves, finally marrying him to a princess of the blood royal. It was received with uproarious applause; but unfortunately for me, I did not get to the end without an interruption. I only sang as far as,

> And there behold me standing,
> A waistcoat for my clothes,
> A hat and boots, striped red and blue.
> And a ring stuck through my nose

when, to my dismay, I heard a voice suggesting that it would be all the better if I were dressed in character. The idea caught like wildfire—two pots of paint were produced, whence I know not, and in an incredibly short time I was daubed from head to foot with rings of red and blue paint, and again mounted on the brass to finish my song.

At last the revelries were ended, and I was permitted to go to my room, thoroughly worn out, and half-stifled by the disgusting smell and feeling of the paint. Luckily I knew something of art, and had a big bottle of turpentine with me, which, with the help of a palette-knife, brought most of the stuff off.

It was broad daylight ere I sought my couch; and when at length I fell asleep, it was only to dream it all over again, and to sing in fancy the chorus of my song,

> Jam-see, jee-mee, jabber jee hoy !
> Jabberee, doree, poree,
> Hikey, Pikey, sikey, crikey,
> Chillagowoolahbadoree !

A CHERUB'S FACE UNDER A FORAGE-CAP.

It was just a cherub's face under a forage-cap which met Colonel Cotherstone's angry gaze, as he sat bolt upright in his chair one Saturday afternoon. A cherub's face, smooth and fair, which had as yet not the faintest signs of a moustache ; a face with languishing azure eyes that went straight to Colonel Cotherstone's heart, in spite of his anger and the popular belief that he was in the fortunate possession of a lump of adamant instead of that too frequently inconvenient organ. The scene was the colonel's quarters in the Cavalry Barracks ta York ; the time between three and four in the afternoon ; *dramatis personæ*, Colonel Edward le Gendre Cotherstone, Sergeant-Major McAllister, and Private Edward Jones, F-troop. It was Private Edward Jones who owned the cherub's face, the languishing blue eyes, the long lithe limbs, and, alas, also a bad character. The description would not have applied at all to the chief, who was largely-made and stalwart, with a sunburnt, rugged face, and hair plentifully besprinkled with grey. Nor would it have either done for the sergeant-major, who, while owning the most irreproachable character, was fat and bald, and moreover did not possess a good feature on his broad red countenance."

"Sergeant-major, you can go," said Colonel Cotherstone, curtly ; whereupon that personage, having saluted, departed, feeling pretty sure that Private Jones was coming in for a severe wigging, or, as he put it, " The colonel's going to give it 'im proper."

But Colonel Cotherstone did not immediately set about the task which he had imposed upon himself. An obstacle, not very often coming between commanding officers and their troopers, presented itself in the shape of that dainty cherub face, with the fair waving hair and the languishing azure eyes, so like another face that he had known long ago *and loved* ! At last, however, he forced himself to speak.

"And how long is this state of things to continue ?" he demanded, sternly.

Private Jones maintained a discreet silence, but he shifted his long legs nervously, and lowered his eyes until the colonel could no longer see them. Once their gaze withdrawn from him he was able to speak fluently enough. Usually Colonel Cotherstone did not find himself at a loss for words.

"Now, look here, Jones," he said kindly, yet with sufficient firmness to make his words impressive, " we must have a change. Almost every day I hear of some fresh misdemeanour, idleness, insubordination, work half done or left undone altogether, infringement of rules, absence without leave. What is the end to be ?"

Private Jones shot one swift glance at his chief's keen angry face, opened his mouth as if to speak, but ended by remaining silent ; the colonel, however, continued :

" By what chain of circumstances you came to enlist I don't know ; but if you imagined for an instant that your birth would permit you to ride rough-shod over everything, why, you made a mistake. Because you are a gentleman, because you can speak half-a-dozen languages, because you have got through your fortune and made an utter fool of yourself, you cannot be excused your duties or have your misdoings passed over without punishment. I daresay it's hard for you to be restricted, to obey the non-commissioned officers, to turn out of your bed at five o'clock, to live with men of a different rank from your own ; but you should have considered all that before you brought yourself down to your present position. With your advantages of education, you might get your commission in the course of a few years, and win back the position you have lost ; but whilst your present bad conduct continues, I can do nothing for you, I cannot pass you over the heads of men who do their duty conscientiously, men whom I can trust. If you do not choose to alter your present ways, you must make up your mind to remain a private always; there is no favouritism in the army. You have now been five months in the regiment, and those five months you have utterly wasted, always shielding yourself behind the fact that by birth you are a gentleman—by birth and by education. I tell you, sir, those two facts are a disgrace, to you, simply a disgrace, instead of a blessing and an honour. As yet I have kept you out of the degradation of the cells ; but I find that punishment by fines is of no avail—the punishment of a fine simply falls upon your mother."

Private Jones lifted his face all crimsoned by shamed blushes, and repeated Colonel Cotherstone's concluding words,

" My mother, sir ?"

" Your mother, sir," returned the chief, sternly. " If you have no consideration for your family, for yourself, for the honour of your old name; no shame at the contempt of your officers, no dread of what the end of all this will be, does the thought of the mother who bore you never cross your mind ?"

The lad turned away in confused silence.

" Answer me !" thundered the chief.

He spoke then for the first time, spoke in such a soft drawling voice, that Colonel Cotherstone absolutely shivered, it was so like that other voice :

" Yes, sir, I do ; only it is so hard," with a heavy sigh.

" What is so hard—your work ?"

" No, sir; I don't know that I find the work so bad. I could always groom a horse well, and the stable-work I soon got used to. And I don't mind the men—they're rough, but they're good-natured, most of them, but it's the non-commissioned officers— I *can't* stand them, sir."

" Why not ?"

" I can do with old McAllister, sir," said the lad eagerly, almost forgetting his drawl ; " but the sergeants in F-troop— Oh Lord !" with another sigh. " If I please one, I displease another. It's having so many masters, and each thinks he has a right to bully me as hard as he likes. Because they've got a few shillings' worth of gold lace on their jackets, I suppose."

"Which they have won by their own good conduct," rejoined the colonel. "I'll tell you what it is, Hamilton: you're a young fool, with only a little further **to** go in the direction you're in to find yourself at the devil."

"You know me, sir!" the lad gasped.

"I knew your—people," answered the colonel, curtly. He had almost said "your mother," but changed the word in time to "people;" "and for your name's sake—not for your own mind—I will give you one more chance. If I move you out of F-troop into Sergeant-Major McAllister's, will you give me your word **to try** and reform?"

The crimson tide flushed anew over the lad's fair face, a rush of feeling (could that darkness be tears?) flooded into his azure eyes. He forgot that he was only Private Jones, and that the tall man with the stern bronzed face before him was that awe-inspiring being "the commanding officer," Colonel Cotherstone, one of the strictest martinets in the service—he forgot it all. He only remembered that he was Hamilton of Glenbarry, and that this was the first real kindness, except old McAllister's, that he had met with for months. In the impulse of the moment he held out his hand, and said heartily, "I'll try, sir."

Colonel Cotherstone just laid his fingers in the outstretched hand for a moment.

"Very well, Hamilton, I'll take your word," he replied, gravely. "Now you can go."

When the door had closed behind the lad, Colonel Cotherstone sat down again in his arm-chair and tried to think. But think he could not. A vision of a cherub's face under a forage-cap came persistently between him and his thoughts. How many years was it ago that just such a head and face had lingered in his memory; just such a cherub's face, and under a forage-cap. And yet there was a difference. The mother's sweet blue eyes had looked straight into his own, with never a shade of the shame he had seen in those of the son that very day, and the forage-cap from under which the mother's golden curls had strayed bore the gold band of an officer, instead of the simple yellow of the dragoon.

He was not altogether easy in his mind, that big bronzed soldier. He knew that, in spite of his stern words, he had treated Private Jones a great deal too easily, else he would not have sent the sergeant-major away. It is not altogether usual for commanding officers to talk to refractory soldiers as he had talked to Private Jones, and yet—

"No," he muttered, "I couldn't be hard on Mary's boy, who came and looked at me with Mary's eyes, and talked to me with Mary's soft tongue. Poor little Mary!" and straightway his thoughts flew back to the little scene enacted ever so many years ago, and which had been recalled so vividly to his memory that afternoon, a scene of which the principal incident was a cherub's face under a forage-cap.

Naturally, before Edward le Gendre Cotherstone had obtained his regiment, he had held the respective positions of major, captain, lieutenant, and cornet. Well, it was when he was only Cornet Cotherstone, and but two-and-twenty, that he was foolish enough to fall in love.

At that time the Cuirassiers were quartered at Edinburgh, and it was in the modern Athens that he and his fate met. This was one-and-twenty years before the opening of this story, when Colonel Cotherstone was forty-three, a first-rate soldier, and, considering all things, fairly popular, though his officers, especially the subalterns, quite believed in a theory, now of many years' standing, which declared him to be *minus* several important internal arrangements, one of which was a heart, the other being the bowels of compassion. He certainly was very hard. They all vowed he had not a single soft spot in his whole composition, but they were wrong. A soft place he had, and the unruly lad with a cherub's face had been lucky enough to find it out.

As I said before, Edward le Gendre Cotherstone was two-and-twenty when he fell in love for the first, indeed the only, time. He was driving along Prince's Street one afternoon, when a small Skye terrier managed to get itself under the horse's heels, and, in addition to that, one of the wheels passed over it. At every period of his life Edward Cotherstone had been as keen as a hawk is popularly supposed to be, and a vision of a golden-haired girl dressed in black, who uttered a piteous cry, and put two little black-gloved hands out to rescue the little animal, who was howling frightfully, caused him to pull up the trap with a jerk, and jump down.

"Oh, I am sorry," he said, bending over the little creature, now whining piteously in its young mistress's arms. "I am so grieved. I hope it's not much hurt."

The girl's blue eyes, half drowned as they were in tears, flashed an indignant glance at him.

"Wouldn't you be hurt?" she asked, bluntly, pointing to the wheel as she spoke, "if that had gone right over your body?"

"What can I do to help you?" he asked, wisely ignoring the question. "Can I drive you home?"

"I live at Portobello," she answered, helplessly.

"Please let me drive you there," he urged. "Let me hold him whilst you get in, and then I'll lay him ever so carefully on your lap."

And so he had his own way; that was a little peculiarity of Edward Cotherstone's. He took the dog from her with the utmost tenderness and without eliciting a single cry; and when she had mounted into the high trap, he restored it to her gentle keeping. On the way down to Portobello he gathered that the young lady's name was Stewart, Mary Stewart, and that she lived with her grandmother, who did not often go out. She told him, too, that she was seventeen; and that Fluff, the injured Skye, had been given to her by her cousin, Hamilton of Glenbarry. She also told him that her father had not been dead many months, and that she had been both to London and Paris. In fact, she was so very communicative, that he thought he knew everything there was to be known about her; but, notwithstanding her apparent candour, there was one trifling circumstance, which, had she mentioned, would have spared him many a bitter heartache. She did not mention it, however!

He took her to her home, and sent his trap away, as she wished him to examine and determine the full extent of the dog's injuries. He was introduced to the aged grandmother, who took quite a fancy to him by reason of having been at school— goodness knows how many years previously! with his great-aunt. She, too, mentioned Hamilton of Glenbarry, and mentioned him, moreover, in a way which did not show that any large amount of love was lost between them.

"He does not always behave very respectfully to grand-mamma," Mary confided to him, in an undertone. "He calls her 'old lady,' and she can't bear it."

"Confounded cad !" thought Mr. Cotherstone.

They found, upon examination, that Fluff was not very much the worse for his accident; and little Miss Stewart was com-forted beyond measure when the young Cuirassier assured her that when the bruises had passed off he would be all right again.

But of course he called next day to ask after Fluff and ascertain if Miss Stewart had recovered from her fright. He was also remarkably attentive to the old lady, and won her heart as easily as he did that of her granddaughter. For some months this kind of thing continued. Edward Cotherstone grew more and more happy ; but little Mary faded somewhat, drooped as does a floweret for lack of water and sunshine. Sometimes she frightened him, she looked so pale, so wan and fragile ; then again she would brighten when he appeared, and throw him into fresh transports of love and happiness ; and so the pretty play went on until it was played out, for one fine morning in June the crash came. He had gone in for half-an-hour, because he knew Mrs. Stewart would not be visible so early in the day. Mary looked so bright and fresh, that the young soldier was tempted to take her in his arms and kiss her, calling her by every fond endearing name he could think of, telling her over and over again how he loved her, how very, very dearly he loved her, his little Scottish lassie, and a good deal more in the same strain. And Mary, what of her ? She never drew back, never whispered the faintest hint of that secret which lay between her and him—the secret which once or twice he had almost stumbled upon. No, she clung to him with an almost despairing passion; which made him feel uneasy in spite of his happiness; she twined her soft arms round his throat, and cried incredulously,

" Do you really love me, Eddie ? "

" Really, my darling," he answered,

And then she broke from the clasp of his loving arms almost impatiently, though the love-light still shone in her azure eyes, the dimpling smiles still played about her tender mouth.

" I shall try on your cap," she announced, coquettishly ; then stuck the golden-bordered little cap on one side of her head, and, turning from the glass, looked at him with passionate love filling her blue eyes, love which she had caught from his. The sound of a carriage stopping without caused her to turn her head, and when she looked at him again the smiles had frozen on her sweet mouth, and a nameless horror had taken the place of the tender light which a moment before was shining in her eyes.

" Oh, my darling, what is it ? " the young soldier cried, in sudden affright.

" It is Hamilton of Glenbarry," she answered, in a hoarse whisper.

" What is he to you ?" Cotherstone cried, passionately.

" He is my—"

" Your what ? For God's sake speak, and let me know the worst ! " he said, fiercely.

" He will be my husband," she answered, in a voice almost inaudible.

With almost brutal roughness Cotherstone thrust her away from him, caught up his cap and gloves, and strode out of the house, where he had spent such blissful hours, and where, alas, he had had such a bitter blow—and he never saw her again.

The following day came a piteous note of explanation—how her father had wished it; how she had given Hamilton the promise to please her father when he was dying; how she had not had courage to tell him earlier, because she had never dreamed he could care for her; how she was very, very unhappy, *very*—with a great dash under the adverb, and a woeful blister just below—how, though she must keep her promise, she would love her darling Eddie best all her life long.

And that was the end of it. A few weeks later he saw the announcement of her marriage in the papers, and then he tore her letter up and set himself to forget her. On the whole he succeeded fairly well. He threw himself heart and soul into his profession, with what result we have seen. He succeeded in making every one, even himself, believe he was a man of the consistency of stone; and yet when Private Jones—brought in to receive a severe lecture, not for one but for a dozen misdemeanours—came and looked at him out of Mary's blue eyes, and talked to him in Mary's soft voice, he could not find it in his heart—his adamantine heart—to be hard upon Mary's boy.

The vision of the cherub's face under a forage-cap threw him back with painful distinctness to the time, one-and-twenty years before, when he parted from Mary. He realised, that Saturday afternoon in November, that perhaps he had been very hard upon her, poor little soul! He might, at least, have stayed and said a few kind words to the poor little woman, who was bound to a man she hated; that she hated Hamilton there could be no doubt, for the look of loathing and horror which leapt into her eyes as she realised his presence proclaimed her feelings plainly enough. Ah, poor darling—she had got from "poor little soul" to "poor darling"—but he felt now that he had been cruel to her; he might, at least, have answered that heart-broken, despairing letter, and so perhaps have made her lot less hard to bear than probably it was. Well, at all events, he had not been hard upon the boy, that was one consoling point. Boys will go wrong, especially when they have no father to keep them straight. He had suspected all along who Private Jones really was, though until that very afternoon he had not been quite certain. He wondered if a letter to his mother would do any good. She was a widow now, poor soul —Hamilton had been dead ten years, he knew—and naturally she would be glad to know there was some one who took an interest in her only child—that Mrs. Hamilton of Glenbarry had had but one child Colonel Cotherstone was also aware—and certainly if he wrote a few lines she could not take them amiss, and they might be a comfort to her.

And so Colonel Cotherstone sat down to his writing-table to pen an epistle to his old love, Mary Stewart, the mother of that exceedingly wayward young gentleman, Private Edward Jones, F-troop, Cuirassiers.

" She called him after me, too," murmured the commanding officer of the Cuirassiers, as he selected a pen. " Poor little Mary ! "

It was easy enough to write " Nov. 14th " under the printed " CAVALRY BARRACKS, YORK," which was already stamped on the paper, but he found the next part scarcely so easy. His most natural impulse was to begin, " My dear Mary; " yet, when he had written it, he thought it too familiar, so took another sheet. Having put another " November 14th " at the top, he began, " My dear Mrs. Hamilton—"

" What shall I say next? " he said aloud.

It took him a long time to write that letter ; but at last he accomplished it. It was not very long, and it was rather stiff. It ran :

MY DEAR MRS. HAMILTON,

    I have only this afternoon discovered that your son has enlisted in the Cuirassiers under the name of Jones. He has been five months in the regiment ; and, though as yet he is impatient of restraint, I am in hopes that we shall make a good soldier of him, and, in the course of a few years, that he will obtain his commission. Any interest of mine, you may be sure, he will not want.

        Believe me, my dear Mrs. Hamilton,
            Most faithfully yours,
                EDWARD LE GENDRE COTHERSTONE.

That was the letter he wrote and sent. Three days passed, during which he received no reply—a fact which worried him somewhat. On the fourth day, however, he received a note, by hand, from Mrs. Hamilton, asking him to call and see her at the " Black Swan Hotel."

He happened to be just going out when the note reached

him, so he thrust it into his pocket—not without a certain feeling of tenderness at the sight of the dainty delicate characters—and took his way into the town. He did not go very quickly, though ; he called at the florist's half-way, and bought a flower for his button-hole—a white rosebud it was. He met some people that he knew, and stayed to chat with them.

But, dawdle as he would, he came to the hotel at last. Every one who has been in York knows that it is not very far from the Cavalry Barracks to the " Black Swan." Colonel Cotherstone went into the hall and asked for Mrs. Hamilton.

" Was Mrs. Hamilton at home ? "

" Certainly. Would the gentleman step this way ? "

And so they led him up-stairs and ushered him into a room, where, seated by the fire, was a lady—a lady with wavy golden hair, with soft blue eyes, and two little white hands outstretched to greet him—his old love, Mary Stewart.

" How am I to thank you?" she cried. " I have tried for all these five months to find out what my boy was doing. I couldn't persuade him to come home, and I have been so unhappy about him."

" Has he never written to you ? "

" Oh yes ; every week regularly. But I did not know that he was in York. His letters came from London ; and the only address was a London post-office. He said he was not in prison, but he couldn't tell me any more."

" No, he has not been in prison," Colonel Cotherstone answered, smiling, as he thought of the near shaves he had had in that respect.

" I didn't quite understand your letter," said Mrs. Hamilton presently. " Why should he be ashamed of the profession he has taken up—too much ashamed even to tell me what it was ? Why should he have any restraint placed upon him ? Have the other officers so much restraint ? "

" My dear Mrs. Hamilton, your son has *enlisted*," said the colonel kindly, wondering at her ignorance.

" How enlisted ?"

" He is not in my regiment as an officer," he said.

" What ! My boy a common soldier ?"

" A private," corrected Colonel Cotherstone, gently. " Yes, that is what he is."

" My boy," cried the little woman, brokenly, " my boy, Hamilton of Glenbarry, a soldier ! Does he have to groom a horse, pray ?"

" Certainly."

" And to do stable-work ?"

" Yes."

" Does he have to salute you ?"

" Of course." In spite of himself a smile broke over his face. " I hope that is not very hard for him."

" Not to you," she said, impatiently. " No one would mind saluting you, of course ; but the others ! You don't mean to say he is obliged to put his hand up so "—with a ludicrous imitation of a salute—" to all the young subs., to the riding-master even ?"

" He certainly has to do so," answered the colonel.

" Hamilton of Glenbarry salute, touch his hat to a riding-master !" ejaculated Mrs. Hamilton. " I tell you it is absurd, utterly absurd !"

" Whilst he remains in the ranks it must be done," said the colonel, smiling still at her vehemence.

" Then he shall not remain in the ranks," she cried. " How soon can I have him released ?"

" Will you take my advice," he asked, " and leave him for a few months, or until I advise you to buy him off ?"

" You would do what is best for me ?" the widow faltered.

" You know I would," touching her hand for a moment. That was a great advance for Colonel Cotherstone ; but the old influences were strongly at work in him.

" I don't know why you should be so good to me," she said, rather forlornly. " I behaved very badly to you, and yet—'"

" Yet what ?" drawing nearer and taking her hand.

" I was unhappy," she said, simply.

They were both standing on the rug ; he, a large, fine,

upright figure in grey tweed; she, a dainty thing in purple velvet looking absurdly young to be the mother of Private Jones.

"Why were you unhappy, and when?" he asked, possessing himself of the other hand.

"When you went away; and—and because—I—"

"Well?" he asked, eagerly. "Because you—"

"Because I loved you so," she said, hiding her face upon his breast.

If Colonel Cotherstone's dream of love was rudely interrupted one-and-twenty years before, when, on that June morning, Hamilton of Glenbarry turned up so inopportunely, he made up for it when he found his little love in the hotel with the sign of the "Black Swan" at York. It would be hard to say who was the most surprised at the event which followed, or rather at the announcement of it. I doubt whether the officers, when, the next evening after dinner, their chief announced that he was going to be married, were as thoroughly surprised as was Ned Hamilton, when, a free man again, he entered his mother's room at the "Black Swan"; and I am perfectly certain that his astonishment did not equal that of his mother when she found how faithfully Edward Cotherstone had loved her all those years. Perhaps the most thoroughly amazed of them all was Colonel Cotherstone himself.

To the intense amusement of the whole regiment, his wife calls him "Eddie." The young ones say that he grew tired of having no heart, so managed to get his brains exchanged for one; but if one of them goes a little wrong in duty or any other respect, he very quickly finds out that the chief's brain is as keen as ever it was in the days when he was popularly believed to be altogether deficient in certain internal arrangements, of which a heart was one.

CALCRAFT—A TROOPER.

THE Cotherstones had been married a few months, and were living at a pretty house in the village of Fulford, which lies about half-a-mile beyond the cavalry barracks at York.

Mrs. Cotherstone was standing at the window of the dining-room, watching for her husband, and, at the same time, taking notes of the interesting process of putting a horse into a cab belonging to the inn opposite. Very slow about his job the man was; the straps seemed to get wrong as each one was fastened. The horse was not particularly anxious to expedite the work, and kept shifting his position every moment, at which proceeding the man expressed his disapproval in a series of " gee-whoops " and " gerrup-ma-lads," of which the animal took but small notice. Then he went inside the inn, for a glass of beer evidently. Mrs. Cotherstone was disgusted. She could, she felt, have put that horse in and been at the house to which it had been ordered in less than half the time that it had taken the man to fasten one strap. She wondered if it was wanted to catch a train? It couldn't be for a wedding—it was after one o'clock; then, but to be sure, it might be wanted for a funeral ! She drummed her little fingers impatiently upon the window-ledge, and wondered indignantly how much longer that man was going to be drinking that glass of beer? Why, she could have drank half-a-dozen glasses of beer in that time, she was convinced, though Mrs. Edward le Gendre Cotherstone was not given to beer !

Then a *divertissement* fortunately came, in the shape of a tall, soldierly figure, in undress, carrying a whip in one hand—a man, with a stern, bronzed face, having, just then, a most pre-occupied expression. It cleared, however, as he perceived the golden-haired little lady at the window, much as a thunder-cloud

I

disperses before the genial influence of the sun, but not before she had noticed the unwonted darkness.

"What is the matter, Ned?" she asked, as he entered the room.

"Oh! nothing particular, my darling," he answered; "it is only that poor devil, Calcraft, again."

"Again?" the little woman echoed, blankly; "and after you gave him such a talking to?"

Her tone implied that since the colonel had taken the trouble to give Calcraft a "talking to," his gratitude ought to have induced him, from that time forth, to become a model of good conduct and amiability.

"It isn't all his fault," said the colonel; "but he is quick-witted and sharp-tongued—the two qualities often go together—and, somehow, he has contrived to get out of his sergeant-major's good graces; you know what that means?"

"Bullying, I suppose?"

"Bullying is rather a mild general term for it," Colonel Cotherstone answered. "In detail it means nagging, continual fault-finding, swearing at, reporting—that is one side. On the other it means, never doing right, always doing wrong, always being late, never being clean enough, everlastingly breaking or infringing rules, being perpetually goaded to the verge of madness, being taunted, scorned, made nothing of; and, like a boil, matters generally come to a head—they have come to a very decided head in Calcraft's case, poor devil."

"Well?" said Mrs. Cotherstone, in a tone implying that he was to continue his story.

"He is rather a favourite of Dickson's—he is in Dickson's troop, you know. He has looked after him as well as he could; but what can an officer do under such circumstances? Next to nothing; and this morning the crash has come. Sergeant-Major Lucas and his wife live at the end of a verandah, which Calcraft has to pass every morning with a big bucket of cold water, and, being an awfully hot night, they had left their window wide open. It seems that this morning Lucas hadn't turned out so early as he ought to have done, not by an hour or more, and as Calcraft passed along the verandah with his bucket of water, some fiend whispered into his ear that the water was very cold, that the window was wide open, and that the Lucases' bed stood immediately beneath it. Of course it was all done in a moment, and Calcraft took to his heels, and then there seems to have been a royal row. Calcraft, the usual scapegrace, was accused, and was marched off to the cells, poor beggar, to await a trial by court-martial. However, there's one thing I can and will do! I can't save Calcraft, but, by George, I'll be down upon Lucas for being late."

"Can't you get Calcraft off?" Mrs. Cotherstone asked in a voice choking with laughter, and wiping the tears from her eyes as she spoke.

"Utterly impossible," he returned, decidedly; "a court-martial must go by evidence, not by private favour."

"I shall give him a sovereign for himself, when I see him," Mrs. Cotherstone announced. If anyone had made such a startling proposal to Colonel Cotherstone a year previously, he would have positively jumped off his seat with horror, and expressed his opinion that such a proceeding would infallibly send the service to the dogs in no time; but on the present occasion he merely possessed himself of one of Mary's little delicate hands, and, with an indulgent laugh, told her she must keep her doings to herself.

"Don't let me know anything about it, for it won't do to have it said that I encourage insubordination in the regiment."

Some of my readers may have seen the interior of a barrack-cell. Such will know that they are not pleasant places. Those who have never entered one must take my word for it! Private Calcraft knew them well, and each experience he had of them he found them less to his taste. During that brilliant summer-day he sat pondering over the fate which had led him into disfavour with Sergeant-Major Lucas. How was it that he hated him so? He was quite sure he had never done anything to merit it: no one else in the whole regiment hated him as Lucas did. I cannot say that he was particularly repentant for what he had done, and there was not a shadow of doubt that he was the culprit, though as yet he had maintained a stolid silence upon the subject; but he found the confinement of his cell irksome, and he would like to have heard what his comrades were saying about his exploit, which would, he knew, be on every tongue in the barracks. Well! he should get it " proper," as he put it, for this business, he had no doubt. They were sure to be pretty hard upon him, he so often got into trouble, and of course they would take the sergeant-major's account before his; not that he had any account to give. He had, as yet, kept quiet, without attempting any explanation, and he thought that would be the best course to adopt, whatever came of the affair; besides, what had he to say?

He leant forward, with his elbows on his knees, and watched a ray of sunshine, which had had sufficient bad taste to weary of the outer world and penetrate, by way of a change, into the cell. Calcraft was very glad to see the sunbeam, though it seemed to him that it couldn't have very much sense to come in there, when it might have stayed outside and be free, and then he fell to wishing that he, too, was free. He wondered how it was that he had borne the tyrant's tyranny so long. Many a man would have made a bolt of it, and trusted to luck that he didn't wake up some fine morning to find himself branded with the letter which would be a shame to him as long as he should live, even to his grave. But no! After all, he wouldn't be such a mean-spirited coward as that. He had fought on for five years, and, come what might, he would fight on a bit longer. Maybe Lucas would be leaving the regiment, or dying, or something of that sort, and then see if he didn't show his officers that he had some good in him, after all! He could just fancy the kindly approval in Captain Dickson's keen blue eyes when he won a good conduct stripe, or was made corporal! Aye! He would keep up his pluck for a while longer, and try if matters wouldn't mend a bit. Just as he arrived at this satisfactory conclusion, the door of the cell opened, and the object of his thoughts appeared—Captain George Dickson.

Calcraft jumped up from his bench, and Captain Dickson sat down upon it.

" Well! you've made an awful mess of it this time, Calcraft," he observed.

" Yes, sir," returned Calcraft, with a salute.

" It's no use trying to keep you straight," the officer observed testily. " I shall have to give you up altogether."

Calcraft made no reply; hitherto he had exulted much over his exploit, but since it was to cost him the kindliness of his captain, he began to look at it in quite another light.

" And, by-the-bye, Calcraft," said Captain Dickson, suddenly, " what the dickens were you doing in the verandah at five o'clock ?"

" Wasn't there, sir" he replied, promptly.

" Sergeant-Major Lucas says it was striking five as the bucket of water came through the window."

" Then it couldn't be me as threw it, sir," said Calcraft, solemnly, " for, when five o'clock struck by Fulford church, I was standing just outside the door of F-troop room, with Private Wells and Corporal Fraser—as they'll both tell you, sir."

" I'll look into the matter," answered the captain, rising ; " and, Calcraft, if you should be lucky enough to get over this business, just let it be a warning to you."

" I will, sir," he said, earnestly enough, but whether some expression in his captain's eyes upset his gravity or not I cannot say, only at that moment his solemn red face relaxed, and the hearty laughter came bubbling up to his lips : it might be at the remembrance of the douche-bath, which he had so successfully administered to his enemy, and, as he dared not laugh outright, his feelings found a vent in a violent fit of coughing, and Captain Dickson beat a hasty retreat; perhaps he wished to laugh in comfort out of Calcraft's sight.

In due time Calcraft was brought before the court-martial. The sergeant-major told his story glibly enough ; in truth. there was not very much to tell.

" On the morning of the 10th of July he was in

window was open at the top, the church clock at Fulford struck five—he was perfectly sure as to the time, because he had compared his watch with it: just as he laid the watch down a bucketful of water was emptied through the window over the bed; he could not see the face of the man who did it, but he saw the hands; he could positively swear to their being the prisoner's hands!"

So ended the case for the prosecution. Sergeant-Major Lucas retired with a well-satisfied smile at Calcraft, who returned it with a defiant stare.

Then—greatly to the sergeant-major's astonishment—appeared two witnesses for the prisoner, Corporal Fraser and Private Wells, who both deposed positively to the truth of Calcraft's statement, that, at five o'clock on the morning of the 10th of July, he was standing with them at the door of F-troop room. Corporal Fraser also deposed that the prisoner was not out of his sight until after half-past five. Accordingly Calcraft was acquitted!

Now Calcraft had made Captain Dickson a distinct promise that, if he should be lucky enough to get over the affair, it should be a warning to him; therefore immediately he found himself a free man he at once proceeded to break it. First of all he informed the non-plussed sergeant-major—who, to save himself from censure for being late, had set the time back a whole hour, and so enabled Calcraft to get off scot free—that the way to catch a bird was by putting salt on its tail, for which valuable information he did not deign even to thank him.

Finding that had no effect, Calcraft, like an idiot—as most soldiers are when left to themselves—occupied himself for a week in taking every available opportunity of passing along the verandah, in which his enemy's room was situate, singing at the top of his voice the refrain of a little song—

> The old old story was told again,
> At five o'clock in the morning!

Finally he brought matters to a climax by asking if he and " the Missis " had found the water very cold? Flesh and blood could stand it no longer. The sergeant-major went to

Captain Dickson, and reported that Calcraft had owned to throwing the water! Calcraft denied it, and repeated what had really taken place. Lucas held to his story, and eventually Calcraft's patience—of which he had not at any time a very large stock—gave way, and, in spite of his officer's presence, he rushed at his enemy, and administered a sound drubbing! That was fatal! There was the tedium of another court-martial: the thrashing—and it was a sound one—counted for a good deal, and the provocation and the bullying, on the other hand, went for next to nothing. Calcraft received the longest sentence which could be given to him, also the prison-crop, and was heard no more of until he was once more free.

August and September slipped away quickly enough to most people, but very slowly indeed to poor Calcraft, in his durance vile. The longest period, however, must come to a close, and the darkest night end in morning. His term of imprisonment did come to an end, in time; but as to his night of troubles ending in the morning in peace and quietness, why, that was quite another matter. Calcraft thought his trials and difficulties grew denser. At first he tried hard to keep straight, for he knew if he could but rise to the rank of corporal, his enemy's power would be considerably lessened; but, try as he would, it seemed quite impossible for him to succeed. The glorious autumn days passed by, each one finding him sunk a little deeper in the slough of despond, each one leaving him a trifle more wretched than the last, and more passionately desirous of lying down to die in peace. Yes! it had come to that. He had begun to look back to the long, dreary weeks he spent in the cells as a time when he had known what it was to have peace and rest. He felt himself a disgrace to his regiment, yet they would not let him do any better, and he did try! He fancied—for he had grown morbidly sensitive of late—that when his officers passed him they looked at him with scorn—all fancy, poor fellow, for they never looked at him at all, or bestowed a second thought upon him, though " Calcraft, poor devil," was their usual way of speaking of him when they did mention him, and most of them hated Lucas as much as they pitied his victim. Still a

contemptuous pity was not calculated to improve the state of a
man on the verge of madness, as Calcraft at that time was;
and had it not been for two persons, he would not have borne
up as long as he did. Those two persons were the colonel's
golden-haired, gentle little wife and Captain Dickson. For
them both Calcraft, in his utter misery, conceived a passionate
adoration. First in his poor tormented heart he held the lady.
She had carried out her intention, which she had announced to
her husband, and, on the first opportunity, had given Calcraft
a sovereign, which he, poor chivalrous fool, had had a ring put
through, and slung it to his watch-chain; and whenever she
met him her gentle " Good morning, Calcraft," fell upon his
ear with such an accustomed sweetness that he could have flung
himself down and kissed her very feet, in gratitude for the
kindness which cost her nothing, but which, to him, was the
one ray of sunshine which brightened his lot. No, not quite
the only ray; he had forgotten Captain Dickson.

Towards the end of November Captain Dickson's servant
died, and he chose Calcraft to fill his place. Then his troubles
lightened somewhat, for he was necessarily less in his enemy's
power; but, unfortunately, the partial reprieve had come too
late—the evil had gone too far, and he was unable to shake off
the effects of the past five years and the continual illtreatment
he had endured—the shame and degradation which had been
thrust upon him during the past few months.

Things had gone badly enough with him since the day he
joined the regiment; but until that fatal July morning when he
had succumbed to the voice of the fiend, which prompted him
to pour a pail of water over Mr. and Mrs. Lucas, he had gone
on his careless way, almost unmindful of anything his enemy
might do to torment him. His long term of imprisonment he
had endured with a considerable amount of cheerfulness and
pluck, expressing his opinion to more persons than one that the
thrashing he had administered was well worth the after-conse-
quences. Alas! he had not at that time counted upon what
was to follow!—it surpassed even his ideas of what bullying
meant, and he had had considerable experience in that respect,

as has been shown. If he had gone into Captain Dickson's service immediately after his release from the cells he might have been able to carry out the good resolutions he had formed during his confinement : as it was, the partial reprieve came too late ; his spirit was cowed utterly, his aspirations after something nobler were crushed, his courage gone! The very appearance of the man was changed ; his fearless blue eyes had acquired a wild unsettled expression, and he seldom looked any one straight in the face ; his face, which had once been of a healthy red, had faded to a sickly pallor, and the flesh had fallen away from his cheeks. He had lost the careless swaggering gait which had once distinguished him and now seemed to have no energy for anything but sauntering—no, trailing is a better word—trailing about the quaint narrow streets, taking no notice of man, woman or child. If Captain Dickson happened to be out or was dining at mess he did not even do that, but stayed in his room—which he had leave to do—being sure there of peace and quietness.

The winter days crept on, and Calcraft's spirit sank lower, his despondency increased, his face grew paler, and his air more dejected. Just before Christmas he got a kick from a horse, which laid him up for a fortnight in hospital. A year before he would hardly have noticed it, but, in his weakened state of body and mind, the trifling accident proved more serious! Not that he minded it : he had a happy time of it in hospital. The doctor always had a pleasant, cheery word for him ; the nurses, if rough, were kindly, and treated him just the same as the others ; his master went across to see him every morning, and lent him more books and papers than his poor dazed eyes could bear to read, and, greatest of all the little pleasures which fell to his lot, Mrs. Cotherstone herself sent him a basket of grapes and oranges on Christmas morning, which threw the poor fellow into a perfect fever of anxiety, until he had despatched a note of grateful thanks, which, if he had but known it, brought the scalding tears into the gentle little woman's soft eyes! Oh! those grapes and oranges! it seemed like desecration to eat them. Willingly would Calcraft have kept them, like the sovereign on his watch-chain, as precious relics!

But at last this pleasant time came to an end and he was pronounced well enough to resume his duties. So he had to turn his back upon his pleasures, and go back to the old routine. He found, to his utter dismay and horror, that Captain Dickson was going on leave for two months and could not take a servant with him. Oh! the agony the news caused to Calcraft's heart. Oh! the bitter, bitter disappointment and dread!

He took the news quietly enough, for his master was rather late and in a hurry to be dressed; but when the long process was finished, and he had gone clanking along the echoing corridor and down the stone steps, Calcraft flung himself down upon the bed, and burying his face among the pillows, broke into such a passionate torrent of tears, that the private's wife who kept the room tidy, happening to come in at that moment, stood stock-still in the doorway, absolutely aghast. Her womanly instinct, however, impelled her to make some effort to comfort him.

"What's up, Calcraft?" she asked, advancing to the bed, and laying a hand—which, if coarse and work-worn, was kindly—upon his head: "is there something else gone wrong? I wouldn't take on so about it if I was you—though I'm sure, poor chap, it do seem never-ending."

She was a good-hearted woman, and she meant to do kindly; yet, if she had quietly gone away and left him to sob the cobwebs out of his brain his agony might have passed; as it was, he jumped up and rushed out of the room, stung afresh by the shame of having been discovered in tears by a woman.

He never stopped to think; he tore across the barrack-square and out of the gates, though the sentry asked if anything was amiss as he passed. Calcraft never heard him! On he sped, seeing nothing for the blinding tears which filled his eyes, hearing nothing for the agony throbbing in his brain. On he went! along the path leading through the drill-field, unaware that Captain Dickson had flung himself off his horse, and, followed by half-a-dozen dragoons, had started in pursuit

with a cry of " Great God ! the river !"   Calcraft never heard or
saw anything save that broad stream shining through the trees
at the other end of the drill-field—the river, where he might
find what he had been seeking so long, a haven of forgetfulness
and peace !

Ah ! the yell which rose up from the on-lookers as the tall
figure sprang headlong into the water, followed, an instant
later, by the officer and a young private, who had been
Calcraft's friend !   There was just one moment of suspense
before the captain's dark, close-cropped head appeared above
the bank, and then that of the private as they dragged the poor
fellow on to the walk.

Colonel Cotherstone just reached the walk as Captain
Dickson gave Calcraft's arm an angry shake.

" What are you thinking of, you d——d idiot ?" he asked,
indignantly.

Calcraft looked at his preserver in a blank, dazed kind of
way.   " You'd best have let me finish it, sir," he answered, in-
distinctly, and then fainted away !

" Dash me !" said the young private, wiping the water from
his face—there might have been a few tears there, too—" Dash
me, if I ever saw anything like that !"

" Here, some of you get him up to the hospital at once,"
ordered the colonel ; " and you, Captain Dickson, the sooner
you get those wet clothes off the better ; you, too, Johnson :
you have acted with great bravery, but there is no need to have
rheumatic fever as a consequence."

＊　　　＊　　　＊　　　＊　　　＊

" I'll tell you what you shall do," said little Mrs. Cotherstone,
when she heard the story a few hours later ; " you shall buy his
discharge—don't you call it so ?—and give him to me."

" But what will you do with him ?"

" Make a butler of him," was the prompt reply.

For many weeks, though, it seemed as if Calcraft would have
no need of interest or of anything else in this world.   He lay
on his bed in the hospital, raving in brain fever, and, when at

last that left him, the doctors found the prostration and weakness almost worse to deal with than the fever had been.

But they brought him round after all, or perhaps, as Dr. Markham declared, the medicine which did him most good was when Mrs. Cotherstone went to see him, and asked if he would like to leave the army and enter their service as a butler.

" But I don't know anything of the work, ma'am," he stammered, though the pleased flush on his poor worn face showed how intense was his delight at her proposal.

" But you can learn," she answered, decidedly ; and so poor Calcraft's future was settled.

He progressed with amazing rapidity after that, and, in order to complete the cure, Mrs. Cotherstone sent him to her Scotch place for a month, where, as he himself said, he was almost too happy to live.

Not very long after this Mrs. Cotherstone presented her lord with a son and heir. Oh ! that child ! How in the years which followed Calcraft worshipped him. No service which the youngster exacted was too difficult for Calcraft to perform ; to him the boy's wishes and commands were law, absolute as " the law of the Medes and Persians, which altereth not !" All the passionate gratitude which the mother had raised in him he lavished upon the boy, and the sweetest music that ever rang in his ears was when the tender, imperative child's voice sounded through the house, with the word which was oftenest upon his lips—that word was " Cal—cwaft !"

THE VICTORIA CROSS: WHY MAJOR CREYKE DID NOT WIN IT.

IT was midwinter. The afternoon of a dull December day was drawing to a close, and as yet the lamps were not lighted in the drawing-room of the house which the Cotherstones called home A blazing fire, however, lighted up the room sufficiently for little Mrs. Cotherstone to study the pages of a book which she held in her hand. The colonel sat opposite, tired out by a hard day's work, and more than half asleep. The boy, now nearly a year old, was on the rug between them, holding a court-martial on his father's boots, occasionally pricking himself with the spurs, and making his tiny hands excessively dirty, his hands and his little embroidered frock.

"Ned," remarked the colonel's wife, à propos of nothing, "I've been looking in the *Army List*."

"Eh, what, my darling?" suddenly rousing himself into an upright position.

"I've been looking in the *Army List*," she repeated.

"Oh, is that all? I thought something had happened to the boy," sinking back in his chair again.

Reminded of the boy, Mrs. Cotherstone looked down, and, seeing his occupation, uttered a scream of disgust, which the child quickly echoed by a loud crow of delight.

"Dir—ty boy!" cried Mrs. Cotherstone, in energetic staccato tones; "such a mess he's in. Ring the bell, Ned dear, please."

The colonel did as he was told, and a moment later our old friend Calcraft appeared, looking quite irreproachable in his faultless evening attire.

"Take him away, Calcraft," cried the little lady; "he has made himself so dirty with Colonel Cotherstone's boots."

As Calcraft advanced, the child put out two dimpled arms to him, and expressed his satisfaction in a series of " Boo-o-o-o-'s."

" How fond he is of the child !" said the colonel's wife, as the door closed.

" Yes," answered the colonel ; he was rather sleepy.

" I've been looking in the *Army List*," Mrs Cotherstone announced for the third time, " and I cannot find anywhere that Major Creyke has the Victoria Cross."

" Of course not," returned the colonel, with a laugh.

" But he has it."

" Certainly not."

" But they always call him ' V. C. Creyke,' " she said, in a mystified tone.

" It is only a nickname, child ;" he often called her " child," though she had a son of age.

" However did he get such a name ? Oh, I am so disappointed, Ned. I have been fancying all sorts of bravery; and now it has gone."

" Oh, he has bravery and pluck enough; you need not be disappointed," he answered. " He gained the name out in the Mutiny, though he did not win the Cross itself."

" And how was it ?" she asked, with deep interest.

" Well, I can only give you the merest outlines of the story," he said, " for it's a good while ago, and my head was in a state of confusion for a long time after that awful business had been cleared up. Creyke's father and mine were, from their earliest boyhood, upon terms of the closest friendship ; their fathers had been the same before them. My father owned the Hall ; Creyke's father was rector of the parish. Well, Creyke was only a year younger than I was, and somehow we fell into the same line as our fathers and grandfathers had done before us, and our friendship was, I really believe, more passionate and tragically inclined than even theirs. We were lucky enough to get into the same regiment, and we were so silly as to get sent to India, soon after which the Mutiny broke out ; it was *just* after you were married, Mary."

" Yes," she replied, " but the regiment did not go."

" No. The 7th Lancers were short of subalterns, having lost several by cholera or misadventure, and I volunteered to go; they wanted two. Of course Creyke insisted upon going, too, though his father and mine came down to us, and did their best to persuade us not to go. It was no good. I had made up my mind, and Creyke's mind was mine; so we went. It was all very jolly at first: we liked India, and there was any amount of splendid sport. We liked the regiment, and Colonel Cornwallis was a down-right good sort, with the sweetest, prettiest little wife you ever saw. The fellows used to fight almost as to whether Mrs. Cornwallis or her sister, Miss Bannister, was the lovelier. For my part I admired the colonel's wife the more of the two—I always did like fair women best : Miss Bannister was very dark. It was no good any of the subalterns looking at her, for the major went out in the same ship with her, and made matters safe; though I don't think they were engaged. Well, the Mutiny broke out, and then we found what two splendid women they were ! They had always been admired, but after the siege began they were simply idolised. How they worked ! Nothing seemed too hard for them : they cooked and washed and nursed until they were fairly worn out, always cheering us on, always ready in any emergency; they seemed to shrink from nothing. Mrs. Cornwallis made no distinction ; it might be the sick baby of an officer's wife or a private soldier, it was all the same to her ; and as for Floss Bannister, I believe any man in the garrison would have walked straight into the enemy's lines at a word from her. Well, towards the end, Major Gurney was killed, and we thought the shock had killed her too ; but an hour after we had buried him, she went her rounds as usual. I never shall forget that night ! Creyke and I were on duty together at one of the outposts, with one gun and perhaps a dozen men. We could see the black brutes moving about, but we couldn't hit them.

" ' I've had two shots at one of those black fiends,' I heard one fellow growl to another, ' and I've missed him both times.'

" ' I don't expect we'll have no luck, since Miss Floss has

given up comin'—not that we can expect it of her, the darlin for I must tell you she had been accustomed, in spite of he pressure of work inside the garrison, to visit the outposts every hour or so, ever since the chaplain died. At his death she took up his work where he left it, poor chap, and she stuck to it bravely right up to the time of the major's death. Every hour or so she used to come. Sometimes she sang a hymn, or read a few words, or just said the Lord's Prayer; if a soldier's wife was ill, and he couldn't get off duty to see her, he might trust Miss Floss to bring him news half-a-dozen times a-day. Well, after the major was killed, we never expected to see her again; for it had been a terrible blow for her, and they carried her away from his poor body in a dead faint. We hadn't been back long from the funeral, and just as the trooper ended, 'we can't expect it of her, the darlin',' she appeared.

"'You ought not to have come,' Creyke said to her, reproachfully; 'no one expected it of you, after such a shock as you have just had.'

"'My duty is to the living,' she said, in a perfectly calm voice. 'I have done my duty to the dead, and I thank God for it. Major Gurney has shown us all how gloriously we may do our duty, and I will not be the first to sit down and say, "I can struggle no longer."'

"If her tears were dried up Creyke's were not, and he turned away his head that she might not see them; he had loved her for months, poor chap, and I believe he would have given his life for Gurney's, if he could have taken that dreadful look of suffering out of her eyes. She turned away from him then.

"'Is Robert Moss here?' she asked.

"'Here, miss,' he answered, stepping out from behind another man, with suspiciously wet eyes.

"'Your wife seems a good deal better,' she said. 'I have just seen her, and she sent her love to you.'

"'Thank you, miss,' he answered, turning away, with eye: overflowing again; then in a choked voice, 'Maybe you'll give my love to Mary, and say I'll come in as soon as I can get off.

"She only stayed a few minutes, and just as she was moving

away, a great hulking Irishman ran after her and caught her gown—a great brute, that had been one of the worst scamps in the regiment.

" ' Shure, miss, darlin',' he blurted out, 'ye won't try to stop the blissid tears from comin'? They'll do ye a power o' good, Miss Floss, an' we can't bear to see ye look like that.'

" She lifted her soft dark eyes to his for a moment, and then she laid her little work-worn hand in his great fist.

" ' My tears are all burnt up, Michael,' she said, gratefully ; ' but I shall not forget what you have said to me.'

" And then she went away, and our watch dragged on. Each day, for the past fortnight, we had been sure matters could not get any worse, but somehow they did.

" It was not many days after this that they drove us back from that very outpost, and we were obliged to leave one of our few guns. The command had by that time fallen upon a man named Hood, a first-rate officer, though still rather young.

" ' It's a pity to let them have that gun,' he exclaimed, vexedly. ' Their fire's bad enough, but to have our own guns turned against us will be too bad.'

" ' Couldn't it be spiked, sir ?' Creyke asked.

" ' Yes, of course ; only the chances are ten to one against it's being done : the fire is so heavy there,' he answered.

" Of course a dozen volunteers stood out immediately, Creyke and I amongst the rest. I was chosen at once, and Creyke insisted upon going too. We were determined that the brutes should not have the gun ; but, upon my word, it was anything but pleasant, running right in the face of the enemy's fire, with only a half-ruined wall for shelter. I can tell you we accomplished our task expeditiously—I know my only idea was how soon I could get out of danger ; for we were in almost as much peril from our fellows' bullets as from the enemy's, as a continual crossfire was kept up the whole time. Just as we turned for a rush from the shelter of the half-ruined wall, I heard a yell from the black fiends behind us ; and before I had gone three yards I came down to the ground with a crash, with what I knew must be a bullet in my shoulder and a

K

second in my hip. Creyke heard only the yell and ran on. I tried to get up and follow him; but I fell back, half-fainting with the pain, and shut my eyes, with a feeling that it was all up with me. I don't remember much more, until I found Creyke bending over me with more resolution in his face than I had ever seen in it before.

"'It's all right, old chap,' he said, coolly. 'The brutes have winged you, but I'll have you inside in five minutes.'

"'Go back, you'll only get hit yourself,' I answered.

"'Can you use your legs?' he asked.

"'Got a ball in my right hip.'

"I saw him take out his penknife and begin ripping up a scarf which happened to be lying near, and then I fancy I must have gone off again; for, the next time I opened my eyes, Floss Bannister was bathing my forehead, and the doctor was bending over me.

"'You're a noble fellow, Creyke,' I heard Hood say. 'If we are spared to get out of this, I shall recommend you for the Cross.'

"'I don't do it for the Cross,' I heard him answer, coolly. 'I'm glad we prevented those beasts getting the gun, and I couldn't leave Cotherstone to die out there. I should never have faced his father again, as long as I lived.'

"'Never mind your reasons,' Hood said, warmly, 'they don't lessen your heroism, whatever they were.'

"Creyke came round to us then, and asked if he could help in any way.

"'Lend me a penknife,' answered the doctor.

"'Oh, by Jove! I've left it behind me,' he said, in a disgusted tone. 'I'll run and fetch it.'

"'You will do nothing of the kind,' put in Hood, imperatively.

"'But it's the only one I have, sir,' returned Creyke mildly.

"'I forbid you to go; I distinctly forbid it.'

"'Oh, I must go, sir,' he said, quietly; 'I shan't be a minute.' And he did so. returning in a few minutes, breath-

less, but unsheathed. " Here's your knife, Doctor,' he said, as
coolly as if he had fetched it out of the hospital.

" ' Now, sir,' I heard Hood say, sternly—I could only just
hear him, for they were trying to move me, and I was turning
very sick and faint again—' you have chosen to disobey my
orders, therefore I shall not recommend you for the Cross. It
is given for valour, not for foolhardiness.'

" And that was how Creyke missed the V.C.," he ended.

" And what became of her?" Mrs. Cotherstone asked, wiping
away her tears, which had been falling plentifully during the
recital.

" The last time I heard of her, she was still living with the
Cornwallises ; and I fancy she would have yielded to Creyke's
prayers, only she promised Gurney just at the last that she
would meet him in heaven—Floss Bannister still. Of course,
you know, Mary, I don't mean that she has forgotten him ; but
perhaps she might have been induced to let Creyke care for
her, but for the promise."

" And Major Creyke?"

" Creyke ! Oh, there will never be any one like her for him.
He will love her all his life, as he will never love any other
human being. I wonder I never told you all this before,
darling. I am afraid I've been so happy myself that I have
never thought of other people's troubles ; and, somehow, I
don't care to look back to the time when I had not found you
again."

Mrs. Cotherstone put her soft hands into her husband's with
a most tender smile upon her fair face. " I hope I may meet
her some day, Ned," she said, earnestly. " I should like to
see the woman who saved your life for me ; and as for Major
Creyke—Ah, now I think, I shall never be able to make
enough of him."

" Only don't make me jealous," he interposed.

" And how was it," she asked presently, " that you came
back to the Cuirassiers ?"

" My darling, at heart we were only volunteers—at least,
that is to say, our interests and pride were all centred in the

old regiment. We always looked upon ourselves as Cuirassiers; and as soon as I had a chance of a troop in the old regiment I took it. The Cornwallisses had left then, for the colonel was too badly wounded to be fit for service again; and, as Floss Bannister was gone, Creyke exchanged at once, though he lost ever so much seniority by doing so."

" Will he ever marry, do you think?"

" Floss would not have him."

" Ah, but I meant any one else. Men do such things, you know, Ned."

" Do you think I could ever have married any one but yourself?" he asked.

" Of course not," she replied, indignantly.

" Well, then, I don't think Creyke will either."

THE CAPTAIN OF F-TROOP.

"Not exactly handsome," said Captain Dickson, in reply to a question put to him by a brother officer, "but the sort of girl that every second man would turn round to look after."

"Ah!" returned the other—by name, Gough—comprehensively, and as if he perfectly understood the description, "and what class?"

"Oh! a lady, decidedly," said Dickson, hastily.

"What a queer thing we've never met her," remarked the other. "Perhaps she's some parson's or lawyer fellow's daughter."

"Very likely," said Dickson, indifferently. "She's a splendid woman, whoever she is. She did fetch me, no mistake about it."

"Where did you see her?"

"At the Minster; followed her down Coney Street, and then she went up Mickle-gate way."

"Lives that way, probably," suggested Gough.

"Probably," returned Dickson; and then they fell to talking of other things.

But the remembrance of the lady did not fade from the memory of the man whom she had so favourably impressed. Try as he would, he could not get her out of his head. Whilst he was dressing for mess that evening, her face and attitude kept rising before his eyes, until he was vexed with himself for being such a fool. Still, she was grand, there was no doubt about it. He had gone to afternoon prayers at the Minster partly because he had nowhere else to go, and partly because the anthem announced to be sung was of unusual beauty, and immediately upon entering his attention had been attracted by a lady in the stalls opposite—a young lady, apparently about twenty, with dead-gold hair and a perfectly colourless face.

Captain Dickson had eyes keen as any hawk's, and he " spotted " the dead-gold hair and the colourless face instantly ; also that she had large dark eyes ; to be sure, they might be grey, or even deep blue, but at that distance they had the appearance of dark eyes.

When the service began, and she rose to her feet, his admiration still further increased, for he perceived that she was of magnificent build and proportions. She was clad in some tightly-fitting, soft material, of a dark blue shade, and round her throat, below her plain linen collar, she wore a broad band of gold. Captain Dickson immediately decided in his own mind that dark blue and gold are the most becoming colours a woman can wear, especially if she chance to have dead-gold hair and a perfectly colourless complexion.

I am afraid he did not attend very much to the service, nor to the anthem which he had gone to hear ; his eyes scarcely ever 'strayed from the grand figure opposite, in the blue dress with the collar of gold. And yet, when the object of his admiration had disappeared over Ouse Bridge, and he had betaken himself back to barracks, snatches of the lovely music kept rising to his lips—

These are they which came out of great tribulation, and have washed their robes, and made them white in the blood of the Lamb.

Ah ! what haunting music it was ! Why—he wondered— why, as the emblem of great tribulation, should there rise before him a colourless face framed in dead-gold hair ? Surely she could not have come out of great tribulation ! It was only a proof of the strange fancies which at times creep into a man's mind. And yet he remembered most vividly how, during the anthem, she had seated herself with what he would swear was a sigh, and, closing her eyes, leant her head back against the carved oak, and remained so until the anthem was ended. It was not a happy gesture —it was the gesture of a woman who, as yet, had not realized the truth of the words they were singing—

They shall hunger no more, neither thirst any more ; neither shall the sun light on them, nor any heat.

They shall hunger—no more! Just then, as she sat down, he caught—or he fancied so, which was almost the same—a wistful glance from those dark eyes which told him very plainly that it had not come to her to hunger no more. He was quite right: there are many kinds of hunger.

Three days later he met her in the town, and her face haunted him more than ever—for it had the rare characteristic of being nicer as you approached nearer to it. Captain Dickson had a good look at her, for she never even glanced towards him. He saw that she wore the same dress as he had seen her in before, and that there was a younger girl with her, evidently a sister, from the similarity of costume and also from the striking resemblance of person. True, she was of a brighter, rosier, more lively type, and looked at the tall dark-haired soldier with interest enough; but, to his mind, she was not half so charming as her sister, who took no more notice of him than if he had been some country clod-hopper on a market day, and who seemed to him to be the living personification of that ideal woman of whom the poet sings—

Faultily faultless, icily regular, splendidly null, dead perfection, no more.

And yet, when he came to think of it, it was hardly an apt description. Each feature was good, and yet the whole was not handsome—faultily faultless, so far good—the face was cold, it was also regular in outline. Good thus far, but for the next clause he had a different opinion—he could not agree with that: a vision of wistful dark eyes came before his mental vision and a pale face, against a back-ground of dark oak ; the face was not null, though the perfection of it might have been described by some people as dead. A great man has said, that every face should be a history or a prophecy : hers contained the history of cruel suffering.

He tried several times to find out who she was, but without success. Then he met her in a shop ; on that occasion, her umbrella, which had been set against a chair, was thrown to the ground, and he had the pleasure of picking it up and restoring it to her. She thanked him with a bow and a grave smile, but without speaking. Captain Dickson wished she had spoken: she had, he felt convinced, a sweet voice, as tender as her face and he would have liked to hear it. Presently her sister asked her a question about something she was buying, but still she did not speak, only bent her head. Captain Dickson wondered impatiently if she had guessed how much he wished to hear her voice, and was trying to tantalize him. But no; the utter unconsciousness of the girl's face was a sufficient answer to his question. Had he been a wooden dummy standing there, she could not have taken less notice of him—nay, had he been a dummy, she might have looked at it.

She moved towards a stand of photographs at the side of the shop, and presently her sister addressed her. "Nell, do you want any of these?" she asked.

Now surely she must answer, thought Dickson, but she did not, only shook her head and turned again to her study of the photographs. How aggravating! Well, he had learnt something—her name was Nell! Nell!—what a lovely name; and then the sisters turned to leave the shop, seeing which Captain Dickson made a rush for the door.

"Permit me," he said, politely, holding it wide open.

"Thank you," said the younger sister, but the elder merely bowed again, with another grave smile, the counter-part of that which she had given him before.

"Who are those ladies?" he asked, when they had gone.

"Their name is Vansittart, sir," the man replied; "they live somewhere on the Mount—Mrs. Vansittart is a widow."

"Ah! really." Captain Dickson's tone implied that he was not much interested in the Vansittart family, yet, for all that he repeated her name a hundred times to himself, just for the pleasure of hearing it: "Nell Vansittart." He didn't know when a name had taken him so! He wondered impatiently why she couldn't have spoken—just "thank you," as her sister had said! Surely two words couldn't have been much trouble! and then an idea occurred to him, which made him hold his breath with the very horror of it. Could it be that she was dumb and had not power to speak? Dumb! could that glorious

creature be dumb?—dumb as the beasts which perish! Was
it that which gave those soft eyes such a speaking language of
their own? Could it be that which gave that gravely sweet
smile such pathetic eloquence? Oh, heavens!—surely not!
Dumb!—why she could not be dumb, for she was not deaf. No,
no!—what an idiot he was ever to fancy anything so repulsive,
so horrible. He would hasten to dress for mess, that he might
go down and forget that so hideous a conception had ever found
a place—even for a moment—in his mind.

But still, he could not shake off the painful impression which
his conjecture had produced, and his brother-officers were not
slow in discovering that something unusual was amiss with
him.

"What's the matter with Dickson?" one asked of another.

"Don't know, fallen in love, perhaps," was the reply.

"Oh, he'll get over it," laughed the one who had spoken first.

"What does Dickson look so blue about to-night?" was
asked at another part of the table.

"Can't say. His young woman's given him the slip,
perhaps."

"Very likely. I say, Dickson, what's up?"

"Up?" said Dickson, stupidly.

"Yes, up—wrong—amiss—anything you like."

"Oh, nothing."

"Has she turned out a failure?"

"She?" repeated Dickson, who, having his head full of Nell
Vansittart, wondered how Gore could know anything about it.

"Why, bless my soul, man!" cried the other, "you might as
well be deaf and dumb, for all the information one can get out
of you."

Deaf and dumb! Captain Dickson started so violently at the
words that a general laugh went round the table. He did not
laugh, only went on quietly eating his dinner.

"Must be in love," remarked a young "sub." to his
neighbour, in tones just loud enough for Dickson to catch.
"And, oh! by Jove! what beastly bad *rissoles* these are!
'Pon my soul, one might get as good in any cook-shop."

Captain Dickson looked up, and fixed his cool blue eyes upon the speaker. "I'll tell you what it is, young man," he said, in a quiet, distinct voice, which could be well heard all over the room; "if we have any more of your nonsense about the mess-cookery, *we'll send you home to rough it for six weeks.*"

"Dickson *may* have fallen in love," said one man *sotto voce* to another, "but his tongue's as caustic and his wit as keen as ever it was."

N.B.—Before I go on with my story, I may as well remark that the dissatisfied "sub." did not venture to open his mouth during the rest of the evening.

Well, not many days after this, the yeomanry ball came off. Captain Dickson went in good time, just on the chance of the Vansittarts being there. As a reward, he had not been in the room five minutes before he perceived the younger of the sisters standing near one of the pillars, in animated conversation with a yeomanry officer. He went straight across the room and asked for an introduction, and having obtained her card, put his name down for the next dance. It was a waltz, and he enjoyed it. The girl was pretty, well-dressed, and a good waltzer; moreover, he was looking forward to being introduced to her sister.

"Perhaps you will introduce me to your sister," he said, when she suggested returning to her mother.

"My sister is not here," she answered.

"Indeed! How is that? I hope she is not ill?"

"Oh, no; but—she does not visit;" and then, having secured another dance, he was obliged to leave her.

She does not visit. Yes, that was what she said. There was not the slightest doubt about her words or her meaning—she does not visit. What could there be to prevent her from visiting? There must be some cause, he argued; young women of twenty, or thereabouts, don't shun the world's pleasures without some very good cause. Then what could that cause be? He danced once or twice with her sister and discovered that her name was Constance; that since their father's death they had lived in Edinburgh, and that they had only been in York a few months. Miss Constance could not say whether they were likely to remain long or not—she thought not; but it would depend chiefly upon her sister.

"I wonder," said Captain Dickson, in his most deferential tone—"I wonder if you would be offended if I asked you a very impertinent question?"

"You had better ask it and see," she returned, with a laugh. "What is it?"

"I have seen you and your sister in the town once or twice," he answered; "and I should like to know why she does not visit."

Miss Constance looked down at her gloves, tore a flower from her bouquet, destroyed it, looked up hesitatingly, as if his question was an unwelcome one, and then looked down again.

"If you would rather not answer it, pray say so," he answered gently. "It was really a most impertinent thing to ask."

"No, no, not at all," she said, hastily. "The fact is, Captain Dickson, my sister had a misfortune a few months ago, and we have never been able to persuade her to go into society since."

"Oh, yes; I understand," he answered.

But understand he decidedly did not! A misfortune! It had an ominous sound about it which he did not like at all. A misfortune! "Why, bless me!" he thought, "there can't be anything wrong with her morals; and what could it be else to make her withdraw entirely from the world?"

She was right in her head, that was very certain; then what could it be?

The following day he walked up towards the Mount, hoping to meet them—meaning the Vansittarts. Just outside Micklegate Bar he saw them in the distance, coming towards him. He stopped and held out his hand to Constance, Miss Vansittart walked composedly on.

And thus during several weeks were his efforts baffled. At length she gave up going into the town with her sister in the afternoon, and, once or twice, when he had contrived to get himself asked in to have a cup of tea, she never went into the room. Once, he just caught sight of the tail of her gown, and a glimpse of her dead-gold hair, but to him she was a very will-o'-the-wisp; it seemed absolutely impossible to reach her presence. But still he did not give up his object; he was determined to know her, and at last he succeeded, for one day he went in with Constance, and entered the room too suddenly for her to escape.

"Let me introduce Captain Dickson, Nell," said Constance, "My sister—Captain Dickson."

Being in her own house, Miss Vansittart could not well avoid laying her hand in Captain Dickson's outstretched palm, and, having done that, she could not immediately leave the room as she would have liked.

"How very cold it is to-day," he said, addressing himself pointedly to her.

Again that little grave bow. He was non-plussed.

"I'll ask her a question," he thought, then said aloud, "Do you skate at all?"

"I do not," she answered, flushing vividly as she spoke.

He understood it all in a moment. Those three words had told him what it was that Constance had called a "misfortune." Miss Vansittart had, through some accident, lost her voice, and could not speak above a whisper. All his soldierly tact and polish came to his aid now. He would not let her feel ill at ease with him. He took a seat beside her, and talked away as fluently and pleasantly as if young ladies who could not speak above a whisper very often came in his way, and presently, when Constance went to take her hat off, and Mrs. Vansittart left the room for a moment, he remarked, coolly, "Do you know, Miss Vansittart, I have been trying to make your acquaintance for ever so long?"

"Yes, I know," in that strange whispering voice, which thrilled his very soul's inmost recesses, "but—I—never see people."

"Yes, I understand exactly. Of course I didn't know until this evening, but I understand now. You won't keep out of my way again, will you?" he asked, persuasively.

"But—" she began, hesitatingly, "is not my voice very disagreeable to you?"

"Disagreeable!" he echoed; "no, indeed. I don't admire your screaming women, whose tongues go five-and-twenty to the dozen until you are deafened."

"I always feel so reluctant to speak," she continued, "for some people look astonished, and others smile, as if there could be anything amusing in having lost one's voice—in such a deprivation."

"When people display a visible lack of brains you should be lenient, Miss Vansittart," he said, gravely.

"Yes, perhaps; only one is apt to think only of one's self," she answered.

Then the others returned. Poor Mrs. Vansittart was so charmed to see Nell interested and pleased once more, that she could not make enough of the man who had wrought the change. He lingered until the irate cook was only forcibly restrained from rushing up stairs to give him a piece of her mind—not a small piece by any means; but at last he did take his leave.

Mrs. Vansittart followed him out into the hall, "I don't know how to express my gratitude to you," she said, "I have not seen Nell so bright and like herself since she met with the accident which deprived her of her voice; and, you know"—with a sound of tears in her tones—"you know what that must be to her mother."

"Mrs. Vansittart," he said, quietly, "I wish you would give me a general invitation to come here."

"With all my heart."

"Thank you much," he answered, heartily, and pressing her hand, departed.

He was too late for mess, but he had some dinner in his room, and went into the ante-room afterwards. He found there one or two strangers who had been dining at mess—strangers to him that is to say. One of them was speaking as he entered the room:

"Have any of you met some people called Vansittart—a mother and two daughters? I heard they had come to York."

" What makes her keep out of sight now?" some one asked.

" Oh! poor girl! She was engaged to Towers-Brooke, of the Drab Horse, and just about a year ago we were all staying at Bullidean—Gylglen's place. Well, Miss Vansittart—Nell, every one called her—slipped into a deep brook one afternoon, and got soaked to the skin. We tried to persuade her to go into a cottage and get dried there, but she persisted in driving home—some six miles. Towers-Brooke was always a queer-tempered fellow, and, of course, he was anxious about her, but he told her—roughly enough, and before all of us—that if she didn't do as she was told, he would never speak to her again. She didn't hesitate a minute : a dog-cart was standing by, so she jumped in and drove off by herself. Towers-Brooke never said a word, he drove the drag back to Bullidean, with a regular pack inside—for four had gone in the dog-cart—and he never once opened his mouth the whole way : I happen to know that, because I sat next to him. We reached the house about six o'clock, and he was off to London at seven, without his dinner even. Mrs. Gylglen was rather vexed about it, but Nell Vansittart was taken so ill with some lung complaint that no one had time to talk or think of anything else, and the end of it was, that she lost her lover and her voice—hard upon her, poor girl !"

" He wouldn't be much loss," remarked one of the audience.

" I think she was fond of him," returned the guest, in a musing tone, " and there was no doubt whatever about Towers-Brooke's feelings, only he was one of those determined chaps that would keep his word if it spoilt his whole life, and killed him in the end."

" Oh ! one of your pig-headed brutes," drawled a Cuirassier, who had not been particularly charmed by the description of Mr. Towers-Brooke, " or what some people call ' firm.' "

" Yes, exactly."

" Ah ! well, I think Miss Vansittart has done well to get out of it. Men of that calibre are all very well in story books, but they are the very devil to live with. I happen to know, because my old governor's one of the sort ; if I were a woman, I'd rather marry ever such a fool."

" A clever sort of chap," put in another.

" Clever as daylight," responded the guest, " as clever as daylight. I dined with the Drab Horse on the day of their last steeple-chases, when Brooke had ridden a horse of Jefferson's and won the cup, which was open to the army. Of course they made a great fuss about it. and toasted the horse ; then they called for the owner, and Jefferson got up in the most approved style, laid his hand on his heart and bowed on all sides. They thought they were going to get a speech out of him, but they couldn't, so they called for the jockey. Towers-Brooke got up and made his bow.

" ' I think my master has said enough for both of us,' said he, and sat down again."

" Very good," laughed the Cuirassiers *en masse.*

" And that same night," he continued, " old Fitz-Hugh, who was Colonel at that time, by way of mixing the company, had asked the R. C. priest to meet the chaplain and another parson. The introduction opened the proceedings : the chaplain, an enormously fat man, very bald and urbane, was walked up to the priest as soon as he entered the room.

" ' Oo-o,' said the colonel—you know his extraordinary way of speaking—' Oo-o—let me introduce you to my very good friend, Father O'Reilly.'

" I never saw a man's face fall as his did in my life ; if old Fitz-Hugh had presented him to the devil himself—horns and hoof and all—his bow couldn't have been more solemn or his face have expressed greater disgust. The priest, who was a jolly sort of chap, saw the joke in a minute. Well, the other parson had just arrived in time to see the meeting between the two, so old Fitz-Hugh took the priest's arm and led him across the room.

" ' Oh ! Lloyd, Oo-o—let me introduce you to my very good friend, Father O'Reilly '

" He looked back at us, as he spoke, to see if we all fully appreciated the crowning point of his little jest, but, to the

general disgust, the new-comer held out a hand, with a hearty
' How are you, O'Reilly ?'

"' How are ye, me dear fellow ?' returned the priest.

"' Oo-o ' gasped Fitz-Hugh; 'then you know Father
O'Reilly ? Oo-o !'

"' Sure, yis. Me good friend Lloyd often comes an' smokes
a pipe with me,' answered the priest.

"I really don't know whether the roar of laughter which
followed was at the colonel's *done* look or at the righteous horror
on the chaplain's fat face. Perhaps it was at the remark with
which the Irishman finished up the colonel's little plot.

"' I'm always deloighted to meet any friend of yours, colonel,'
he said, taking a glass of sherry and bitters from the tray as he
spoke, 'but I make a rhule of drawing the line *after* the
Establishment.'

"And now we must be going, Russell," he said, rising, " or
your wife will be locking us out."

Captain Dickson, after a while, went up to his room in a
strangely meditative mood.   There was a roaring fire blazing up
the chimney and a newspaper lying on the table.   He sat down
in his accustomed chair, for the first time since he had joined the
army, thoroughly dissatisfied with his life.   All at once it seemed
to have grown utterly distasteful to him.   He looked round the
little room, with eyes no longer blind to the many makeshifts and
shabbinesses which it contained.   There were the common deal
legs of the table protruding from beneath the torn, stained
cloth which covered it;   there was the usual make-believe
dressing-table, with its cretonne hangings and the petticoated
chairs—how his soul loathed them !—and there in the corner,
with which regularly every morning he barked his shins, was
the big bath, with huge patches of paint knocked off; and there
were the window curtains, which made a point of coming down
every time he tried to draw them.   Hitherto he had merely
suffered all these things because he felt it was not worth while
to have anything better, to be at the mercy of soldier servants
and railway porters ; but, somehow, of late a great craving had
taken possession of him—a craving for a home ; a home in the

country, with decent hunting and shooting; with pleasant
society, where there would be no practical jokes nor after-dinner
songs, such as he could hear them singing in the ante-room at
that moment—

> Oh! my Jem—Jemima,
> She's left her loving Sam!
> And gone to be a Mormonite.
> In new Jerusalem.

Ugh! how sick he was of it all. No wonder: he had heard
Gore sing that song almost every night for the last five
years. He invariably got on a chair and see-sawed his
arms up and down whilst he sang it. He didn't know, or
rather he never attempted, any other, and he could not be
said to *know* that. Oh, how weary he was of it all! The
stale jokes! He knew every one's story, and just at what
part of the evening it would be brought in. A new story
or joke was a perfect godsend to them! Would they never
grow tired of trying how much mustard and pepper Martin
could take without finding out his food had been tampered
with? Would they never cease to treat old Barber's bald
head as a round of toast, and butter it? Would they never
discover that life may be of better worth than turning men
out of their beds as soon as they have got comfortably into
them, and marching them about draughty corridors in scanty
attire, at the risk of rheumatic fever and lung complaints?
He wondered, with a long sigh, how he had managed to live
to thirty years of age without finding all this out? It was
because—and his heart told him the reason quickly enough—
he had never taken a fancy for a country house and a wife
who should have dead-gold hair and a colourless complexion.

He leant back in his chair and gave himself up to the
pleasure of contemplating his castle, which, as yet, was *in
nubibus*. How different it would all be. What long, quiet cosy
evenings they would have together. She must sit always
close beside him, else he would not be able to hear what she
said—the girl he loved—the girl with the strange whispering
voice and the serious eyes, with their wistful, pained expression. Curse the fellow who brought that shadow in to them

L

And yet, if things had been otherwise, Nell Vansittart would be to him as nothing. He must not forget that.

There was one thing, however, that he forgot completely— or no, he could not be said to forget it, for the idea had never presented itself to his mind—that was, that it was possible Miss Vansittart might not find herself able to care for him as he cared for her, nor did he admit, even to his own mind, that it was probable. She still cherished some of the old tenderness for the man who had once loved her—Towers-Brooke.

George Dickson never thought of these possibilities and probabilities, so they did not trouble him. For the next few weeks he went on his roseate way with a brave joyous heart and eyes which saw not the tiniest cloud upon the horizon of his future. Day by day he found his way to Mrs. Vansittart's house, and with each visit Nell was more gracious to him, more at ease, more friendly, until at last he summoned up courage, when one afternoon he found her alone, to unfold to her his glowing visions of the future.

" You care for me ?" she repeated, incredulously.

" Yes, dear; is there anything astonishing in that?" he said, with a tender smile.

" Oh ! Captain Dickson !" she gasped, her whispering voice growing louder because of her pain, "indeed, I never thought of this—I expected it was Constance."

" Oh no; it is yourself."

" But I never thought of it !"

" Will you not think of it now ?"

" Oh—no, no !"—it would be hard to say whether the pain in eyes, or voice, or face, was the keenest—" you do not understand; you do not know."

He guessed instantly that she was thinking of Towers-Brooke. " I know all about the man who treated you like the hound he is," he said, savagely.

" Don't say it," she said, holding out her hands imploringly ; " I cannot, will not hear a word against him."

" You love him still ?" he asked, incredulously.

" Love him!" she repeated, heedless of the pain she was inflicting, " oh ! how I do love him—still."

" You would take him back—now?" Dickson asked.

" Take him back !" she echoed, " oh yes, indeed—if he came to me maimed and tattered, crippled and blind, deaf and dumb, I would still take him back gladly : " but," with a sad smile, " he will not—he will keep his word."

And then he left her.

It was all over. He went back to his barrack-room and hated it worse than ever. He had thought to escape from it all, but he had been mistaken. There it all was : the stained table-cloth, the deal legs of the table, the sentries pacing up and down outside, Gore singing in his room next door—

> Oh ! my Jem—Jemima,
> She's left her loving Sam,
> And gone to be a Mormonite
> In new Jerusalem.

There was the quarter-master's baby squalling just across the corridor, and the adjutant's wife scolding her servant. There was that poor devil, Calcraft, in the hospital, and the man he had got in his place knew as much about varnishing boots as he did about making mince-pies. He was thumping at the door at that moment.

" Sergeant-Major Lucas wants to speak to you, sir."

" Very well." What could that be for? Nothing to do with Calcraft, for he was safe in hospital. He had a good mind to cut it all, but for the present he was obliged to hear what Lucas had to say : for, however ill the world used him, he was still the captain of F-troop.

THE SIGN OF THE "GOLDEN SWAN."

HE made a very bad senior sub., there was no doubt about it. In the first place, he had ten names, a circumstance which told against him ; in the second, he had a great many distinguished relations, and as these " salt of the earth " were not permitted to remain quietly at home with their wives, but were ostentatiously paraded on every occasion as, " Getty, my cousin, you know," or " Sir Lucian Boodsworth, my old uncle," and a dozen such others, they told against him likewise. As the Cuirassiers—those who were as distinguished and those who were not—frequently said, it is doubtless a fine thing to be fifth cousin to an earl—called, for shortness, Getty—and to have an uncle in Parliament, with the additional charms of being a baronet and a millionaire : still, even of those good things, *other* people might have too much.

Then also he had no money, and he had, worst of all, a mother ! Yes ! he had a mother, and she called him " Lucy." Now, since he possessed such a superabundance of names, she might as well have called him by any of the others, but, by one of the absurd freaks of coddling love which some mothers indulge in, she called him " Lucy ;" his brother officers called him " The Alphabet ;" his name, however, in all its glory, shone thus — Lucian Boodsworth John George Lawrence Gettandine Sholto Montague Cosmo Abdy—ten of them— and his mother called him " Lucy," and his brother officers " The Alphabet."

Mr. Abdy was an only child, indeed, at the time at which the little incident I am going to relate took place, he was the only son of his mother, and she was a widow, Mr. Abdy *père* having died some fifteen years previously, to the very great detriment of his son's bringing-**up** !

He was not ornamental, and he was certainly not useful; in person he was singularly unprepossessing ; his height was considerably over six feet, and in width he might be, perhaps, about one-sixth of his height—barely twelve inches ; his shoulders were of the class known as "champagne," in truth, they were so very much of the champagne order that he seemed to have no shoulders at all, only an enormously long neck, to which, somehow, his arms were attached ; he had also remarkably long legs, slightly inclined to knock about the knees ; and, to crown all these charms, he had a foolish round face, with boiled-gooseberry eyes and white eye-lashes, a nondescript nose, a huge mouth, bad teeth, and a mop—a perfect mop—of curly flame-coloured hair.

So much for his personal appearance ! now for his accomplishments.   Well, he had a personal appearance, though to be sure it was not much of a one to look at, but accomplishments he had none ! Shoot—he couldn't. To many other pursuits the same description accurately applied—to polo, cricket, riding, swimming, and indeed to most of the hundred-and-one amusements to which soldiers devote themselves. He was once known to drive the drag back to the Blankhampton Barracks, the others having stayed in the town, and on reaching his destination was hailed by an impudent young sub., who hadn't quite got licked into shape, with " Hollo ! Abdy, what have you done with the others ?—killed 'em all, eh ? " To finish the list of Mr. Abdy's charms, I need only add that he wore his hat on one side, and fancied every woman he met was in love with him ; now there was no doubt whatever about the hat, but as for the other—

Oh ! wad some power the giftie gie us
To see oursels as ithers see us ;
It wad frae mony a blunder free us,
        And foolish notion.

The Cuirassiers had been quartered in Blankhampton nearly a year, and had naturally made a large circle of friends in the town and neighbourhood. Shortly after Christmas Mrs. Abdy arrived, and took up her abode in private lodgings, announcing her intention of remaining some time—several months, at least.

Her first proceeding was to take advantage of her son's absence at a house in the vicinity, where he had gone for a couple of days' hunting, to go up to the barracks with her maid, and—what she called—"put poor dear Lucy's things tidy," to the intense delight of such of the officers as were in the barracks.

Now probably the last person a cavalry officer would like to set loose in his rooms would be his mother—excepting, perhaps, his sweetheart—and "poor dear Lucy," not dreaming that such an onslaught would be made during his absence, had left everything in the utmost disorder, it having never occurred to him that such an idea would present itself to the old lady's mind. The very first thing, therefore, that she was enabled to do was to read his love letters, the result of which was that she indignantly declined offers of help in her self-imposed task from any of the officers, and betook herself back to her lodgings, without having put any of "poor dear Lucy's" things straight at all, having, in truth, left them rather more untidy than she had found them.

Having thought the matter over, with the help of her luncheon and a glass or two of sherry, Mrs. Abdy came to the conclusion that the sooner she could get "Lucy" married the better. That happened to be exactly "Lucy's" own opinion, and, like his mother, he, too, inserted a clause in the matrimonial scheme—the clause was *money*. What he wanted was youth, beauty, birth, amiability, talent, style, and money. Those were what he *wanted*. What, however, he had made up his mind to have was money—as many of the others as he could get, but money first and foremost. He had tried a good many young ladies with the requisite amount of gilding, but, unfortunately, he had not been able to induce them to see things in the same light as himself. Young ladies who have twelve or fifteen hundred a-year of their own have usually an exalted opinion of themselves, and look for a little, or, if they marry a poor man, they take care he is something to look at, at all events.

Up to the time of the opening of this story Mr. Abdy had been evidently unappreciated, for he was a bachelor still.

The more his old mother turned the matter over in her mind the more puzzled did she become, and at last she put on her hat—she was sixty-five at least, but she wore a hat—and sallied out for a promenade down the High Street. She had walked the length of the narrow street, and, having crossed over the road, was proceeding leisurely back, by the other side, when a voice exclaimed,

" Why, can that be you, Mrs. Abdy? Who would have thought of seeing you in Blankhampton ? "

" Mrs. Chillingly ! " cried Mrs. Abdy, in as great astonishment, " and who would have thought of seeing you, indeed ? "

" Ah, who indeed? I'll tell you how it is. My daughter is perfectly wild about hunting, and having tried all the other hunting districts in England, I think, made up her mind that she should never be happy until she had had a few weeks with the Blankhampton Hunt. It ended, of course, in our coming, and she has gone out for her first run this morning."

" Then have you taken a house ? "

" Oh, dear no ! We are at the ' Golden Swan '—a very comfortable hotel, too. I want to go as far as the Post Office; will you walk with me, and then come back and have a cup of tea ? "

" Thanks, very many," returned Mrs. Abdy, willingly.

" And what has brought you into this part of the world ? ' Mrs. Chillingly inquired.

" Oh, Lucy's regiment is here. My son, you know."

" Oh, really ! Very nice for you. I suppose you are in lodgings ? "

" Yes," she answered, " my son has gone to stay a couple of days at Sir Hugh Brooke's—the great iron people, you know; but he will be back this afternoon."

" I never met him," remarked Mrs. Chillingly. " I never was so surprised as when I saw you walking quietly along."

This was just the chance Mrs. Abdy had been looking for. Miss Chillingly was an heiress; her father had been something in the cotton-spinning line, and had left three hundred thousand pounds between his wife and daughter. She was young, very pretty, a splendid horsewoman, and a charming girl. Could anything be devised to suit " Lucy " better?

For the next few weeks her whole attention was devoted to the task of bringing the two together. " Lucy " himself was more than willing. Rosey Chillingly seemed very well pleased at his attentions, and Mrs. Chillingly, whose influence went for a good deal in Mrs. Abdy's calculations, having become utterly tired of being dragged about the country at her daughter's sweet will, was charmed at the idea. She didn't in the least care who Rosey married so long as he was a gentleman, and of " Lucy's " family there could be no question.

Amongst the officers of the Cuirassiers the marriage was spoken of as a settled thing; they were expecting every evening that Abdy would announce the news; but one afternoon an accidental carelessness made just all the difference in the true state of the case—in this wise: Miss Chillingly was not entirely unknown to the regiment—indeed, with one of the officers, Mr. Bernard, there had been some very, very tender love passages, which had been broken off through a misunderstanding—broken off and never quite cleared up. It happened that when she was returning from a long day's hunting, with " Lucy" in close attendance and her groom behind, Geoffry Bernard had overtaken them, and, seeing a certain softness in Rosey's face and a certain defiant swagger in Abdy's manner, he greeted her and rode on with them. He fancied—could it be all fancy?—that she seemed suddenly relieved, and at parting he was bold enough to ask, in an undertone, if he might call on the following day?

" Surely," said the girl, turning a pair of brilliant blue eyes up wistfully; " come in and have a cup of tea. My mother will be delighted."

Then he thanked her, and with Abdy, who had not overheard the little arrangement, slowly rode back to barracks.

But although " Lucy" had not overheard the conversation between Rosey and Bernard, he knew the latter well enough to be aware that he was more than inclined to go in on his own account, and he determined on the morrow to have the whole thing settled and done with one way or another. What was the use, he argued, of shilly-shallying any longer? Faint heart ne'er won fair lady—and a good deal more.

"Walk down into town with me, Abdy?" said Bernard, suddenly, as they entered the gates.

"All right; come round to my rooms when you are ready," he replied.

"After all, it would be as well not to lose sight of Bernard during the next few hours.

So presently Bernard went round to Abdy's rooms—he had been lucky enough to secure two.

"Ready, Abdy?"

"Not quite," returned a voice from the inner room, and evidently from behind a towel. "Shan't be a minute."

Now Geoffry Bernard was very much in love, and considered all things fair in love and war; therefore, seeing a letter lying open on the blotting-pad, he made no more of reading it than if it had been his own. Dishonourable, of course it was, but true for all that! It was not long, and the ink was still wet.

My Dear Miss Chillingly,

Will you meet me at the Seven Willows to-morrow afternoon at three o'clock? I want to ask you a very important question, and at your hotel one is never free from interruptions. Devotedly yours,

L. B. J. G. L. G. S. M. C. Abdy.

"How the deuce does he remember them all?" murmured Geoffry Bernard, as he strolled to the pier-glass and began admiring himself. When, a few minutes later, Abdy entered, Bernard was resting his arms upon the chimney-shelf and his forehead upon his arms, staring into the fire in the brownest of brown studies.

"Asleep, old man?" Abdy asked.

"Very nearly," with a start and a laugh. "What tiring work hunting is."

"Awfully so," returned Abdy, folding the letter up and directing it.

But all the same, Geoffry had not kept very closely to the truth when he said he was very nearly asleep; he never

was further off from sleep in the whole of his life. His quick
brain was busy, and the result of his cogitations was that, when
they got down to the club, he wrote a note, and the effect of
the note startled the whole of Blankhampton the following
morning in such a manner as had not happened for years. In
this way : the hotel of the " Golden Swan" was in the centre of
the principal street of the town, a narrow thoroughfare, having
barely room for two carriages to pass ; the business of the
hotel having increased, the owner had secured the house opposite
to the original one, and thus the hotel was in two parts, one
on each side of the street. In order to attract notice, he had
over either entrance door a huge gilded swan, and extending
across the street from one house to the other, a sign about a
foot broad and placed about sixteen feet from the ground, thus :

THE GOLDEN SWAN.

Well might the respectable inhabitants of Blankhampton be
startled the following morning, when in the *Blankhampton
Daily Herald* they read the following announcement :

A LONG JUMP.—We understand that Mr. L. B. J. G. L. G. S. M. C.
Abdy, of the Cuirassiers, has undertaken to clear the sign of the "Golden
Swan" without assistance of any kind. See advert.

Of course everyone turned eagerly from the local news to the
advertisement sheet. Yes ; there it was :

THE SIGN OF THE "GOLDEN SWAN."—Lieutenant Abdy. of the
Cuirassiers, will jump the above sign, IN FULL UNIFORM. at 3
o'clock this (Wednesday) afternoon.
The public are invited to attend !

Had Colonel Cotherstone been at home, Bernard's *ruse* would
not have succeeded so well. As it was, no notice was taken of
it, for the major was not out of barracks during the morning,
and Bernard took good care that the paper containing the
announcement should not come within his reach. Mrs. Abdy
was away, having gone to visit the Brookes—"the great iron
people, you know"—and so at half-past two " Lucy" went
quietly out of barracks to keep his appointment with Miss
Chillingly. Just about that time a little regiment of up-

holsterers were busy laying down straw and mattresses in order to break the fall. The windows of all the houses and the hotel were full of ladies; there was a crowd of gentlemen about the steps of the hotel and at the coffee room windows, and *the public* had gathered in great force in the street itself.

" What does it all mean?" exclaimed Rosey, as Geoffry Bernard entered their sitting-room about twenty minutes to three.

" Haven't you seen the papers?"

"The London papers—yes."

" The *Blankhampton Daily Herald*, I mean," he answered, taking a copy out of his pocket and pointing to the advertisement.

As Miss Chillingly read, an angry light came into her eyes, and she bit her lips nervously. So Mr. Lucian had simply been trying to make a fool of her. Well, thank goodness, she had not intended to go.

She laid the paper down and walked to the window, whither Geoffry followed her.

" He will never jump over *that*," she said, with a look at the sign.

" I should think not," Geoffry answered.

" Why is he going to attempt it?"

" I really cannot say."

And so they waited and waited, until three of the clock struck—the hero of the day did not appear. The crowd began to grow impatient; so did Rosey Chillingly.

" Is he coming, do you think?" she asked at last.

" I daresay not," said Geoffry, coolly. " He has a trick of forgetting his appointments."

Again she turned to the window with that sudden flush upon her face. Geoffry took advantage of it.

" Rosey," he said, in a low tone (they were alone, for Mrs. Chillingly had gone out of the room to fetch something), "can you forgive me for what took place two years ago? It has made me very unhappy."

" Has it?"

Then somehow his arms found their way round her, and she felt his passionate kisses upon her lips. Poor "Alphabet," waiting savagely in the wind about the Seven Willows, was quite forgotten by both of them, until a series of groans and hisses from without recalled them to what was going on in the street.

"They have given him up," she cried; "the men are taking the mattresses away. Oh, I do believe, Geoffry, it is all a hoax!" At which Geoffry burst out laughing.

Yes; it was all a hoax. Towards five o'clock Mr. Abdy found his way into the room to see the lovers sitting together on the sofa and Mrs. Chillingly busy writing a letter. Unfortunately, the homely comfort in the cosy room was too much for him, and he lost his temper.

"Of course, you have had a fine view of all this foolery that has been going on," he said to Rosey.

"Well, we saw the preparations and the crowd," she answered; "but you never came—why did you not?"

"It is a hoax," he almost shouted. "I have been nearly mobbed on my way here; but, never mind, I know whom to thank for it, and I'll be even with him yet," at which Geoffry burst into a fit of smothered laughter.

"Oh, don't be angry," the girl said, soothingly. "If it was only meant as a joke, you should take it as such. 'Give and take,' you know, should be the motto for the army." But well-meant as her sympathy undoubtedly was, the sight of "Lucy's" livid face and flaming eyes was too much for her, and she, too, relapsed into a perfect agony of hilarity, in the midst of which the enraged officer rushed out of the house.

"I hope I shall never see him again," she laughed, "for I shall never be able to keep a grave face. Oh! won't he pay you out for this?"

"Not he," returned Geoffry, carelessly, "because I shall not give him the chance."

After dinner that evening he announced his engagement to his comrades, receiving the congratulations of every one present excepting Abdy.

" Won't you wish me joy, Abdy ?" he asked.

" No, sir ; and, what is more, I shall report this disgraceful hoax to the colonel to-morrow," he thundered.

" Very well," returned Bernard, carelessly. " You might as well be pleasant about it, for I shall leave the regiment immediately; and, if it's any comfort to you to know it, you never had a chance from the first."

That was quite true, but during his whole life Lucian Abdy cherished the most bitter hatred against his successful rival, and if any one desired to throw him into a transport of rage he had only to mention the hoax, which, as he thought, cost him the heiress—the sign of the " Golden Swan !"

HUMPTY-DUMPTY.

When he first joined the regiment he was called "Fatima," but before very long his *nom de fantasie* was changed to "Waugh." However, just before he obtained his troop, an incident took place which gave rise to a third sobriquet—that of "Humpty-Dumpty;" all three names suited him fairly well: "Fatima," for he was frightly obese; "Waugh," because it was the expression most often on his lips; "Humpty-Dumpty"—but no, that requires a story to itself!

The regiment was the Drab Horse, and had succeeded the 52nd Dragoons at Mollington, where they became great favourites with all the people round about, and that, mind, was a very great credit to them, for the departure of the 52nd had been looked upon almost in the light of a public calamity, and the good folks of the neighbourhood regarded the new-comers with anything but favourable eyes, until their unaffected pleasantness won for them as golden opinions as Mollington had ever bestowed upon any regiment before.

The yeomanry ball was over, the two county gatherings—the hunt and the officers had both done their duty, and there had been private dances *ad libitum*, but the neighbourhood was not satisfied—they wanted a fancy ball!

"Have you heard about the fancy ball?" Hills asked at mess one evening.

"No, what fancy ball?" said Paget.

"There's to be one on St. Valentine's day," he answered.

"Subscription?" some one asked.

"Of course, at the assembly rooms."

"Awfully jolly!—what shall you go as?" cried Hartley.

"Never thought of it; I suppose we shall be obliged to make asses of ourselves—uniforms not admitted"

" Quite right, too," put in a third man, warmly ; " I always myself thought uniform a scurvy way of getting out of it— nearly as bad as pink."

" I say, Jimmy," Hills called out, " what are you going as ? "

" Waugh," returned Jimmy Desmond, scornfully

" Oh as ' Waugh ; ' well, my man, keep on eating Bath chaps at the rate you've done lately, and you'll be able to do the part to perfection," Hills laughed. " 'Pon my word," he added, *sotto voce*, " it won't be long before he turns into a veritable pig, that ' Waugh ' of his is inimitable."

" I know—a—chawictaw that would suit ' Waugh ' to per— fection," drawled a high-toned deliberate voice from the other end of the room, " suit him—down to—the ground."

" What is it ?" Hartley asked.

" Hump—ty-Dump—ty," returned Carruthers, coolly, and continuing his dinner as unmoved by the roar of laughter which followed his suggestion as if he had remarked that the day was cold, and no one had taken any notice of it.

" Waugh," exclaimed Desmond, savagely, " I think ' Champagne Charlie ' would suit you as well as anything."

Carruthers looked up deliberately, and settled his glass so as to " fix " the speaker ; the others waited in silence to hear what the smooth silver tongue would rap out—more than equal to the occasion, they were sure.

" My dear—chap," he said, calmly, " Champagne Charlie in the owiginal—er—was—ah—a vivacious person ! Now—my deadliest enemy—ah ! excuse the twagic element—could hardly accuse—*me*—of being vivacious."

" By George, no !" put in Hills, amid a roar of laughter.

" And ' Champagne Charlie ' was—undeniably—a cad—and I weally don't think," he went on, plaintively, " that I am—a cad."

" Perhaps you intends to go as Hadonis ?" put in a rough voice, from the extreme end of the table—it belonged to the quarter-master.

Carruthers turned his melancholy dark eyes upon the speaker, with just the faintest expression of contempt on his handsome face.

" Ah! no—I had—some thoughts of—er—taking your *rôle*— that is, if you don't mind lending it to me, once in a way."

" Oh! no, not at all! what is it?" Groves replied, seeing his way to what might be a good thing.

It was a good thing, but scarcely in the way he expected, for after a long pause, Carruthers said gently,

" I—er—thought of going—as—sixty—*per cent!* And I fancy I had the bwute there," he added in an undertone, for the benefit of the others, who—most of them—knew what it was to borrow money from the gentleman in question, at something like *sixty per cent.* interest.

As the days passed by, the fancy ball was the subject uppermost in every one's thoughts, and many were the suggestions for " Waugh's" costume : one thought the " Fat boy in Pickwick," another " Magog"—only where was Gog to come from, the Drab Horse not being able to produce him?

" Waugh," however, put all their ideas to flight by announcing grandly that he intended to go as *Cœur de Lion!*

" *Cœur de Lion*?" repeated Carruthers, for once taken aback.

" Bless my soul!" put in Hills again.

" Take my advice, Carruthers," quoth " Waugh," drily, " and go as ' Champagne Charlie,' " and then he bolted out of the room before any of the men assembled could answer him.

" *Cœur de Lion*," Carruthers said again; " but—oh, by— Jove!—you never shall."

In his desire to be emphatic he was quite eager, he almost forgot his drawl.

Captain Carruthers said nothing more upon the subject that afternoon. It wanted but three days to the ball, and many were the speculations as to how he would manage to prevent Desmond from being present in the character of *Cœur de Lion*; that he might be unable to do so never occurred to them —they knew him too well for that.

That evening Carruthers sat next to Desmond at dinner, a most unusual circumstance.

" **Carruthers** means mischief," remarked one officer to another, "just watch him keep filling up ' **Waugh's**' glass every time he turns his head."

" ' **Waugh's** screwed already," responded the other.

But Desmond proved that he was not more than half-seas-over, and, as the re-filling process went steadily on, he very soon showed that he was *all*-seas-over by rising to make a speech, and after stammering out " Gentlemen, I—I—" collapsed, all of a lump, under the table.

" The beast's drunk again," said Carruthers, disdainfully ; " here, some of you fellows, get him off to bed."

So off half-a-dozen men carried him, swinging him up and down, and shouting at the top of their healthy voices—

With a hilly-haulee, hilly-haulee, Ho!

*   *   *   *   *

" Officers' call " had just sounded, and the officers of the Drab Horse had assembled in the orderly room.

" Where is Mr. Desmond ?" asked the chief.

Mr. Desmond was not forthcoming, that was evident.

" Orderly, go and let Mr. Desmond know that ' officers' call ' has sounded."

The orderly departed hastily, and, after an absence of five minutes or so, returned, with a purple face and without Mr. Desmond.

" Mr. Desmond says he can't come, sir."

A look of astonishment passed among the officers, and Colonel Norreys, for a moment, positively stared at the orderly, as if he could not believe his ears.

" God bless my life and soul, sir !" he thundered, " am I the commanding officer of this regiment or NOT ? *Can't come!* Upon my word, the service is coming to a pretty pass ; an officer *can't come* when I send for him. Mr. Hills, have the goodness to tell Mr. Desmond to come here immediately ? *Can't come!* Upon my soul !" &c. *ad libitum* until Hills returned, quicker than the orderly had done, but, if anything, slightly more purple about the face, and with eyes steadily bent downwards, and lips tightly compressed.

M

"Mr. Desmond will be here in a moment, sir," he said to the irate chief.

"In a moment," he growled, turning angrily as the door opened to admit the culprit.

"Now, Mr. Desmond—er—why! God bless me—what—*the* devil!—"

His interjaculatory remarks were lost amidst a smothered explosion of laughter from the officers, in which he himself, though he gallantly tried to keep grave, was compelled to join. The only person in the room who did not laugh was James Desmond. There he stood, in his undress, with his forage-cap stuck jauntily on one side of a perfectly bald head, his long moustache had disappeared, also his short whiskers, hair, eyebrows—it was all as bare as the back of your hand! Yes, there he was, with his great, round, red face, his little pug nose, with one arm akimbo, the other hanging by his side—the personification of "Humpty-Dumpty."

I have said that the only person in the room who did not laugh was Desmond, but I must make another exception—that one was Carruthers, who put his glass carefully in his eye and surveyed his comrade gravely

"By—Jove!" he remarked, at length, then dropped his glass and looked at nothing.

"What is the meaning of this, sir?" the chief demanded, making a great effort to keep his countenance.

"You know as much as I do, sir," Desmond replied, grandiloquently, looking only at his commanding officer, and folding his arms, in which position he looked so supremely absurd that the smothered mirth bubbled out again.

By a mighty effort Colonel Norreys frowned his officers into silence once more, and turned to the indignant "Waugh."

"Let me hear about it," he said, sternly.

"I went to bed, as usual, last night, sir," he answered, "and this morning, when my servant came in he dropped his can of water and rushed out of the room. I thought that perhaps he might be ill, but when I got up and looked in the glass—I perceived the cause."

"And you mean to tell me that such a change could be brought about without your having *some* idea of what was going on?"

"I do, sir."

"Humph!" Colonel Norreys's face was a very expressive one, and he looked more than sceptical on the point. "You say you went to bed as usual last evening?"

"As usual," returned Desmond.

"Humph! Well, gentlemen, you are all subject to suspicion in this affair. I must ask you if you considered Mr. Desmond ' as usual ' when he retired from the mess-room?"

"Mr. Desmond," answered Carruthers, calmly, "was considerably the worse for champagne when he left the mess-room last evening."

"Ah!" muttered the chief, comprehensively, "does that mean that he was drunk?"

"*Vewy*—dwunk," returned Carruthers.

"Ah!" remarked the chief again, if possible with more comprehension than before. "Mr. Paget," addressing a notorious practical joker, "may I ask why you are laughing?"

Paget pulled himself up and straightened his face, without making any reply.

"This is a very serious matter," said the colonel gravely, whereupon Desmond gave a malignant leer at his brother officers. "Mr. Desmond goes to bed very drunk, and gets up in the morning minus his *hair*. Either he has done it himself, or the blame rests with one or more of you."

A murmur of denial ran along the line, only Carruthers put his handsome nose two inches higher, without condescending to speak.

"You hear, Mr. Desmond," said the colonel, coldly. "This is not the first time I have had to speak to you about playing pranks with your personal appearance. However, since your experiment this time has failed as signally as did a previous one, I will give you a couple of months' leave, and request you to return to your duty a less conspicuous object than you appear at present. You are excused all duty to-day."

Surely that was the most cruel part of it all. Some ten years before " Waugh " had been intensely desirous of possessing a moustache, and since Dame Nature considered him too young to have the coveted adornment, he had denounced her for an old-fashioned stupid, and foregathered with the regimental surgeon, who told him, in strict confidence, that he had a recipe which would bring out a pair of moustaches with the rapidity of lightning.

" It will sting a bit, but you mustn't mind that," said the surgeon, gravely.

" Waugh " was heroic. Bless you, he didn't mind a little more pain. What would that be in comparison to the delight of having a pair of moustaches of his very own ?

Reader, do you know what a cantharides blister is ? Well, that was what Dr. Hale gave " Waugh" to bring out his moustaches ! It didn't hurt him at first, and he put it neatly along his upper lip, with a little defiant twirl at either end, to make him look fierce—but he didn't look fierce very long : the blister did that part of the business. In vain did " Waugh " writhe and tug ; he couldn't move it. It held on to his unfortunate upper lip like grim death or a leech, until eventually the epidermis thought the discussion not worth going on with, so bade a friendly adieu to the *cutis vera* and set off on his travels with the blister. That was bad enough, but the roars of laughter which greeted him when he appeared at breakfast the next morning, with a clearly defined raw patch, just the shape of a moustache, extending along his upper lip and perfectly correct in detail, even to the knowing little twirl at either extremity, they were much worse.

And to have that raked up now, and made an excuse to let the real culprits off, Desmond felt and said, in no measured terms, that it was disgraceful—utterly disgraceful !

But it was no use attempting to argue the point with the colonel, so he took himself off on his leave in dignified silence and—a wig, returning at the expiration of it, looking all the better for his mysterious shave, for his hair, which before had been persistently straight, grew curly, and really improved his appearance immensely.

And thus, though he did not go to the fancy ball in any character, life, so far as he was concerned, was a perpetual fancy ball ; for as long as he remained in the regiment he was never allowed to forget how he had once appeared in the character of " Humpty-Dumpty." And—he never got drunk again as long as he lived.

WHO was he? Why, the colonel, of course! What other man in that big family of over-grown children occupies the proud position of absolute monarchy? And what was his name? Thomas Crêvecœur.

He was an autocrat—an absolute monarch—a martinet of the fiercest and most unreasonable description, and he commanded the gallant regiment known as the 18th (Royal) Dragoons. Behind his back they called him "Tommy," "Our old man," "Old Fireworks," and the like; but to his face it was "yes, colonel," and "no, colonel," in the most mealy-mouthed manner.

Occasionally the youngsters played very judicious pranks on him; that is to say, when "Tommy" got three sheets in the wind he was wont to unbend considerably, and they therefore had to fall in with his humour, and if he joked—joke back again; but it was unsatisfactory work—so akin to playing with lighted matches over an open barrel of gunpowder.

Well, one evening, after an extra big night, Colonel Crêvecœur retired to his rooms, rather nearer to being half-seas-over than was usual even with him, who could stow away a bottle of cognac a-day with ease and comfort. He was desperately sleepy—almost too sleepy to walk at all; the night was awfully cold; on the ground outside the snow lay thick, and the fires in his rooms burnt brilliantly—as fires do in frosty weather—casting mellow pleasant glow over everything. Up to the sitting-room fire-place Colonel Crêvecœur went, meandering thereto in graceful curves, which so delighted him that he unburdened his soul by a burst of language, popularly called "choice Italian." And, somehow, his legs seemed more inclined to continue the graceful meandering movements than the rest of him did, so he caught at the chimney-piece to steady himself; a liberty which—as it was merely a sham shelf of wood and fringe, put to hide the hideous regulation finish to the hideous regulation grate—that article promptly resented by breaking down, with all its freight of letters, horse-shoes, candlesticks, photograph frames, and odd little Indian ornaments and figures. Happily the glass was safely screwed to the wall, and the fire happening to flicker up just then into a brilliant blaze, Colonel Crêvecœur caught sight of his own handsome countenance, and suddenly became aware that he had been having too much.

"What a demmed red face you've got, Crêvecœur, my boy," he remarked, confidentially, gazing idiotically at the reflection of cheeks flushed scarlet, white moustaches fiercely waxed, and close-cropped white hair, all rumpled up on end.

" Been having too much—very wrong—shouldn't do it—bad example to set the young 'uns—gerrabed—gerrabed—sooner the better."

Now since a roaring fire was alight in each of the rooms, the use of a candle was entirely superfluous; but Colonel Crêvecœur, being in as great a state of absent-mindedness as was ever Sir Isaak Newton when he made the little hole for the kitten—though, to be sure, the cause was a very different one—troubled himself to stoop for a candle and stick from among the *debris* on the floor. He fished up the stick first; then the candle. But, alas! the candle was broken, and being slightly too small for the candlestick, required fitting to a greater nicety than his head was capable at that moment of conceiving or his fingers of carrying out.

" Dem the candlestick!" said Colonel Crêvecœur, flinging it across the room.

Still it did not occur to him to betake himself to bed without any extra light; stooping, he placed the broken candle between the bars, with the effect of making a big blaze in the fire, but none where he wanted it at the end of the candle.

" Dem the candle!" he exclaimed, tossing it into the fire;

then sat himself down to recover his breath—his eyes closed, and in two minutes he was off to sleep as sound as a church.

He must have slept for about a couple of hours ; for he awoke, with a start, to find the fire burned very low in the grate, the room in darkness, and the big clock in the gate tower striking three.

Colonel Crêvecœur sat up in his chair, as sober as a judge. " I must have been asleep," he muttered ; " gad ! how deuced cold it is."

As he passed the window to go into the next room, he drew aside the curtain to look at the night. The square was as light as day—on the great expanse of newly-fallen snow the full moon shone down bravely, bringing each sentry-box and each snow-capped range of troop-rooms into view, with the startling distinctness of a photograph.

He only stood there for a moment, but, as ill-luck would have it, a man in plain clothes came quietly out from between the chief block of officers' quarters and the commanding officers' house, and passed quickly towards the nearest troop-room— *unchallenged* by the sentry immediately below Colonel Crêvecœur's window. He did what, of course, any other commanding officer in the service would have done, he flung up his window, and demanded angrily the reason of the non-challenge ?

" I didn't hear him, sir," stammered the unfortunate sentry, in dismay.

" You—didn't—hear—him," in tones of the most withering scorn, " and what the devil did you mean by *not* hearing him, sir ? What are you there for, sir ? Who is he ? What is he doing out, prowling about at this time of night ? Up to no good, I'll be bound. I'll not have men prowling about at all hours."

The man in plain clothes had quickly enough vanished at the first sound of the colonel's voice, but the old autocrat was not going to be done in that fashion. It was just the time for relieving guard, and whilst he was yet speaking, the corporal of the guard made his appearance, and performed that ceremony.

" Put this man under arrest !" thundered the autocrat, " and turn the guard out."

So there was a scurry back to the guard-room, a hoarse " Guar-r-r-r-d tur-r-r-r-n out," a great scramble and scuffling and catching up of carbines plainly audible across the silent square—then a tramp of spurred heels, as the guard marched down to the commanding-officer's quarters.

" Sound réveillé !" shouted the colonel.

Out rang the trumpets and out came the regiment, wondering if a big riot was on, or a monster fire or maybe an invasion. But after all, it was but a great to-do about nothing !   Who had been out in the square during the past half-hour ?

The delinquent stood out instanter.   " Me, sir," he announced, without any circumlocution whatever.

" Oh, *you !*" with a frightful sneer on his handsome old face, " and pray, what were you doing out of your quarters at this hour ?"

" I'm Mr. Bartholomew's servant, sir," the man explained ; " I've been helping Dr. Scott to put 'ot flannins on 'im, but when he dropped orf to sleep the doctor said I might as well go to bed, as he could do werry well by his-self for the rest of the night."

Now as young Bartholomew was suffering from a severe attack of inflammation of the lungs, there was nothing further to be said—therefore, with a very bad word, the old colonel banged down his window, not even condescending to dismiss the regiment, and whilst the orderly-officer was hesitating whether to take that responsibility upon himself, one of the men broke into a hearty laugh.

Up went the window again !

" Ah, ah, my fine fellow, I'll teach you to laugh on the other side of your mouth," the colonel roared.   " Mr. Mordaunt—let the regiment be ready in full marching order in half-an-hour."

Full marching order—at three in the morning, with the thermometer at ten degrees below zero, and snow a foot deep on the ground !   In two minutes that barrack might, with reason, have been likened to Pandemonium ; such a cursing, such a swearing, in truth, in the space of five short minutes you might have heard as great a variety of oaths as would have served to fill this volume; such a hasty blacking of boots—such a polishing of helmets—such groanings over soiled gloves and facings, which there was no time to clean—such a hurrying, such a scampering of orderlies to apprise the married officers living in the town—such a rousing of whole streets to find the married men living out of barracks—such a grooming and stamping and kicking of sleepy, frightened horses—such a plunging and slipping and neighing, until, at last they were ready to start.

All through the town! Such a flinging up of windows—such thrusting out of sleepy heads to know if an enemy had suddenly invaded the country—such wonder as the loud strains of " Auld Lang Syne " and " The girl I leave behind me " rang out upon the frosty air—such bitter tears of sweet little modest maidens, who did not like to appear *en demi toilette,* and made sure the brave 18th were off to India at least—such hurried mental totting up of unpaid bills !

Then out into the country ! Rousing the inhabitants of village after village, and making them wonder if the Queen was dead, that the soldiers made so much fuss? One—two—three —four—five—six—seven long, slippery, dismal, miserable miles by a round which brought them back through the town again, where the worst was to come. A good mile from the town clouds quickly drifted across the moon, and the snow began to fall again in heavy blinding wreaths ; several horses suddenly became utterly unmanageable and frantic, lashing out every minute when they were not stumbling, and stumbling when they were not occupied in kicking—one fell, breaking his rider's leg in two places in the fall; a second came down a couple of hundred yards further on, smashing a foreleg horribly; a third ran his head bang against a lamp-post, tumbling over as dead as a door nail, at which another terrified animal made a clean bolt of it and tried to jump a house, with the result of turning a somersault and landing in the gutter with a broken back, jerking his rider off, with, happily, no more serious injury than a couple of broken ribs.

It was a ghastly night's work, and truly morning light rose upon a ghastly sight. Three gallant chargers lay stretched stiff and stark upon the trampled blood-stained road; two hospital cots were filled that before had been empty; anger and disgust was on every face, well-nigh rebellion and mutiny in every heart!

Amongst it all Colonel Crêvecœur stalked, grim, silent, vigilant, like an avenging spirit—a mighty big spirit for such a very trivial a misdemeanour.

In due course the story was wafted to headquarters, with what effect never transpired. The dignity and the authority of a commanding officer must be kept up of course—yet many in the regiment suspected that when, not many weeks later, Major Forde was gazetted to the command of the regiment, *vice* Thomas Crêvecœur, resigned, the retirement had been politely compulsory.

So he passed out of the regiment which he had ruled so long with a rod of iron, and with him—with one exception—passed away the last of the old race of martinets.

HIS PRINCESS.

DICK CARTER stood in front of the ante-room fire, with his hands behind his back. It was Christmas-eve, and on the last day of the year the regiment was to sail for India's coral strand. For his part, Dick wished India's coral strand was at the deuce; but then, since neither his nor any other Cuirassier's wishes could alter either the position of India's coral strand or the sending thither of the regiment, Dick had no alternative but to accept the situation, which he did with much swearing—what his Princess called " choice Italian."

" Who is to have the depot?" some one asked presently; " are you, Carter?"

" Can't afford it; I've too many of those beastly bills. Why don't you take it?"

" If I can get safe on board, I shall be in luck," he laughed.

" I can't say I altogether look forward to being on board," put in Dickson, in accents of great disgust; " for I overheard Mrs. Newcombe telling Mrs. Hey, in Jones's shop yesterday, that the voyage will be great fun, for they will dine with the officers every day."

" By Jove!" murmured three or four voices, half in surprise, half in indignation; for Mrs. Newcombe was the adjutant's wife, Mrs. Hey that of the quartermaster.

" Mrs. Newcombe having been out before knew all about it, and was initiating Mrs. Hey into the mysteries and delights of ship life. Mrs. Hey was, I fancy, rather taken aback by the prospect of the daily dinner, and gasped out ' Oh! lor.' "

A perfect roar of laughter greeted the words, and he continued. " They neither of them saw me for ever so long, and then Mrs. Hey made a clean bolt of it. I wasn't sorry, for I'd been wanting to laugh for some time."

The only one who did not join in the laughter was Dick Carter, who, still before the fire, was gazing abstractedly out of the window, past the rows of ugly barrack-buildings, to the murky sky beyond. Almost unconsciously his lips screwed themselves up, and he whistled softly the notes of a song, which he had heard the night before—

Will you think of me and love me, as you did once long ago?

"Curse it," said Dick, savagely.

"What?" Scott asked, innocently, never thinking of the words of the song, indeed it was doubtful if he knew them.

"Oh! everything," Dick returned, volubly; "India—bills —everything." But, all the same it was neither India nor the bills which made that vigorous anathema slip off his tongue just then.

He snatched up the poker and stirred the fire energetically— to speak with entire correctness, he did not stir the fire at all but smashed it, as if it was the coral strand of India, and he had a special mission to send it to the deuce.

Then, seeing that the chatter of voices had gone on again, he straightened himself up once more and went back to his occupation of watching the sky, thinking the while. He had one or two very unpalatable things to think about just then : first of all, there were his bills—not that he objected to a few bills, he had had them, bless you, ever since the days when he had emerged from frocks and tunics into knickerbockers—he would have bills, as he very well knew, to the end of the chapter; he rather liked them, there was something so uncom- fortable in paying ready-money, counting out the coins, haggling over the change, and getting discount. Dick felt rather ashamed of that discount; but then, to be sure, the times when he had received it were few and far between—like angel's visits. No ! he hadn't the least objection in the world to a few bills; he had never been what he called " a ready-money devil; " but, unfortunately, there were other people concerned who were not so easy-going as Dick was—those were the creditors. He had been forced to put his pride in his pocket a good many times of late, and, like several others of the

Cuirassiers, he knew that if he could manage to get on board the *Jumna* without being arrested, he should consider himself very lucky. Then, besides the bills, he would have on the morrow to be present at the men's dinner—just to say a word to them; and on the following day he would have to make a regular speech, for he was to give a dinner to his troop, which would cost a lot of money—not that he grudged a few pounds; but he was so awfully hard-up just then, there was no doubt about it. Well! he supposed he should get over the bills and the confounded speech in time; but there was another matter at which Dick could not look so philosophically. Unconsciously his whistling broke out again—

"*Che faro senza Euridice*——" but there he stopped with a suddenness which was a shriek of pain in miniature, and stood looking blindly at nothing, with such pain in his blue eyes, that it would have made your heart ache to see it. Not that his brother officers noticed anything, more than that "Carter was down in the mouth to-day, poor chap;" they were busy, one in retailing, the others in listening to the story of a quarrel which Captain Long had had with his wife that morning, and which Mr. Scott had overheard from his room, which stood at right angles to the Long's dining-room. What do you say? you don't believe cavalry officers descend to such little mean tittle-tattling as to discuss matrimonial squabbles? Then that only shows all you know about cavalry officers!

Ordinarily, Dick Carter was as good a hand at talking scandal as any officer in the regiment; but on that occasion his mind was otherwise engaged. He was wondering how he was to get over the parting with his Princess. A fine fellow he was, this same Dick, lithe of limb, tall of stature—for he was but slightly under six feet, square in the chest, strong, graceful, careless— a very *beau ideal* of a cavalry officer—with a sensible face, clean shaven, save for a heavy moustache of reddish-brown, a face which would have been handsome had it not been for a certain squareness in the jaw, but which could not be thought ugly, for the beauty of the keen blue eyes and the brightness of the fair hair above it. Looking at him for the first time across a room or a street your first impulse would probably lead you to remark, " What an ill-tempered, haughty face ;" but if you were brought close to him, and he wished to be civil—that just made all the difference in Dick—in two minutes you would be entirely won by his fascinating smile ; but then, perhaps, his persuasive voice and manner might have had a good deal to do with the change.

And whilst Dick was thinking rather dismally of the immediate future, the orderly officer for the day entered hastily.

" Oh, you're here, Carter !" he exclaimed ; " there's an uncommonly suspicious-looking chap asking for you !"

" Where ? Who ?"

Dick was on the alert in an instant ; for a moment his Princess was forgotten.

" A writ, I should say," Havers laughed ; " and the bearer of it has just been bundled ignominiously out of your room by your man, who informed him you had gone to Paris, and were not coming back to England at all; but would join the regiment at Malta."

" Clever chap," Dick murmured, as he put on his hat and caught up his gloves and stick, departing hastily.

It was but a step from the back door of the mess-rooms to the house in which he was quartered. Dick's long legs took him up the stairs four steps at a time, and with such haste, that he almost annihilated Craddock, who was occupied in washing the flagged landing between his master's rooms and those of Mr. Scott. He paused in his task, and sat back upon his heels with the flannel floor-cloth in his hands.

" Just had a bum-bailiff here, sir," he said, coolly.

" Yes, hang it! I know," returned Dick, savagely. " Can you keep him out if he comes back here, do you think ?"

" I'll punch his 'ed if he comes up my steps," Craddock replied, in a matter-of-fact tone, though a slow smile of delight overspread his fresh, good-looking countenance.

Dick laughed outright. " All right, then, I'll trust to you."

" Very well, sir," and Craddock went on deliberately washing the landing and then the stairs.

In order that he might hear anything which transpired, Dick left his door open, and presently he heard an oily voice asking if Lieutenant Carter had come *yet?*

" *No;* Leefetenant Carter hain't come *yet*," replied Craddock, calmly.

" I've heerd as 'ow he's in this 'ouse," remonstrated the visitor.

" Oh ! you're like for to know best," was the sarcastic reply.

" I must come up and see for myself," he went on, emboldened by Craddock's unlooked-for mildness.

" Oh ! yer must, must yer ? Then let me tell yer, me fine gentleman, that I'm a 'onest dragoon what serves her Majesty the Queen, and I don't take Government pay for washing steps for the likes of you to walk up and down."

" Oh ! I won't make no dirt," the bum promised, eagerly.

" I don't expect yer will," returned Craddock, affably.

Now the emissary of the law—I suppose a bum-bailiff *is* an emissary of the law—being a small spare man of ten stone or so, felt that a personal contest with a dragoon standing over six feet in his socks, and riding about thirteen-stone-ten, would hardly suit his purpose ; therefore, taking up his position against the jamb of the outer door, he proceeded to try and discover whether Craddock was of the class which, like the deaf adder, refuseth to hear the voice of the charmer, or whether he was open to blarney ? Now, upon certain occasions, Craddock was open to blarney, but then that was when the donor of it was of the softer sex ; to a bum-bailiff Craddock was as hard as iron.

" It's only bad sort of weather," remarked the emissary, pleasantly.

Excepting for a suppressed growl, Craddock did not condescend to return any reply.

" Sort of weather when one wants something warm inside, eh ?"

" You'll get something warm *out*side if you hain't orf soon," returned Craddock.

" Did you feel dry at all ?" said the emissary, presently,

gnoring his opponent's last remark. "I must admit I feels dry myself."

"Ah! there's a pump over yonder, **at** the stables," answered Craddock, significantly, "and there's some water in this 'ere bucket, though, to be sure, it hain't over clean."

Having finished off the first half of the stairs, he rose from his knees, stretched himself, and coolly planted his back against the wall. Seeing that, the emissary returned to the charge again, this time with a ludicrous assumption of authority, which made Dick and his man both laugh out aloud.

"Come, come, young man, you must let me come up them stairs."

"You'd better try, that's all," said Craddock.

"I know Lieutenant Carter's up there."

"Leefetenant Carter *hain't* up there, I tell yer," thundered Craddock, with utter disregard of the punishment in store for fabricators.

"Now look 'ere—speaking confidently—"I'll give you 'arf-a-crown for yourself if you'll let me come up them stairs."

"Chuck us yer 'arf-crown," answered the dragoon, sus-piciously.

With much fumbling the emissary produced a shilling, which he held poised on his finger.

"Arf-a-crown," said Craddock, stolidly.

"Say a florin."

"Arf-a-crown," was the dogged reply—"not a ha'penny less."

After a good deal of circumlocution, the half-crown was thrown from the emissary to the servant. Dick, leaning against the door of his room, wondered what was coming next.

"Now, I've paid up fair, so let me see into them rooms," said the emissary, eagerly.

Craddock cast a glance of most thorough contempt at him, and dipped his floor-cloth once more into the bucket. "I'll see you d—d first," he returned, deliberately, as he wrung it out, and went on washing the landing, at which Dick burst into a wild fit of uncontrollable laughter.

N

Craddock glanced up carelessly. "It's all very fine for you to laugh, Jinks," he said, in his stolid imperturbable way; "it hain't your turn to wash the steps down, or may be it wouldn't be so funny. Is Mr. Scott's mastiff in his room?"

"Yes," grunted Dick, disguising his voice.

"Then just let 'im out, there's a good chap; he'll make pretty short work of this cove down here." Then, as Dick opened Scott's door, "'Ere, Lion, come along—set 'em orf"—but the emissary had departed, a good deal faster than his wont.

Seeing the result of his *ruse*, Craddock sat down on the stairs and just roared with laughter, till he could roar no longer, and Mr. Scott going in found the laughter of master and man so irresistible that he could not ask what was the joke for the merriment which absolutely choked him.

"Craddock, go and see which way the brute's gone," said Dick, presently.

"Just going out of the gates, sir."

"Then come along," cried Scott, hastily; "there s a cab just driven up to the mess, and I told him to wait, thinking you might want it."

"Thanks, old man," said Dick, gratefully.

For the present the danger was over. As they drove towards the gates Dick uttered a sigh of relief—a sigh which quickly, however, turned to one of impatience, as a few bars of "Auld Lang Syne" floated out from one of the buildings they passed.

"Practising that thing already," Dick said, with what was almost a groan. "Goodness knows it's bad enough when it comes to the last, without hearing it every day for three weeks previously."

"Auld Lang Syne" was the farewell air when the Cuirassiers departed from old quarters for fresh ones. Like many another, Dick hated it as though it were poison, but he had never before detested it so cordially as he did then. I know one regiment which always used to play "When other lips and other hearts"—I daresay they play it still, only they have been

frizzling in India for ten years, so I have not had an opportunity
of judging; I knew another which kept to the hackneyed
" Girl I leave behind me ;" and another which of late has
played " Sweethearts " for the march out. Of them all, I
consider " The girl I leave behind me " is the best. There is a
certain jollity about it—it is almost impossible to feel affected
by it. Once, though, when a gay and gallant regiment, of
famous Peninsular and Crimean memory, was leaving a town
prior to embarking for India, there was an unusual amount of
weeping and wailing over the departing heroes ; bitter were the
tears shed to the strains, which somehow always make me
laugh :

> My love, I will come back again
> To the girl I leave behind me.

Oh ! the tender partings—the fond women folk who clung to
the stirrups and tramped some miles of the way for a last hour
together. Oh ! the passionate injunctions, " You'll not forget
me, Jack ?" I doubt not that under their gay trappings many
a poor fellow's heart throbbed painfully, many an eye was dim
beneath the shelter of the busby, with an emotion none guessed
aught of save themselves. " A change came o'er the spirit of
my dream, and it was eventime." Past the gate came two
girls, who in the morning had been especially and particularly
demonstrative in their leave-taking, and with them—if you
please—two men of the relieving regiment.

" Sarah," said one to the other, as they passed, " now isn't
these chaps a deal better than the 'Leventh ?"

" 'Leventh !—bah !" returned Sarah, scornfully.

Oh, Sarah ! Sarah !—I minded me of the sore heart and the
moist eyes I had noticed in the morning, and I was sorry till I
remembered that Jack and Bill were probably playing the same
old drama at the first halting-place.

" Where are you going, Dick ?" Scott asked, as they neared
the town.

" ' The Swan.' "

" Ah !"

Scott asked no further questions

Dick's Princess, who with her brother had come to see the last of him, was staying at "The Swan."

And what was she like, this Princess? Not handsome, certainly, as Dick once said to her himself: " You are perhaps not exactly handsome "—he had hitherto stoutly maintained that she was—"but then, don't you see, you are the sort of girl that every second man would turn round to look after."

" That's the prettiest compliment any one ever paid me in my life," laughed the girl, gaily.

She was standing by the window as Dick entered the room, a tall girl, in a closely clinging gown of black ; a girl with good dark eyes and a perfect form. She would, perhaps, have been better-looking had the eyes been more often filled with laughter, had there been a less haughty expression of the mouth, less resolution in the whole face, voice and gestures. She never looked haughty to Dick, though, to him, voice and gestures were always tender : when her eyes rested upon him, they always shone with that tender love-light which comes to the eyes of all of us at some period of our lives or other.

" Are you going to take me for a walk, Dick ?" she asked; " it is late, but still, you may as well."

Dick explained the circumstances which had prevented him from going earlier, and added, moreover, that it would be as well, perhaps, not to venture out that day more than was absolutely necessary.

" After to-morrow it won't matter," he ended ; " a writ must give eight days in which to pay up, and by that time we shall have sailed."

" Oh, Dick !" said the girl, with a suppressed sob. Alas ! the love-light had been dimmed by tears very often of late, and there was a suspicious brightness in the dark eyes upturned to him then.

Dick bent down and kissed her very tenderly.

" What has my Princess done with all her pluck ?" he asked, then hurried on with an earnestness which showed how little trust he had in himself. "When 't comes to the last, my darling, you won't give way, you'll be strong and brave, that I may be able to keep up too? You'll just say 'good-bye,' quietly, without any fuss."

"I don't know—but I'll try," she answered.

"You know, Princess, you are strong and brave; not like some women, who have no pluck! Gather up all your resolution and let me remember you smiling to the last."

"I only have one weakness," she said, with a wistful tenderness, which showed how firm a hold upon her that weakness had.

"And that is——"

"Yourself," she replied, simply.

"And you call me a weakness?"

"My love for you is a weakness, because—oh! Dick, you won't go away and forget me?"

"Of course not. My love, it will soon be over : just two years, till I get my debts paid, and then I shall come home, and we will laugh together at our fears at parting. It will only be two years, Princess—three, at most—before I come home to you."

"You never will," she said, calmly. "Dick, dear, sometimes you wonder that I am low-spirited, what you men call 'down in the mouth,'" with a gleam of laughter struggling through the sadness in her eyes; "but you are careless, and I am not. You, if you have what you wish in the present, are content—you don't look into the future. I do, and I count the hours, almost the moments, that are left to me, because I know that they are the end."

"They are not the end," he cried, passionately; "when I come back, we will go to Italy together, and then I will make you cry *peccavi* for your foolish fancies now."

"Yes, we will go to Italy together," repeated the girl, dreamily. "What a pity it is that we cannot go to Italy now, whilst we are young, whilst we love each other. Oh! what a nuisance money is—how vexed I am that I am poor."

"I don't care," he said, defiantly.

"Don't you?" she asked, wistfully; "but then, don't you see, you have not any money either."

" No, by Jove ! I havn't ; I only wish I had," he exclaimed, ruefully.

" What a pity one cannot sell one's pedigree," she said, musingly.

" Is it long ?   What do you value it at ?" he laughed.

" Why, where do you think those came from ?" she asked, holding a row of filbert nails just in front of his nose.

" Came from ?   I should think you growed 'em," he replied, making an effort to kiss the fingers.

" Growed 'em, of course ; but they don't grow by chance."

" No, perhaps not ; the Greeks did not admire filbert [nails," he said, coolly ; " too near an approach to the claws of a beast, you know."

" I should have given the Greeks credit for more sense," remarked the Princess, superbly ; " but, since I live in the nineteenth century I am very glad to possess my filberts, without worrying about the ancient Greeks."

Just then a knock was heard at the door, to which Dick called out, " Come in."

" There's a gentleman wants to see you, sir," said the waiter.

" A gentleman.   What sort of a gentleman ?" Dick asked, suspiciously.

" Well, sir," returned the man, looking round cautiously, " it's Mr. Goodenough's clerk."

" And who the dickens is Mr. Goodenough ?" demanded Dick, rising.

" Oh, he's a lawyer, sir."

" Oh ! a lawyer, is he ?   Well, don't let Mr. Goodenough's clerk come up here, that's all.   By-the-bye, how did he know I was here ?"

" Saw you come in, I think, sir."

" Ah ! where is he ?"

" In the bar."

" Then let him stop, if he likes.   I suppose all customers are good for the house—eh ?" with a laugh.

" Well yes, sir, of course," the waiter replied.   " I believe he means to wait until you come out."

At this intelligence Dick and the Princess laughed aloud.

"He'll have to wait a good while, then," Dick laughed. "I suppose you've some spare rooms?"

"Oh! yes, sir."

"Then I'll sleep here to-night. I didn't intend to turn my rooms upside down until Monday, but a few days won't make much difference. Don't let that brute up here, waiter, that's all."

"Well, sir, I'll try, of course; but if he insists on coming up?"

"These are *my* rooms," put in the Princess, with sudden dignity; "you had better tell him that these are Mr. Villiers's rooms, and that he cannot enter them. I wish," she continued to Dick, "that Jack would come in, I don't know where he has gone."

"Oh! it's all right," he laughed.

"I should have thought, now," she went on, plaintively, "that you were quite capable of breaking a clerk's head for him; when I first knew you, you used to talk very largely about twisting any one's neck, who presumed to look twice at me, but it seems to have been all idle swagger."

"Oh! I would break his head or twist his neck with the greatest pleasure, only, don't you see, if he sees me, he will be able to serve the writ on me."

"Oh! I didn't know," she said, rather blankly.

Presently the waiter came back, and closing the door behind him, set his back against it.

"If you please, sir," he began, solemnly, "he says he won't go away, not if he sits in the bar till morning; and I don't believe he will, he's a determined sort of fellow is Johnson "

"He's very welcome to sit in the bar till he turns to a mummy," Dick replied politely; "you can tell him so, with my compliments, if you like."

"Well, sir, but if he steals up here?—I can't be watching the staircase all the day."

"Look here, waiter, just keep Mr. Johnson out of my way and I'll give you a sovereign. Here it is."

" Well, I'll do my best, sir "—the sovereign had made all the difference to Joseph—" but, if you'll take my advice, you'll keep this door locked, and go in and out through Mr. Villiers's bed-room." The brother of the Princess occupied an apartment opening out of the sitting-room and having a second door on to a landing, connected with the principal corridor and staircase. "If he stays, as I think he will, I'll bring dinner up by the billiard-room and the back stairs."

" What fun," cried the Princess, clapping her hands, as Dick turned the key behind the retreating servitor ; " I feel as if we had gone back a few hundred years and were being besieged—this was the sort of thing my crusading ancestors went in for. It is like the siege of Jerusalem in miniature, only we are on the wrong side of the barricades."

" Did your ancestors go to the Crusades ?" Dick asked.

" Of course ! We came over with the Conqueror and did all the Crusade business, and finally settled down in Ireland, intending to become respectable gentry ; unfortunately, we got mixed up with royalty, and learned from experience that ' he who increaseth riches increaseth care.' The elder branches of the family—the semi-royal family took good care of themselves— couldn't keep to their quiet, respectable country life, but must needs get attainted for high treason, so, of course, forfeited their estates. Perhaps they had got a few drops of the wild Irish blood mingled with the cool determined Norman stock—any way, instead of being a belted earl now, Jack is only a poor sailor, with nothing a-year but his pay. Our men could never keep their money ; they could make it, or—in the elegant fashion of former times—take it, but they could not keep it. My own grandfather, after serving through the Peninsular, after being with Abercrombie in Egypt, and with Picton at Waterloo, after being in twenty-four engagements, besides skirmishes, hadn't sense to stick to what he had got, but went and put— ' invested ' he called it—all his money in some manufacturing concern, as a sleeping partner. He woke up one fine morning to find the others gone and himself saddled with all the liabilities—a fine end that was for Abercrombie's *aide* to come to."

"So your grandfather was an officer?"

"Yes—his brother too; and a good way back on my mother's side we have more fighting blood. I have some letters of my great-great-grandfather, written to his wife from Flanders, where he went with his regiment, the 1st Dragoon Guards."

She left the room, and presently returned with a bundle of old letters, very yellow and frayed, in her hand.

"Oh! are they not old?" she laughed, sitting down upon the rug, and untying the string. "What is this? Oh! listen:

"Cornet Villiers.   Dr. to Henry Tilley.

			£	s.	d.
1760.	Feb 5.	For a pair of water-gilt Bosses	0	12	0
		For a superfine web sercingle, leathered with neat's leather	0	4	6
1761.	Jan. 10.	For a Rich officer's cap of black and scarlet velvet, embroider'd with gold, and a guard over the Head chac'd & water-gilt &c. ...	6	16	0
		A green oil cloth cover for Do. lin'd with baize & for a deal box to pack it in	0	1	0
		Paid the carriage of the Cap by the coach to Leeds	0	2	6
			£7	16	0
		Allow'd for Yr old boss	0	3	6
		Due to Balance	£7	12	6

9th April, 1761.   Received then the full contents and all demands,

"HENRY TILLERY.

" Here is another:

"Guildford, December 27, 1759.

"DEAR LOVE,—

"I doubt not that you will be surprised at never receiving a letter of so long a time from me, but I hope you'll excuse me as we never have been quartered above two or three days at one time at any place, this seven weeks; nor do we expect to stay here above a month, as we shall relieve the Queen's Dragoon Guards, now on the Coast-duty, near where my uncle lives: but I expect to have the pleasure of seeing you in Yorkshire, for I hope to come 'a-recruiting in ye spring. My servant asked me leave to go to London for a week, which I have given him. I gave him money to buy a barrel of oysters and pay carriage to Yorkshire as soon as possible. I shall send you something from London, as I shall ask leave for a day or two to go there, for I am but thirty miles from Town. It is a fine place and a pleasant country that I am quartered in. I command a party of forty men and horses. The troop is divided into three different quarters—this place, Farnham, and Godalming. Cornet Jeffreys desires his compliments to you, and the rest of the gentlemen, though unknown to you. You were acquainted with Jeffreys in Chelmsford—he lived with Oldham in Cope's. My duty to my mother, love to brothers and sisters. Please, Dr. Love, you and my little ones accept the same, and I wish you a happy Christmas and a-many of them, from your affectionate husband,   WM. VILLIERS.

"This place is in Surrey.

"It is very good writing," the Princess laughed, "but the spelling is queer, and half the words abbreviated."

"I daresay he could fight," Dick said, with great contempt on the subject of spelling. "Go on."

"Dingen, April 17, 1761.

"DR. LOVE,—

"I have got safe to this side the water. I at this time lie at anchor in the River—

"I cannot make out the name of the river," Princess put in—

"and in a few hours disembark and go to the place I have dated my etter from. The men and horses of the party I belong got all safe here but two horses, which died in the passage here, for we had two or three very rough nights, though I never was sick at all. We are got into a very fine country, and the people are very civil, but I don't know one word they say. We are ordered to lie at this place nine days to rest, and then we march for the army, which lies at a place called Hamlin, from which place I will, as soon as I arrive, write to tell you how to direct to me. though I believe I am come too late for fighting, for we are told here that a peace is concluded on. But it is very certain to have a—

"I don't know what that word is," she broke off, "'p-s-a-tion'—Oh! it must mean a passage—yes—

"a passage of arms betwixt the French and our army. I have got a very good and sober servant. He comes from Gisbourne, in our neighbourhood. I'm ordered to get another servant and two more horses, which I shall get in three days, but the fresh servant I only hire from month to month, as he is for nothing but to lead and take care of my bought horses. I assure you, the sea has made such an alteration in me that from eating very little, I am become a *glutton*. I am healthy and very well. I don't know what more to say, as we at present have no news, but I am quartered at a gentleman's house, and the quarter-master says—for he has just been to wait upon me—that I shall always be quartered in such houses on our march till I get to the army for I do assure you I am at

present a very great man, for the colonel has gone forward to join the
army, and I am at present the commanding officer of our men and horses,
which consist of 230 men and horses, besides two cornets and two
quarter-masters, all under my command, and will be, until I join the
regiment. I am allowed hay and corn for seven horses every day for
nothing. Wine here is no more than ninepence a bottle. Brandy at four
shillings a gallon. Eating we don't pay anything for, till we get to the
regiment, but wine and brandy we are obliged to carry with us to our
quarters, for their beer is worse than water. The beer the common
soldiers drink is brewed from nothing but straw.

"S. Wildman is with me and Thomas and David Nuthall and the
Lilleys, and almost all the men I enlisted; J. Foster and both Briggs are
with me.

"Beg my duty to my mother, and love to brothers and sisters and my
little ones. I beg the blessing of God may attend you all is the sincere
prayer of your affectionate and loving husband,

"WILLIAM VILLIERS.

"I send this letter back by the captain of the ship that brought me
over. My old friend, Major Lichfield, is here, and desires his compliments to you. I have just been on board his ship to breakfast with him.
General Douglas commands us all to the army; he is a very good-
natured gentleman—it was he that reviewed me on Blackheath when I
was in Sir F. Cope's regiment.*

"The next two letters," observed the Princess, as she paused
and scanned them carefully, "are from my great-great-grandfather."

"Very likely—go on," that was what Dick usually said when
his Princess was talking—"go on."

* Rolstadt, June 12, 1761.

"DEAR LOVE,—

"Since my last, dated 21st May, from Barringtroop, we marched
to this place, which is situate but nine English miles from Padarborne.
It is a very pleasant country all round us, if ye army had not distressed
ye poor inhabitants so much by their being situate in and near this neighbourhood for two campaigns before this. We expect marching from
these quarters in a day or two to a place called Dryburg, which is about
sixteen English miles from this, where we are to encamp. The army of
the allies are to have three different encampments; one commanded by
Duke Ferdinand, the others by the Prince Hereditary and General
Sporkon, which are to act in three different ways, to observe the movements of the French army. We are very quiet, and by what appears at
present, shall continue so, for at this place there is nothing talked of but
a peace. A cornet in this country ought to have, besides his pay, four or
five hundred a year. We cannot do with less than five horses, and, if we

* Cope's Foot.

should have a vigorous campaign, I shall be obliged to keep six horses and three servants. I myself keep two servants besides a dragoon at present, which I pay twenty shillings a week to, and two shillings a week to the dragoon, out of my two pounds two a week. I do assure you this place for a gentleman of ye cavalry is the most expensive I ever saw, for no officer in this regiment can live upon less than twice his pay, but all our gentlemen are men of very great fortunes and never regard the expense, which they are in fact obliged to be at. I have no news at present, but, if anything extraordinary should take place, I will give you a line; but I cannot think why my brother has not answered any of my letters that I have wrote to him. I beg in your answer to this you will be so good as to let me know the reason. I would write more fully in regard to my affairs but that letters are very apt to miscarry. When you write to me, you must pay the postage out of England or the letter will not come to me. I have my health very well, which I hope you and my children enjoy, which is the constant prayer of your affectionate husband till death,

"W. LEACH.

"Direct for me as under:

"To Cornet Leach, of the first Regiment of Dragoon Guards,
"With the Allied Army in Germany.

"N.B.—I beg you will not let one post slip before you write me an answer to this.

"You may tell Joshuay Andisty that his brother has left the regiment he was in, and they do not know where he is.

"My duty to my mother, &c.

"How strange to read all those little tender private details written nearly a hundred-and-twenty years ago," said the Princess, dreamily. "I wonder what your letters will read like a hundred and twenty years hence, Dick?"

"Or your's?"

"Mine!" with a wry face. "Any one who gets hold of my letters to you will be sure your Princess was neither more nor less than a housemaid. I write horribly. But, still, it is strange, is it not? Ah!"—holding the yellow-brown carefully folded paper out at arm's length—"how my great-great-grandmother watched for that! How she kissed it and perhaps cried over it and loved him—'her affectionate husband till death.' He was getting very home-sick when he wrote that! You see, Dick, it was not 'do this and do that' in those days —it was 'I beg you will not let one post slip.'"

"Why, do I not pay my Princess homage enough?" asked, tenderly.

" Too much, Dick," with a quick sigh. " Well, do you care to hear any more—I believe there is some account of an engagement in one. Yes, here it is :—

" House of Hanover Camp, July 17, 1761.

"DEAR BROTHER,—

" I take this opportunity of writing to acquaint you that yesterday we had an engagement with the French army, a few miles from the ground we are encamped on, which is the same ground we were on before the action began. On ye 15th, at 9 o'clock at night, we were ordered to strike our tents and march, which we did. The French army lay in the front of us, and they marched off from their left a few hours before we did. Yesterday morning, at daybreak, they began their attack, which lasted till six or seven o'clock. Our cannons and small arms played very brisk and continued till near nine, when the French found it too warm to stand and were obliged to retreat with great loss, the ground being covered with dead. The loss on our side is very few, their loss in killed and wounded and prisoners amounts to upwards of 8,000 men, 11 pieces of cannon, four of which are 18-pounders. Amongst their killed are several officers of distinction, the report is that we have two lieut.-generals of theirs prisoners. As to anything more, I must refer you to the newspapers, only that if they had not retreated when they did, they would have lost a body of 6,000 men more than they did ; and that this battle has added great honour to Prince Ferdinand, for their army are at this time three times our numbers. I am very well and safe. From, dear brother,

" Your most affectionate,
"WM. LEACH.

" My love to my wife and children.
" Duty to mother and love to sisters, and please accept the same yourself.

" What battle would that be, Dick ?—Minden ?"*

" I believe Minden was in 1759. It must have been a pretty sharp engagement—how many did the French lose ?"

" Killed, wounded, and taken prisoners, 8,000, 11 pieces of cannon—four 18-pounders. I wonder what they would have thought of the 81-ton gun and the ' Devastation ?' "

" I wonder what fighting will be like in another hundred years?" Dick laughed.

" Scientific slaughter, I should think."

" Well, finish the letters."

The girl turned them over in silence for a few minutes,

* The Battle of Villenhausen, July 16th, 1761.

heedless of Dick's injunction to go on, and then she suddenly gathered them up, with a resolute face. "I can't read any more," with a gasp of pain, "there is only parting and poverty. I do not find either subject pleasant just now, they both cost me so much."

"Sing to me then," he answered. "I want you to sing to me as much as possible this week, Princess, for heaven only knows when I shall hear you again."

"After this week, never any more, Dick," she told him, with grave sadness.

"Oh! nonsense!—are all the foolish fears back again?"

"I do not think," she said, simply, "that they have ever been away"

And then she sang for him a tender song, with a passionately pathetic refrain—

> Oh! my love, I loved her so,
> My love that loved me years ago.

That song had lived in Dick's memory for months; would he ever quite forget it while he lived?

"I cannot sing!" she cried, with feverish impatience, rising from the piano and going back to her place at Dick's feet. "I can do nothing but dread—Oh! the future, how afraid of it I am. I wonder, Dick," with sudden wistfulness, "how soon it will take you to forget me?"

"When the bullet goes through my heart," Dick answered, earnestly, "I *may* forget you."

And the Princess laid her head back against the heart which was to beat for her always, with a smile, and was comforted.

And the days crept over, until the last had come. Jack Villiers had left the pair pretty much to themselves, feeling that, except at meals, he was an unwelcome addition to their company. Dick took his Princess for long walks—he had now no fear of writs, and they were positively showered upon him—he showed her all the little sights of the place, and she helped him to buy such of his outfit as he had not procured in town; and, in time, the last afternoon came—the very last time that she would put on her hat and go out with him; the last time they would go into a shop like two children and buy *nougdt*, or toffee —the last time.

" Dick," she said, when she came into the sitting-room, dressed for walking, " let me have the cross."

" Yes, child, of course."

It was an " Iron Cross of Prussia," which some friend of Dick's had found in Berlin and which the Princess had vainly coveted for some time.

" Buy me a steel chain to wear with it. I want to have one of your choosing," she said, softly.

And so they went to some dozen shops before they could get what they wanted; but they got it at last, and went back to the hotel together.

" Dick," she said, as they reached the door, " **you** won't have champagne to-night?"

" Oh! we must, child—the last night."

" Yes, I know," impatiently, " and then you will drink to our next merry meeting, and I cannot bear it—indeed I cannot, dear."

" I won't, indeed."

"Not one word?"

" I promise."

Dick kept his promise faithfully, but just as he raised the first glass to his lips, he looked full at her; the girl threw her glass down and, with a passionate burst of tears, rushed into the inner room, weeping as if her heart would break. But presently, mindful of her promise to be brave, she went back and held her glass for Dick to fill.

" To our next merry meeting," she cried, courageously.

Her tears were all gone, there still lived in the girl some of the cool determined spirit of her crusading fore-elders, and she had, for Dick's sake, forced the scalding drops back—it must have been—even to her heart. And so, on that last night, she sang and laughed, wearing a brave smile to hide the utter agony within her.

" I want you to keep my helmet for me, whilst I am in India," Dick said, during the course of the evening.

"Very well!" she answered, "I will take care of it."

The moments sped quickly on and midnight had come. More than once Jack Villiers had dropped asleep before either of the others thought of bed.

"I don't think it's wise to sit up all night," Jack said, at last, sleepily.

"No, no—I am going to bed at once," the Princess answered.

She made no attempt to undress, but threw herself on her bed and drew a fur rug over her, lying listening to the sounds about the house until all was silent. Still she did not sleep: she heard the clock in the hall strike one—two—three; then, very soon, the sound of the boots—she supposed it was the boots—hammering at Dick's door. Evidently Dick had been already up when the servant went, for when she, a few minutes later, entered the sitting-room, he was there, trying awkwardly to fasten his belts.

"Let me do that," she said, hastily.

"Are you there, my darling?" he asked, turning quickly at the sound of her voice.

She fastened the belts in silence, her shaking fingers scarcely able to perform the task. She spoke no word, only her face grew more and more deathly pale, her eyes more intensely dark, the weight of pain on her heart more and more crushing; once she looked at him, but what she saw in his face made her keep her eyes resolutely away from it, was she not nerving herself to get through the next hour bravely? But the silence was broken at last, when she saw him trying to force some things into a bag, more than it would hold.

"Let me do that," she said, calmly, taking them out of his hands.

She dared not look at him, the hands trembling so nervously before her told her what she would see if she should look up into his face, and a great tear which fell with a splash upon her wrist warned her that she must be strong, for Dick's strength was fast deserting him.

"It is snowing fast," Dick said, turning to the window, and drawing aside the curtain.

"Is it?" said the girl; her voice sounded almost indifferent, so great was her effort to keep her tears back. Oh! if he would but go now, she thought, passionately; now, without a word.

But Dick did not. He crossed the room to her side, and stood watching her packing the bag.

"Linda!" he said, using her name almost for the first time since he had known her—for he had passed from "Miss Villiers" to "My Princess"—"Darling, it has come."

She dropped the bag and its contents, and turned to him, looking then with sad hungry eyes into his white quivering face.

"You—won't—forget—me," she managed to say; "you'll —think of me—sometimes."

But Dick never answered; he took her in his arms for a moment, as if he would never, never let her go again. The girl felt her head swimming and her heart sinking yet lower— then her kisses, the last she would ever give him, fell upon the brass guard of his helmet, and its icy coldness brought her to herself.

It was all over then—at the door he turned and looked at her for the last time. A pair of blue eyes beneath an Indian helmet, a pair of dark ones under a mass of red-brown hair, and in both such dire misery, that I can write no more. The door closed, and he was gone.

She heard him clatter down the stairs and tramp along the stone-floored hall, then she ran to the window and flung it open wide for yet the very last look. The tall, soldierly figure passed out of sight amid the driving snow; but the girl sank on her knees and stayed there, half unconscious of aught but that the end had come. Jack, coming out of his room, found her there, wet with snow and almost frozen to death.

"Come in, old woman," he said, persuasively; "you will get your death."

"I am past that, Jack," she answered.

o

"Am I to give him any message?" for **he was** going up to the barracks for Dick's cabin trunk.

"Tell him I am not crying or anything; that I'm quite quiet and cool," she answered, and turned to the window again.

Oh! why did she want to hear it? What was she listening for? It came presently.

> We twa hae paddl't in the burn,
>   From early morn till cline;
> But we've wandered mony a weary foot,
>   Sin' the days of Auld Lang Syne.

"I feel nothing!" cried Dick's Princess, stretching her cold hands to the wild snow; "I am past feeling."

But it was not so when Jack returned, on his way to the station.

"Let me go, too," she pleaded.

"No," he said, soothingly; "poor Dick's awfully cut up; and you'll break down, and make it harder for him."

"I am as cool as—as an iceberg," she cried. "I must go, Jack."

So he let her go.

They were too late to see him again—the doors of the station were closed. The cabman drove them up close beside a low railing, from whence they could see the long train. They could see three or four officers of other regiments, who had come to say a word of farewell; but she could not see Dick. Once, amid her tears, she saw the waving of a handkerchief, and wondered if it was his? The band struck up again, and the train moved. One by one the instruments ceased—there was an attempt at a cheer, which ended in a huge sob, and the Royal Regiment of Cuirassiers was gone; they had passed away into the distance, and Linda Villiers stood in the dim grey mist of that December dawn, alone. She might have cried:

> My eyes are full of tears, my heart of love,
> My heart is breaking, and my eyes are dim;
> And I am all aweary of my life.

BY-AND-BYE;

OR, HOW RICHARD CARTER SHOT AT A PIGEON AND BROUGHT DOWN A CROW.

AND by-and-bye Dick's letters to his Princess grew shorter and more constrained! With each one the girl lost her pluck and her brave on-looking to the future. She was troubled at the change, though she hardly knew in what it consisted.

At first Dick's letters had been one passionate outpouring of an imprisoned spirit—imprisoned in that huge gaol known as India. Oh! how he hated India and everything Indian. He should die, he cried out, away from everyone he loved; he had no one to care for him, no one to think of him. He had heard of the splendours of Indian scenery, of the magnificent profuseness of nature there. Bah! it was hideous, hideous, hideous— a dirty, dusty, dismal, deserted, miserable hole, something like Aldershot, only, compared to India, Aldershot was a perfect paradise. He believed there was fine scenery in Kashmir, but all that Dick had seen on his march to Unapore was hideous, hideous, hideous—that was what India was in Dick's opinion. He didn't know which he hated most—Bombay; the railway carriages; the bungalows, where they put up for the night; the half-barrels, which were provided as baths, and against the unfinished edges of which he had nearly broken his legs twice, or the station at which they ultimately arrived. He hated it all! If he had a preference, it was for Bombay, because it was so many miles nearer to England than Unapore.

For a month or two his detestation of India and everything Indian increased. He wrote to Linda that he had been to a ball at which there were thirteen ladies present, balanced by two hundred-and-fifty men; the *belle* was Mrs. Newcombe, a fact which so utterly disgusted him that he went home before the end of the first dance, and gave Indian society up as a failure.

Then he got leave and went to Simla, where the ladies came
under his especial censure : " I don't like the women here at
all," he wrote to his Princess, " they are vulgar to a degree :
they call you by your surname and talk very loudly, they smoke
and drink B. and S. and positively guzzle champagne whenever
they can get it, as for their morals, they are *nil !* Here they
are during all the hot weather carrying on no end of a life,
while their poor devils of husbands are frizzling down in the
plains. I cannot do with them after a pet like you," followed
by a good deal of tenderness, which the Princess read and
smiled at, and, worst of all, was foolish enough to believe.

And then Dick fell ill—his letters were brimful of that one
subject ! His leave was almost up and he should have to go
back to Unapore and die—there was not the least doubt about
the dying ! The men were dying off like sheep, the only times
the band was heard was when the " Dead March " was played—
that, the Princess gathered, was about every hour or so. Three
officers had died within a few hours of one another—to be sure
one was in consequence of a fall from his horse, and another
had steadily killed himself by drinking, she had seen that in the
papers—the colonel had had a very bad go of fever, Creyke was
very ill, and Dickson, so Dick had heard, was a perfect wreck.
Poor Dick !—in one week more his leave would be over, and he
must make his mind to go back to Unapore and die.

Ah ! how she wept over that letter, with a wild sense of
rebellion against the ill-fortune which had made her anything
but a great heiress, who could have given her soldier-hero
all he wished in a country more suited to his tastes than
India had proved to be. Poor Princess ! Alas ! she had a
passionate adoration and fair prospects, but passionate adoration
is unfortunately not good to eat, neither will it provide shelter
and raiment ; and, as for prospects, she knew as most people
do—or, if they don't they will very soon find out—that it is
but ill work waiting for dead men's shoes. And so she could
only weep over Dick's letters, and gather such papers as might
interest him, or make her eyes ache by writing long letters.
telling him over and over again how she was always thinking

of him all the day—aye, and for the matter of that—half the night too.

By the next mail came a still more disastrous letter! His health was worse: so ill, indeed, was he that a medical board was to sit on him at his rooms with a view to further leave. At the end of that epistle was a postscript to the effect that the board had obtained for him four months' sick leave. Once more her spirits rose, she breathed freely ; she went about the house singing like a lark, so glad to heart was she that her boy had been successful. She carried the letter about with her, she read and re-read it, she talked to the photograph she wore in her locket, and she wrote Dick the longest letter she had ever written to him or to anyone else, during her whole life. She took his helmet out of the case and cleaned it carefully, until it shone like burnished gold. Never had Dick's soldier servant bestowed such tender attention upon it. She put it on her own head and looking in the glass, tried to cheat herself into the belief that they were not dark eyes which she beheld beneath it but the true blue orbs, which she had seen there aforetime— that the heavy knot of brown hair which tilted it up behind was not there in reality, but only the back of Dick's close-cropped head. It was of no use, the face under the helmet was that of the Princess, and Dick's was thousands of miles away amid the lovely scenery of Simla—yes, he had retracted his first opinion somewhat, and admitted that Simla was lovely. She fell then to wondering what was he doing? Thinking of her, of course—thinking of his Princess, and calculating how soon he could save sufficient money to take him back to England and her. Oh! Princess! Princess! why did you go about all that brilliant September day, with the self-same song upon your lips, which Dick had cursed so heartily on Christmas Eve ?—

In the gloaming, oh ! my darling, think not bitterly of me,
  Though I passed away in silence, left you lonely, set you free ;
  For my heart was crushed with longing, what had been could
    never be,
  It was best to leave you thus, dear, best for you and best for me.

Why did your heart's gladness find its vent in words like those? Could it be that they were a fore-shadowing of what was to come, the first of the by-and-bye? Presently a letter came, not less profuse in terms of endearment than the former ones had been, and yet the scalding tears rushed into the girl's eyes as she read it, a blank pain settled down upon her heart, never to be quite lifted any more—she could not have told what manner of pain it was nor why it had come, therefore I use the word "blank" advisedly. The letter was loving, but it was evidently written in great haste; it ended "God speed my darling," and yet, in his carelessness, he had blotted the words. He wanted this, he wanted that; Princess, was to do this, to get that. Why should it pain her so sorely? She could not tell, it was the undefinable *something* which had begun the *by-and-bye!*

Amongst other news which this letter contained was that there was to be a fancy-ball, to which Dick was going in the character of the Earl of Leicester, "of the time of Queen Elizabeth, you know," he added. Ah! surely that was the unkindest sting of all—"the time of Queen Elizabeth." What had come to Dick that he took it for granted that she did not know to what period of history *the* Earl of Leicester belonged? And so the pain settled down upon her heart and stayed there!

The bright September days crept over and chill October came in, but there were no letters from Dick. The girl fretted and worried and pined to know what could have chanced. Surely he must be ill that he did not write. She got the helmet out and cleaned it again, she looked up his old letters and read them a dozen times over—all of them save the last one, there was but one line of that she cared to remember, that was the "God speed my darling" at the end.

The days crept on. Twenty of October's thirty-one sons had come and gone, the Indian mails were in, but there was no letter from Dick. All that day the Princess stayed in the house, lest the precious missive might come, and coming, lie one moment unread; but no, it came not—

It came not, no, it came not,
The night came on alone,
The little stars sat one by one,
Each on its golden throne.

So the Princess went to her bed and slept, for a wonder, long and heavily; and towards morning she had a dream. She dreamed that at last the longed-for letter had arrived, and that it was but a letter of farewell, conveying the announcement of his approaching marriage. She awoke with a gasp of relief that it was, after all, *only* a dream. How could an idea so idiotic have got into her brain, she wondered? Dick marry! The idea was too absurd. What, to one of the women who " are vulgar to a degree, who call men by their surnames and talk very loudly, whose morals are *nil*, who drink B. and S. and positively guzzle champagne, whenever they can get it?" How supremely absurd to think of Dick's marrying one of those.

And yet the impression produced by the dream could not be shaken off, it was so distinct; she had seen the letter so plainly —the bluish foreign paper stamped with the crest of the regiment, Dick's careless yet firm writing—it had been all too real. There was only one thing unlike Dick—its utter coldness. Whatever his failings had been—and, dearly as she loved him, she had not been blind to them—no! though she had loved his very faults, because they were his, coldness had not been one of them. She tried to argue herself into the belief that, since dreams always go by the rule of contrary, Dick's next letter would bring her good news—perhaps! Ah! the thought which flashed across her mind made her very heart stand still for a moment; perhaps he had somehow contrived to get leave and was coming home. And so, amid hopes and fears, the next few days slipped over, and at last the letter appeared.

" It's a very thin one," murmured the Princess, ruefully, as she opened it.

The first thing that caught her eye was the end. No " God speed my darling," not even the more usual termination, " Your own Dick "—no, nothing of his usual tenderness. It

was a new sensation which thrilled through her heart as her
eyes fell upon the four words which concluded the letter, for
they were, " Yours truly, Richard Carter ! "

The by-and-bye had come !

It is not necessary to give the letter in detail. It was
incoherent, *very*. The handwriting was shaky, the tone half-
tender, half-bland ! The latter was indeed one of the ex-
pressions he used :   " You don't know how it pains me to tell
you thus blandly—"

" Blandly," repeated the Princess, with a passionate sob
" fancy Dick bland—to me."

And what was it that he told her, thus blandly ?

It was merely the fulfilment of the dream which she had not
been able to banish from her mind. Dick had—well not
exactly forgotten her, but he had made up his mind that the
only way out of his difficulties was by a rich marriage, and so
he was going to be married !

The lady—he called her a *lady*, so the Princess concluded
that she was not a girl—was called McPhearson ! She was
rich ! She was handsome ! She was loving ! She was going
to pay off all his debts—or at least, her father was going to do
so, which amounted to the same thing ! Her people lived in
London, and she was staying in India for a little while with a
married sister. Dick was quite sure if the Princess knew her
she would like her awfully. Linda was not so sure of it—she
was rather doubtful on the subject, but that was nothing ; and
that was all—excepting " yours truly, Richard Carter," over
which the Princess wept most bitterly of all. And then, when
her first grief had passed somewhat, she began to put two and
two together, to think the matter over. She was not exactly
a fool and she knew life pretty well, indeed—considering her
short experience of two-and-twenty years—better than most
people.

The lady was Scotch ! There could be no doubt of that.
Her father lived in London—then what was she doing out in
India ? She must have gone out on " spec," husband-hunting !
The Princess wondered was she oldish ? Probably she was

older than Dick or he would never surely have spoken of her
as " this lady!" And Dick owed some four or five thousand
pounds, which Mr. McPhearson was going to pay! To the
Princess's tolerably keen mind that hadn't a Scotch sound
about it! If Dick had been a nobleman she could understand
some rich city man " shelling out," but for a simple sub. in a
cavalry regiment—why, it was absurd—it hadn't a Scotch sound
about it.

The result of her calculations was that she wrote and recommended Dick to get his debts paid before he was married.

" Ladies," she wrote, " who are young, rich, and handsome,
have no need to go out to India husband hunting, unless there
is something very very shady in the background. If she has
gone all the way to India to catch a husband, I don't believe
her father will be willing to pay four or five thousand pounds
for him—it hasn't a Scotch sound about it, Dick."

But Dick did not wait to receive her advice. His anxiety to
secure his pigeon was too great, and it was not many weeks
after she had received the news of his intended matrimonial
venture, that she saw an announcement in the *Times*—

On the 7th ult., at Simla, by the Rev. ———, Richard Carter, Esquire
(the Cuirassiers), of Breakdown Castle, County Cork, to Lily, youngest
daughter of Andrew McPhearson, Esquire, of 17, Tollington Crescent, W.

And so it was all over—the bullet, which was, in piercing
Dick Carter's heart, to make him forget his Princess, had
found a billet—perhaps neither of them had looked forward to
its being a bullet of gold. Well! the end had come: Linda
Villiers might sit down and weep her very heart out, or laugh
and forget him. Dick wouldn't care which—at least, that was
what she told herself, and she had a fair knowledge of life—
considering her years.

During the week which followed, she got very tired of seeing
that same announcement—in every paper in which the notice of
a marriage could be put was it found: *Times*, *Telegraph*,
Standard, *Daily News*, *Illustrated London News*, the *Graphic*
—nay, when one day turning over some numbers of the *Queen*,
she came upon the following, over which she laughed out aloud

—and, be it known, she had of late done very little in the way
of laughter. It came under the heading of the " Upper Ten
Thousand at Home and Abroad " :—

A marriage has been arranged between Mr. Richard Carter, Cuirassiers,
of Breakdown Castle, County Cork, and the youngest daughter of Mr.
Andrew McPhearson, of 17, Tollington Crescent, Kensington, W.

Poor forsaken Princess ! She laughed till she cried, and she
cried till her head ached, and then she went to bed and sobbed
herself to sleep—but she cut the announcement out and put it
away with that of the marriage.

" The Upper Ten Thousand "—No, I won't be quite sure
that it was not under " Marriages in High Life," but any lady
reader will know—it makes no matter, for both were equally
absurd. The Princess was certainly anxious to know which of
the two families had inserted the numerous announcements of
the marriage. One of them must be very proud of the
alliance—of that, there could be no doubt. She rather fancied
it was on the McPhearson side, for she had an idea that the
Carters had not a great deal of money to spare—at least, Dick
had always said so.

And that was the end of it all. Dick Carter had found himself a bride in India, and the girl whom he had called his
Princess had to get over the change as best she could—she
did get over it in time. The old obstinate spirit, which had
fought so bravely in the Crusades under Cœur de Lion, lived
in the girl still; the cool determined brave heart with which
her grandsire fought through the Peninsular—for the Villiers
had all been gallant soldiers for generations—which carried
him into Egypt, (one of Abercrombie's chosen staff), and to
Waterloo with Picton, it lived again in the girl. She was
heart-broken, ill, weary of her life : she had lost what she
valued most upon earth but she struggled on—on to the time
when the fair prospects had become substantial realities ; to the
time when she could look back to the old days and see only the
brightness ; when she could admit that, as they were, things
were best ; when, thinking of Dick tenderly still, she could
bear to listen to the strains of that old Scotch melody, which

had wrung her heart so sorely as they floated to her, through the driving snow, that chill December morning, when she and Dick had said " good-bye," to meet on this side of the grave never more—though then they had both looked forward to the by-and-bye.

But that was not quite the end. Not many months after Dick Carter entered the bonds of holy matrimony a series of announcements appeared in the papers, which made the Princess—I call her by the familiar name still—come to the conclusion that it was from the McPhearson side that the numerous notices of the marriage had emanated—not that this one was in connection with a wedding, on the contrary. It ran thus :

On the 25th, at 17. Tollington Crescent, Kensington, W., Andrew McPhearson, Esq., aged 80 years. Dearly loved and deeply regretted. Indian papers please copy.

" How strange," remarked the Princess, " to say ' Indian papers please copy,' when he has two daughters married in India."

Yes ! It was perhaps a little strange, and something else rather astonished her—his age. Eighty years ! She came to the conclusion that—and all her information was by that means—Mrs. Richard Carter was in all probability a good deal older than her husband, who was seven-and-twenty. To be sure Mr. McPhearson *might* have married late in life, and " Lily " *might* be the youngest of a very large family ; but, still, the chances were ten to one against it. Of that, however, she had no means of knowing, except she had troubled herself to write to some of her friends in India, which she did not do. No ; she saw the notices of the old man's death in the papers with a sigh and a certain feeling of sadness.

Dick had soon come into his kingdom ! No doubt he had quite forgotten her by this time, she thought, quite ceased to regret her, that is. That he could forget her was, of course, utterly impossible—as long as he lived, he could never remember leaving for India without a thought of the girl who had risen at four o'clock in the morning and bidden him adieu, to the strains of "Auld Lang Syne!"

And time crept on. It was some months after the death of old Mr. McPhearson that the Princess was in London with her mother, on their way to the sunny Rhineland. They stayed in the great city, to see the Academy and one or two theatres, at one of which they witnessed that old-world comedy, "She Stoops to Conquer!" The play began.

"I wish people would come earlier," remarked the Princess, plaintively, as she rose, for about the twentieth time, to allow some people to pass.

"The places on this row are all filled now," returned the mother, consolingly.

At the last comers she scarcely glanced, except to notice that one was a tall lady in a grey opera cloak, the other a young man, apparently her son.

The play went on, and to it the Princess gave her undivided attention until it was ended.

"Splendid play," she observed, when it was over.

It was to be succeeded by a farce, and during the interval the audience behaved as an audience at a theatre generally does behave. The men got up and moved about, speaking to their acquaintances, the usual trays of ices and wine were sent round, women criticised other women's dresses, there was general bustle and hum of voices. Suddenly the Princess became aware that a gentleman had come behind her, and was speaking to the lady in the grey opera cloak.

"Oh! we are in Tollington Crescent," she said, evidently in answer to some question.

Tollington Crescent! She pricked up her ears immediately; it was a magic sound to her. She turned her head, and saw that the lady was in mourning, then she turned it away again.

"Oh, my mother's gone down to Exmouth!" she said—again the Princess had missed the question—"my brother's got a little son. She has gone down to see her grandson."

"But your brother has been married some time," said the gentleman; "this is not the first?"

"Oh, no ; but the first boy—the son and heir."

The last words were, however, spoken in a tone which plainly showed that the addition, "and heir," were intended as a joke, and meant to be received as such.

" Ah ! the first that counts, I suppose ?"

" Er—yes !"

A moment's silence, then the lady spoke again,

" I have not seen you for some time."

" No; I have been out of town for six weeks."

" Really ! I thought that perhaps you had already gone to India."

" Oh, no."

" When do you go ?"

" In about six weeks. And have you heard from Laura and Lily lately ?"

" Oh, yes ; they are both very well."

" Still at Simla ?"

" Oh, yes."

If the Princess had been a fainting sort of young lady, she would probably have fainted; but, as she was not, she did nothing of the kind. She turned rather pale, and a deadly sickness crept over her ; but she preserved sufficient presence of mind to carefully examine the appearance of the lady from Tollington Crescent ! Now, up to that moment, she had never for one instant doubted the reality of the riches in the McPhearson family; but, after five minutes' survey of her neighbour's dress, they took unto themselves wings and fled away—as the reader may have known reputed riches do before to-day.

Mrs. Richard Carter's sister—for, of course, she was a sister —had taken off, or rather thrown back her cloak, after a fashion ladies have when a theatre becomes too warm; the Princess was glad of it, for it gave her a more favourable opportunity of studying her person. She was a tall woman, perhaps six or seven-and-forty—she might be a little less, but that was what she looked. She had—the Princess began with the crown of her head and worked slowly downwards—she had

Scotch stamped on her ! Her hair was of that peculiar hue
just now so fashionable, and known as "cardinal red;" not
ordinary red hair, but a deep scarlet. By way of a head-dress,
she had a bit of rusty-black feather, what, I am told, is best
described as feather-trimming, and which, as the Princess told
herself scornfully, she wouldn't have picked up in the street,
much less have worn it about her person. Her face was long,
with an undeniably good nose, high cheek-bones, a hard mouth,
and lack-lustre eyes of the description known as "boiled goose-
berries;" it was a face without any softness in it, which might,
perhaps, have been accounted for by the brick-dust colour of the
complexion and the scarcity of eye-brows and lashes—it might
be that the Princess was a little prejudiced !

But to continue : Mrs. Richard Carter's sister wore a gown of
some thin black material, "not worth ten shillings," Princess
said afterwards. The bodice was cut square—it was cut very
square : so square, that, had the wearer been a lady of Venus-
like proportions, it might have been thought by a fastidious
person to be cut too square. As it was, the Princess's eyes beheld a broad expanse of fleshless bony chest, which absolutely
made her shiver. "It was like a dead woman's neck !" she said
afterwards.

The sleeves of this gown did not come down to the waist, but
ended at the elbow—probably they were what ladies describe as
elbow sleeves—at all events a pair of very sharp angles protruded
under the frilling which fastened them off. On her arms she
wore black mittens of open-work. Now, I take it, that,
possessed of a pair of beautiful hands and arms, a lady can not
do better than pretend to cover them with open-work mittens.
Mrs. Richard Carter's sister had got the mittens, but, alas ! she
had neither the beautiful arms nor hands. The wrists were long
and large, the hands had no breed about them ; the nails were
square, and they were not *very* clean, moreover they had those
white blemishes upon them which are commonly known as
"gifts "—

A gift on the thumb is sure to come ;
A gift on the finger is sure to linger.

If there be any truth in old sayings, Mrs. Richard Carter's sister had a great many presents in store. Not only had the nails "gifts" on them, but the surrounding skin had grown over them so as to almost hide the half-moons which most people admire. Not only were the nails objectionable, but the fingers also, for they turned up with a thick lump of flesh beyond the nail, and gave them the appearance of being bitten. She wore a considerable quantity of rings, but there was not— Princess especially noticed that—a diamond amongst them, or, indeed, one of any value. She thought of the filbert nails and the four or five valuable rings hidden away beneath her own gloves !

On one arm—no bailiff's man ever took more careful account of the knick-knacks of a house than the Princess did of this lady's personal adornments—on one arm she wore a fourpenny black snake bangle, on the other a heavy bracelet of gold ! She took especial notice of that bracelet—it was a huge onyx, as large as a walnut, and set in " a broad band of gold." She knew, as most people do, who have given their attention to such things, that the onyx, like the amethyst, is not a very valuable stone, and when set in gold of good quality diamonds and pearls are used also—there were neither diamonds nor pearls in the bracelet, so the Princess came to the natural conclusion that the gold massive setting hailed—perhaps from Abyssinia.

" I don't believe," she said afterwards, " that there is any money at all."

" Cannot be much," answered the mother.

So the Princess went back to her hotel and thought it all over. What a strange coincidence, that she should be thus brought in contact with the sister of the woman who had succeeded in marrying Dick, and still more strange that by her conversation she should have known who she was.

The result of her cogitations was, that on the following morning she suggested that they should take a hansom as far as Somerset House and just have a look at the old gentleman's will.

Her suggestion was soon carried into effect. They drove

through the grand quadrangle, and were set down at the will department. On entering, they were informed that they must purchase a shilling stamp, and then she was given a big book, and told to look out the name. She had but small difficulty in finding it :

> Andrew McPhearson,
> 17, Tollington Crescent,
> Kensington, W

There it stood.

Then they were directed to the reading-room, and told that the will should be sent in a few minutes. They found the room, in which were a few chairs, a bench or two, a long table, and two grave-looking clerks, watching to see that the documents were not tampered with.

And presently *the* will appeared.

" You must read it at the table," said one of the grave clerks, as the Princess stretched out her hand to take it.

" Oh! must I? I did not know," she said apologetically. " *Under* twenty thousand pounds," she said, with a little gasp, to the mother.

There was the usual legal preamble as to the soundness of the testator's mind, then everything—" all my houses, lands, furniture, books, pictures, carriages, horses, domestic animals, and things "—was left to the wife for life, with the exception of the sum of one thousand pounds, to be paid at once to the trustees of his granddaughter, Mary Bagot, the interest of which was to be applied for her schooling and maintenance.

" I don't like that word ' schooling,' " said the mother critically.

" It has rather a third-rate ring about it," replied the Princess, continuing her perusal of the will.

At his wife's death or marriage the testator directed that to each of his daughters, Marion Bagot, Janet Neville, and Laura Ashburnham, he gave the sum of two thousand pounds, to be invested for them—though only with their written consent—by the trustees named in the will, the interest to be paid to them, or only upon their written receipt. In the case of any of them dying without children, their money was to return to such brothers and sisters as might be living or have left children. To Mary Adelaide Lucy, if, at the time of her mother's marriage or death, she should be unmarried, he gave *three* thousand pounds; but if she should be married, she was only to receive two thousand, as her sisters—in either case, less one hundred pounds " had in anticipation."

" Bless me," the Princess ejaculated, blankly, " whatever can that mean ?"

" To take her out to India, of course," returned the mother, " and little enough, too."

" It wouldn't buy her outfit," gasped the girl. " But to continue :

To his son, Donald, the testator bequeathed the sum of one thousand pounds, unrestricted (at his mother's death, that is to say). To his son, McIvor, the sum of one thousand pounds, less three hundred " had in anticipation." The remainder of the money to be equally divided amongst his six children.

" And that is all," said the Princess, " but look, it says ' late of Calcutta ;' I wonder what he has been ?"

" He has evidently made his money himself, and he does not intend some idle extravagant fellows to marry his daughters and spend it," Mrs. Villiers replied.

The Princess turned the document over thoughtfully. " I wonder which is the codicil ?" she said, aloud.

" There is not one."

" But it says the ' Will and Codicil.' "

" I think," put in one of the grave personages at the end of the table, " that it is merely a clerical error, but I will inquire."

It was merely " a clerical error."

Princess thanked him, and said " good morning." She did not speak until they had got half-way across the quadrangle.

" Then when her mother dies—which may be twenty years hence—she will have, at the outside, about a hundred-and-forty pounds a year strictly tied up to herself—Dick being able to touch neither principal nor interest—and if she dies without children, it goes back to her family. Of course she *may* have

money of her own ; but, no—if that were so, he would not have
provided the other thousand.   No ! a hundred-and-forty pounds
a year !   I wonder if he is very fond of her?   He didn't use
to like red-haired women !   If not—why I should have been
the better match by far—but then, to be sure, I had no money
then."

The Princess's money had come, as many things do come in
this world, too late.   Oh, the pity of it !   Oh, the pity of it !

SUPERSEDED.

CHAPTER I

Sʜᴇ was always called " Pretty Polly." When she first came from school (that grand London school, where the terms were a hundred a-year *with* extras) her mother made an effort—not a small one, for when Mrs. Hugh Antrobus made an effort it was usually one which might be classified as prodigious—to have her called by her proper name of Mary ! Perhaps that was one of the very few instances on record in which an effort of Mrs. Hugh's had proved a failure ; but a failure it undoubtedly was, and a very signal one, too. No one could or would remember to call her anything but " Polly ;" and so, at last, Mrs. Hugh gave it up, and even fell back herself into the old familiar habit of calling her eldest daughter " Polly."

Polly's father was a lawyer, not a particularly distinguished one—indeed there were people in Blankhampton ill-natured enough to say what money he had he had not come by in too honest a fashion ; but that is rather beside the question. Certain it is, that Mr. Antrobus was a lawyer, and hardly at the top of the tree ; he had married a lady whose father was in the cotton-spinning way, without much money, but with remarkably large ideas. One of Mrs. Hugh's ideas was that Polly was the most utterly beautiful young woman who had ever been born—many mothers think the same ; another, that Polly was destined to make a brilliant matrimonial alliance—Mrs. Hugh never said anything so common-place as marriage. Having made up her mind on these two important points, Mrs. Hugh felt that Polly would have small opportunity of encompassing that desirable end so long as they remained in the house at forty pounds rent, which they had occupied since their marriage ; so she cast about in the neighbourhood of Blankhampton, and finally decided upon the River House as a suitable abode.

Now, the River House was quite the best in the vicinity, and was, in fact, a mansion in miniature.

"It will suit us exactly, Hugh," she said, when they had finally arranged with the landlord, and were inspecting it with a view to re-decoration; "a charming hall; and these glass doors will keep the vestibule and upper gallery as warm as possible. And the library—I should think we should have enough books to fill up the shelves, Hugh! As for the dining-room, it is a superb apartment; we shall require nothing but a carpet—and really, Hugh, I think we might afford a Turkey The drawing-room : ah! the girls must look after this; Mary" —she was as yet in the Mary period—"Mary will be able to exercise her ingenuity. Back-stairs *and* servants'-hall : well, Hugh, when we can afford a billiard-table, this will be the very place to put it in."

She had probably forgotten that in a billiard-room a side-light is objectionable; perhaps she had never known it : but that is not *à propos* of the subject. Upon one point she was right—inside and out the River House was all that could be desired. It stood in the midst of tastefully laid-out grounds, sloping in terraces down to the river's bank, or rather to the public promenade which led to the city, half-a-mile away. Not quite so far off, in the opposite direction, were the Cavalry Barracks, from whence Mrs. Hugh—though she did not say so —thought it not improbable Polly's splendid match might come.

In due time the Antrobus family removed to the River House, and Polly began to feel she had taken her proper position in the world. Now that her home was a mansion in miniature, with a servants' hall, a housekeeper's-room, a courtyard, and stabling for twelve horses, she felt she could invite, or at least feel equal to inviting, any of the city heiresses or noblemen's daughters with whom she had associated at Miss Neville's. True, there was only one nobleman's daughter in that establishment : her father was an Irish earl, and not even a representative peer; her dresses were always shabby, and her bills were a long time unpaid. And equally true was it that the Antrobuses could have done without a servants' hall; and had not a housekeeper to occupy the room set apart for her; nor yet horses to fill the stables. Still, the stables, and the housekeeper's room, and the servants' hall were indisputable facts, just as it was that she had been at school with an earl's daughter, and Polly felt that the several circumstances added to her dignity not a little.

And so Mrs. Hugh received her friends in the big drawing-room with bland complacency, and Polly swept her trains along the polished floors of the vestibule and passages as if she had been accustomed to *parqueterie* all her life; while the younger girls, To-To and Baby, narrowly escaped breaking their necks by daring rambles on the roof itself.

It was April when they entered upon their new domain; soft balmy weather, so that Polly was able to parade about the garden paths in an evening, with a scarlet shawl twisted about her shoulders and a natty little sailor hat, with a ribbon of the same colour, perched on the elaborate *coiffure* of twists and coils, in which her fair hair was arranged. She certainly was very pretty, everyone acknowledged it. She was tall, being rather above the middle height, but, when you had said so much, that was about all that could be said for her figure—it was not actually a bad figure, but, most assuredly, it was not a good one; she had pretty hands, with long slender fingers, and her face was as fair as a blush-rose; her forehead was low and white, and her flaxen hair fell on either side in the rippling waves you may have seen in a Greek statue; her nose was slightly inclined to be aquiline, and her mouth, it must be owned, was the least prepossessing feature in her face—it was undeniably a foolish mouth, weak and without character, yet the lips were red as cherries and, when parted, displayed a row of even, pearly teeth, so beautiful in themselves that few persons noticed the weakness of the mouth. Her eyes were blue, not particularly large or expressive, but of a lovely turquoise tint, and her complexion was glorious—there was not the least flaw in it, it was perfect : of the delicate whiteness of Parian marble, with an apple-blossom flush upon it—it was a complexion which would have made a plain face charming. Now Polly was most emphatically not plain !

She was a nice girl too—good-natured and gentle, and though somewhat given to romancing and very much given to dreaming, had no bad habits. She played very nicely Thalberg's " Home, Sweet Home !" and other pieces of that calibre ; she kept the flower-vases in the drawing room carefully arranged, and she spent a good deal of her time in the garden—" the grounds " the Antrobus family called them—sitting in a careless, yet graceful attitude, on some rustic bench, with a book in her hand, of which she read but little. Polly never did a stitch of sewing, but for the most part dreaming of that grand future which was coming, and trying how near she could model her person and her manners to those of a young duchess.

" A young duchess " was Polly's favourite ideal, though she had never seen one herself, and Lady Edith O'Shaughnassy's description of the young Duchess of Ballycorum was not at all the same class of person as Polly's Duchess of Dreamland.

" Just a slip of a girl, with a wide mouth and two great staring black eyes," Lady Edith had said, " and dressed nine days out of ten in a gown of rough homespun and a thick grey jacket, with no end of pockets, and her boots—just regular brogues."

" And for church ?" Polly had asked.

" Oh, not much better. A brown velveteen dress, with a jacket like it, and a brown felt hat, with a scarlet wing in it— sometimes a sealskin jacket, but not often, for Ballycorum is three miles from the church, and the duke's a big man, so she's warm enough walking."

" And does a duchess walk three miles to church ?" Polly gasped, all her most cherished ideas thus being turned topsy-turvy.

" Of course—no one has his horses out on Sunday in our part," Lady Edith answered, promptly ; " but when old Lady Ballycorum is at the Castle she uses the pony carriage."

It was very evident that her grace of Ballycorum did not belong to the same order as the Duchess of Dreamland—perhaps it was because she was an Irish duchess! Polly's " grace " lived in an atmosphere always heavy with perfumery, surrounded always by masses of hot-house flowers and rare exotics. Upon every occasion she made a *toilette*, and even her *négl gées* were of the richest silk and velvet, profusely decked with *priceless* old lace ; with *her* diamonds were so much a matter of course that even her bedroom slippers were adorned with buckles glittering with those costly gems—only the Duchess of Dreamland had nothing so common as a bedroom, she had a sleeping apartment ; she summoned her footman by means of a silver bell, and when she felt " a little low "—which she did sometimes, in an exceedingly refined manner—drank rare wine out of a fragile goblet of Venetian glass ; she was quite too luxurious to walk a step, and apparently did not stand in need of exercise like less privileged mortals.

As for the duke, he was but a lay figure. Once Polly had exerted herself sufficiently to begin a novel, with herself in the character of a duchess for heroine, but she came to one sentence so thrilling that she straightway fell a-dreaming, and the novel was never finished—

" May laid her hand on the embroidered sleeve of the duke " ——after that it was impossible to go on.

Well, the glorious summer months passed over, and the family at the River House seemed no nearer to attaining their object. Their intimacy with the barracks did not altogether progress—Mr. Antrobus called on the mess and received a few days later a couple of cards, left by two gentlemen, who did not even ask if he was at home ? Mrs. Hugh called on all the officers' wives—for the Cuirassiers had been ordered to Blank-hampton a month after the Antrobuses went to the River House—but the calls had been returned and their invitations declined : the Cuirassiers would not have them at any price. However, they did manage to scrape a tolerable intimacy with the pay-master, whose back windows overlooked the River House gardens ; and when, in due time, the invitations for the officers' ball were issued, through Captain Lewis's interest one went to the River House.

Polly was almost roused out of her habitual serenity. As for Mrs. Hugh, she folded her fat arms and beamed about the house with benignant triumph.

" You must have a new dress, Polly," she cried.

" Oh yes," Polly returned—that was a matter of course.

" Have you thought of anything nice ?"

" Yes," answered Polly, after a moment's pause; " I will have azure and silver."

Chapter II.

"There was a sound of revelry by night."

So there was : the Blankhampton Assembly Rooms were brilliantly lighted and superbly decorated. At the entrance stood two sergeants, each bearing a silver salver, one to receive the cards of invitation, one to dispense the programmes. Between them and the outer entrance stood a guard of honour, and within the room itself was stationed the regimental sergeant-major, ready to bawl forth the name of each fresh arrival.

On the right of the doorway, some yards within the room, stood Colonel Cotherstone, and opposite to him his officers *en masse*—only they were not exactly *en masse*, for they stood in a straight row, for the most part with their hands behind them, looking for all the world like a class of very gorgeous school boys just about to say their lessons. And so, after all, they were. My simile is not far wrong, for were they not one and all about to repeat the lesson which officers seem to be so proficient in learning, and which they are all so willing to teach to others ?

" I wonder," muttered Anthony Creyke to his next neighbour, Eliot Cardella, " if old Dare expects I shall dance with his daughters, because if he does—" he broke off suddenly, for into the Honourable Eliot's grey eyes had come a gleam of surprise, and he exclaimed, " Gad ! what a pretty girl !"

It was Polly—and Eliot Cardella was the Earl of Mallinbro's second son!

Major Creyke looked after Polly and remarked, " Pretty well." He did not admire pink and white Dresden-china sort of girls.

Eliot Cardella dropped out of the line at once and marched off to where Mrs. and Miss Antrobus were standing with Captain and Mrs. Lewis.

" Good evening, Mrs. Lewis. May I ask for the first ?"

Under any other circumstances Mr. Cardella would have seen Mrs. Lewis on the top of the guard-room clock before he would have asked her to dance, but to all general rules there are exceptions, Polly made one that night.

" I believe the second is a galop?" he said to Polly, with that deferential air of courtesy which implies so much and really means so little.

" I believe it is," returned Polly, glancing at her card.

" I'm afraid I don't dance very well, excepting a polka," he began ; " but if you will do me the honour——"

" I shall be pleased," said Polly, serenely.

" May I take a polka also ?" he asked.

" Oh, yes," Polly answered—she would have danced an Irish jig with Lord Mallinbro's son.

And so the ball began ; Cardella walked through the mazes of a quadrille with Mrs. Lewis, and Mrs. Antrobus sat blandly watching her daughter do the same with Captain Lewis. She thought she had never seen Polly looking so well. Her dress of sheeny, shimmering blue silken stuff was wreathed with frosted silver gauze, and studded here and there with large frosted water-lilies ; round her white throat she wore a string of pearls, and half-hidden in her flaxen hair were half-opened water-lily-buds.

" Who's Cardella talking to ?" one Cuirassier asked of another ; " very pretty girl."

" Ya-as," returned the other, with the instinctive hauteur a soldier invariably puts on when speaking of some one a shade beneath him " fathaw's a lawyer fellah !—always hanging about the barracks.   Keep clear of attorneys myself, one never can be sure they havn't a writ or two in their pockets—combining business and pleasaw at the same time, you know. Cardella seems taken."

"Young fool," said the first speaker, emphatically.

Meantime the band had struck up, and our couple started; but, after two turns, Eliot Cardella abruptly stopped.

"I must apologise for bringing you into this mess," he said, in a tone of concern.

"It is of no consequence," said Polly, sweetly, regardless of the strip of torn silk floating behind her, and the big frosted water-lily tossed to and fro amongst the dancers like a cork on a stormy sea.   She was unaware that her substantial foot had come down like a half brick on that of her partner, and he gallantly kept the knowledge to himself.

"I won't put you into further risk," he said politely.   "Shall I find you another partner, or will you forgive me and sit this dance out?"

"I do not think there is anything to forgive," said Polly, in a soft, murmuring voice, and raising her turquoise blue eyes artlessly to his; "I would just as soon sit out with you as dance with anyone else," but there was the faintest emphasis on the word *you*, as if she preferred sitting out.

"You are too flattering," returned the incorrigible flirt, sinking his voice to the level of hers, and bending his eyes tenderly on her face.   "Shall we find a seat here?"

"Here" was a small lounge, almost hidden behind a folding-door and a screen of flowers, and just the very place Polly felt was best for a *tête-à-tête* with an earl's son.   She sank down in a languid attitude, her azure and silver draperies falling in graceful folds about her.

"I am so sorry," said Cardella, when he had squeezed himself into the small space left for him, "to have spoilt your beautiful dress!   What a bore you must think me."

"I do not think it was you who did it," Polly answered, innocently; "I believe it was Colonel Cotherstone."

"Very likely."

In his heart he did not in the least care who had done it, and thought the colonel much more likely to be the delinquent than himself. When a man gets to the chief's age he ought to give up capering in a ball-room.

" I say, Cardella," said Dickson, ten minutes later, " look out what you're after, that girl's father is a lawyer—not of too high repute either. I don't deny that she's awfully pretty— only be careful."

" Oh! she's awfully pretty," Cardella said, readily, " but have you seen her feet? By George! they are heavy! The major's mare, Bonny Bell, trod on my foot last week, and it was a thing to hers, glancing in Polly's direction.

" Same foot?"

" Yes, worse luck."

" Poor devil," laughed Dickson.

Who, having overheard the above conversation, would have expected to see Mr. Eliot Cardella make his way to Polly's side as soon as she was free? And yet that was what he did. Probably the mere fact that there was a sharp father in the background only made him more ready for the fun of flirting with her. Everyone knows that an Englishman enjoys sport the better when it has an element of danger in it.

" Mr. Cardella," said Polly, in her soft voice, " who is that strange-looking officer over there?"

" The elderly man?"

" Yes."

" Oh! that's our surgeon-major—' Chronohotontologos ' we call him."

Polly opened her blue eyes very wide indeed.

" What do you say?" she gasped, at last.

" His real name is Williamson," Cardella laughed, " but we call him ' Chronohotontologos.' "

" It is most—extraordinary!" ejaculated Polly.

Chrono——why her mouth would be out of shape for ever if she contrived to pronounce half of it.

" Why do you call Dr. Williamson strange?" he asked, present'y; " I assure you he is one of the very cleverest men you ever knew. Let me introduce him **to you**; you'll be charmed with him."

"No thank you," returned Polly, icily, "I would rather not."

"But why?"

"I do not take much interest in—doctors," she said, calmly.

It was all Cardella could do to avoid expressing his amazement by a long whistle. Fancy this lawyer's daughter turning up her nose at a man like Williamson, particularly when she had gone to that very ball under the auspices of Lewis, whose father had been master tailor of the 17th Hussars, and who himself had risen from the ranks.

"Must be a complete fool," thought Cardella, with an intense desire to burst out laughing. But when he took Polly back to her mother's side, and a partner immediately claimed her, something in Mrs. Hugh's fat bland face made him seat himself beside her. Dickson happening to pass just at that moment felt "the young fool" must have utterly taken leave of his senses.

"May I take you to have an ice, or a glass of wine?" he asked, courteously.

"Oh, no, thank you! I enjoy looking on."

"And so do I," he responded. "I suppose I ought to be hard at work introducing people, and so on, but I really hardly know a soul here, and I looked after most of the decorations."

"You look tired," said Mrs. Hugh, blandly.

"I am a little tired," he admitted.

"Ah! those tiresome field-days," she responded, sympathetically; "I am sure they must be trying. I really do not know how you sacrifice yourselves so cheerfully, there must be so much restriction and general unpleasantness."

"Well, it isn't so bad as Oxford," he laughed.

"Oh! are you an *Ox*-ford man?"

"Yes," wondering what she could find so astonishing in that.

'My brother," said Mrs. Hugh, with the air of a person playing the last trump, "is the Dean of Brazenface."

"Brazenface," Cardella repeated; "what is his name?"

"Fullerton," said Mrs. Hugh, more blandly than before.

"Not Billy?" the young man cried, forgetting his manners and suddenly recalling the dean.

"Ye-es," her tone was a trifle less oily.

"Oh, I remember Billy well enough"—utterly forgetting that it was her brother of whom they were speaking; "yes, I knew Billy and Billy knew me. Little fat man, with a squint." The expression on her face made him, all at once, remember how completely he had set his foot in it; and, to cover his own embarrassment and her discomfiture, he began to speak volubly. "And so he is your brother, Mrs. Antrobus? Why, what a little world it is after all! I daresay you and I have lots of mutual friends, if we could only compare lists."

Mrs. Hugh's fat countenance literally shone with delight. He thought, in a good-natured way, that she really was a very jolly old lady, and was evidently not prone to take offence; for he had certainly been extremely rude, and ninety-nine ladies out of a hundred would have never taken any notice of him again, but this one seemed to enjoy the joke as much as he did.

Now, if Eliot Cardella had been in the Palace of Truth instead of the Blankhampton Assembly Rooms he would have learned one or two things which would have surprised him not a little. First, that Mrs. Hugh Antrobus did not consider herself at all *old;* and also, that her beaming did not arise from the joke concerning Dean Billy, but from his having so completely put himself upon a level with her: it was a new sensation for her to be thus chatting amicably with an earl's son, and, like the young gentleman in *Locksley Hall,* she

Looked into the future, as far as eye could see.

In fact, she looked rather further, for she saw Polly, Polly no longer, but the Countess of Mallingbro'—she disposed of Viscount Cardella without any ceremony—a coronet on her fair brow and costly diamonds flashing upon her fair throat and rounded arms. Seeing all that, she might well beam.

"*Good*-night, Mr. Cardellah," she said, when he saw them

into their cab, an hour or two later, " we shall be charmed if
you will call."

That cab was a great trial to Polly, but with a little make-
believe, it was easy to fancy it had C-springs and brocaded
cushions ; but still, she was not sure that to Mr. Cardella it
might make a difference.

Chapter III.

It was the day after the ball.   Major Creyke and ten or twelve
officers, chiefly juniors, were at luncheon, and there was one
guest, the chaplain.

" I say, Mr. Brandon," said the major to the guest, " did
you happen to hear the riddle the colonel asked the Dean last
night ?"

" No ; what was it ?"

" Why are two young ladies, kissing each other, performing
an act of the highest Christian virtue ?"

" Give it up," said the chaplain, at once.

" It was quite ecclesiastical."

" Give it up," he repeated.

" Because they are doing unto others as they would that men
should do unto them—*men*, you know."

" Oh ! the point isn't exactly obscure," laughed the chaplain ;
" what did the Dean say ?"

" He bolted."

" I should think so."

At that moment a discussion arose at the other end of the
table, almost amounting to a squabble, in the midst of which
one of the youngest officers rapped out an ugly word.   The
major rose at once and rang the bell.

" Mr. Brandon, will you take cherry brandy ?"

" Yes, thank you."

" So will I.   You," looking at the others present, " will have
what you like ; and," turning to the servant, " put it down to
Mr. Cogner, for using bad language in Mr. Brandon's presence."

For a moment the subaltern looked a little dismayed, but

since there was no remedy for the major's fiat but cheerful acquiescence and an avoidance of evil speaking for the future, he was obliged to get over his chagrin as best he could.

"By-the-bye, Brandon," remarked the major, presently, "do you know anything of a man called Antrobus—you've been here longer than we have?"

"Lawyer?" the chaplain asked.

"Yes!—lives at a big house near the river, and has a pretty daughter."

"No, I don't know them personally—they had not been there very long when you came; Captain Kennedy had that house before them."

"And you don't know anything about him?"

"No, I can't say I do, except that he does a good deal in the money-lending way. Why do you ask?"

"Because they contrived to get to the ball last night— through Lewis, I suppose; if I'd known anything about him, I'd have struck his name off the list."

"He's coming down the square now," put in Dickson, suddenly. "I'm off!"

"So am I," cried the major. "Come up to my rooms, Brandon, and have a cigar."

In consequence of this, when Mr. Antrobus arrived at the ante-room it was tenantless, and having left the regulation amount of paste-boards, he was obliged to go away, as wise as he went. Even Eliot Cardella cleared out with the rest. It was all very well, he argued, to amuse himself for an hour or two with a pretty girl, but to entertain the old money-lending father, when all the other fellows had cleared out at his approach, was rather more than he felt inclined to do. Moreover, he had half-promised the old woman to call, and, if he saw Mr. Antrobus then, he could hardly do that. Not that he had quite decided to call—he did not know, he was sure, whether it would be exactly wise—it would be almost like putting his head into the lion's mouth; and yet, she was awfully pretty, there was no denying that.

He went up to his room in a very undecided frame of mind.

He wanted to go and see Polly—what he did not want, was the objectionable father and mother. He wondered, impatiently, why nice girls need have objectionable belongings, how much nicer it would be to "shunt" them, as they do in the States.

He drew a chair to the fire and smoked a pipe, then he changed his clothes, and sat down again in a greater state of indecision than before. They say that a certain road is paved with good intentions. Now Eliot Cardella's intentions were undeniably good— in fact, they were rather better (in a worldly sense) than good, for they were cautious; and yet—yet he hesitated a little longer, and finally succumbed to the voice of the tempter, and betook himself to call at the River House. Polly was very pretty, and Eliot Cardella was particularly susceptible to feminine charms—as a consequence, four o'clock found him chatting pleasantly in the drawing room at the River House with Mrs. Antrobus and Polly.

That visit was quickly followed by an invitation to dinner, which occasioned a little more hesitation on Cardella's part, and ended by being accepted.

Oh, that dinner party! It lay like a leaden weight on Mrs. Hugh's mind for a week; she could not get rid of it, night or day—it was like a lump of indigestible pudding, and much worse than a bad conscience. Polly never worried herself about anything; she superintended the decorations of the table and put fresh flowers in the vases—then she dressed herself carefully and went down, in good time, looking very graceful in a gown of pearly-grey silk, finished at the throat and wrists with some antique rose-point, which Mrs. Hugh *said* had been her grandmother's. At her throat she had a bunch of large sweet-smelling purple violets, secured by a tiny brooch of seed pearls in the form of a leaf, and in her hair she had several clusters of the same fragrant blossoms. Polly certainly had some very good points, she was never impatient, and if she tried rather too much to model herself after Tennyson's heroine, who seemed to be very *haut ton*—" Faultily faultless, icily regular, splendidly null, dead perfection "—why she never condescended to anything so vulgar as quarrelling, and upon all occasions she was very pleasant to look upon. Some people may think that a very small virtue, for which Polly deserved no praise, but *men* will all agree with me, that it is a very great matter indeed.

As usual, Mrs. Hugh was late, and only scurried into the room as the first vehicle rolled up to the door. Polly, who had been gazing reflectively into the fire, turned, as Cardella's voice fell upon her ear, with a pretty pleased smile of welcome and—well, for once, she was vexed, for there stood Mrs. Hugh, with her dress well tucked up about her, displaying a not too clean white petticoat, the long folds of silk gathered up under her arms, just for all the world as it was when she went into the kitchen in the morning to look after the *cuisine.* Polly could have shaken her; but, since that was impracticable, she interposed her own slight person and flowing draperies as much as she could between the Honourable Eliot and the vast bulk, which she called " mother," and at the very first opportunity gave the dress a vigorous tug.

" Do let your dress down, mamma," she said, in a sharp whisper.

" Dear me ! how absent-minded I am," remarked Mrs. Hugh, blandly. " I don't know what I should do, Polly, if I had not you to look after me."

Which, for Polly, was out of Scylla into Charybdis. She needn't have troubled herself : Cardella was not sufficiently interested in Mrs. Hugh to notice her ; he only saw Polly, and thought she was looking prettier than usual, with that sudden deepening of the apple-blossom flush on her cheeks, and that shy uplifting of her blue eyes. And oh ! by Jove ! what a jolly gown she had got on. That jolly silvery grey, with such lace as his mother often wore, and those velvety, sweet-smelling violets, fastened by the little pearl brooch. He did not know much about dress, but he thought she looked very distinguished and quiet.

" I was so disappointed not to meet you at the Deanery last night," he remarked, somewhat awkwardly for Polly, who had never been asked to the Deanery in her life, but fortunately he did not give her time to reply. " Such a lot of hideous women

Q

there were too," he said, resentfully, as if they had all been asked for his especial annoyance.

"Perhaps you are very bad to please," she said, softly.

"Oh! I know a pretty woman when I see one," he returned, coolly. "What lovely violets you have; I smelt them the moment I entered the room."

"The children got them for me," Polly said, deprecatingly. "We generally have plenty in the hot-house."

"I wish they would give me some," he returned.

"You shall have some of these," unfastening her brooch as she spoke.

"I will keep them for ever," he said, in a low voice.

"Or throw them out of the cab window," she laughed, "like the gentleman in ' Sweethearts.' "

"I thought he threw them overboard," Cardella murmured, lazily leaning against the chimney-shelf, and regarding Polly with the well-satisfied air with which all men regard a pretty woman, leaving the tender passion quite out of the question.

"Oh yes, of course ; he threw them overboard after all the protestations he made, but she—kept hers."

"Never make protestations myself," he remarked ; " awfully bad plan."

"I thought you said you would keep those violets for ever," said Polly, raising her blue eyes for an instant.

"By Jove! what pretty eyes," thought Cardella ; then, aloud, "So I shall."

"Oh, nonsense!" the girl laughed, twisting one or two of the flowers in her slender fingers.

"Don't you believe me?" throwing a little extra warmth into his tone, that he might make her look up again. A moment later he wished he had not succeeded ; the full glance of her eyes had disappointed him. They were pretty in colouring, but there was no soul looking through those blue windows ; the face was nearly perfect, for the only approach to a fault lay in the mouth, and he noticed nothing beyond the red ripe lips and the even pearly teeth, but it was quite expressionless: there was no fun playing about the mouth, there was no awakening of that fierce fire which lived in his susceptible heart; it was an artistic mask—"icily regular, splendidly null, dead perfection."

"Do you never keep your *souvenirs* ?" he asked.

"*I !* Oh, no !"

For the first time a gleam of expression came into her face and eyes—a half-quizzical, half-dismayed look, which made him forget his disappointment, and think how awfully pretty she was. If her sense of humour was somewhat latent it was there, and Cardella was just in the frame of mind to enjoy calling up an unusual trait in her character, more than if she had been clever enough to see and appreciate every little joke that cropped up.

She contrived—quite accidentally, of course—to pilot her "gentleman" to the seat next to Eliot, who had taken in Mrs. Hugh, and presently, under cover of the general chatter and Mrs. Hugh's benignant attention to her right-hand neighbour, contrived to inform Polly that he thought her name remarkably pretty.

"Mary ?" she said, enquiringly.

"No, Polly ! There is something very soft and sweet-sounding about it, and really, in these fine days, anything homely and old-fashioned is pretty."

"It has the advantage of being both," Polly said, with a laugh.

"It has. Now my mother is called Gladys Elizabeth Tudor, but my father always calls her ' Nancy.' "

"I like that," remarked Polly, with great decision. It was true. If the Countess of Mallinbro' was called "Nancy," it would create no surprise if her daughter-in-law was named "Polly." All the same, she made up her mind that, if she ever came to be the Honourable Mrs. Eliot Cardella, she would spare no pains to have the name of Polly put aside in favour of May.

Practically, Polly finished the Honourable Eliot off that night, for after dinner she sang—it was only a simple ballad she chose, and her voice was not a fine one, though she sang expressively. He had heard the song scores of times: he had heard it sung by the great Canadian singer at amateur concerts; in drawing-rooms such as this; ground out of barrel-organs, and yet there he was listening to it again, with all his soul in his eyes and a strange yearning and fluttering at his heart, such as Polly's dead perfection by itself could never have had power to bring there.

> What made the assembly shine?
> > Robin Adair!
> What made the ball so fine?
> > Robin was there!
> What, when the play was o'er,
> What made my heart so sore,
> Oh! it was parting with—
> > Robin Adair.

Music had always been a passion with him: that dear quaint old ballad conquered him—the earl's son, and Polly was the daughter of a not too reputable attorney. What an odd world it is!

CHAPTER IV.

A few weeks had passed! Two men were talking in Captain Dickson's room—at least, Eliot Cardella was talking and Dickson lounging in a chair, with a pipe in his mouth and clothed in very much-be-splashed cords and pink, was listening attentively.

"And so you've regularly got let in," he remarked between the puffs at his pipe, when Cardella had finished what he was saying; "and what are you going to do?"

"Dashed if I know," he said, ruefully.

"What'll your father say?"

"Say—he'll tell me to go to the devil, as sure as fate. You see, Dickson, blood is his hobby. He wouldn't care if Cardella and I married girls without a farthing, so long as their pedigrees were all right, but——"

"The daughter of a money-lending country attorney, with rather a shady reputation into the bargain," suggested Dickson. "will hardly be likely to meet with a warm welcome, eh?"

"Just drive him frantic," returned Eliot, promptly.

"'Pon my soul, you are an ass," Dickson laughed, with delightful frankness; "because, you know, I warned you from the beginning what it would lead to."

"So you did; but then I never dreamt of its coming to this."

"But they did. I should exchange into a regiment in India and cut the whole concern, if I were you."

"Oh! I couldn't very well do that," Cardella returned, doubtfully, "what would she think?"

"Oh! well if you want to marry her——" Dickson began.

"Why, I like Polly well enough," he said, hesitatingly, "and, if it was not for the governor, I'd marry her at once and cut the lot, though I'm not exactly——"

"In love with her?" Dickson suggested.

"Yes, just so."

"Well, my dear chap, I don't see how I can help you—I'd go in and make violent love to her myself, if I thought she would throw you over for me, but I am sure she would not."

"You are a much richer man than I am."

"But you've got a handle to your name," rejoined the other. "No, really, I don't see what you are to do but go on with it, or get out of the country and cut the whole concern."

"Cardella's coming to-morrow, for a fortnight's hunting," said Eliot, dismally.

There really seemed to be no loop-hole for escape. The more Eliot Cardella pondered over the fix into which he had got himself, the worse did his situation appear. He had gone through the whole family programme; Mrs. Hugh had attempted—ineffectually, it is true—to embrace him; her husband had wrung his hand and pretended to dash away a few tears at the same time; the two younger sisters at once began to call him Eliot with, what seemed to him, unnecessary distinctness and vain repetition; and the young cub of a brother, who was, he believed, "articled" to his father, had linked his arm in his future brother-in-law's and walked the whole length of the High Street with him—after which he had gone back to barracks in a towering rage and relieved his mind by making a confidant of Dickson, who could see as far through a milestone as most men.

And the cream of the whole affair was that he was not in love with Polly a bit; he liked her well enough, and certainly admired her ; but her belongings—they very nearly maddened him ; what effect they would have upon his father he was afraid to think—the courtly old earl who had married the dark-eyed, olive-skinned daughter of a duke, and who would see no charm in Polly's fresh, fair, apple-blossom loveliness. Why, he would not admire Venus herself if a drop of plebeian blood ran in her veins. What would he think of Polly?

The following day Viscount Cardella arrived at Blank-hampton, and established himself at the sign of the " Golden Swan." Between the brothers there was a striking likeness, but the viscount was larger, fairer, handsomer than Eliot, and with even more of the old earl's courtly grace about him, and decidedly a greater capacity for flirting than his brother.

As soon as he had asked after home, Eliot plunged head foremost into the subject just then uppermost in his thoughts.

" I'm going to get married, Cardella," he announced, abruptly.

" Going to get married, are you ?" returned the viscount, whom for the future we shall call Cardella ; " what a fool you must be," with great cheerfulness. " Is she good-looking ?"

" Very." Eliot wished everything was as satisfactory as Polly's looks."

" Who is she ?"

" Her name is Antrobus."

" Antrobus—never met her. Got any money ? Who's her father ?"

" I don't think she'll have much money," Eliot said, dubiously, " and her father's a lawyer."

' A *lawyer !*" Cardella exclaimed, all the cheerful interest vanishing from face and voice. " You mean a barrister ?"

" I mean a lawyer," returned Eliot, firmly.

" Good life !—what will the earl say ?"

"I daresay he will cut me," Eliot answered, with a nervous laugh, which he tried vainly to make defiant.

"And you've fallen in love?"

"No, I haven't. I like her very well, but—oh! damn it all, Cardella, I've got let in, so I must take the consequences. I always was the fool of the family."

Cardella said nothing, but sat looking into the fire, with a grave face.

"There be all the more money for you if the governor cuts me off," Eliot said, bitterly.

"Don't suggest anything so horrid, my dear old chap; there will be enough for both of us," Cardella answered, soothingly. "I was only thinking, if you really don't care for this girl, it seems a pity to spoil your whole life. I tell you what, you must take me to see her. Can you take me to dinner to-night?"

"They told me to take you—like their check!" he cried, angrily.

"Then send a note up at once. I shall know better what to do when I've seen them."

The result of this was, that Lord Cardella and the Honourable Eliot went that evening to dine *en famille* at the River House. Eliot thought his brother had taken leave of his senses, for the moment he beheld Polly he, metaphorically speaking, fell down and worshipped her, which, with the utter unreasonableness of human nature, he highly resented. Hang it all, but it was too bad of Cardella to go poaching on his manor like that. Of course, if he chose to marry Polly, the earl's pleasure or displeasure would make but small difference to him, since the personal property was nothing in comparison with the entailed estates. Therefore, when Cardella went back to his hotel, Eliot turned in the direction of the barracks with a sulky "good night," at which the viscount laughed out aloud.

It happened that the next afternoon, when returning from hunting, he fell in with Dickson, and after a little desultory chat, suddenly remarked:

"By the way, Dickson, can you tell me anything about these

people my young brother's got mixed up with?"—Eliot was five-and-twenty.

" I don't know them myself," Dickson replied, " but I understand the father's a third-rate attorney, who does a good deal in the money-lending line."

" Ah !" murmured the viscount, comprehensively.

But Captain Dickson's information made no difference whatever in his manner towards the family at the River House. He told Mrs. Hugh that Polly was a perfect aristocrat, at which Mrs. Hugh beamed so intensely that the viscount caught himself wondering what he should do if any part of her skin gave way.

He assailed Polly on her weakest points. He from the first refused to call her Polly, as a name utterly unsuited to her delicate style of beauty : he invariably called her *May !* He monoplised her altogether. Eliot looked sulkily on, whilst Cardella sauntered about the town with his *fiancée*, or hung over her at the piano. His horses stood idle in their stables, for though he had gone to Blankhampton for the express purpose of hunting, he spent all his mornings in the drawing-room at the River House, *tête-à-tête* with Polly, and invariably to the intense astonishment and surprise of Mrs. Hugh, when he made his appearance in the dining-room, and begged, with the courtly grace which had broken a score or so of hearts, for luncheon.

Polly's manner to Eliot grew colder and colder. He was all very well, she argued, but *only* a second son after all. Lord Cardella was more her style ; the way he made love—and he made very desperate love indeed—was so different to Eliot, who had seized hold of her, and almost crushed her to death. Lord Cardella was accustomed to lift her hand to his lips in a manner Polly thought most entrancing.

Of course, to be the Honourable Mrs. Eliot Cardella, would be an enviable position, but the Countess of Mallinbro'—ah ! that was her true sphere !

And so the days crept on, lengthening as they passed, and Cardella still lingered at Blankhampton. The breach between the brothers grew wider and wider, and bets began to pass freely among the Cuirassiers as to which would come off the victor. They all thought them both a couple of fools for their pains, but, of course, they knew their own business best.

Cardella's devotion to Polly grew more and more tender, Eliot's face sulkier, and his temper more uncertain, until, at length, Mr. Antrobus took him into the library, and asked if it was true that his income depended entirely on his father's caprice?

"Quite true," Eliot returned, "except for ten thousand under my mother's settlement."

"Then I think it will be best for the engagement between you and my daughter to come to an end," he said, gravely. " I am not a rich man, and I have three other children to provide for. It had best end."

"I decline to give her up," Eliot answered, hotly, "excepting she writes and tells me she does not care for me."

"I think she will do so," said Mr. Antrobus, quietly ; " I believe I am doing what is best for the happiness of you both."

When Eliot got back to barracks, he found his brother in the ante-room, having, for a wonder, gone to lunch there, instead of to the River House. During the meal a note was brought in, addressed in Polly's well-known caligraphy :

The Hon. Eliot Cardella,
Cuirassiers.

Eliot knew its purport before he opened it. It ran :

MY DEAR ELIOT.—

    I think my father's decision is for the best, but I hope we sha'l remain all our lives sincere friends.

Believe me, always truly yours,
MARY ANTROBUS.

That was the end of it. He put the note in his pocket, and asked Cardella presently to go up to his room—

"I've something to show you."

Cardella, who had resolutely refused to acknowledge any cloud between his brother and himself, followed him, and Eliot put the note into his hands with a laugh and one word—"Superseded."

" Look here, Eliot," he said, when he had read it, " I have got you out of the most confounded scrape you ever were in in all your life. I shall go back to town this afternoon, and I hope you'll be as grateful as you ought to be, when you've got over this a little," at which Eliot Cardella burst into a fit of hearty, uncontrollable laughter.

The sulks, like the devotion, had been put on, but though the brothers had been playing at cross-purposes, their plan had succeeded.

I will leave the reader to imagine how the family at the River House felt the next day, when Mrs. Hugh received a card :

VISCOUNT CARDELLA.

P.P.C.

THE LADY-KILLER-IN-CHIEF.

Chapter I.

"Most awfully shabby," said Dorothy St. George, calmly; "but then, since I have not another, what am I to do? I am not a spider, therefore I cannot evolve a new gown out of my own inner consciousness."

"Let me give you a gown—two gowns," pleaded Jack Sinclair, flushing a little under the girl's steady gaze, yet looking very handsome and soldierly in the brilliant June sunshine.

"My good Jack," returned Miss St. George, quietly, "have you sufficient money to pay your debts?"

"No," he admitted, unwillingly.

"Then how can you afford to buy me gowns? And how can you imagine for one moment that I should take them, if you could?"

"If you loved me——" he began.

"My good Jack," said the girl again, gravely, lifting her azure eyes leisurely to his, "it seems to me you are a great deal too well assured of the state of my feelings. Some people, you know, have a habit of counting their chickens before they are hatched."

"Oh, Dolly, you do love me!" he cried.

"Perhaps, just a little," half indifferently; "certainly not enough to let you buy me—*clothes!*" with a sudden shamed flush at the bare idea of it.

Jack Sinclair sighed impatiently. He had no such pride himself; but then, to be sure, no cavalry officers ever have, except they are rank men. He, that very morning, had shaved himself in Broughton's room. because Broughton had just had his razors ground; he had passed on to the next room to sponge the remains of the lather off his face, because Broughton was using his sponge and basin for a like purpose; he had borrowed a collar-stud on his way back to his own quarters, because his laundress had sent his shirt home minus a button at the throat; and before he finished dressing he had lent his last clean cotton tie to Dickson, who had got two days' leave; he had surrendered his hair brushes to Squints, who had walked in for no apparent reason—perhaps because some one was using his—and had helped Ponto out of a difficulty by the loan of a shell jacket. Thus Jack Sinclair, accustomed to regard his belongings and those of his brother officers as public property, could not understand why the suggestion that he should buy his *fiancée* a gown—which, goodness knows, she stood sorely in need of—need bring that shamed flush to her proud face.

"Then how will you do?" he asked at length, rather ruefully.

"Stay at home," she laughed; then sang, in a rich mellow voice,

> "Stay, stay at home, my heart, and rest,
> Home-keeping hearts are happiest!"

"Oh, I daresay!" Jack put in, very ruefully indeed. But the girl only laughed and sang on:

> "For those that wander, they know not where,
> Are full of trouble and full of care;
> To stay at home is best."

"But, Dolly, my darling," he interrupted, "couldn't Mrs. St. George lend you a dress?"

"Mrs. St. George," answered Dorothy, regarding him gravely, yet with laughter in her brilliant eyes, "is possessed of *one* presentable gown besides the one you see her in every day."

"I'm sure she would lend it to you," cried Jack.

"It is a *moiré antique*," said Dorothy, as if there need be nothing more said upon the subject.

"Well, what of that? I remember, the last time I was at home, my mother was wearing one, a bright green one it was, with white-pot buttons—she said they were porcelain, but I knew better."

" Ah !" remarked Dorothy, without much interest.

" Then you'll come to the sports to-morrow, darling !"

" *The moiré*," returned Dorothy, " is of the most startling rose-colour you ever saw. Why, Jack, all the women would be laughing at us."

" Let them," he rejoined, fiercely ; " who cares ?"

" I do, for one. No, Jack : some day, when we are rich, I will go to the sports; and I'll give a cup, and you shall run for it."

" I don't see why you can't come in the gown you've got on," he grumbled, " it looks awfully jolly :" but, all the same, he was very well aware that the garment in question was very, very shabby ; it was so entirely out of keeping with its wearer. Jack thought, as he watched her that lovely June day, that he had never seen a more perfect picture than she made as she sat upon the river's bank, the willows and the turf making a background against which her radiant loveliness shone out more like a gem in a dark setting than anything else he could think of. She had taken off her hat, and the sunshine streamed down upon her golden head, giving the heavy braids the appearance of a diadem. Jack wished passionately that he could have given her a crown of rubies and diamonds ; and yet he knew that no gold would ever become her as did these imperial coils of lustrous hair, no sapphires could ever equal the beauty of her azure eyes.

And yet she was so very, very shabby ; her brown stuff gown was positively threadbare—" bright as a sixpence," she said. One little foot was visible beneath the frill of her gown, and an inch or two of a slender ankle : they, the foot and the ankle, were all right, Jack had admired them dozens of times ; but the boot which covered the foot, oh, it made him absolutely shiver ! —seven-and-sixpence a pair, with square toes that seemed to be of an inquiring turn ! Ugh ! Jack looked from them to his own patent leather and canvass boots at thirty-five shillings a pair, and thought of the dozen or two of others which stood all in a neat row in the lowest compartment of his cupboard, and he had the grace to feel ashamed of himself. If Dorothy St. George could case her little slender feet in such boots as those and keep out of debt, why need he, a great hulking brute, with feet like potatoes, have a bootmaker's bill as long as his arm?

He looked, too, at her little hands folded idly before her, such pretty hands, with pink-tinted filbert nails; then his eyes fell upon a certain mark along the forefinger of the one which lay uppermost, and, bending down, he kissed it as if he would fain kiss that disfiguring seam away. Oh, why should she have to work so hard, whilst his sisters, not half so fair, dawdled their time away, and gave dresses to their maid such as Dorothy could never afford to buy? Oh, why should it be? A flush mounted to the young man's brow, and his eyes sank before the glory of hers: the question was easy to answer. He had " sown the wind " in a long course of reckless extravagance, in the raising of his father's just anger; now he was " reaping the whirlwind " in banishment from home, and in the pain of knowing that between Dorothy St. George and him lay a long array of debts which he had no money to pay.

And there are people who say our sins do not find us out in this world!

" Oh, my darling!" he cried, with a sudden burst of passion, " how I will make up to you for all this some day!"

" Some day," she repeated, wistfully; " if, by the time you come into your kingdom, you have not repented, Jack!"

" Repented! Why?

" You will be rich, I still poor."

" Supposing I remained always poor and you became very rich, would you desert me, Dolly?"

" I cannot say, I am sure," she laughed. " I have always been so awfully poor, you see, that if I were suddenly lifted up in the world I might tiptilt my nose even at you."

" Ah, you don't mean that," he said, coolly.

" ' There's many a true word spoken in jest,' " she quoted, gravely.

"'Then, thank God, there is no chance of it!" he cried vehemently.

"No, indeed," with a smile, half bitter, half sad. " Do you know, Jack, that I don't know who I am? I never shall know it."

" Yes, yes; you told me. Don't talk about it."

" But I must talk about it. I'll tell you now," she answered. " To begin at the beginning, I must tell you my mother's name was Meredith. At sixteen she was left to the care of her uncle, a clergyman in North Wales. Her father also had been a clergyman. She had not been many weeks at Llangwylt before she met my father, who was staying in the neighbourhood for the trout-fishing. He fell in love with her and married her; my great-uncle married them himself. After the marriage they went abroad; and one day it came out quite by chance that he had been married under a false name—George St. George. He assured her that the legality of the marriage was certain. He told her also that his reason for deceiving her was because his uncle, who had very large unentailed estates, had arranged a marriage for him; and if he heard anything of my mother, would probably cut him off with but a very small property. My mother never troubled herself about it; she loved him, and she had perfect faith in him, and so a few months passed over. He seems, although quite young, being only seven-and-twenty at the time of the marriage, to have had a most passionate and unforgiving temper, as my mother found to her cost—and mine; for one day she angered him so much that he left her. I fancy she had been in a passion herself, and had cried out that she no longer loved him. Whatever it was, he never forgot it or forgave it. ' You shall never see me again,' he told her; ' *and you shall never know who you are.*' From that day to this she has never seen him. For anything we know to the contrary, he may have been a chimney sweeper. Mother went back to Llangwylt, and I was born there; and when her uncle died six years ago we came here, to starve upon seventy pounds a year," she broke off, bitterly.

" Did she never try to find him out ?"

"Uncle Meredith wished to do so but mother was too proud."

"What a strange story!" Jack said, thoughtfully; "and, oh, by Jove! what a beastly temper he must have had!"

"Ah! that's where mine comes from," rejoined Dorothy, calmly. "Who's that, Jack?" as a boat passed them, a graceful outrigger, with a man in white flannels, who came as near to the bank as he could venture, evidently to stare at her, and who, after a salutation to Jack, sculled away, and was out of sight in no time.

"That, my darling, is the handsomest man in the service," Jack answered. "We call him the Lady-Killer-in-Chief."

Chapter II.

The Lady-Killer-in-Chief had changed his flannels for his ordinary clothes—light grey trousers, and a coat of grey velveteen. He certainly, as he sauntered down the High Street at Blankhampton, merited the homage which was paid to his personal appearance when his brother officers spoke of him as the handsomest man in the service. The only fault in his face was its extreme coldness : cold classic features ; cold blonde hair, irreproachably parted down the middle, and brushed straight away behind his ears without a hair being out of place : cold hazel eyes, large and beautiful in themselves ; and a cold smile, like the flickering of a feeble winter sun over snow-topped mountains. An utterly cold manner, too—which to women seemed irresistible—and perhaps the most cutting caustic wit that had ever made itself felt in the mess-room of the Blankhampton Barracks. Swaggering leisurely down the High Street he met with Dickson, who, as a matter of course, stopped.

"Where have you been?"

"I've been for a pull. The river's awfully jolly to-day, and, by-the-bye, Dickson "—plunging at once into the subject uppermost in his thoughts—" can you tell me who that girl is Sinclair goes about with—tall girl with golden hair?"

" I don't know her name. I believe Sinclair's going to marry her."

" Going to marry her ! Ah ! is it settled?"

" I really don't know. She's a very handsome girl," remarked Dickson, carelessly.

" Uncommonly," Montagu replied, with what, for him, was great warmth. " And so Sinclair's serious ?"

" Oh, quite so !" adding with a laugh, " has she ' taken ' you rather ? No use ; she's awfully in love with Sinclair."

" Pooh! I'll cut him out in a week," cried Montagu, confidently.

" I don't believe she'll look at you."

" Won't she? Well, you'll see ;" and then the two men parted, and went their respective ways, neither of them in the least aware that the subject of their conversation was just within the door of the shop behind them, and had heard their whole conversation, with proud scorn filling her violet eyes, and utter contempt on her imperious mouth.

Bryan Montagu did not find the task he had set himself altogether easy to accomplish, for he could not succeed in making a start. In the first place he did not know who she was, nor where she lived ; and since he never met her anywhere he could not obtain an introduction. However, at last, he happened to meet her with Sinclair in a shop, and asked boldly to be introduced.

Miss St. George was very gracious to him. She smiled so enchantingly that Jack straightway went off into a towering rage and scolded her all the way home, at which she laughed more heartily than he had ever heard her laugh in his life. To add to his wrath, Montagu informed him during dinner that Miss St. George was really very decent-looking ; " and I believe I passed you on the river one day last week," he ended.

" Yes, and you turned and stared at her as if she'd been some little milliner-girl," Jack returned, sulkily.

" The penalty of beauty, my dear chap," laughed Montagu, lightly. " Now I assure you I'm so accustomed to be ogled that

I should feel quite uncomfortable with people who didn't admire me."

" Miss St. George doesn't admire you at all events," retorted Jack, with a short laugh ; " for she says she never saw such a ' screw ' in her life."

At which Bryan Montagu, who was really a very pretty oar, though, perhaps, with a slight tendency to " screw," was, for once, taken aback ; and registered an inward vow that before many days were over he would pay Miss St. George out with interest for that unflattering remark. And pay her out—how ? As he had made many another girl suffer before—broken-hearted for the cold hazel eyes which for her had been wont to have no coldness in their clear depths ; for the straight-featured classic face which had made itself her heaven ; for the sound of the smooth persuasive voice which would fall upon her ears never more, or if perchance it did so, fraught only with slighting indifference, more hard to bear than silence. That was the plan Mr. Bryan Montagu marked out as Miss St. George's punishment.

Accordingly, the following afternoon, instead of betaking himself to the club, or his more favourite river, he turned in the direction of the village in which Mrs. St. George's little house was ; and, as luck would have it, just as he passed the Cotherstone's house he saw Miss St. George emerge from the gate of her cottage, and turn down the lane leading to the river. He followed instantly, and reached her just as she was about to pass through the little gate which opened into the River Fields.

Mr. Montagu lifted his hat with his most fascinating smile. Miss St. George blushed becomingly, and half drooped her splendid eyes. Mr. Montagu thought he had never before beheld so lovely a face. Miss St. George thought—well, she *looked* as if she found herself in Arcadia.

" You are going for a walk ?" he asked.

" Well, no. I am going to sit by the edge of the river and read," she replied.

" May I come with you and talk instead ?" he asked imploringly.

"Oh yes, if you like," she replied, calmly, thinking what a lucky thing it was that Jack was safely out of the road, being on duty that day.

Any one who could have heard their conversation that afternoon must have laughed, even if it had been Jack Sinclair himself; they were so awfully polite, to begin with ; each seemed to be trying how fascinating he or she could be ; each seemed so desperately anxious to make the other pleased. They got along like a house on fire, which is, as every one knows, a tolerably rapid rate. In fact, they got on so well that Mr. Montagu had already advanced as far as personal compliments ere Miss St. George found out she really *must* be going home, with an emphasis on the " must," by which she evidently intended to convey to him the fact that only stern necessity compelled her to move at all. But they got still further before they reached the gate of Mrs. St. George's cottage; for after a little circumlocution, she promised to meet him at the same time and place the following afternoon. All the same, she raised but very little objection before she consented, and Mr. Montagu felt he had never come across a cherry so ripe and ready to fall into his mouth.

" Hollo, Sinclair !" he called out to Jack, whom he met in the square. " Down in the mouth, eh ? Ah, it's an awful nuisance not being able to get out of the square, isn't it ? Particularly when there's a nice young woman half-a-mile off waiting for you. And she *did* look so nice this afternoon."

The hot anger leapt into Jack Sinclair's grey eyes, but his heart grew cold as lead within him, for he had never felt very sure of Dorothy ; and if Montagu made up his mind to go in for her, he knew well enough that he would spare no pains to accomplish the desirable attainment or putting his (Jack's that is) nose out of joint.

" How do you know ? " he growled.

" Because she has been with me for the last three hours," Montagu returned, coolly.

" I don't believe it ; " poor Jack thundered ; but all the same he felt from the other's manner that it was true.

" Just as you like, of course, my dear chap," said Montagu, carelessly ; " but go along the path leading through the River Fields to-morrow afternoon between three and four, and you will see for yourself."

Sinclair turned away without answering, for Montagu's quiet manner had left him without hope. Of course the following afternoon he went, and saw for himself that his comrade had spoken truly. There, just visible above the river's bank, was Dorothy's hatless golden head, and in suspicious nearness to it Montagu's sleek blonde *caput;* and whilst he stood there watching and half-hidden by the hedge, her merry laugh rang out upon the still summer air in a peal which re-echoed in Jack's heart like the death-knell of all his dearest hopes. Oh, he was reaping the whirlwind, and no mistake about it !

" Now, did you do as I advised?" Montagu asked him at mess that night, in a tone of sneering triumph. " Are you convinced ? "

" Hang you ! " cried poor Jack, passionately.

" By no means," returned Montagu, calmly, going on with his dinner as if that was the chief object of his existence. " You shouldn't allow yourself to fly in such transports of rage, my dear chap; it's not good form, to begin with ; it's bad for the digestion—bad every way. You're a deuced good fellow, Sinclair, but you go into everything with such terrible earnestness. It spoils you, my dear fellow ; and it will be getting you into trouble one of these days, take my word for it."

But during the weeks which followed Jack's rage had time enough to cool. As far as Dorothy was concerned, he had resigned in favour of Bryan Montagu, who had contrived to get the *entrée* to the house, and who pretty nearly lived there. Twice Dorothy had written to know why he kept away, and to ask him to come ; and both times he had sent a formal reply, declining the invitation. He scarcely went outside the barracks, and when he did so, went between six and seven—a time when he knew Dorothy was very unlikely to be out.

At last, however, he was one day compelled to go into the town early in the afternoon ; and about half-way down the

High Street he saw Dorothy and Montagu coming on the same side of the street.   They were close upon him before he perceived them, but he did not hesitate a moment.   He turned sharply to the right, and crossed over to the other side without so much as a look, and without any recognition whatever. Dorothy turned very white, but she kept a brave front to the world, and laughed it off as usual.   Montagu tackled Jack upon the subject that evening.

" Now, I tell you what it is, Sinclair," he said, leaning back in his chair, and surveying Jack with much amusement in his eyes, " your behaviour is what *I* call uncommonly shabby. Blow-hot, blow-cold, you know."

" Mind your own business," returned Jack, sulkily.

" Ah, conscience touching you up a bit, eh ?   Well, it's what you must expect, whilst you behave as you've done lately.   Oh, Sinclair, you've a great deal to answer for !   You've brought desolation into a once happy home, grief to a once happy heart. Of course, it's right and proper that you should pay attention to the fair sex ; their youth and beauty demand it ; the honour of your regiment requires it; but you should not concentrate your attentions, my dear chap—you. should not concentrate : they should be more general and less marked."

But Jack was as sulky as a bear with a sore head, and would have no argument on the subject, so Montagu was obliged to have it all to himself.   Not that that had any effect on his tongue ; he never let Jack rest a moment.

" Ah, you may well look so blue," he would cry, " with such a conscience as you must have—enough to give you the blue devils for the rest of your life !   Think of the young affections you have blighted, think of the irreparable injury your heartless conduct has wrought, think of the gay hearth now made desolate, the light heart which will be light no more. Look at him, gentlemen "—appealing, after the manner of a counsel in a court of justice, to the grinning officers round about—" look at the depraved individual who stands before you, the male flirt.   Ah, well well, Sinclair, of all my sins, and they are many, I do not carry on my conscience the shameful weight of young fresh affections trifled with, won, and thrown aside."

Poor Jack! he met Dorothy often enough now. Dorothy always alone, with no Bryan Montagu in attendance, but with, oh, such a blanched face, such a world of woe in the azure eyes, that if Jack had wished for revenge, there it was. But Jack wished for nothing of the kind. The sight of his false love's white face only made him miserable, so utterly miserable, that he could have fallen down upon his knees in the very street, and prayed her to try and look happier; he could have choked the very life out of Montagu as he sat sneering and jibing at the mess-table, only that would not give him back to Dorothy, or take away that piteous woe from her face. And then Montagu took his long leave, and Dorothy grew whiter and whiter, until at length he missed her altogether, and feared she must be ill.

Once or twice he felt half inclined to ignore the past and go and see her, but the remembrance that she was fretting for Montagu kept him back. She wanted Montagu, and Jack Sinclair would be of no use; and so when his turn came for long leave he went away, sore at heart as was ever Dorothy St. George, with her's breaking for love of the man who bore the nick-name of the Lady-Killer-in-Chief.

Chapter III.

THE Cuirassiers had left Blankhampton for Colchester, *en route* for India, and Dorothy St. George had seen nothing more of her two lovers since the day that Jack Sinclair went away on long leave. True, Bryan Montagu had called twice; but Dorothy had not seen him, being indisposed—otherwise lying on her bed in the exhaustion which usually comes after violent weeping. Mr. Montagu had stayed half an hour each time, talking serenely with Mrs. St. George, and left, with graceful regrets that Miss St. George was not well enough to see him; and that had been all, that was the end. And yet she could not forget the past; she was not allowed to go out of the house, for a terrible cough had taken hold of her; she could not rest anywhere : she thought herself that she was going mad. As the year drew to a close, and the day fixed for the embarkation of the regiment drew near, she persuaded her mother to take a daily paper, that she might see the latest, and indeed last, intelligence of them. She was not hard to persuade, for a great dread had come over her, lest her child, who was all she had in the world, should be taken from her; and so for a time the paper was left at the house daily. The news about the Cuirassiers was but scanty, and Dorothy used to fling the paper down and sigh piteously each day, hoping that the next would tell more. And at last the sight of their own name caught her eye, and she for the first time looked at the paper with an interest unconnected with the Royal Regiment of Cuirassiers.

If this should meet the eye of Florence Meredith, who in September, 1s—, was married in the parish church of Llangwylt, North Wales, by the Rev. David Meredith, to George St. George, gentleman, she is requested to communicate with Messrs. Owen, Lucas, and Co., Gray's-inn-road, London, when she will hear of something to her advantage.

Dorothy read it aloud to her mother.

" What does it mean? " she cried, thinking it might have something to do with—with—

" It is to say your father is dead," Mrs. St. George replied, an ashen hue overspreading her face.

" And you will write ? "

" At once," she said, in a trembling voice. " If he has relented, things may be very different for us."

Two days passed by, and no reply. Dorothy was wildly curious, fretfully impatient, and, when on the second morning the postman passed the house, intensely disappointed.

" I believe it is a hoax," she cried.

But it was not so. Towards noon an imperative knock resounded through the house, and the woman who had gone every day to help since Dorothy's illness ushered into the tiny sitting-room a small grave gentleman, clad in black, and with an irreproachable white neckcloth.

" Mrs. St. George? " he said, with a grave bow.

" Yes," she answered, rather faintly.   " Are you——"

" My name is Lucas.   May I ask if this is your daughter? "

"That is Miss St. George," she answered, haughtily : the words "your daughter " rather angered her.

"Pardon me," said the little old gentleman, politely, " this lady," taking Dorothy's hand and leading her a step forward, "is the Countess of Beaurivage.   You are now the countess dowager ;" at which theatrically-told piece of news Dorothy burst out laughing, and her mother sat down and quietly fainted away.

Not only had great honour come upon them, but also great wealth.   The lately deceased earl had managed, shortly before his death, to pick a violent quarrel with the heir-presumptive, and to annoy him had left a will giving an exact account of his marriage and what had taken place since, and leaving every farthing he possessed to his daughter ; his wife he left unnoticed ; but then, as Dorothy said, it didn't much matter. And so the sailing of the *Crocodile* passed apparently out of mind.

The romantic story of the Earl of Beaurivage's marriage and the succession of the beautiful young girl to the title was naturally enough wafted into all the papers.   Those containing it were handed on board the *Crocodile* at Malta, and read almost simultaneously by the two men who had known Dorothy St. George most intimately in her days of poverty.

"Think what you've missed, Sinclair," drawled Montagu ; " who would have thought of little St. George turning out a countess in her own right?   By Jove ! it almost equals a novel !"

" I suppose you'll find it worth while to go back and marry her now ?" said Jack, bitterly.

"Pooh!   Not I!   I amused myself with her ; but as for marrying——" He did not finish the sentence, for Jack flew at him like a tiger, and flung him head-foremost down the companion ladder ; whence Mr. Bryan Montagu was picked up extensively bruised, and very careful to give Jack as wide a berth as was compatible with the capabilities of the ship.

"Curse you!" Jack shouted after him. "I don't believe she would have you at any price!" And yet it puzzled him to guess why Dorothy had acted as she did.

One week the regiment remained after landing, at a place called Deolalee; and when they went forward to Unapore, they marched without Mr. Bryan Montagu, who returned to England by the next steamer. He had seen enough of India during these seven days, he said; but Jack Sinclair always felt, with a thrill of satisfaction, that he had something to do with his return. He had not forgotten the time, not far distant, when Bryan Montagu had talked of the delights of India with what was nothing short of rapture.

Chapter IV.

Three years passed away before Jack Sinclair returned to his native shores. He did so then because he had come into his inheritance; for his father had gone into that higher region where such things as earthly riches and troubles have no place. But he died, blessing Jack to the last; and Jack had been sent for, reaching his home, alas, too late.

And so he was no longer Jack Sinclair the dragoon, troubled with numerous debts and other difficulties, but Sinclair of Cleve, the owner of a good estate, the head of a good county family. It was perfectly astonishing how nice every one seemed to find him. The self-same people who had looked very much askance at "that dreadfully wild fellow, Jack Sinclair," found out that, after all, young men will be young men, and that wild-oats are best sown. Some ladies even went so far as to affirm that the wildest young men make the best husbands. *Those* were ladies with marriageable daughters.

But they angled and baited their traps for him in vain. Jack would have none of them. His mother remained the undisturbed mistress of Cleve, and his sisters declared he must have left his heart in India.

Jack said, " Exactly so ; " and then they wondered why he hadn't married her ? Effie suggested that perhaps she was married already ; but the more strong-minded Laura scouted that idea altogether. She was sure Jack would not be such a fool as that. No, depend upon it, Jack did not feel altogether satisfied about her. Perhaps her family was not to his liking. That the lady might be unwilling never entered their heads. Was not Jack " Sinclair of Cleve," with seven thousand a year ?

However, their conjectures brought them no nearer to the truth, since Jack turned a deaf ear to all their hints, and invariably answered them with the same word, " Exactly."

" You ought to marry," Laura told him one day.

" Exactly," said Jack, easily.

" Then why don't you ?" she asked. " I'm sure you're in love."

" Exactly."

To say the least of it, the answer was discouraging.

However, in love or out of it, Jack did not change his condition. He went about in the character of an eligible bachelor, and seemed to find the position a very pleasant one; at least, he certainly made no attempt to alter it. He had returned from India in the summer, and during the autumn and winter seemed as if he was trying to make up for the society he had missed during his sojourn in the East. The family at Cleve saw but little of him until Christmas, when he remained at home a whole fortnight. At the end of that time he went northwards to pay a long-promised visit at the house of a man who had been in the Cuirassiers when he first joined the regiment. He had a long and cold journey, arriving about an hour before dinner. Major Holroyd went out to the door to meet him, with a thousand apologies for not having been at the station, three miles away.

" The fact was, my bailiff came in just as I was starting; and as his business was urgent—roof of a cottage tumbled in worse luck !—why, I was obliged to go round and make some arrangements for the family until it can be attended to," he explained.

"It really did not matter," Jack answered. "How is Mrs. Holroyd? Oh, there you are !" as he followed his host into the inner hall. "How are you? And how's our old friend, Ethel ?"

"Grown a monster," Mrs. Holroyd laughed. "You'll see her presently, no doubt. You'll have a cup of tea, Captain Sinclair ? I remember your old weakness for it. I think you must know every one here, excepting perhaps Lady Beaurivage."

Jack turned from a young lady who was greeting him effusively with a great start. Yes, there she was! The one love of his life. No longer pale, no longer with that look of hunted pain in her great azure eyes ; but calm, smiling, self-possessed; and sitting near to her was Bryan Montagu. Jack determined, as he held out his hand with a grave bow, that his visit at Lark's Nest would be cut short on the following day by a plea of "urgent private affairs."

"Then you do know her ?" Mrs. Holroyd cried, seeing the friendly, yet half-distant salutation.

"I used to know Captain Sinclair," answered Lady Beaurivage, distinctly, "very well indeed ; but, for some reason or other, he cut me."

"Dead as a door-nail," Montagu affirmed.

"I cannot believe that," cried Mrs. Holroyd, emphatically.

"It is quite true," answered Lady Beaurivage, calmly ; "ask him if it is not so."

"I won't ask you, Captain Sinclair, because I have too much faith in you to believe it," said the hostess.

"Unfortunately it is perfectly true," Jack returned, gravely.

"Why ?" some one asked, thoughtlessly.

"Why ?" he repeated. "Oh ! you must get Lady Beaurivage to tell you that !" at which the young countess blushed so vividly crimson that every one laughed ; and Mrs. Holroyd, to spare her further confusion, made a move, and carried her off to dress.

" Of course there's no truth in all that nonsense about your cutting her ?" Major Holroyd asked, when he and Jack were left in possession of the hall.

" Oh yes ; it's true enough," Jack answered, bitterly. " If I'd known she was staying here, I shouldn't have come, and as it is, I think I had better leave you to-morrow."

" But what on earth has she done ?"

" It was just this way : Lady Beaurivage was engaged to me, and jilted me—for Montagu. That's the whole story, Holroyd, and the less I see of her for the future, the better."

" Then why doesn't she marry Montagu ?"

" Sure I don't know," Jack returned, forlornly.

" Because," Major Holroyd continued, " he has been running after her for three years, to my certain knowledge. He worships the very ground she walks on, and she always *seems* as if she detests him. To be sure, one never can tell what a woman is up to," he ended ; " but, at all events, Jack, I don't see that they need drive you away from us ; you've done nothing to be ashamed of."

" No, exactly," Jack answered.

" Then you'll stay ?"

" Yes, I'll stay," holding out his hand and gripping his friend's hard, a display of feeling of which he repented instantly, and marched off upstairs, wishing he hadn't made such a fool of himself. All the same, Major Holroyd, standing, staring reflectively into the fire, did not consider he had made a fool of himself at all.

" Queer concern that," he muttered. " I'll keep an eye upon them."

So he did, but he learnt remarkably little. The intercourse between Lady Beaurivage and Mr. Montagu was exactly as it had been aforetime—abject worship on his part, persistent snubbing on hers. Jack Sinclair kept aloof from both of them, and spent most of his time with small Ethel, a child of ten, who had been a great pet of his in the old days, before he fell in love with Dorothy St. George, otherwise Lady Beaurivage— and time slipped on.

He came in one afternoon after a long day's hunting, tired and wet, having missed all the others and returned alone. Just as he reached the hall he saw Lady Beaurivage, with three of the children clinging about her, coming down the stairs; and as he never met her, if by any chance he could possibly avoid her, he slipped into the library, thinking they would be going on to the drawing-room. A moment later, however, the door of the library opened, and the four, not seeing the red-coated figure in one of the deep window-seats, entered, and went to the other end of the room, where was the fire-place. His first impulse was to get up and go away, but he could not do that without speaking to Dorothy, and if he did so, Ethel would instantly entreat him to stay; therefore he remained where he was, almost hidden by the curtain, and listened patiently while Dorothy related a long fairy tale.

"And then they were married, and lived happily ever after," said the soft voice, tenderly, bringing the story to an abrupt termination.

"Well, and what then?" Dick asked, eagerly; "what then, Dolly?"

"Oh! nothing more than that," she answered, with a soft laugh : "what more would you have?"

"People are always happy when they get married," put in Ethel, wisely.

"Who told you that?" Dorothy laughed.

"Captain Sinclair said so, because this morning I told him Jinks was going to be married, and he said, 'Happy Jinks!' Would you like to be married, Dolly?"

"It would quite depend," Dorothy said, guardedly.

"If it was Mr. Montagu?" Ethel suggested.

"Oh no, not at all!" very emphatically.

"If it was Captain Sinclair? He's very nice, you know, Dolly."

"Is he?"

"I like Captain Sinclair best of any one I know," Ethel returned, critically; "and he's got the prettiest dressing-case I ever saw. And he's going to buy me a watch and chain when he goes back to town—a real one you know ; so, Dick, you may have the old one mother's keeping for me. I say, Dolly, if it was Captain Sinclair?"

" Captain Sinclair would not have me," said Lady Beaurivage, with what sounded to Jack like a sigh.

" I'll ask him, if you like," Ethel cried, obligingly.

" No, thank you," with a genuine laugh.

" Tell us another story, Dolly, do," put in Jim, imploringly.

" Do you know that the bell has rung for the nursery tea ?" Lady Beaurivage asked, " and that you were promised some honey ?"

" I forgot. Come, Dick, Ethel, let us be off:" and away the three youngsters scampered, leaving the library to the other two occupants.

" And so they got married and lived happily ever after," said one of them, moving forward into the firelight.

Lady Beaurivage started violently, and jumped up from her seat.

" I did not know you were there," she exclaimed, confusedly, wondering anxiously if he had heard what Ethel said about himself.

" My little friend, Ethel," he said, coolly, " asked you if you would like to marry Montagu, and you said, ' Oh no, not at all !' If it is not too impertinent, may I ask why you did not give the same reply when she asked you another question ?"

Lady Beaurivage remained silent, and Jack continued :

" Would not the same reply have done? And how is it you have not married Montagu ?"

" Ugh !" cried Lady Beaurivage, without much dignity, but with a very large amount of expression, at which Jack laughed out aloud. It might be that the laugh gave her courage, but certain it is that she put out her two pretty hands with an imploring gesture, and faltered, " Don't be cross with me any more, Jack !" She seemed to have parted with her dignity altogether.

A heart of adamant must have melted before those azure eyes shining through a mist of tears ; and Jack's heart was not of an adamantine quality, so far as Dorothy was concerned; and so somehow his arms found their way round her, and the golden head was pillowed on his breast.

" What did you do it for ?" he asked after a while, without much regard for grammar.

And then she told him of the conversation she overheard, and how she had determined to pay the Lady-Killer out in his own coin, never considering that Jack would object.

" And I thought afterwards," she stammered, " that perhaps you only wanted an excuse to get out of it."

" Oh, my darling !" Jack cried, reproachfully.

And so they were married, and lived happily ever afterwards.

THE SAD HISTORY OF BOB SABRETASCHE.

"Fools climb to fall : fond hopes, like seeled doves for want of better light, mount, till they end their flight with falling. '—*J. Reading.*

WHEN Bob Sabretasche was a youngster old Sabretasche *père* was frequently asked a question, to which he always made Bob reply—this was the question :

" And what are you going to make of Bob ?"

The major invariably passed the question on to head-quarters.

" Bob ! what are you going to be?"

' A soldier," was Bob's prompt reply.

And what branch of the service are you going into, pray ?" he would further question, with many signs of suppressed delight on his sun-burnt face.

" Well—I won't be a dirty mud-crusher "—only five-year-old Bob pronounced it *cwusher.*

" Now, sir," or " Now, madam," as the case might be, the major would cry, with honest pride, " there's a proof for you that ' what's bred in the bone will come out in the flesh.' "

" You need not be vulgar, major," put in Mrs. Sabretasche, with quiet severity. Mrs. Sabretasche was a large, fair, placid woman, possessed of very decided ideas as to right and wrong; but without sufficient energy of mind or body to do more than utter a feeble protest against the latter, while she did nothing at all to further the cause of the former. She folded her large white hands, lifted her expressionless blue eyes to her laughing husband, and remarked quietly—as if she was saying " How fine a day it is "—

" You need not be vulgar, major."

" Pooh ! nonsense, Maria, my dear—nonsense ! The lad's vocation in life is chosen—it was born with him. Bless you—he is but just five years old."

"Six next month," interposed the wife of his bosom, indifferently.

"Well, nearly six then—what matter does it make? He's a mere baby still; and," turning to his visitor triumphantly, "I assure you he runs up his 'ticks' in the village as regularly as if he were five-and-twenty."

"And who taught him that, I should like to know?" asked Mrs. Sabretasche, with something like warmth. "He ought to have been whipped."

"Pooh! nonsense, my dear. I tell you 'what's bred in the bone,' etc. It's born with the lad—born in him. He's a regular dragoon in miniature at five years old—well, nearly six, then—that is five, isn't it? A clever little chap he is, though I say it, that shouldn't. Bob!"

"Ya-ath," returned the youngster, in a drawling voice, which sounded delightfully absurd on his juvenile lisping tongue.

"What do you say when you don't want to go to bed? Hey? What a—what a—"

"D—d bore," finished the baby, in a tone of quiet indifference, which showed he was ignorant of the signification of the words. Then, interrupting his father's proud noisy mirth, "I say, father, mother took me to church to-day and I saw—" dropping his voice and speaking very impressively—"I saw—*the Devil!*"

"Eh! bless my soul—WHAT!" exclaimed the major, jumping almost out of his chair.

"Now you see the result of your teaching," put in Mrs. Sabretasche, in a tone of desperate resignation; "it was old Sir George's monument that we went in to see."

"Ha! ha! ha!" laughed the major, uproariously, "the boy's not so far out of it, after all! Old George Leroy was as nearly akin to the old gentleman as human beings ever go. Bless the lad, he's a real Sabretasche—a chip of the old block; bless me, and only five years old."

"And father," Bob continued, climbing on to the major's knee and sitting with one hand squared on his hip, like a dragoon on horseback, "Tom Leslie put his tongue out at me this morning and said I was a molly-coddle. I'm not a molly-coddle, now am I?"

"That depends upon what you said to him," answered the major, gravely.

"Well," said small Bob, with a long sigh, "I said I *might* be a molly-coddle, but if he called me so again, I'd just punch his head."

"Quite right too," remarked the major, with infinite satisfaction, and looking as stern as his pride and laughter would permit.

"Such a volley of abuse Bob poured out," complained Mrs. Sabretasche; "I would have given him a good whipping, only, it's no use beating the child for your fault—and it is your fault, major."

"Now look here, Maria," said the major, with much decision, "a soldier's one thing and a parson's another. If you wished for a parson, you should have married a parson; but you didn't, you married a Sabretasche, of whom you must just make the best, and, what is more, you must not grumble if my boy takes after me, it's only natural that he should. The Sabretasches have always been soldiers—they take to the army as young ducks to water, and I wont have the Sabretasche traits of character knocked out of him—you must simply make the best of us both."

That was the principle upon which young Bob's education was completed—the result of that education I will relate in the pages which follow.

Young Bob went through the usual course of training which boys of his class undergo. From the hands of a tutor to Eton, and from Eton to Sandhurst, at which place he lost a year's seniority for insubordination, or some such misdemeanour. He received the news with characteristic coolness—characteristic of both parents, for it combined his mother's quiet calmness with his father's spirit of don't-carish dare-devilism; that is to say, he touched his cap when the decision of the powers-that-be was communicated to him, said, "Very well, sir," and went out of the awful presence—and laughed.

" What will your governor say ?" a friend asked him.

" Say ? That they're a set of thick-headed old idiots," answered Bob, laughing yet more. " Just the way they served him—so he can't say anything to me, if he feels inclined."

However, when Bob went home, with two months' leave and a commission as sub-lieutenant in that most distinguished regiment, the Scarlet Lancers, old Sabretasche was far too proud of him to cavil at so trivial a matter as the loss of a year's seniority. He superintended all the details of Bob's outfit with a delight only to be equalled by that of a bride selecting her *trousseau.* He coached him in all the etiquette of the mess-room—no small task that—and on parting he gave one piece of advice—one only.

" Now, look here, Bob," he said, as they were driving through the green lanes on their way to the station, " there's one thing I should like to say to you before you go."

" All right," said Bob, cheerfully, flicking at the flies as he spoke.

" I lay no restrictions upon you," said the gallant old major, rather wistfully; " I never have done, I don't think I have ever bullied you in any way."

"'Deed, no," returned Bob, readily.

" And I should like to feel that I can trust to your honour, never to play a woman false. It's a wrong once done, Bob, that you never get over as long as you live, a remembrance of that kind comes back to you years after you'd fain forget all about it."

Bob looked down from his high driving-seat a little curiously at the handsome flushed old face, which his own so strongly resembled.

" I say, father," he remarked at last, " are you speaking from experience ?"

" Perhaps I am," he admitted, " but take my advice about it, Bob."

" I think I will," said Bob, quietly.

Not another word was spoken between them till they reached

the little country station, whence Bob departed for Colchester, where his regiment was quartered.

"Good-bye, Bob, my boy—bless you," cried the major, rather huskily, as the train started.

"Dear old chap," murmured Bob, as he lit a cigar and put his feet on the opposite seat. "By Jove! though, who'd have thought he had ever gone in for the character of a gay Lothario?"

Arrived at Colchester, Bob betook himself and his belongings in a fly to the barracks, drawing up in front of the mess with considerable clatter and dash—taking into account that after all it was only a fly.

He jumped out and addressed himself to one of two officers in undress uniform, who were standing in the door-way.

"Er—good morning," said Bob, in no wise abashed.

"Good morning," said the latter of the twain, with civility.

"I suppose you are officers of the Scarlet Lancers," Bob remarked, blandly   "My name is Sabretasche, er——"

"Oh! Sabretasche-er, is it?" interrupted the officer, with an amused smile. "Well, Mr. Sabretasche-er, I suppose you've come to join?"

"Exactly-er," returned Bob, easily. "Where shall I find my quarters, and can I report myself to the colonel at once?"

"Well, as I happen to be the colonel, you can," said his new friend, smiling, while the shorter man laughed outright.

Bob was, however, thoroughly equal to the occasion, awkward as it was. He took off his hat, displaying a handsome curly head, and said, with the utmost gravity, as if he had not spoken before, "I have the honour to present myself, sir."

"As for quarters," the colonel continued, "this is Mr. Smithers, the quarter-master."

Taking this as an introduction, Bob looked at the quarter-master and said, "How do?" with a nod of the curtest description.

Just at that moment, two other officers appeared round the corner, to whom Colonel Keith introduced the new arrival.

"And Wingfield," he said to the younger of them, "just

look after Mr. Sabretasche to-day, and put him in the way of things generally."

" Certainly, sir," answered Wingfield.

He entered the cab with Bob, and drove off to the quarters allotted to him. The colonel stood where they left him, looking after the retreating vehicle.

" I've no doubt he'll make a smart soldier," he remarked, when he had watched it quite out of sight, " but he'll want a good deal of his d——d cheek taking out of him."

Notwithstanding that such was the opinion of their commanding officer, the Scarlet Lancers did not find Bob Sabretasche's " cheek " so very easy to eradicate. He had been too well coached by his old father to make any mistakes in his intercourse with his senior officers—the respectful " sir " with which he addressed his colonel or major, the quiet air of deference with which he received their opinions, when they were contrary to his own, at the same time sticking resolutely to his original sentiments—all were faultless, and the senior sub. had no occasion to polish off Bob's education on that point. He submitted to be drawn with imperturbable good nature ; in fact, so good that they soon found there was no fun in disturbing him, for was he not always as ready for a midnight frolic as they were ? He was thoroughly well up in mess-room etiquette, and was never to be caught tripping in those little matters which necessitate the imposition of a fine.

And so the first terrible months—or what are usually so— passed over for Bob Sabretasche very easily ; and then he was summoned home by a telegram, telling him that the large, handsome, serene woman, who had been so placidly careful of his morals, was dead, and his father left alone.

Bob took the news badly. In all his twenty years of life he had never had such a blow as that. In truth, he had never had a blow of any kind except in the matter of that year of seniority, which he had taken as a joke. When the telegram arrived he was at lunch, and, just when about to put it into his pocket, he saw, with a great start, that it was from ——,
near which town was his father's house. He happened to be

sitting just opposite to the colonel, and asked, by a look, if he might open it.   The chief nodded, and Bob, under cover of the cloth, tore open the yellow wrapper.

" *Your mother died this morning ; pray come.*"

For a moment Bob sat perfectly still, then, feeling his composure giving way, flung the telegram with etiquette to the winds, and rushed out of the room.

What's the matter?" asked the chief, as the door closed with a great crash.

The man nearest to Bob's vacated place picked up the telegram and glanced at the brief sentences which conveyed so much.

" His mother is dead, sir," he said quietly.

" Ah !" murmured the superior, comprehensively, with a sigh to the memory of a gentle woman who had passed away twenty years before.   He continued speaking, but, later, he went up to Bob's room, and told him to get home as soon as possible.   " I'll arrange your leave," he ended, kindly.

And so Bob Sabretasche went home to the old house where he had lived and been happy, but, alas ! in which he would live and be happy never more.   That telegram was but the beginning of the end.   The death of the fair placid woman whom he had loved broke the old soldier down utterly, and within six months Bob found himself alone in the world, with no near relatives, but one-and-twenty years of age, and with a fortune of as many thousand pounds entirely at his own disposal.

Just at first he was too much stunned by his double loss to do anything more than his duty.   He did do that in a dull, mechanical way which presently put him on the sick-list, and gave the doctor no small amount of trouble ; and then Time, the comforter—who does such wonders for all of us—took him in hand, and smoothed the harsh lines of his sorrow into the more tender lineaments of a loving recollection, so that by the time the regiment moved its quarters to Liliminster, he was able to enter with great zest into all sporting pursuits, and found a good deal of enjoyment in the pleasures of society.

The better to cultivate both, Bob set up a stud of fourteen

hunters, likewise the smartest Stanhope phaeton which could possibly be procured; for that he had two high-stepping chesnut cobs, which, with a couple of chargers, brought the total number of his stud up to eighteen—and, be it remembered, his income was about a thousand a-year. For a year or so he certainly went the pace. Quoth one of his friends to him one day,

" I don't know what your income is, Bob, but if it is anything under eight thousand a year, you must be a fool."

" Income be bothered," returned Bob, carelessly. "Come round and look at my coach—it's a clipper, out-and-out the smartest I have seen for ever so long."

Yes, the crowning point of Bob Sabretasche's folly was to set up a coach and team of his own. He threw his money right and left like water—water which cost him nothing—and, at three-and-twenty, had managed to get so nearly through his one-and-twenty thousand pounds, that he pulled himself up sharp one fine morning, and wondered what the deuce would be the end of it all ?

His sudden awakening came in this wise. A few days before he had received an intimation from his bankers to the effect that his account was over-drawn. He at once telegraphed to his lawyer for money, and from that acute gentleman had by return of post a letter suggesting, since his patrimony was reduced to five thousand pounds, the advisability of not further lessening it. Bob awoke from his course of reckless extravagance like a somnambulist suddenly recalled to consciousness. Since his father's death he had never given money-matters a thought. He had been terribly cut up by the loss of his parents so near together, and had taken to spending money more for something to do than from any other cause. He had fancied it would be very jolly to have fourteen hunters, a coach and team, and the cleverest cobs in the service, but as to how those luxuries were to be paid for had simply never occurred to him. Had he not, from earliest childhood, been accustomed to have anything or everything for which he felt the smallest inclination ?

He sat, with the lawyer's letter in his hand, for a long, long time, looking thoughtfully into the fire. Well, he had gone the pace, there was no doubt about that. It had been great fun whilst it lasted, but, after all, he didn't know that he was not growing rather tired of it all. This continual visiting, the dodging of gracious mammas with young and lovely daughters, and daughters also neither young nor lovely. How they had tracked him down, to be sure! He glanced up at the dozens of pressing invitations for the month to come, which were lying about the chimney-piece, and in spite of his suddenly sobered senses, burst into a fit of hearty laughter at the thought of the time and pains which had been taken, and wasted, in trying to hook him—really wasted, for was he not, after all, of the worst class of detrimentals : a poor man, with expensive tastes ? The laughter soon ceased as the stern reality came back to him again with ten-fold vigor.

"By George! what a fool I have been," he said, emphatically.

Still, it was no use crying over spilt milk, no man can eat his cake and have it. Bob had undoubtedly partaken very greedily of his. As he sat there in the twilight of that cold March day, with the red fire-glow playing over his handsome face—from out of which all the carelessness and fun had been driven—two or three lines came into his mind, lines which he had read ever so long ago, when he had been young—Bob felt that he had grown awfully old since then ; when he had not taken to squandering money like an idiot or a cotton-spinning cad—as he told himself, wrathfully ; when he had had a dear, good, gallant old father, to whom he could have carried all his troubles and had kindly advice. Yes! it was in those far-away happy days, which were never to return again, that he had read them, little dreaming how soon the time would come when they would be applicable to himself :

Fools climb to fall : fond hopes, like seeled doves for want of better light, mount, till they end their flight with falling.

"And—oh! Lord," Bob groaned, " I have been a confounded idiot, and serve me right to come such a cropper."

And then he roused himself, with a mental shake, and looked round the pretty room. It was pretty, in spite of the take-to-piece-able barrack-room furniture. The walls were hung with pictures from cornice to dado—yes, Bob had the room decorated in that style; there were velvet-hung brackets, a superb flounce of lace, worked by the hand of some fair lady, adorned the chimney-valance; there were hot-house flowers and rare old china in profusion, so that the whole was tasteful and pretty. Well, he thought, with a sigh, there would not surely be any need to disturb that. The little trifles had cost a good deal, to be sure, but if sold they would fetch very little, and he did not exactly wish all his brother officers to know how deeply he was dipped, therefore, he concluded to let the room remain untouched. He got a bit of paper, and jotted down what he had left out of the wreck of his fortune :

£5,000—capital.

Well! that wasn't so bad to begin with, he thought, with an attempt—a very poor one, too—at self-comfort. Five thousand pounds! Why, it was only the other day that he met a man —a cotton-spinning fellow—at Lord Agate's, who had given as many guineas for a necklace for his daughter, and thought nothing of it; and now that sum was all Bob had in the world, except what he might be able to realise from the sale of his horses and so on. Queer little thing that same daughter was —little, slim, rather ugly thing, with a wide mouth, very soft eyes, and no shape to speak of.

" I believe she was spooney on me," Bob said, aloud, to the walls or his reflection in the glass, maybe; " yes, sir, sure she was, and she was engaged to a fat, vulgar old brute, thirty years older than herself, she told me. Poor little soul. Queer sort of taste, though, he must have. Lord ! I wouldn't have kissed her for a thousand pounds."

But it was no use thinking about Lily Ray or Lily anybody else. So he returned anew to his calculation, as to what he might reasonably expect his horses to bring him. Bob didn't quite know whether fourteen hunters were not too many for any man—it was hard work to keep them all fit. Fourteen

hunters—put 'em at a hundred a-piece. Very few of them were
of less value than that, whilst most of them were worth a good
deal more. If they fetched a little more, the difference would
pay off any little debts that might be standing. We must do
Bob the justice to say that he had no debts to speak of.
" Well, then :

" Capital..........................	£5.000.
" Hunters........................	£1.400.
" Coach...........................	£150.
" Team...........................	£400.

" The coach cost three hundred guineas," Bob thought ruefully,
and I've only had it a few months : it ought to fetch a hundred
and fifty—I'll put it at that. The team is worth six hundred
—every penny of it—but I suppose I shall have to throw them
away at four. Oh—h ! Lord ! but this is a bad business—

" Capital..........................	£5.000.
" Hunters..........................	£1.400.
" Coach...........................	£150.
" Team...........................	£400.
" Pay.............................	————

" Umph ! goes in expenses !

" Total...........................	£6,950.

" Total, six thousand—nine hundred—and—fifty," Bob mused ;
" call it seven thousand. Well, se-—ven thousand, at five per
cent.—three-fifty a year. How the deuce am I to live on
three-fifty a year and a subaltern's pay ? I suppose the
phaeton and the cobs must go—though I did hope to be able
to keep one of them, at least."

He sat working out this unpleasant problem for a long, long
time, without much success, and then, somehow, his mind
wandered off to Lily Ray and her five-thousand-guinea necklace. What a little ugly thing she was. At least, perhaps
not exactly ugly, but she'd a very wide mouth, and no shape
at all. She was, somehow, *unkissable.*

" Now, Jinks ; what is it ?"

" Well, sir—it's a lady," returned the man, holding the door
in his hand.

" A lady! Oh! the devil—tell her I'm out," Bob answered, shortly—he did not want troubling with any ladies, just then.

The man departed, closing the door after him, and Bob thought to hear no more of his visitor, but, a moment later, a querulous, imperious voice rang through the corridor, which caused Bob to spring from his seat in double-quick time.

" Which are Mr. Sabretasche's rooms? Show me at once. I will wait until he comes in," it said.

Bob flung his door open, and a tiny creature, robed in rich furs and closely veiled, stepped out of the darkness into the circle of light cast by the fire. In the background stood Jinks in silent amazement—perhaps he doubted for a moment if the small creature might be a fairy or not, only the ordinary cavalry soldier is not a speculative animal—but as his master shut the door in his face, he concluded that all was right, and departed about his business.

As the door closed, the visitor tore her veil aside, and flung —literally flung herself into Bob's astonished arms.

" My dear Miss Ray," he gasped, " what does this mean?"

" Dear, darling Bob," cried the poor little person, clinging to him convulsively, " they've been so cruel to me—oh! so cruel to me. Look," pulling back the furs from her small wrists and displaying the white skin all bruised and livid. The sight elicited a cry of horror from Bob, and an ugly sharp word from between his teeth. " Oh! I hated him so—I couldn't marry him," Lily went on, with a great shuddering horror in her tones and in her soft eyes—the eyes were really pretty, if nothing else was—" and papa said he would *make* me love him; but he could not," triumphantly, " for I love—you."

" But you don't mean to say he used personal violence towards you?" Bob cried, aghast.

" I'm black and blue all over," she answered confidently.

" Low beast," cried Bob, with emphasis.

" Just what I told him," remarked Miss Ray, with a long sigh. " However, it doesn't matter, I'm all safe with you."

Poor Bob trembled in his shoes—did this little body expect

him to *marry* her? Bob was absolutely sick at the bare idea of it.

"What made you think of coming to me?" he said, abruptly.

The soft eyes turned upon him in reproachful surprise. "Why—have you forgotten your promise?" she asked, with quivering lips.

"Did I promise you anything?" he said, tenderly, for, after all, if he did not admire her, she was a woman, and he was mindful of those cruel bruises. "What was it that I promised?"

"Oh!" cried the poor child, with a sob of terror—she was but seventeen—"you promised me, if ever I needed a friend, I might come to you and trust you to take care of me. Don't you remember? It was the night of the ball at Lord Agate's. You *cannot* have forgotten it," she ended, with a wail of despair.

"To be sure not, certainly not," he said, soothingly, though he had no recollection of it whatever.

"I don't believe you even remember it," she said, sorrowfully, "you *said* you liked me and I believed you, but, after all, you don't want me, and if I go back they will kill me. Oh! they will kill me!" shrinking back with every appearance of terror. "So cruel they were—how they hurt me. I didn't care so much then. I thought I could get away to you and be safe, but you did not mean it at all, and you don't want me."

For a moment Bob stood irresolute, trying to think! He looked at the swollen, bruised wrists of this poor little soul, who had flown to him for protection, relying on his promise. Then a sudden recollection came over him of the day when he joined his regiment: how he had driven his father to the station, and the dear gallant old man had asked him—the only favour he ever remembered him asking—never to play a woman false! In that brief moment of reflection he remembered that he had squandered his father's fortune—that his father was dead! Should he then fail to keep his promise to his dead father, the very first time he was tried? Assuredly not! If his whole life was to be sacrificed, it would only be a slight reparation to the gallant memory he had so soon forgotten.

" You may trust me to take care of you, Lily," he said, kindly, bending down and laying his hand on her shoulder. She flinched from the touch, gentle as it was, thereby forcing another oath from between Bob's teeth.

" Good heavens, child!" he cried, passionately incredulous, you don't mean to say that they really struck you? That you cannot bear to be touched?"

" I daresay it will soon go off," she said, trying to be brave, though the tears were stealing down her cheeks, " and—and you won't send me back?"

" On my word—no!" he answered.

And then he turned to the fire, trying once more to *think*— to realize his position. He was not at all sure, since Lily was only seventeen, that he could marry her legally without the consent of her father; of course, he would have to marry her, and equally of course, Mr. Ray would not consent. Then again, what the deuce were they to live upon? Three-fifty a-year and his pay? It was absurd! He sat down on the sofa beside her and took her hand in his—very carefully this time.

" Do you know, Lily, that I am a poor man?" he asked.

" Really? I thought you were very well off," she said, placidly.

" But I am not, indeed. I have been very reckless and extravagant since my father died, and I have only about four hundred a-year left."

" Ah! I am so tired of being rich," she cried, gladly; " it will be ever so much nicer to be poor; you don't know."

" I don't, indeed," said Bob, doubtfully.

" I've ever so much money with me," Lily went on, producing her purse. " I wish you would take care of it, please, I might have it stolen; and Bob, dear, will you go and pay the cabman, and tell him to bring my luggage up here?"

" Your luggage!" Bob gasped; " my poor child, you *cannot* stop here. Don't you know that this is a barrack?"

"To be sure ; I told the man to drive here," she said innocently ; "why, soldiers always live in a barrack, don't they ?"

Bob fairly groaned aloud ; however, he went and paid the man, and had the luggage—a goodly pile of it—taken upstairs.

"How did **you** manage to get off ?" he asked.

"Papa went to London with—*him*, to get a special license," she said, simply, "so I packed up all I thought I should want and—*me voilà.*"

"And when does he return ?"

"Not until to-morrow morning," clapping her hands gaily, "when he will find me—gone."

"Well, I must be 'gone,' too, to make some arrangements for your accommodation," Bob said, ruefully.

"But you will come back ?"

"Oh ! yes—in a few minutes."

He went hastily to the colonel's house, and knocked at the door of his sitting-room.

"Are you busy, sir ?" he asked, as he entered.

Colonel Keith looked up from his writing, "Oh ! is it you, Sabretasche ? Yes ! I am rather busy. What is it ?"

"I've got into a terrible mess, sir," Bob said, wistfully ; "but perhaps the major will help me, if you are too busy."

"No, no, sit down and tell me all about it," the chief replied. He made a rule of always encouraging the confidences of his subalterns, whenever he could ; so Bob sat down and told him all about it.

"What had I better do, sir ?" he ended.

"Do you say the girl is here ?"

"Up in my room, sir."

"She can't stop there, that's very certain," said the chief, hurriedly ; "we'd better see if Mrs. Wilson will take charge of her." Mrs. Wilson was the adjutant's wife, and lived in the upper part of the colonel's house. "You see, Sabretasche, I can't help you in this matter, as I'm not a married man ; if I had been, I would have taken her home at once."

"You are very good, sir," Bob said, gratefully.

" It's a very unpleasant business to be mixed up with," he went on ; "you see, if the father chooses to be awkward, he can withold his consent altogether."

" Exactly ! That is what I thought," said Bob.

" And you say they have positively beaten the child ?"

" Her wrists are as black as my coat, sir," Bob returned, indignantly.

" And I suppose you've been in love with her all along ?"

" In love with her !" Bob echoed. " Oh, dear no ! The fact is, she has come to me, relying on a foolish promise, made in jest, from which, of course, I cannot go back now. Well, sir, I'll go round and see what I can do with Mrs. Wilson."

" I'll come with you," said Colonel Keith, kindly.

The adjutant's tender-hearted little wife did not, however, wait to hear the whole of Bob's story, but rushed impulsively to his room, and did not so much as wait to put on her bonnet. A few minutes later Lily found herself by her new friend's fire, her feet on a stool, a cup of tea in her hand, her adoring eyes fixed on Bob's face, and her ears filled with the muttered exclamations of half-a-dozen stalwart officers, who had already heard the story, and were one and all ready to pay Mr. Ray and—*him* back in their own coin with ample interest. Poor little Lily had never been made so much of during all her seventeen years of life : to her it was all delightful. The tall, and for the most part, good-looking officers in their handsome mess dress, the kindly affectionate hostess, and her lover, Bob. Oh ! it was like fairy-land to her. She gave no thought to the future, she had almost forgotten the past, and so little did she look below the surface of the present that she never noticed how sorely troubled Bob was. How was she to know that his very soul was sick at the thought of his marriage, while his poor brain was puzzling over the miserable question, how were they to live on four hundred a year ? If she had known precisely what was passing in his mind, she could scarcely have understood his feelings—she loved him. She had never looked at the other side of the question. As for money, she had always had so much of it that poverty was only a name to her : she knew nothing of its stings. For the present she was exalted into a heroine, and the worship she received was very pleasant to her.

The following day Colonel Keith and Bob went over to Weystone Hall, Mr. Ray's residence. They found him at home and apparently in that state of calm which invariably succeeds a storm. He was a little, burly, ill-tempered looking man, evidently standing in much awe of the stern-looking gentleman commanding the Scarlet Lancers.

Colonel Keith stated his business in a clear and concise manner, ending by *demanding*—not asking—for a written consent to his daughter's marriage with Mr. Robert Sabretasche.

"I'll never speak to the hussy again!" roared the irate father, breaking into a passion once more.

"Will you have the goodness to sign this paper?" asked the colonel, calmly

"She's no daughter of mine, sir," screamed Ray *père*.

"The law, however, rules otherwise," answered the colonel, with provoking coolness ; "will you sign it or not? If not, we shall procure a summons immediately for assault and battery."

"Sign it, yes, and be glad to be rid of her!" Ray roared; "only, young gentleman, don't think as 'ow you're going to get any of my money"—in his excitement long disused terms cropped up again—"you've played fast and loose with me, and the girl's all you'll get."

Bob turned his nose skywards in huge contempt, but kept silent : he had immense faith in his chief's conversational powers.

"Now, sir," said Colonel Keith, when he had put the signed and witnessed paper carefully into his pocket-book and buttoned his coat over it, "let me tell you, sir, that you are, without exception, the most scoundrelly, cowardly cad I ever spoke to or ever heard of in my whole life. You say *you* disown your daughter, but, if ever she speaks to you again she'll be a confounded fool—there, sir."

After which the pair stalked out of the house, leaving the astonished owner literally beside himself with rage and fury.

"Sabretasche," said the chief, when they were in the train again, " we've done that fellow in the eye; I've not only got a written consent to the marriage, but also resigning all claim to any personal property, money, or jewelry, which Miss Ray may have taken away with her—properly witnessed, too."

"It really is awfully good of you, colonel," said Bob, even in the moment of victory unable to repress a sigh.

"I'm sorry, though, that you don't think more about her, poor little thing," he continued.

All the chivalry in Bob's nature rose up at the words. " Oh! it's all right, sir," he said, hastily; " I shall not illuse her," at which assertion Colonel Keith laughed heartily.

A fortnight followed, during which Lily Ray remained as the guest of the adjutant's wife, and Bob contrived to make arrangements for disposing of his horses and setting his affairs somewhat in order. The hardest pang of all was parting with the cobs, but they had to go—happily for Bob's peace of mind, not much under their proper value.

On the whole, his " effects " realized more than he had expected, so that he was able to pay just over three thousand pounds into his banker's hands. His small *fiancée*, having had this step in view for some months, had spent very little and saved the pocket-money her wealthy father had lavished upon her. Thus they had nearly three hundred pounds between them to go on with, which, considering the doleful condition of their joint circumstances, was not so bad. Still, how to keep a wife on five hundred a-year was an unsolvable problem to the man who had been living at the rate of some seven thousand a-year.

" I don't know how we shall manage it, Lily," he said, the day before the wedding.

" Manage what?" she asked.

" Why *living*, of course—we shall only have about five hundred a-year, all told," he answered, gloomily.

The poor child slid down upon her knees before him. " Am I a great bother to you?" she asked, wistfully.

If worried and unwilling, Bob was still a gentleman and

1

kind of heart. "No, no, child," he said hastily; "only we must live somehow, and neither of us have tried pinching before."

"I shall not want any clothes for an age," she said, confidently. "I've been expecting something of this sort—though I didn't know you were so poor—so I bought a few silk dresses. I have them at the bottom of one of my boxes—not made up, you know."

"Oh! but I don't know that dresses cost so much," said Bob, carelessly.

"Oh! but they do, indeed—a lot. That jacket cost a hundred guineas," pointing to her sables lying on the sofa; "but, of course, it will not last a lifetime."

"Well, but, Lily—it is servants and housekeeping and all that," he said, in a perplexed tone.

"Oh! do you want many servants?—they're such a nuisance —poking and prying into everything one does, and counting the mouthfuls one eats—I hate them."

Bob shivered—he did not hate servants.

"And you know, Bob, dear, there are my jewels. We can sell them. I don't care for them. I shall love your two rings better than all the diamonds on earth."

"Oh! we can't sell your jewelry—besides, it won't be worth much," Bob answered.

"Not worth much!" she echoed. "Ten thousand pounds, if a penny. Why, my necklace cost five thousand guineas."

"But you don't mean to say you brought *that* away with you?" Bob cried.

"Do you suppose I left it behind?" Lily asked, opening her eyes very wide.

"Why, bless me, what a clever little soul you are," he said, with a laugh. "Who's that? Oh! is it you, colonel? Come in, sir."

"I say, colonel," he said, after a while, "did you not tell me that you made some arrangement with Mr. Ray as to his daughter's belongings?"

"Certainly—he signed a paper, giving up all claim to any

personal property, money, or jewelry, she may have taken away with her. Why, is there likely to be any trouble?"

Bob burst out laughing. "She has brought all her jewelry with her," he answered; "that is all, but it may make a great difference to us," for he had made a clean breast of his misfortunes to the colonel long before.

Nevertheless, they had hard work to make both ends meet. Bob, at three-and-twenty, and Lily, but seventeen, knew as much about house-keeping as did the babes in the wood, ergo—they were not a little imposed upon. Then, on the other hand, Bob could never allow himself the luxury of a growl, for, as surely as he began, did the tears well up into Mrs. Bob's eyes and she immediately went in for the luxury of a good cry. Bob, like a good many other men, hated a scene, and tears invariably acted upon him as does a red rag to a bull; so he came to the conclusion that his best plan was to abstain from growling. On that score, matters went rather more smoothly, but there were other scores upon which they persistently declined to go smoothly at all. Lily *would* make a practice of spooning him. Poor Bob! He had never got over his first feeling that Miss Ray was *unkissable*, and now that she was transformed into Mrs. Bob Sabretasche, he did not find his original opinion altered. But that was not the worst of it. Mrs. Bob made a rule of being more openly demonstrative in public than in private. She liked, poor little soul, to make a display of her affection for her handsome stalwart husband; to sit with her hand in his; to call him by all manner of absurd and endearing names, regardless of the presence of his brother officers, who, one and all, treated him to a volley of nursery names and spoony terms, whenever he ventured to show his face in the ante-room.

"Now, 'Bobbie-wobbie,'" the first would cry, "come and sit next to me, 'Duckie-wuckie.'"

Whereupon Bob would shut the door with a crash, and betake himself back to his mismanaged home, to endure the same from Lily, only with the difference that poor little plain Lily was most thoroughly in earnest. Poor Bob; the great

change in his life told upon him frightfully—the brightness
faded from his eyes ; the soldierly, swaggering gait grew quiet
and preoccupied, the smartness in his person vanished, and the
officers of the Scarlet Lancers one and all agreed that poor old
Bob really had gone off woefully.

And then, a new trouble came upon them.   In spite of her
childish ways, little Mrs. Bob, as they called her, was a great
favourite with the whole regiment.   Most of them remembered
the poor little bruised and swollen wrists, and admired her for
the pluck she had shown in cutting the home lot and flying for
succour to the man whom she loved.   To the officers' wives
she was so good-natured and gentle that they, too, admitted
her into high favour, and thus it happened that by-and-bye
she began to notice the behaviour of other men towards their
wives.   It was an eventful day for both of them when Mrs.
Bob's eyes were thus opened.   She perceived that Bob, though
long suffering and courteous, never made love to her, and
although there are many, many wives who would prize those
two desirable qualities before a little love-making and a lot of
bullying (is not that the usual mixture?), Mrs. Bob began to
pine for that which was denied her.   She cared nothing for
courtesy, less for long suffering, and she did crave for Bob's
love.   She one day, in a burst of confidence, said as much to
one of the married ladies.

" My dear Mrs. Bob," said she, kindly, " you should never
judge one man by another, they show their affection so differ-
ently ; and, I assure you, Mr. Sabretasche never was of an
effusive nature.   I never knew him flirt with any one."

But the little woman remained unconvinced, and immediately
adopted a new demeanour towards her lord and master.   She
ceased all the little caresses and endearing terms which had
so *worried* him, but which, with the usual contrariety of poor
human nature, he somehow missed.   He looked at her as she
ate her dinner in silence, and wondered if she were " seedy ? "

" Oh, Lily, the colonel's coming down to dine to-morrow,
there's something on at the theatre, so we'll dinner at seven,"
he remarked.

" Very well," said Lily, quietly, and without lifting her eyes.

Then, not a little to his astonishment, instead of bringing her dessert plate round to his side, she left the room without speaking. Not that Bob minded that much, but it was rather stupid alone, and an awful bore having to pick his own walnuts; Lily certainly was an indefatigable walnut peeler, there was no doubt about that. Ugh!—he flung the unoffending nutcrackers down with a crash, and broke a plate in so doing, which brought him to himself again.

" Queer thing to go off like that," he mused ; " she's such a good-tempered little thing."

It never occurred to him that the trodden worm will turn at last. This poor fragile little worm, upon whom he had been treading so ruthlessly for months, had turned at last, and Bob did not like it. He felt as if some soft little bird had suddenly repaid his caresses by trying to peck his eyes out. Well ! no, he admitted, not *caresses*—he could not shut his eyes to that fact.

However, it was no use sitting looking at that broken plate all night, so he roused himself and went into the drawing-room. His wife was sitting in a huge chair, with a novel in her hand. She never looked up when he entered, and did not, as was his wont, fly to fill his pipe—bless you, no, she did not mind smoking—to give him a light, to fold his paper just where he wanted to read, or to do the hundred-and-one things, in the doing of which she had made a veritable slave of herself. Bob felt himself personally aggrieved. No sooner was he settled in his chair than he discovered that his tobacco-pot was missing.

" Do you know where my tobacco is, Lily ? "

" I believe it's on the dining-room chimney-piece," she answered, indifferently.

Bob fetched it with a groan—an inward one. Then he filled his pipe, but a lighter or a match there was not. He had not a scrap of paper or a fusee about him, and at last he flung the offending pipe into the fire.

" I say, Lily."

" M—m ?" said Lily, reading on.

" Have you a head-ache ?"

" Oh, no."

A moment later the book shared a similar fate to the pipe, being unceremoniously banged under a sofa.

" Then what is the matter ?" Bob asked. " Why did you go off without any dessert ?"

" I went off," said the little woman, bravely, " because you did not want me. I don't like making myself too cheap, and I've done a great deal too much in that way lately."

Bob stood irresolute. He had schooled himself so carefully in the belief that he did not want her, that he felt it would be like telling a lie to say otherwise, and yet, the prospect of peeling his own walnuts, of filling his own pipe—in fact, of doing the hundred-and-one things that Lily had regularly done for him, was absolutely appalling—therefore he compromised matters by saying,

" I never said so."

" Not in words," retorted Lily, significantly.

" What do you mean, child ? "

" Just what I say !" she cried, with hysterical passion. " You don't want me, though you swore to love me—to love and to cherish me. Yes ; I suppose you married me for pity, for you don't really want me, and I wish I was dead !"

Bob Sabretasche was not a very clever young man, and it dawned upon him that he had really trodden upon that meek little worm very unmercifully As always happened when he was in a dilemma, a vision of the kindly, handsome face of his dead father rose before him, and the frank voice rang through his ears : " Never play a woman false, Bob ; it's a wrong once done that you never get over as long as you live ; a remembrance of that kind comes back to you, long after you'd fain forget all about it."

" I wish I was dead," Mrs. Bob went on tearfully, " and so, I dare say, do you."

" I do not," he cried.

" But since I am not "—with a great sigh—" I think I

will go away. Perhaps *they*"—she always spoke of her people thus—"perhaps *they* will take me in again."

The handsome old face vanished, and in its place came a vision of himself as he would be in the long years of the future—*alone*, growing middle-aged and old—*and alone*.

"Don't speak like that, Lily," he cried, taking her in his arms, "I cannot bear to hear you."

"But you don't want me, I *know* you don't."

"On my word, I do."

She had taken his word before—she took it again.

And, after all, when old Ray died, they came in for something like a million of money, and they did not have to wait so very long for it either.

A SATANIC A.D.C.

Lucy Moore was cook in the family of a well-to do pro-
fessional man in the old city of Liliminster, and, to use her
mistress's words, was a perfect treasure. In these days perfect
treasures are very bad to meet with in any class of life, but
most of all in the kitchen; a fact of which Mrs. Johnson was
very well aware, and for that reason took great care of Lucy
and did everything she could to make her satisfied with her
place.

Many people maintain that servants are what the mistresses
make them, so perhaps Mrs. Johnson's own disposition may
have had something to do with the excellence of Lucy's. Never
had a girl so kind and good a mistress—so Lucy said; and
never had any mistress a better servant—so Mrs. Johnson
said. Her kitchen was always the very picture of neatness
—the dish-covers and pans shone like burnished silver in the
sunshine, the range was never dull, the oven was always clean
when required—a little circumstance most housekeepers understand the value of. And best of all, was the appearance of
Lucy herself. Her plentiful brown hair was always smoothly
brushed and coiled into a neat knot at the back of her head,
she had a bright intelligent face with soft grey eyes, good
teeth, a white throat, and *invariably* a clean collar. Small
wonder was it, therefore, that Mrs. Johnson was for ever
haunted by a great fear, lest some unprincipled young man
should discover Lucy's charms and carry her off in triumph
—still, as Lucy was turned three-and-twenty and seemed bad
to please, she was not without hopes that the evil day might
yet be put off for an indefinite period.

But Mrs. Johnson had reckoned without her host, for one

fine morning, when she went as usual into the kitchen, Lucy took her breath away by expressing in the much-dreaded formula, that she " should like to leave this day month, m'm."

" To leave!" the poor lady gasped ; " why, Lucy, what is the matter ?"

" Well, m'," returned Lucy, with a blush, " it isn't that anything's the matter, but—I'm going to be married."

" Married," with a great sigh ; " well, Lucy, I am glad for your happiness, but, oh dear, what *shall* I do without you ?"

" Oh ! there's plenty more to get, m'," said Lucy, with a pleased blush, " and it's such a good place, you are sure to get suited."

" Well, we must hope so," returned Mrs. Johnson, not very hopefully. " And so you are going to be married, Lucy ? I hope you have made a careful choice—marriage is a serious business."

" Yes, m', but he is a very steady young man," Lucy answered, proudly.

" And what is he ?—what is his name, Lucy ?"

" His name is Jinks, m'. Yes, m', Henry Jinks, and he's a soldier."

" *A soldier*—oh, Lucy !" Mrs. Johnson almost screamed. " Oh, I am sorry—I am sorry !"

" There's no call for that m', *I'm* sure," said Lucy, in an offended tone, " he's a very fine young man."

" But, my poor girl, you don't know the life you have before you," cried the mistress—being old-fashioned, and classing all soldiers as " bad in a lump "—" you don't indeed. A soldier has some four-pence-half-penny a day, when his expenses are paid, and how can you live on that ?—after being accustomed to a good table, too. Why, even if you can get put on the strength of the regiment, you will only have one room— perhaps not that—and seventeen dirty soldiers to wash for."

" Well, m'," Lucy answered, " I never saw a dirty soldier yet, and I fancy if one was to keep himself dirty he would very soon get himself into trouble ; and as to washing for them, I'm not going to do that. He's got leave to be married, but I'm

going to live as cook with Mrs. Sabretasche, **one of the officers'
ladies.** My young man is servant to Mr. Sabretasche and lives
in the house, and so as Mrs. Sabretasche has had a deal **of**
trouble with her servants, being a **very young lady, I'm**
going to be cook-houskeeper for her."

" And, how will you do, if you've half-a-dozen babies?" the
mistress asked.

" Why, m', Mrs. Sabretasche say's **she'll risk that**," Lucy
answered, with another blush.

And so in due time Lucy Moore was transformed into Lucy
Jinks, and took up her abode in the Sabretasches' domicile.
Everyone was benefited by the change excepting Mrs. Johnson,
who got an idle, dirty, incompetent person in Lucy's place, and
never ceased bewailing the loss of her perfect treasure. On the
very first evening of Lucy's rule Bob Sabretasche had a dinner
as well-cooked as he could have got at the mess, and his satisfaction reflected itself upon Mrs. Bob. Not that she cared much
about cooking, but it was nice to see Bob pleased.

" Tell your wife, Jinks," said Bob, when the dessert was
placed on the table, " that I've the very highest respect for her
—she's a very clever woman." And so Mr. and Mrs. Jinks
were pleased also, for every one likes well-merited praise.

" It's a great piece of good luck, Lily," said Bob, when Jinks
had departed; " we must take care of them both, for Jinks is a
clever servant, and a woman who can cook like that is not to be
met with every day."

" No, it is a comfort," Lily answered.

For a few months this delightful state of things continued.
Lucy was a careful, conscientious manager, and made everyone
around her comfortable, Jinks was as happy as a man could be,
and the Sabretasches positively revelled in little dinner parties.
when all at once there came a change. No; the change was
not in the housework, that was as well done as ever. No; the
change was in Lucy herself. She all at once grew nervous,
listless, almost sullen. Her hair was rough, her collar awry, and
she complained perpetually of headache. Jinks was beside
himself and forgot half the duties he had to perform, for which

Lucy rated him soundly, reducing him thereby almost to tears. Mrs. Bob told Bob she was very uneasy about Lucy; and Bob, who had noticed the change in her personal appearance, asked the doctor to step in and look at her.

The doctor did step in, and immediately asked if she had anything on her mind?

Lucy looked nervously round and stammered,

"No, sir," whereupon he promised to send her a little soothing medicine.

In due time the medicine arrived and Lucy took it—she also took some wine, which Bob sent down for her; but neither medicine nor wine had the slightest effect upon her nerves, and after a few days she confided to Mrs. Bob that she must leave the house.

"Leave!" Mrs. Bob echoed, blankly. "Oh! Lucy, why?"

"I never!" exclaimed Jinks, the plate in his hand falling to the ground in his consternation.

"The devil!" ejaculated Bob, aghast.

"Ah-h-h-h!" shrieked Lucy in terror, then sank down upon the nearest chair and, covering her head with her apron, burst into a torrent of tears.

It was an unusual and impressive scene. Mrs. Bob sat in her chair weak and trembling, she was just then in delicate health, as Bob remembered; Bob himself stood staring at her, and Jinks—very white and open-mouthed—held on by the end of the sideboard, looking alternately from his wife to the broken fragments of the plate lying at his feet. At the door stood the scared housemaid, having been attracted by Lucy's prolonged scream, and in the midst sat Lucy herself, sobbing and shuddering and, after the manner of her class, swaying to and fro, as if in the most dire agony of mind and body.

"Now come, tell us all about it," said Bob, persuasively.

"I dare not stay, sir," Lucy sobbed.

"But why? Jinks hasn't been ill-using you, surely?"

"Why, Jinks isn't that fond—" muttered the owner of the name, under his breath.

"Well, what is it, Lucy," Bob urged, "if it's not Jinks?"

"Oh! sir, he's as good and kind," Lucy said between her sobs, "as a man can be, and I'm that fond of him, it would break my heart to part from him. And I like Sarah—we never have no disagreeables in the kitchen at all. I like you all, sir and I thinks a deal of mistress, I do—but I dare not stay. I'm not safe in this house, and I must get away somewhere."

"Has any one been annoying you?" Bob asked. "By Jove I'll break his head for him."

"Me too," put in Jinks, stolidly.

"Not safe," Mrs. Bob repeated, incredulously, while Sarah scurried in and shut the door; "why, Lucy, who can do you any harm here?"

"I'll tell you all about it, m'," said Lucy, wiping her eyes with her apron. "You know I always gets up early, for master's breakfast must be had punctual."

"Yes, I'm sure you do, Lucy," Mrs. Bob answered. "You know, dear, when Jane was here, you *often* had to go without your breakfast and get something to eat in the mess."

"Yes. Well, go on, Lucy," said the master.

"When I awoke on Monday morning—a week yesterday as was—it was nearly half-past seven, and I hurried to get down, thinking of master's breakfast, you know, m'. Thinks I—I shall have to run to get it in in time, but, if you'll believe me, sir, when I went into the kitchen all was done. The floor had been fresh washed, the grate black-leaded, the fire was burning—a big fire, too, it was, such as I never keeps—the kettle was filled and hanging on the bar, even the plates and cups that you'd had on Sunday night was all washed and put away. All was done—the steps had been washed, the hall swept out, and it's been just the same ever since. I went up to see if Sarah had been helping me, which I thought was queer, as in general she isn't a very good getter-up; but there she was in bed, sound asleep, just as I'd left Jinks. Oh! I must go," she ended, with a fresh burst of tears, "I must go, for I'm not safe here."

"But Lucy," said Bob, at last, "why are you not safe?—who do you think has done all this?"

Lucy looked cautiously round, puckered up her apron into a thousand creases, glanced furtively at her husband and Bob, then at her mistress sitting astonished and tired and finally said, in a frightened whisper, " I think it's *the devil!*"

As I am writing a true story, I must confess that at this point the four persons who had been listening breathlessly to Lucy's tale began to laugh, not merely did they begin, but they continued—they laughed until they were obliged to sit down and cry with the effort, while Lucy, thinking the whole world—nay, two whole worlds—were against her, once more threw her apron over her head, and absolutely wailed aloud in her terror and dismay.

" Now come, Lucy," said Bob, still struggling with his laughter, " go down and get your breakfast, whilst we think over this business."

" But supposing he should really come, sir," Lucy protested, " and I should see him—tail and hoof and all. Oh! I don't know what I should do."

" Jinks or Sarah will stay with you," he said, soothingly, " and you know he never shows himself to more than one person at once."

" But perhaps he'll come in the morning and carry me off."

" Oh! nonsense, Jinks and I will sit up to-night and watch for him, and if a loaded revolver does not settle him, we must call in the police. Now go and get your breakfast. Mrs. Sabretasche is quite upset by all this."

The two women left the room, and Jinks followed more slowly, looking thoroughly mystified.

" A Satanic A.D.C., eh, Jinks?" remarked Bob Sabretasche, cheerfully.

" The very rummest go as ever I 'erd on, sir," Jinks replied, as he closed the door.

" Well, it really *is* odd, Bob," said his wife, in a puzzled tone; "now isn't it?"

" Very. I say, Lily, all this has upset you. Of course, Lucy's a very clever cook and all that, but it's very tiresome of her to have her heroics just now. She must be rather touched in the upper story."

" Well, do you know, I always thought her a remarkably sensible young woman," Lily answered, gravely. " However, to-night, you and Jinks will see what you will see. What a bore, though, sitting up. I wish, Bob, you would let me sit up, too."

" Certainly not," he replied, with much decision. He did, however, let her sit up an hour later than usual—partly because she was excited and wakeful, and partly because he looked forward to the long night's vigil with not a little disgust. He had many and many a time sat up all night in his bachelor days, gone to bed at cock-crow to snatch an hour's feverish sleep, and tumble up cross and heavy to his duty ; that was all very well, but to spend the long hours of the night in a silent house, with only a book and a pipe to keep him awake, was a decided nuisance.

" I knew it was too good to last," he said, thinking of Lucy's little dinners. " Jinks," he said, when the others had gone to bed, " go into the dining room and pile up a good fire ; I will do the same here—and remember, whatever happens, the women are not to be frightened."

Jinks obeyed, and in a very few minutes the house was as silent as the grave.

One—Two—Three—Four.

" This is becoming tiresome," Bob yawned, rousing himself out of his chair, with a great stretching of his long limbs. " Hollo ! what's that ?"

" That " was the opening of the door above, followed by the sound of a footfall on the stairs—not a quick, light tread, but slow and somewhat shuffling. He strode to the door, just in time to see Jinks appear at the opposite one, poker in hand, and, looking up the stairs, he saw Lucy herself descending them, her eyes set in the fixed glassy stare of a somnambulist. He stepped lightly across the hall, seeing that Jinks was about to speak.

" Not a word, for heaven's sake !" he whispered. The figure

in her long loose night-dress passed more swiftly by them, and
the young man caught Jinks by the arm, perceiving that he was
trembling and had grown ghastly pale. "Don't you see that
she is walking in her sleep?" he whispered.

"Lord! sir," returned Jinks, prosaically, "blest if I knew
what to think, except she'd gone out of her mind."

They watched her, in silence, for nearly an hour, whilst
swiftly and with wonderfully little noise she performed all her
morning's duties—then she went as quietly back to bed again,
and in two minutes was sleeping as peacefully as a tiny child.

"Now then, Jinks, the quicker we get to bed the better,"
said Bob, with a shiver and a yawn, then thanked his stars
that it was his cook and not his wife who had a fancy for
roaming about the house in her night-dress during the small
hours of the morning.

"And so you see, Lucy," he said, with a laugh, a few hours
later, "it wasn't such a very bad devil after all."

"I don't know for that, sir," Lucy retorted brightly—she
had taken the teazing very pleasantly—"most of us finds ourselves quite bad enough to manage. Jinks tells me that A.D.C.
means an orficer who helps the general, and I think most of us
might apply for that post to him, as I thought it was."

"You are right there, Lucy," said Bob, in answer to this
somewhat incoherent statement.

He looked across the table at Lily's wan face, which of late
had seemed all eyes, and thanked God that he had sent in his
resignation of that not too creditable post before it was too late.
He kissed her very kindly before he went out, even more kindly
than usual.

"We must tell Jinks to lock the door for the future," he
said. "I cannot have you worried, for you have grown very
precious to me."

"How is that?" she asked, with a flush of intense pleasure.

"Because Lily, my child, you have taught me that I can
get surer and better promotion than as A.D.C. to his Satanic
Majesty," Bob answered, gravely.

"Kiss me," said the girl, simply.

SERGEANT THE HONOURABLE HUGH BRABAZON.

CHAPTER I.

THE HONOURABLE HUGH BRABAZON had come to the end of his tether, and, as most people know, that is a remarkably unpleasant position. I was going to say that most people know it from experience, but as it is not very long since I myself did feel such a thrill of indignation from a similar supposition, I will refrain from inflicting the like upon any one else. Yes! I went to a military temperance meeting—a kind of mission from soldiers to civilians—but I cannot say that I went as a sympathizer. I heard very bad speeches, shocking singing, and I think the very worst pianoforte solo I was ever condemned to listen to. Assuredly I did not go to hear any of those things. I went to hear the band, which was an exceptionally fine one, but I was none the less disgusted when the quarter-master got up and told us, he was quite sure we all knew, *from experience*, that "drunken joy brings sober sorrow." If *he* had "touched pitch" and seen the error of his ways, it was rather too bad to cry out that the whole world was—or had been—as bedaubed as himself. However, we have been leaving the Honourable Hugh to be what the stock-brokers call a "lay-bye," and must return to him without further ado.

In the first placé, Hugh Brabazon was a younger son of a very noble and mighty house. He was fair to look upon, exceedingly so, standing over six feet in his socks, and being well-built, active, and very graceful ; he had merry blue eyes, well-cut aquiline features, and chesnut hair, which grew in little short curls all over his head.

He had come of a race accustomed for many generations to

be extravagant, and the family trait was not less marked in Hugh than it had been in any of his ancestors. He was extravagant, with a generous open-handedness which might have been all very well if his purse had been proportionately long, and, in fact, inexhaustible; but, unfortunately, such was not the case: he tried the experiment of running a race between his inclination and his purse, and, as generally happens, the latter got the worst of it and made a bad second. What was still more deplorable, Hugh's tether pulled up with a jerk so sharp, that, as the most expeditious way of settling matters, he left his "engagements" to arrange themselves, and—'listed for a soldier.

Taking all things into consideration, it was an utterly idiotic move to make; for if the House of Brabazon had not much money, it had considerable influence, and in a little time he might have been pushed into something, or he might have married some wealthy young lady hailing from the City, who would gladly have given her thousands for the sake of obtaining those six magic letters, "Hon. and Mrs.," before her name. However, Hugh did not give the House the opportunity of exerting the influence it undoubtedly possessed, but brought his affairs to a climax by pushing himself into the Scarlet Lancers as Private Hugh Brown.

Of course, the officers saw at once that he was a gentleman, though the truth concerning him did not creep out for some time; therefore, they put him into B-troop, commonly known amongst the men as "the gentlemen's troop."

There he found his old chum, Bertie Le Mesurier, in all the dignity of a lance-corporalship. The sergeant-major was a scion of one of the oldest north-country families and an M.A. of Oxford to boot. There was the son of a major-general; the son of a high dignitary of the Church; the son of a major, and Teddy Lloyd, who had been at Eton with Hugh ten years before.

As he recognized one after another he laughed and declared the new life would be glorious fun. Poor Hugh! He did not laugh very long!—he had to grow accustomed to a good many

U

things before he learned to laugh again in the old, gay, light-hearted fashion; for, when the novelty of his surroundings had worn off, he was supremely miserable.

He was always forgetting!—that was his great stumbling block. He meant well, but remembering was such hard work. When he met Joey Parsons, who had fagged for him at Eton—a little snub-nosed imp, whom he had bullied and thrashed, and now had to salute—well, it was hard work. Not that Hugh cared a fig for the actual fact of saluting, not a bit of it. He was Lord Brabazon's son—a scion of one of the oldest and proudest families in the kingdom, and his position—his birth that is—was unalterable. He knew that nothing could make Parsons *père* anything but a brewer, with no claims to any other distinction than the possession and pride of a certain income. Besides, Hugh had the old *noblesse oblige* feeling very strong in him; he was Private Hugh Brown, No. 842—worse luck—and Joey was Sub-Lieutenant Parsons, and must therefore be respected as such. No! it was not that at all that bothered him; but when he met Joey, dressed like a tailor's advertisement, strutting into the town, with a cigar in his mouth, and the most perfect unconsciousness that the man who passed him was anything but one of the "men," was in fact Hugh Brabazon, who had thrashed him dozens of times, his inclination to give him a dig in the ribs and shout "Hallo, Joey!" was at times almost too strong for him; and usually, the nearly-forgotten salute was so hurried that, had not Joey himself been taken up with the novelty of *his* surroundings, and so full of his own importance, he might have recommended Sergeant-Major Green, M.A., to see that Private Brown, No. 842, was properly instructed in the manner of saluting his officers when out of barracks.

And then there was the food! Hugh really did not know whether, taking the life all round, the food was not the most trying part of the whole business. It might be wholesome, he confided to Bertie Le Mesurier, but oh! dash it, it was unpalatable. The restriction, the work, the horrible drill, drill, drill, the more horrible uniform, in which he was so uncomfortable and felt such a long-legged idiot, the most horrible riding-school, and the lack of a corner he could call his own, were all very bad, undeniably bad things, but he didn't know that the food was not the worst. The bare table, the tin plates, the coarse food, and the three-pronged steel forks—oh! how he did prick his unfortunate mouth, until at last he went in desperation to the town and bought himself a silver spoon, knife and fork, with a case to keep them in. As he said, with grim humour, he had stood god-father to Private Brown, and was bound to come down with a christening gift.

Just at first it did not ooze out in the regiment who Private Brown, No. 842, was when at home. Those in B-troop who knew him were gentlemen, and respected his *incognito*, as he did theirs. But "murder will out," and before many months had elapsed, the secret of his real name was generally known. It came out in this wise. It happened that Sub-Lieutenant Parsons desired to change his servant. It occurred to him that Private Brown was an exceptionally clean, smart-looking fellow, and he intimated that he should be glad to select him for that purpose. I am bound to say that Hugh immediately went off into the most agonizing paroxysm of laughter that ever embarrassed a private or ruffled an officer's dignity—Sub-Lieutenant Parsons's dignity was undeniably ruffled.

" What the devil do you mean, sir ? " he demanded.

For a moment Private Brown struggled against it, but it was of no use, the laughter broke out again, in a more exhausting burst than before.

The little officer looked up at the big private in utter astonishment : this was a breach of discipline too awful to realize, but, as he looked more closely, a gleam of recognition came into his short-sighted, boiled-gooseberry looking eyes.

" I have seen you somewhere before—where ?" he asked, authoritatively.

The laughter bubbled up to Hugh's lips again, but in moderation this time.

" It would be rather turning the tables, if I became fag for you, Joey," he said, with good-natured contempt. " Excuse the familiarity, sir, but one is apt to forget sometimes that you are anyone but that young limb of evil, Joey Parsons, and I anyone but Hugh Brabazon."

"Hugh Brabazon!" Joey repeated, "and in the Scarlet Lancers!—I must have been blind!"

"I often thought so," Hugh said, easily. "Well, sir—Lord fancy my saying ' sir ' to you!—I am very much flattered that you would care to have me for your servant, but——"

"No, no, of course not," said Joey, hastily, and resuming his official tone. "Well, Brabazon, I'm awfully sorry that you've come down to this, the life must be an awful change for you, and if I can do anything to brighten it, you may count on me, for the sake of old times."

"Thank you, sir," answered Hugh, simply.

He saluted him as usual, as he walked away, but stood watching the small receding form with a huge scorn on his mouth and in his handsome eyes.

"What is it, Hugh?" asked Bertie Le Mesurier.

The scorn changed into a sigh. "A new sensation, Bertie," he said, with a short laugh. "Ah! I wish I could go back to the old ones, when I didn't have a brewer's snobbish son inviting me to clean his boots and brush his clothes for him."

"Did he do that?"

"Yes; did me the honour to wish me for his servant."

"What did you say?"

"Say? I didn't say anything; I just roared."

"Laughed?" Bertie echoed.

"I should think I did," laughing again at the remembrance. "I believe he thought of putting me under arrest, only he didn't."

"I wouldn't do that again, though, Hugh. Ridiculing your officers is a serious thing; besides, he may make life very much more unpleasant for you in many ways, if he thinks fit."

"But he won't," returned Hugh, confidently, "he won't. You are heir to a baronetcy and I am Lord Brabazon's son, so we are both sure of Joey Parsons's ' civility.' "

"My good chap, I am Corporal Black and you are Private Brown," he expostulated.

"He knows us both, take my word for it," Hugh laughed. "Moreover, he wants to marry one of my sisters, who won't look at him. I never met him after I left Eton, but I heard all about it from the girls : they used to make awful game of him."

The danger-signals mounted up to Bertie's face, and he asked, with a great assumption of carelessness, which sister the little cock-sparrow was after ?

" Gwen," Hugh replied. " Yes ! it was Gwen, who—oh ! hang it, Bertie, she hasn't forgotten the old days, any more than you or I have."

"Bertram Black, lance-corporal of the Scarlet Lancers," said Bertie, in a hopeless voice, "and she is the Honourable Gwendolin Brabazon, one of the most beautiful women in England."

"With a heart to match her face, bless her," cried Hugh. "She won't forget the heir of the Le Mesuriers for a low little scrub of a Cockney brewer."

" I wish I dared think so," Bertie returned, wistfully.

" Well, now look here, old man : Gwen's the only one of the lot who has stuck to me through thick and thin. Eva's not so plucky as Gwen, and she is the only one who knows where I am. I send my letters through her maid, and Gwen writes to me every week regularly. I heard from her this morning. If you care to see her letter you can, she won't mind."

" Care !" Bertie repeated.

" Yes, I see you do. You will see what she says about you, and, since she has sent me two photographs exactly alike, she must have meant me to give one to you. You can take your choice."

He handed him the dainty, perfumed letter and left him— glad of his friend's pleasure, but with a sigh on his lips, a dull pain in his heart, an utter sense of weariness and restless impatience with everything around him, and a vision before him of a fairy figure, most often clad in scarlet and white garments, of two soft brown eyes looking into his own, of two red-ripe lips upraised to his, of the feeling of two rounded white arms about his throat, and a soft voice whispering, " I love you."

He folded his arms upon the railing of the verandah, and gazed through the December gloom across the scarcely visible rows of barrack buildings to the twinkling lights of Liliminster, two miles away, and, as he leant there alone, an exceedingly bitter cry rose to his lips.

"Oh, Nell, Nell, Nell! If I could only bring the old days back again. Oh, Nell!"

All was quiet around him! There was an occasional clatter of spurred feet on the corridor behind him; a bad piano went "ting-ting-tum-tum" in the officers' quarters; there was, now and then, a sound of laughter from the next block, where the married people lived, and he could hear the measured tramp of the various sentries. Still, the great deserted square was quiet, and Hugh Brabazon leant on the railing, gazing across it into vacancy—vacancy as utterly blank and empty as his troubled heart.

A shower had fallen during the afternoon, and it might be that the raindrops were still hanging from the roof of the verandah, and so had fallen upon his uncovered head and down his face upon his clasped hands; and yet surely the rain-drops would not have been warm; warm?—the drops which fell upon Hugh Brabazon's hands were scalding hot. Poor Hugh? He had got over the roughest part of the new life, but the little glimpse of the old, which had come to him in his conversation with his whilom fag, Joey Parsons, and with his sister's lover, Bertie Le Mesurier, had been more bitter to him than all the changes he had yet undergone, and most bitter of all was the fierce yearning which rising in his heart had forced that passionate cry from his quivering lips—"Oh, Nell, Nell, Nell!"

CHAPTER II.

Two years had passed away, and Hugh Brabazon was still in the Scarlet Lancers, not as private, but as Sergeant Brown.

During that period of time many changes had taken place in the regiment. Sergeant-Major Green, M.A., had resumed his own honourable name as a commissioned officer, and his place had been taken by the son of the major-general, who, if wild, was a first-rate soldier.   Bertie Le Mesurier had gone back to society, as Sir Bertram, some months before the brilliant August days on which I take up the threads of my story; and if there was no Gwen Brabazon down in the old Devonshire house, there was an Honourable Lady Le Mesurier to be found at a certain Elizabethan mansion, styled Rest Court, who bore a strong resemblance to that very beautiful young lady, and who frequently wrote to Hugh as "your very loving sister." The son of the " dignitary " was doing as well as might reasonably be expected, considering his training, which must have been on the principle of "the shoemaker's missis going the worst shod." Teddie Lloyd they had left behind them at Liliminster, in his quiet grave, and Hugh was advanced to the dignity of sergeant. Such were some of the changes which two years had wrought in the " gentlemen's troop " of the Scarlet Lancers.

It was a blazing August afternoon—most people know what that means, but happily for them, only a limited portion of the community know what it means when the words *at Aldershot* are placed after it.   The sun literally poured down, it teemed, it shone cats and dogs, if one may be allowed the expression; and every living thing in Aldershot was probably nearer to sunstroke and heat apoplexy than he or she had ever been in his or her life.   Reader, have you ever been to Aldershot?   Do you know the bare, bleak, shelterless combination of flints and grit of which Aldershot is composed?   For my part, I think Burns was rather out of it when he described his farm as the " riddlings o' creation," he could never have seen Aldershot.   I never knew a soldier yet who did not hate it, and it has often been a source of marvel to me to determine how it is that any one can live there from choice, and there certainly are people who do so.

The Scarlet Lancers were in barracks—not camp—and on that particular afternoon Sergeant Hugh Brown was very busy helping Sergeant-Major Todd—otherwise Geoffrey, eldest son of Major-General Colquhoun, V.C., C.B.—to do nothing. Each was in possession of a door post of the sergeants' mess, that being the only spot where anything approaching to a draught of air was obtainable. Within the long room various bundles of scarlet and gold lace were lying about in more or less advanced stages of the two complaints I have just mentioned, which, as the heat of the day wore off, might end in nothing, or in the hospital and the " Dead March in Saul."

" Awfully hot," murmured Hugh, sending out great clouds of smoke from a well-coloured meerschaum, and thereby making himself very much hotter.

" Beastly hole, Aldershot," returned the other; and I'll be shot if there are not some tourists coming to look round. Fancy any one sufficiently idiotic to come to Aldershot for a ' hairing !' Why, town must be cool to this."

Hugh turned his head in the direction his friend had indicated.

" Mr. Sabretasche," he exclaimed, in disgusted tones; " Mr. Sabretasche *and* ladies. Hi! you fellows," putting his head inside the room ; " here's Mr. Sabretasche bringing some ladies round the barracks."

The several bundles of scarlet and gold, struggled up from their various recumbent attitudes, and there was a general buttoning of jackets and straightening of ruffled locks.

" Mr. Sabretasche might know better, on a day like this," one growled, with a great sigh, as the last button slipped into its place.

Hugh took no notice—he was too lazy, and the weather was too sultry to admit of argument with any one. He straightened himself once more against the door-post, and thanked Heaven it was Mr. Sabretasche and not himself who was making the round of the barracks.

" Can we come in, Sergeant Brown ?" said Mr. Sabretasche, at his elbow.

" Certainly, sir," Hugh answered, with a bow for the little lady, who never would, under any circumstances, pass him without recognition, and who persisted in calling him " Mr.— *Brown.*"

" Good day, ma'am."

"Good afternoon, Mr.—*Brown*," she returned, "is it not warm? Too warm for sight-seeing, is it not? But we have a lady staying with us, who has never been in a barrack in her life, so we braved the heat."

Hugh was about to make some courteous rejoinder, when he looked past Mrs. Sabretasche at the face of her visitor, visible for the first time, since, as yet, she had carried a large white sunshade. For one moment his heart seemed to stand still— then it went hurrying on again in such fierce throbs that his brain was in a whirl, and he felt as if he must fall. By a mighty effort he controlled himself, and bent courteously down to the little wife of his officer.

"It is very hot! Will you not rest here awhile, ma'am?" he said.

If he desired and intended to meet Mrs. Sabretasche's guest without recognition and as a stranger, she did not fall in with his views. On the contrary, she went a step nearer to him, and laid her two little hands on the gold embroidery of his sleeve.

"Oh, Hugh!" she said, in a piteous voice.

Sergeant Brown moved a step away from her, and the little hands fell to her side again.

"Why, Nell!" cried Mrs. Sabretasche, in surprise.

"What are you doing here?" the girl called Nell asked, blankly.

"This is the sergeants' mess, ma'am," Hugh replied, coldly; "and I being a sergeant—sergeant Brown, at your service— live here."

"You—live—*here?*" the girl echoed. She looked around her with eyes which saw no comfort, no beauty in the room, which was, in truth, both comfortable and pretty. She took in every detail: the long table with its green cover, the prints, and one or two water-colours on the walls, the pair of silver cups, the various presents given by sergeants who had left, either as officers, or to go back to their own position, at the vase of flowers on the side table—it was really a very pretty room, but she saw in it only misery, discomfort, and ugliness, and elevated a nose already inclined that way by nature. "You, Hugh Brabazon—*live*—here?" she repeated.

"Sergeant Brown, if you please, ma'am," Hugh said, by way of correction.

"Don't tell me," she cried, imperatively. "Do you think I do not know you?"

"It would be more kind, then, to pass me," he said, in a low voice.

"I will not pass you. What have I done that I should not speak to you?"

"It is what I have done," he answered.

At this point, Mrs. Sabretasche betook herself into the billiard room, whither her husband and the other members of the sergeants' mess had gone. Nell, perceiving that they were now alone, put her hands on Hugh's arm again, and, as the wall was behind him, he could not escape; in fact, the tall man was at the little woman's mercy.

"What have you done?" she asked—then in sudden alarm, "not got married, surely, Hugh?"

"Married," he repeated, scornfully, "to whom?"

"Oh! well, I didn't know. One never knows what may or may not have happened. I can't say I should have been surprised, after the horrid way you treated me."

"Nell!" he said, reproachfully.

"Oh, you may say 'Nell!' as hard as you like." She laughed—a suspicious laugh it was, for there was a sound of tears in it, and there were glistening drops in her soft eyes. "Pray, since we cannot stay talking much longer in a sergeants'-mess, are you coming to call upon me whilst I am with the Sabretasches?"

"My dear child—I am sergeant Brown, and your host is Lieutenant Sabretasche," he answered. "Do be reasonable—it is not likely I can be on visiting terms with them."

"Cannot you come for once as Hugh Brabazon?" she asked.

"It is impossible. Here I am only Sergeant Brown."

Just then Bob Sabretasche came out of the billiard room, followed by his wife.

"Brabazon," he said, simply, "will you come to my house, as soon as you can this evening?"

Hugh looked down upon his uniform and hesitated.

"Never mind that, I'll send Jinks out," said Bob; "I'm sure you and Lady Helen are dying to—to—talk old times over."

"I am, I frankly admit it," said Lady Helen, with saucy coolness; "but my opinion is that Mr. Brabazon wishes to shirk the acquaintance."

"Yes, do come," supplemented Mrs. Bob, "and I will show you my babies."

"Come and show me the rest of the barracks," said Helen, in a whisper so coaxing that Hugh hardly knew whether he was standing on his head or his feet. "Do come, Hugh; don't be nasty. Yes, Mr. Sabretasche, he will come this evening; and, in the meantime, he is going to show off the rest of the barracks to me."

"Very well—come, Lily, let us go on in front," Bob answered, with a laugh.

As the two figures passed the windows, Sergeant-Major Todd and another sergeant went to the door and watched them out of sight—the tall man in scarlet and gold, and the little woman in scarlet and white.

"She's a deuced pretty girl," Todd remarked; "I wonder who she is. Seems to have her own way with Hugh."

"She is Lady Helen Fairfax," Smith answered.

"Oh, you know her?"

"Yes! She didn't see me, though. Yes, I know her: my sister married her cousin, the earl. Lady Helen was engaged to Brabazon ever so long ago."

"Then you are Harry Tyrrwitt—how well you've kept your secret."

"Yes," with a laugh; "but don't let it go any further."

"Oh, no. So that is Lady Helen Fairfax, is it? I've often heard of her. I didn't know old Hugh was spoons on her. How was it they did not marry at first?"

"Hugh got into debt and other difficulties, gave her freedom

by letter—and bolted. I didn't know she cared for him still,
or I might have let her know his whereabouts long since—
however, I suppose it will be all right now."

But later, when Hugh turned up again, he did not look at all
as if it was all right; of a truth, he was most woefully
puzzled. Little Nell, whom he loved so, had crossed his path
once more, and would not be treated as a stranger. Poor dear
little Nell, who had no money, and ought to marry a duke at
least. The delight of seeing her was still visible in his
brightened eyes and in the tender smile upon his lips, still with
him in the passionate throbbing of his heart; and yet—what
was he to do? He was Sergeant Brown and she was an earl's
daughter, as poor as she was proud and lovely. Even if he left
the army, they could not live upon air.

He spoke to no one, being like a man asleep. Nor did he
rouse out of his reverie until he found himself in Mrs.
Sabretasche's drawing room, admiring the younger of her two
babies, and—as his quickly beating pulses told him—once more
near Nell Fairfax.

Bob was not in the room. Mrs. Sabretasche went the
length of weaving a polite fiction about an important letter, at
which Lady Helen had the audacity to laugh aloud.

"We expected you to dinner, Mr. Brabazon," said little
Mrs. Bob, when the baby-worship was brought to a close.

"Oh! you are very kind," Hugh answered, "but I couldn't
very well come to dinner."

"Why not?" Nell asked.

"My uniform," he began.

"Oh! we sent Jinks and his wife to the theatre," Mrs. Bob
laughed, "and the other two servants brought the dinner in for
us. We did capitally, did we not, Nell?"

"Yes, all but the visitor."

"Well, I must take this little lady up to the nursery. Will
you excuse me for a few moments, Mr. Brabazon?"

"Certainly!" He opened the door for her, and Nell, watching him, thought that, although he could not have seen much
of ladies during the past three years, he had lost none of the

courtly grace for which the Brabazons had ever been distinguished.

"Now," she said, as the door closed and he came back to the window, "what have you to say to me?"

"I don't know what to say," he answered, drawing her to him and looking down into her clear eyes. "I think, Nell, you are making it harder for both of us."

"Do you know," she asked, gravely, "what I think of you?"

"No, how should I?"

"I think, when you went off as you did, that you behaved abominably. Yes, Mr. Hugh Brabazon, disgracefully, and now you are going to do penance for your sins. You are, in fact, going to marry me."

"My darling, we cannot live upon nothing," he expostulated. "You cannot live in barracks, on a sergeant's pay."

"Of course not, you foolish man."

"Child, I have no money besides."

"But I have; did you not know it? Yes, Aunt Winny left me eight hundred a-year, with a recommendation to marry for love, if I could. Now Mr. Sabretasche, who is quite the most charming man I know, tells me that in a year or so you will have your commission. Until then I shall live 'retired.' Meantime, you are going to marry me at once."

"I won't do it," he said, stoutly.

"Oh yes you will," she replied, quietly. "If you don't, do you know what I shall do? I shall take lodgings in the town and loaf about the barrack gates, watching for you; and every time you appear, I shall cry aloud in heart-rending accents, 'Will you—will you—will you?' _ad libitum._"

"My darling, you cannot marry a sergeant," he cried, fighting desperately against himself.

"I not only can, but I will," she replied. "Why, bless the man, I shall not be Mrs. Sergeant Brown, but Lady Helen Brabazon; and it may only be for a few months."

"Then why not wait?"

"Because I won't. No, no, no! I tell you, I will not go away from Aldershot as Nell Fairfax. _I'll drown myself first!_

—there !" she laughed. " Oh ! it will be great fun. I shall
have a nice house—say in Trinity Terrace—and a couple of
maids, and a nice little carriage. Why, we shall be as jolly as
possible—only, they tell me, you may not live out of barracks."

" And you shall not live in them," he said, with much determination ; " to that I have made up my mind."

" Oh ! then you have made up your mind to do as I tell you
—otherwise ?"

" I suppose so," very reluctantly.

" Hugh," she said, suddenly growing grave, " you do care for
me still ?"

" Oh ! my darling," he exclaimed.

" As much as ever ?"

" A thousand times more !" he cried, passionately ; " never a
day that I have not thought of you ; never a night that I did
not see you in my dreams ; never a church-parade that I did
not pray for your happiness, never mind what my life would be
without you."

" Very considerate of you, I'm sure," she remarked, nodding
her head sagely ; " very considerate, ve—ry ! And did you
ever wonder if I sometimes thought about you ?"

" Often !"

" I'm glad of that. I might have been married heaps of
times, but, somehow—I say, Hugh, when you get your
commission, we shall be quite ' swagger' people : with our two
absurd titles, my eight hundred a-year and your pay—why we
shall be positively affluent."

*   *   *   *   *

It was less than a year after this, that the following
announcement appeared in the *Gazette :*

15th Lancers—Sergeant the Honourable Hugh Brabazon to be Sub-
Lieutenant, *vice* William Muirhead Tayte, promoted.

N ——; OR, AS WE GO ON.

Sooner or later—it may be sooner or it may be later, *but* sooner or later, and generally sooner—we find our evil deeds, words—nay, even our evil thoughts—come home to us: we get paid out—*as we go on!*

My pet theory is that no place of eternal punishment exists —if one does, our treatment is unfair, for do we not each and all expiate our sins—as we go on?

If we do something we know to be wilfully wrong, why it won't be very long before Nemesis comes down upon us with a crash and makes us wish we had left that particular thing undone; if, on the other hand, we err through ignorance or foolishness, N—— swoops down upon us as relentlessly as a music-master's pencil on the knuckles of his pupil—we rub our knuckles and wish we hadn't done it, but the pain is there, all the same.

The rule applies equally well to every phase of life—from the highly criminal misdemeanours down to those little flirtations with sin, so slight that one can hardly tell if they be right or wrong. It is as universal as that we were all born and that we shall all die—the only variation N—— permits is, that he sometimes pays his bills sooner, sometimes later; but I fancy most of my gentle readers will agree with me that he does not make a rule of taking long credit.

And not only to us of the present day does the theory apply —you may look as far back through the by-gone ages as you will, even to Adam and Eve, a period when our friend N—— had only just gone into business and had had but two customers, and there he is in full force. In many—nay, in most cases—the " paying out " seems inadequate to the particular evil deed, word, or thought for which our friend N—— has awarded it: just think of the lengthy punishment which followed—and faith! is still following—the purloining of that one apple!

There was Lot's wife—it could hardly have been agreeable to be turned into a pillar of salt, though probably she knew but little about it; and there was Hagar, who sniggered at Sarah! Aye! but N—— in the shape of Sarah herself, pulled her up sharp one fine morning, and I wonder how often after that did Madam Hagar wish she had kept a civil tongue in her head? I am afraid that is what a good many of us wish, besides Hagar, the bondwoman!

Of course, you have read the story of a wise old gentleman called Merlin, who lived ever so long ago—so long, that neither you nor I can fix the precise date—a wise old man, who knew the artfulness of womankind as well as any wary woman-hating old bachelor in this, the enlightened nineteenth century: a wise old man, who knew pretty nearly everything there was to know. Who, I wonder, would have believed that he could be such an old fool as to lend an ear to Vivienne's blandishments—an utterly unscrupulous young person, whom he did not even like, possessed of a reputation which, like many other things, would not wash: an adventuress of the most pronounced type? N—— did not delay very long in presenting Merlin with his account——

> And in the hollow oak he lay as dead,
> And lost to life and use, and name and fame.

From imaginary history into real is but a step—as many a one finds who slips ever so little from the realms of truth into the region of fiction—and there, staring us straight in the face, is the history of a certain king, who stuffed himself with lampreys *and died*. In that case N—— evidently considered a moderate paying-out of no use. Possibly he had tried it in the form of indigestion many times before, and without much effect, so clinched the matter by quietly putting His Majesty out of the way of lampreys for the future.

Out of the pages of history I might go on swelling my number of proofs *ad libitum*. There was Elizabeth of gracious memory—good Queen Bess; a bad-tempered termagant she was, gad-zooks! Every child knows a story in which Bess, Essex, a Countess, and a ring, played important parts—who, I wonder, would have been any of them? There was the Martyr King!—what of his promises? As I said, one might go on multiplying instances for ever, but that is what I must not do, for my story is strictly of the present day.

Perhaps in no class of life is my theory so indisputably apparent as it is in the service. Over every camp or barrack N—— keeps an eye, and careful indeed is he to keep his accounts in strict order. No vestige of a rule may be infringed, no duty shirked, no ill-temper pass unpunished, no honour remain unnoticed; and among the Scarlet Lancers no longer credit was given than in any other regiment.

The Scarlet Lancers had been nearly six months at Liliminster—quarters with which they were very well satisfied. They had good hunting, good society, roomy, comfortable barracks, a convenient hospital, and an excellent cathedral service on Sunday afternoon. Better than that, there was a circus—at least, during three months, one had been settled in the town—a respectable little theatre, and a subaltern who bore practical jokes with the most angelic and lamb-like demeanour. Nay, I am not by any means sure that Anthony Geohegan's disposition might not have ranked higher than either of the two standards I have quoted, for I fancy by the end of a month or so even an angel or a lamb would have rebelled against the course of treatment he was expected and, in fact, did undergo. Yes, he might have taken a very high rank, the first prize, indeed, if he had gone in for competition at a patience show, had not a circumstance occurred which caused a change. Every form of practical joke did he experience that the ingenuity of man could devise, but at last, after two year of martyrdom borne in uncomplaining silence, the trodden worm turned with such a vengeance that the gentlemen known as the officers of the Scarlet Lancers began to think it as well to run up no more " ticks " with N——, by means, that is, of Anthony Geohegan.

x

The awful change came about in this wise. Like many Irishmen, Anthony was of a fair-haired, blue-eyed type, a tall strong man, much given to laughing, and scarcely seeming to possess a temper at all. He was fairly well off, had no debts, and was not a little sick of barrack life and broken rest. So he fell over head and ears in love, and announced to his disgusted comrades that he was going to be married. The Scarlet Lancers were utterly taken aback.

"Tony going to be married!" exclaimed Clarke, when Tony had departed, after making the announcement. "Oh! that's the very devil."

"Make the most of him whilst we have got him," suggested Hartog.

"Who's the girl?" asked Joey Parsons.

"Miss Linden," returned Bob Sabretasche, "her father was Colonel of the 60th Hussars. Awfully nice girl, but I fancy rather a sharp temper."

A comprehensive "Ah!" came from the lips of the several officers assembled, and in the mind of more than one an idea suggested itself that out of Miss Linden's sharp temper not a little fun might be had. Whilst they were still talking over Tony's engagement, he passed the windows of the mess-room, apparently with the intention of going into the town,

"Hollo, Tony!" shouted Hartog, throwing up the window beside which he was standing.

"Yes," was shouted back.

"Do you dine here to-night?"

"No—concert in town," was the answer.

"An idea has occurred to me," said Hartog, shutting the window. "Tony is going to dine in town—with Mrs. and Miss Linden, of course—afterwards going to a concert."

"Yes," said the others, crowding round him.

"Dundas five minutes ago got out of a hansom with his gun and eight or ten brace of young rooks dangling to a string."

"Well?" they cried, impatiently.

"Well!" Hartog laughed; "Tony's man will lay his

things out early of course, and whilst he is at his tea we
will place the young rooks—bless 'em—in connection with
Tony's dress clothes, and then, in all probability, we shall
have considerable diversion at the concert this evening."

" I don't see the joke," said Joey Parsons, at which three or
four of the others laughed again.

" That's because you are a Cockney, my child," Hartog
laughed. " But just try the experiment of shaking a few
young rooks over your own clothes, and you'll very soon find
yourself in the plight our young lover will be in to-night."

" Not fleas?" Joey ejaculated. " Oh, I think that will
be rather beyond a joke—we've no business to worry the girl."

" The girl had no business to hook one of our best men,"
one growled in reply. " We shall *never* get another Tony."

All unknowing of the plot against him, Anthony Geoghegan
rushed into barracks at the very last minute to dress, and
without going into the mess-room jumped into a cab and drove
off to his *fiancée's* domicile. Before he had got half way there
Tony was woefully uncomfortable. *They* had found their way
to his skin and were biting as if they had fasted for a month.
Probably they found Tony better supplied with blood than the
young rooks had been.

" Ugh! dash it," muttered Tony to the cushions of the
dilapidated cab, " I must have got a flea."

A flea—dozens if he only knew it, but he didn't. He shook
himself like a Newfoundland dog just out of the water, but,
although perhaps he momentarily displaced them at their
operations, they returned to the charge with more fury than
ever, and Tony went into his lady-love's presence in as
uncomfortable a state as ever any lover was in. Uncomfortable!—he was undergoing torture !

Miss Linden was alone in the drawing-room. Such a pretty
girl, sharp as any hawk, with brilliant hazel eyes, nut-brown
hair, and a complexion like cream, with just a dash of pink
across the cheeks ; a lovely girl, and at the sight of her
Anthony Geoghegan forgot his bodily discomfort for a
moment, and took her in his arms and kissed her.

x 2

" You have not been very long," she said, smiling up at him. Mother is not yet ready."

" I'm glad of that—crsche !" with a great jump and a mental ejaculation of " Lord, how the devils do bite."

" What's the matter?" said Evelyn.

" Nothing, darling, just a twinge here, that was all," laying his hand on his left side,

" Your heart is not affected, Anthony ?" she said, in sudden alarm.

" No, no, a mere stitch—crsche !"

" Anthony, it is there still," she cried.

Another mental ejaculation of " yes, dash it—it's there safe enough."

" Suppose you give me a kiss—that will cure me safe enough," he suggested.

Miss Linden was not averse to the cure he proposed, and put her arms round his neck very affectionately—her arms were very pretty, Tony particularly noticed that, and her throat and bosom were as white as snow.

" What a pretty dress that is, Evelyn," he remarked. " I've not seen you wear it before."

" No ; I'm glad you like it, dear. Do you think this colour suits me ?" she asked.

" I believe there are two," returned Tony, absently.

" What?" said Evelyn, opening her brilliant eyes very wide. " Two what ?"

" Er—, I believe I was thinking about something else," he stammered, reddening a little. " Forgive me, darling, you were speaking about the dress. Yes ! I like that soft creamy colour very much, and those quaint yellowish trimmings are charming."

Soon after, Mrs. Linden appeared, and they went in to dinner. At first Evelyn talked a good deal, but gradually relapsed into comparative silence, and Mrs. Linden had all the conversation to herself.

" This is dreadful," said Tony to himself; " I shall never be able to exist through the concert."

He watched his *fiancée* furtively, and presently noticed an uneasy movement of one shoulder, and saw one little hand steal up the sleeve of her gown.

" She's got one," he thought; " there must have been ever so many."

However, at last the repast was ended; and after a cup of coffee, they betook themselves in a cab to the concert room ; Mrs. and Miss Linden, of course, occupying the back seat. That fatal drive ! No sooner did Mrs. Linden, who was a lady of ample proportions, get settled in her chair, than she whispered to her daughter, who sat between her and Tony—

" My dear, I've got a flea about me."

" So have I," returned Evelyn, tragically ; " I believe I have got two."

Then she had to listen to a tender little speech from Tony— he had a lull just then—but as soon as she turned her head, Mrs. Linden claimed her attention again.

" My dear, I shall never be able to stay all the evening. This thing is driving me crazy. I never could sit quiet with a flea about me."

" Hus—sh—sh—sh," whispered Evelyn, with a nervous glance behind her. She just looked aside in time to see Tony make a vigorous attack upon one arm ; he had taken the opportunity, whilst her head was turned, to give his sleeve a good scrub up and down. He reddened so visibly, that an unworthy and suspicious thought made its way into her mind.

" Dear me," she reflected, " I've heard Irish people are dirty, but—" She gave one swift side glance at Tony's fair skin and spotless linen, and immediately went off into a fit of laughter, impossible to explain, in spite of his entreaties that she should do so ; but for all that perfectly intelligible to half-a dozen pairs of eyes, looking on from the other side of the room.

Assured of the success of their plan, Jack Hartog and his confederates continued the treatment, and for a fortnight or so the three victims were submitted—by means of poor Tony—to a perfect plague of fleas.

"It is a most extraordinary thing," exclaimed Mrs. Linden, one evening, after Tony had taken his departure, and she had been entertaining on a more lavish scale than usual, "that when Anthony comes, I seem to have these things worse than ever. I'm sure it's far too early in the year for them. I can't think where they all come from."

It happened that on that very same evening Tony went back to his room rather earlier than the mischief-makers expected, and surprised them at work with the batch of young rooks, which daily fell victims to become the means of discomfort to three unsuspicious and unoffending people. Tony entered the room quietly, not from any desire to creep in unawares, but simply because his thoughts were occupied and he was therefore walking slowly. The scene which presented itself was decidedly a novel one. Round the sofa-bed with its bearskin cover, stood five or six officers, and in their midst Jack Hartog, with the bunch of birds tied on the end of a stick. He was shaking and rolling them upon the fur rug vigorously, amidst roars of laughter from the entire assembly.

"What the devil are you doing?" exclaimed Tony in very genuine and open-mouthed astonishment.

The group confronted him, with a start, but Jack Hartog turned round coolly, with the stick still in his hand.

"Oh! it's you, is it, old man? What's brought you back so soon?"

"It's half-past ten," Tony answered. "What on earth are you doing here, and what the deuce are those birds for?"

"Birds!" Jack repeated; "what birds?"

"Why those young rooks, you've got tied to that stick, of course," Tony retorted.

"Well, the fact is, we were going to put them into your bed," Hartog said at last, with a great air of making a clean breast of the matter. "Little joke, you see, Tony. There, now, don't turn crusty, old chap. We've let you alone lately, and we haven't much more time left to plague you in."

The light began to dawn upon Tony's mind. He crossed the room, and in silence took a pistol from its case on a side table.

" Now," he said, quietly, "you fellows clear out of my room or, upon my soul, I'll fire. I've found you out at last, but take my word for it, you've played your last joke in this room."

After a faint show of resistance, they did leave the room, Hartog allowing the birds to remain on the floor. Tony picked them up, slipped them off the stick, and flung them after the retreating party, catching Hartog just in the nape of the neck, and, as Tony said to himself, with a grim laugh, making him thoroughly uncomfortable for the rest of the night.

He shut the door and locked it, flung the fur rug from the bed into a remote corner, and sat down to think. Now, nine times out of ten, when a man or woman sits down for the express purpose of thinking, the matter on hand is of an unpleasant nature! So it was with Anthony Geoghegan. His thoughts were very bitter, for not an hour previously Evelyn Linden had spoken to him very seriously, and asked him to take back his ring and consider the engagement at an end. Naturally, he had pressed her to give him some reason, but in vain. She only repeated that she wished the engagement at an end.

" Tell me you no longer care for me," he said to her, " and I'll go away and never trouble you again."

" I cannot marry you," said Evelyn, evading his question.

" What have I done ? " the poor fellow cried. " Oh ! Evelyn, I would have made you so happy."

Miss Linden shuddered—yes, positively shuddered, as Tony particularly noticed.

" It is of no use, Mr. Geoghegan, I have not been happy the last fortnight, neither has my mother, and, believe me, it is best at an end."

Until he reached his room her decision had puzzled him, but the little episode of the rooks had enlightened him considerably—poor little darling, she had been eaten alive as he had been. However, to-morrow he would go and ask her plainly if that was the cause of his dismissal, and then, surely, everything would come right.

Unfortunately, he was on duty the next day and could not get out of barracks, but on the day following that, he hurried to Mrs. Linden's house and found—*the place shut up.*

For a moment Anthony was bewildered—then it dawned upon him that, after all, the fleas could not have been the cause of Evelyn's desire to close the engagement: evidently, she wanted to be rid of him; evidently, she cared nothing about him. He remembered how, on the night of the concert, she had put her soft white arms round his neck and kissed him, but it had all been a sham—make-believe love—counterfeit coin!

He never thought of writing to her or of trying some time in the future to win her woman's heart. Oh! no. The Scarlet Lancers had accomplished their end finely, but the process had left Anthony Geoghegan with a decided distaste for practical jokes; indeed, if the truth be told, he vowed a mighty vow that his brother officers should get no more fun out of him.

Nor did they! During the morning of the following day, a couple of intelligent workmen appeared, asking for Mr. Geoghegan. He took them up to his room, and they spent about a quarter-of-an-hour measuring the dimensions of the doorway with a foot rule.

"Going to have an iron door put, Tony?" was the careless question of an officer passing.

"Oh, no!" returned Tony, in as careless a tone.

For a week nothing new appeared in Tony's quarters, but at the end of that period the intelligent workmen came on the scene again, one carrying a bass full of tools, the other having a large, light burden, carefully enveloped in cloths. They made their way to Tony's room, the door was closed, and, beyond a little screwing and hammering, no one could guess what was going on.

Tony himself gave them no opportunity of discovering. He did not go to dinner until the very last minute, and when one who had waited to see him leave his room tried the door, it was locked. Evidently there was some mystery in Tony's apartment, but whatever it was, Tony did not enlighten them. He was a little quiet throughout the meal, but not in the least sulky, and towards eleven o'clock betook himself to bed, with a civil "good-night."

The conspirators waited half-an-hour or so before they followed him, as they had done regularly every night since he had caught them with the rooks. They stepped softly along the corridor and tried the door.

It was open!

Yes: the handle turned easily and the door opened. Clarke and Hartog stepped into the room lighted only by the fire-glow, when "Hur—r—r—r—ah!" was their simultaneous cry.

"What is it?" asked those in the rear, pushing them forward again to meet that invisible enemy, which once more extracted that shuddering cry from both of them.

"What the deuce is it?" cried another, pressing forward. "Oh—h! Lord, what's that?"

"Galvanism," replied Hartog; "but where is it? Hi! get a light, somebody, and let's find out what and where the confounded thing is."

Clarke fetched a light from his room opposite, and beheld, if you please, a square cage, fitting completely over the door, made of strong brass wire, and attached to it an electric battery, which stood on a table by Tony's bed.

"Oh, there can't be much strength in that," said Hobbs, scornfully, "I'll pull that down in two minutes."

"Try," returned Hartog, shaking his fingers.

He put his back against it and tried to force the wires through, but Tony turned on such a current of electricity that the youthful Hercules fell to the ground in something very much like a swoon.

"Oh! hang it, Tony, don't kill the poor chap!" exclaimed Hartog.

"Take the poor chap out of my room, then," returned Tony, from under the bed-clothes, "and don't trouble yourselves to come drawing me any more. I am perfectly sick of it, and bedad, I won't have any more of it;" after which, he rolled himself afresh in the bed-clothes, and refused to utter another word.

And that was all about it! The *dénouement* is awfully flat, is it not? Yet, when a thing comes to an utter and complete close, one can make neither more nor less of it.

So the officers of the Scarlet Lancers felt flat—very! It was no use attempting any more fun with Tony. They began to wish his engagement had gone on, for it would have been better to have lost him altogether than to have had that tantalizing birdie inside that impregnable electric cage. And Tony was so wonderfully good-tempered about it, too; if he would only have sulked, or been disagreeable, it would not have been half so bad. Ah! N—— had taken a novel way of paying off old scores that time.

And Evelyn Linden—what of her? She and her mother remained some months away from Liliminster, on an allowance of so much a week from N——. His coinage was varied— bitter tears, sad sighs, sleepless nights, yearnings, longings, re- grets. Poor Evelyn!

It was not long after their return home that Joey Parsons, in a burst of confidence, told her all about the plot of the rooks and the electric cage. She said very little; but when the good- natured young soldier had gone, she wept—tears so bitter, that N—— relented and put an idea into her mind to write Tony a note, asking him to call on her. She sent it by the man-servant, expecting he might perhaps come the next day, but within an hour he appeared—flushed with expectation and hope.

"Oh! Tony," she cried, springing from her seat; and Tony kissed her——.

A REGIMENTAL LODGE;

OR, HOW JACK HARTOG WAS MADE A FREEMASON.

Chapter I.

' Take my advice, Jack," said old General Hartog to his son, when he joined the Scarlet Lancers, " never be surprised at anything. Take everything as a matter of course, and if the laugh happens to turn against yourself—laugh harder than any of 'em."

" Very well, sir," said Jack, cheerfully.

" And remember this, if—and of course they will—if they attempt to hoax you, always let them play the game out, before you show them you are not such a fool as you look."

" I suppose I do look a fool," said Jack, rather ruefully, stealing a glance at himself in the glass opposite.

" Well, my dear lad, you're an uncommon fine fellow, there's no doubt about it," the old soldier answered, eyeing his son's six feet of splendid manhood proudly; " but men who don't manage to get into the army before one-and-twenty—and then do it by the back door, otherwise the militia—can't be said to be particularly distinguished in the brain line."

" No, I daresay not," returned Jack, carelessly. " Well, never mind, sir, I'm a first-rate shot, good cross country, A-1 at lawn tennis, and a very decent hand at whist; and if there's any fighting, I'll let them see that I'm worthy of my name—see if I don't."

" I don't fear but that you'll do that, Jack," said the old man, with something like a mist gathering before his keen blue eyes. " I need not have said anything nasty about the back-door, I might have remembered there were no examinations in my time."

"Oh! never mind," cried Jack, lightly.

He was not thin-skinned concerning his mental accomplishments; did any one of his own standing chaff him about past failures, he would quote coolly—

" No, I tarn't speak Frenss au' I tarn't speak German, but I tan punss your 'ed."

A speech which, with the addition of a certain swaggering gesture of his strong right hand and arm, generally had the effect of diverting the current of the conversation into widely different channels.

A few days later this handsome, swaggering young fool left the paternal mansion for the quarters of the Scarlet Lancers, just then at Blankhampton, where, as is not invariably the case, he met with a cordial reception. His brother officers " took " to him. He was very goodly to look upon, for he had a nice, fresh, fair face, with blue smiling eyes and a pleasant mouth, disclosing good even teeth; he was tall and straight, too, with firm, strong, graceful limbs, and an inexhaustible fund of good humour. They all declared he was " awfully " good tempered. Their most trying jokes he bore with blissful good nature; which, though it perhaps took a little from the zest of their amusement, decidedly won their admiration and esteem. When they amused themselves by smashing his furniture, he set to work and smashed with the best or the worst of them.

" Do you think I'm going to see my things smashed and have none of the fun ?" he demanded, coolly.

When he found every coat, tunic and jacket he possessed carefully sewn as to arm-holes and pockets, instead of flying into a rage, as they expected, he sat down on his bed, and cried " Splendid !" And when they got into his room one night, when there had been a big mess, and cropped his fair-curly hair like a convict or a Frenchman, he sold them all by going into raptures of admiration over his appearance every time he came within sight of a mirror. After that they left him alone; they said it was no use chaffing such a fool.

If Jack had quietly allowed matters to remain there, I need never have written this history; but unfortunately, from his youth up, he had been impressed with an idea that the inner life of a cavalry regiment is absolute Pandemonium. No doubt in the general's younger days it was so; for his stories so far threw the doings and misdoings of the Scarlet Lancers into the shade, that his son, so far from perceiving that they were tired of playing their practical jokes upon him, only imagined the calm preceded, instead of succeeded, the storm. He was therefore, more closely on the look-out for chaff than ever; and bearing in mind that he was always to let them play their game out, before he shewed the extent of his wisdom, expressed no surprise on hearing that there were a good many Freemasons in the regiment, and that they had a lodge of their own.

He simply did not believe it! He had never heard of anything of the kind from his father, and imagined in the casual mention of the institution that a deep-laid plan was brewing for his especial delectation.

"I suppose you are not a Mason, Hartog?" said the major, one evening after mess, a few days after Jack had first heard of the lodge.

"No, sir—wish I was," said he, with apparent innocence, though he was ready to burst with laughter.

"Do you? Oh! there is no difficulty about the matter. There is no lodge here in Blankhampton, and a good many are glad of the opportunity of joining ours. I fancy when we leave they will form one. We have a lodge to-night, shall I propose you?"

"If you please, sir," said Jack, cheerfully.

"I encourage soldiers to join—though, as you probably know, we are not allowed to *invite* persons to join our body—I always encourage any desire to do so. A soldier never knows to what part of the world he may not be sent at an hour's notice; and if he is a Freemason he will always find a lodge open to him, or brother Masons to hold out the hand of fellowship to him.

"Exactly," said Jack, rather hazily.

"Perhaps, Scott, you will second him?" the major said, turning to a grizzled old captain on his right.

"To be sure, major," with a merry twinkle in his hard blue-grey eyes—or what seemed so to Jack.

"You're in for it. What a fool you were to say yes," laughed a subaltern afterwards.

"Oh! I always was a fool—all the Hartogs are," returned Jack, with praiseworthy good nature. "I wonder what they do? Are you one of 'em?"

"Oh, no! I'm a Catholic."

"Well, what's that got to do with it?"

"Priests won't let us have anything to do with 'em. Never knew what it was to be thankful on that score before; shut the major's blarney up in a moment."

"What do they do?"

"Stick you on a red-hot gridiron, and chivvy you round the room with a poker."

"Oh! come, now," incredulously.

"So they say, but of course I can't speak from experience. By Jove, though, what a fool you were to say yes."

"Well if they begin any of that stuff on me, I shall take to my fists," laughed Jack, of course thinking Vane in the secret also.

"I wonder what kind of a jumble they'll make of it," quoth he to himself that night, as he slowly undressed. "Of course, their game will be to gull me enough to make me long to get into a genuine concern, and get kicked out as a consequence. Lord! what a joke to tell my old governor; it beats his yarns hollow."

CHAPTER II.

By means of moveable furniture, ornaments and jewels, the members of the Scarlet Lancer Lodge of Free and Accepted Masons had made a very pretty interior. A spare troop-room had been divided by temporary partitions into the correct form of an oblong square, vestibule and outer room. They were ne-cessarily obliged to dispense with the three grand pillars—the Doric, Ionic and Corinthian; but the ceiling was painted in a representation of a celestial canopy of divers colours. They had a very handsome floor-covering of moveable parquetry work to represent the mosaic pavement, the blazing star, and the indented or tessellated border; the tracing board, rough and perfect ashlers, were also in due position, and all the other paraphernalia of skull and cross-bones, coffin, tassels, and the like.

It was to this room that Jack Hartog made his way on the evening appointed for his initiation into the secrets and privileges of Freemasonry. He was met by a sergeant, acting as Steward, who was waiting in the outer room to prepare him for entrance. It occurred to him, when the man explained his duties, that it was scarcely the right thing to bring a non-commissioned officer into the working of a practical joke upon a subaltern; and for the first time he, like his father, pronounced the non-purchase system a mistake.

" It has lowered the tone of the army," said Jack to himself.

" You'll have to take your jacket off, sir," said the Steward.

" My jacket; why ?"

" It is necessary, sir," was the answer.

Jack shrugged his shoulders, but off came the jacket. " Any more ?"

" Your waistcoat also."

Off came the embroidered waistcoat—he began to wish himself out of the business safely.

" You must bare your right arm, sir," the Steward continued.

" I say, they're not going to tattoo me ?" he asked, apprehensively.

" No, sir," with an amused laugh. " Now, undo your shirt at the throat, and pull up your left trouser so as to leave the knee bare."

" Anything more ?" Jack asked, satirically.

" Oh, yes ! slip your right heel out of your boot."

" Well, of all the tom-foolery !" Jack began, too hopelessly surprised to be in the least amused.

" And empty your pockets and take your rings off."

"Lord bless me!" he ejaculated, blankly.

" Hollo ! what's that for ?" as the sergeant lifted a rope with a running noose.

"To put round your neck—it is technically called a cable-tow."

" Then let me tell you, you are not going to put what is technically called a cable-tow round my neck," said Jack, with considerable decision.

" Must be done, sir, if you mean to be initiated to-night."

" Oh ! blow your initiation—and what's that for ?"

" To blindfold you."

" Blindfold me ! Not if I know it ! Why, I might be scalped, before I could say ' Jack Robinson.' "

" No fear of that," laughing outright.

" Well, all this tom-foolery," glancing down at his odd figure, " is quite enough, without the rope or the bandage, and I don't intend to submit to either of them."

" You cannot enter the lodge without them," was the decided reply. " Wait a moment, sir, and I'll fetch one of the officers out, who will convince you that it is really necessary."

He went to the door of the Lodge, giving one distinct rap—so Jack thought, but it was the Tyler who performed the ceremony—and after an instant's parley, Captain Scot came out and asked what was amiss ?

" Why, they want to put that rope round my neck," said Jack, indignantly.

" Of course."

" And to blindfold me ?"

" To be sure—the two most absolutely necessary parts of the ceremony."

" Then I'll be d——d if I will," said Jack, emphatically, sitting down on the chair and beginning to straighten his apparel.

" You can do as you like, of course, my dear chap," said the grizzled captain, good-naturedly ; " but as the colonel and the major are both enthusiastic Masons, and as the major has proposed you himself you will seriously offend them both, besides making yourself the laughing-stock of the regiment. They will all say you were too big a coward to join."

That decided him, and, with a great sigh, he resigned himself to go on.

" Now look here—if there is any red-hot iron business, I shall kill the first man I get hold of," he said, as his senior left him.

" All right," with a laugh.

" Now, sir," said the Steward, leading him to the door.

It was as well that he was in ignorance of the pointed sword held to his breast as he walked, or he would probably have turned tail, in spite of that significant hint about making himself the laughing-stock of the regiment.

There was a moment's parley between the Steward and the Tyler; then the latter gave three distinct knocks. This was followed by a rap from within, the signal of alarm, and, after a slight pause, a voice asked,

" Who is there ?"

" A poor candidate is in a state of darkness," answered the Steward, " who comes of his own free will and accord, and also properly prepared, humbly soliciting to be admitted to the mysteries and privileges of Freemasonry."

(" Draw it mild," put in Jack, *sotto voce.*

" Be serious, sir, it is a grave business," exclaimed the Steward, earnestly.)

" How does he hope to obtain these privileges ?" asked the Inner Guard.

" By the help of God and the tongue of good report."

" Halt, till I make due report."

Then there was a repetition within concerning the poor candidate in a state of darkness, during which Jack resigned himself to the inevitable, with a murmured protest on the utter profanity of the proceedings.

" And I don't go in for being saintly myself," he ended.

" You'll get into serious trouble if you are not quiet," came in a warning whisper from his guide.

Y

Then the door was flung wide open that they might enter; it closed behind him, and retreat was effectually cut off.

CHAPTER III.

It was about two hours later that Jack Hartog, once more clothed in his mess-dress, went into the mess-room, where those who had dined at the late dinner still lingered. He was hailed with a shout of laughter and " Now then, brother, how did you get on?"

" Frightened you out of your wits, hey ?"

" Have a glass of champagne, my boy," and the like.

Jack seated himself and made a grave survey of the faces assembled round the table.

" I don't go in for being straight-laced," he remarked deliberately, " I wasn't brought up in that way; but upon my word, they went beyond a joke to-night."

" What did they do, Jack? What's it like? Did they stick you on the gridiron ?"

" Not a bit of it ! Never heard of a tamer sell in my life."

" Well, what did they do ?"

" They just made a fool of me," said Jack, ruefully.

" Impossible, Jack ! that was already accomplished," laughed one.

" But what did they do? come tell us," cried another.

" Well, first they undressed me."

" Undressed you !" with a great yell of laughter.

" Very nearly ; I had to take off my jacket and waistcoat, empty my pockets and pull off my rings, my shirt was undone at the throat, my right arm and my left knee bare, and my right heel pulled out of my boot. Then they stuck a rope round my neck and a bandage over my eyes—under which, all the same, after a little judicious frowning and wrinkling of my nose, I could see beautifully."

" Yes, what then ?"

" Oh ! a lot of blarney about a poor candidate in a state of darkness begging for light, and all that rot. Oh ! it was splendidly got up, only the ceremony was awful trash; any fool could have seen through it in a moment."

"Why, Hartog, you don't think it was a joke—a trick?" said one of the listeners, suddenly perceiving the truth.

"Of course it was; never heard such twaddle in the whole course of my life."

"My dear chap, it was the real thing," Kerr asserted.

"Oh, yes! no doubt," with a knowing laugh. "You're all in the joke, and think you'll be able to gull me into trying to get into a real Freemasons' club, and get kicked out. Ah! but I *ain't quite* such a fool as I look."

"Hartog, I assure you there is no joke at all about it," he persisted.

"Well, now look here," said Jack, "I've an uncle, who's ever such a great swell in the lodge the Prince of Wales belongs to, and I've often tried to get the secrets and things out of him; though of course I never could. Whenever I chaff him about Freemasonry, he invariably turns as solemn as you please, and says it is a very impressive and grave ritual, requiring a great deal of thought and care to under-stand and get proficient in. He *couldn't* say that of all the humbug and tom-foolery that went on to-night. Why, *every* one knows that the Freemasons' signs and secrets are awfully difficult to learn, and this was wha: they showed me to-night—that's the first sign," making, as he spoke, the sign of an entered apprentice.

One of his hearers rather recoiled. "Don't do that again, Jack, it's so horribly suggestive—particularly with knives about. Ugh! it gives one the shivers."

"Well, that was it—the first. No, I'm wrong, the first was a kind of goose-step; then that; then the grip, which,"— holding out his hand for any of them to take—"was just that and nothing more. As if I was such a foo' as to swallow all that."

"Did you swear much, Jack?" some one asked.

"Oh! no end—on my knees too—most profane I consider it. Yes, on my knees, with my right hand on the Bible, and holding one point of the compasses to my heart, so. Well, I cannot say what I did not swear, all sorts of impossible things. There was something about cutting my throat, and tearing my tongue out by the roots, and burying my body in sand of the sea at low water mark."

" What! Burying yourself?" cried a laughing voice.

Jack looked puzzled for a moment. "No, I suppose they were to bury me," he replied ; " and, between you and me, gentlemen, I am thoroughly ashamed of having had any part in the affair. I don't go in for being saintly, as I told you, I wasn't brought up in that way, but I have some respect for sacred things, and I don't approve of bringing the Bible and the name of the Almighty into practical jokes, and I'm very much surprised at a man of the major's age for doing so."

" Well, don't let him hear you say so, that's all," laughed Lucian.

" Hartog, it is not a joke," repeated Kerr, emphatically, for the third time.

" Kerr, it was a joke," returned Jack, with equal emphasis. " I tell you there was something about that chap that was after Ruth—I forget his name—and what could he possibly have to do with Freemasonry ?"

" Oh ! that was——" began Lucian, then broke off short, for in the doorway leading from the ante-room stood the major himself, looking straight at Hartog, with a face of thunder.

Lucian's sudden stop and look of blank dismay caused every head to turn that way, and a hush, as of death, fell upon the excited group. In an instant Jack realised the truth ! For the first time in his life he knew what a sensation of sickening fear meant—he could not think or speak, he was conscious of nothing but that those terrible cold eyes were fixed upon him, and that he had made a mistake which would probably wreck his whole life.

Amid that death-like silence, Major Bernard advanced into the room, and laid his hand upon the back of a vacant chair at the head of the table, his cold eyes—like the flash of steel, several of them thought—were still fixed upon Jack's fast-whitening face.

At last he spoke—not loudly, but in the suppressed voice of a man utterly possessed by a storm of intense passion.

"Well, sir," he said, at length, in accents of cutting scorn, "you are a credit—to—your regiment—a cred—it—sir."

Jack spoke no word—only his widely-opened blue eyes remained fixed upon his superior's, with a fascination piteous to behold.

"You have this evening," the major went on, in the same terribly low tone, "taken solemn oaths before God and your fellow men, which you have broken. Do you know, sir, that you have ruined your life—that you have forfeited your claim to be called a gentleman, and earned the contempt of every honourable man?"

"I—I thought—" Jack began, piteously, but Major Bernard cut him short, and continued—

"Your evidence would not be accepted in any court of justice in the world, sir," he said, scornfully, "do you know that?"

Jack looked despairingly around, and caught at the arm of the man next to him, that he might steady himself. The major went on—

"How is it possible that your father's son can have so little value for his honour, so little respect for himself, so little respect for a stainless name, which to honourable men is in itself alone another term for chivalry and valour, I cannot imagine. Have you no notion of the value of your word? Have you no respect for your solemn oath?"

Again he tried to speak, but this time his trembling lips refused their office, and the sound died away in his throat. Only he held Kerr's arm with a harder grip, and his blue eyes remained fixed on his major's face, as they had done from the beginning, while in his brain and heart one question was repeating itself over and over again, "What will the general say?"

"All I have to say is," said the major, "that you will be formally expelled from the body of Freemasons, and that my private acquaintance with you is, from this day, at an end. I have done."

He turned on his heel, as if to leave the room, but Jack suddenly loosed his hold of Kerr's arm, and with one despairing look at the major, staggered out. As the door crashed behind him Major Bernard turned back to those standing about the table.

"I suppose, gentlemen, he has told you everything?" he asked.

"Everything," replied one or two voices.

He was once more turning away, but Kerr stopped him.

"Wait a moment, sir," he said, hastily, "I must give you some explanation of this, since Hartog seemed unable to do so. He really believed the whole affair was an elaborate practical joke. I have been trying to convince him that such was not the case, ever since he came in here. Is it not so?" appealing to the others.

"Yes—certainly."

"A joke!" echoed the senior, indignantly, "I play a joke upon him—a lad like that— or, indeed, upon any one. He must be a fool."

"I don't think he is particularly clever, sir," Kerr answered, "and as for what he told us, it didn't amount to much, for we couldn't make head or tail of it—neither for the matter of that did he seem able to do. I think you may trust him to divulge nothing further, and you have our word that what he has disclosed is safe with us. Is it not so?" turning to the others once more.

"Oh, yes—yes, of course!" they all cried.

But the major was not thus easily to be mollified.

"Utterly without principle," he muttered, grimly. "Hollo! What's that?"

That was the sound of a pistol-shot, followed by a heavy fall on the floor above.

"Good God! the young idiot has shot himself!" cried Kerr, pushing the major unceremoniously aside. He ran along the verandah and dashed up the stairs of the quarters adjoining, just as a trooper's rough voice rang out vigorously for help. The adjutant's wife ran out of her rooms on the same floor, and several officers and servants followed Kerr, who forced the door open with one shove of his strong shoulder, to find Hartog lying on the floor, bleeding profusely from a wound in the shoulder.

"I was in his room when he came up," said the servant, as they turned him over. "He told me to go out, and I seed something was up—I heard the click of the pistol, and I must just have tried to bang the door in as he took aim, and startled him."

"Hollo! what's this?" exclaimed the old surgeon-major, entering.

"It's your damned Freemason tom-foolery!" returned Kerr, savagely. "Is he much hurt?" in a gentler tone.

"No, no, nasty flesh wound through the shoulder—have him off the sick-list in a fortnight. Now, clear out, all of you; Mrs. Gray will stay with me, and Ford, you stop; all the rest clear out—we can do better without you."

They went back to the mess-room, where they found the major, very white and grave, and with all the anger and sternness faded from his face.

"How is he, not dangerously hurt, I hope?"

The intense anxiety in his tones rather touched Kerr, who had mentally determined as he descended the stairs to make out the worst possible case, and give him as great a fright as he could.

"Moore seems to think the danger lies in possible contraction of the muscles," he answered, "the ball has gone clean through the top part of the shoulder.

"There is only one way in which his life can be saved from ruin," said a young officer, coming forward, "and that is for us all to get made Masons at once."

"You are right; I had thought of it," Major Bernard answered. "It is not customary—indeed it is forbidden that we should invite others to join our body, but I have the greatest respect for his father—a braver soldier and a truer gentleman does not live—and I had already determined to ask you, who have heard his folly to-night, to save him from further trouble concerning it."

"I shall be very glad," said Kerr, without hesitation.

"And I—and I," in a chorus from the others.

"And what about Vane—he is a Catholic?" asked Major Bernard.

"I have been sitting with Gwynne all the evening, major. I only ran out when I heard the pistol-shot."

"That is all right," in a relieved tone; "oh, here is Moore. How is the patient?"

"Conscious again, and crying on Mrs. Gray's shoulder like a baby. What a nice little woman she is. I say, what was the matter?—a quarrel?"

"Oh, no—only a mistake," said the major, who, now that his anger was gone, did not care to further publish Jack's misdoings. "Perhaps, Kerr, you will go up and set his mind at rest. I will come and see him in the morning. For the rest, gentlemen, I need not ask your silence and your forbearance."

"No, major, no—certainly not."

"And the request comes with a good grace from you," growled Kerr, as the door closed behind him.

"Poor Jack wasn't far out of it," remarked Lucian, when the still angry Kerr had betaken himself to comfort poor crest-fallen Jack upstairs, "it must be a precious tom-foolery business. They won't get me there a second time, I can tell you."

"Poor old Jack! how the major did slang him," laughed another. "I say, what was that about Ruth?"

"It wasn't Ruth," returned Lucian, "It was Boaz."

CONSCIENCE.

Chapter I.

He was alone; a handsome, grey-eyed, sunburnt man, in a fairly-comfortable room. I am not going to describe it; only so far as to say that the chair in which he sat was a very big one, and that the fire, to which his long legs were stretched, blazed half-way up the chimney, though it was but the beginning of October.

"Oh! confound—*every*-thing," he observed disconsolately to the walls, or maybe the fire, and clasping his hands at the back of his smooth sunshiny head. "I don't know what to do. I'll be hanged if I know what to do. Poor little Pussey, how her face did cut me up. I can't get it out of my head; nor the widow's either, for that matter. Poor little Pussey! and yet I can't help myself."

He upheaved himself from the depths of the big chair—a fine fellow, nearly six feet in height, with clean active limbs and a perplexed handsome face; grey as to the eyes, and fair, if a good deal sunburnt, as to the complexion; just the man every one calls "Charlie" on the very slightest provocation.

As he marched about the little room, his long legs sadly inconvenienced by its narrow confines, the door opened, after a knock from sturdy knuckles, and a lancer in the usual cavalry soldier's *déshabillé* of unbuttoned jacket and his cap at the very back of his head, entered, carrying carefully a small parcel, a pair of newly varnished boots and a sword.

"What's that, Fraser?" the officer asked, wheeling round.

"Parcel, surr!" returned Fraser—not his regular servant, who was on sick leave.

Opened, it proved to be a box containing a bunch of dainty

blue forget-me-nots, over which, despite Fraser's presence, Charlie Kerr fairly groaned aloud.

" Here! stick 'em into water and get me dressed for mess— sharp," he said, smothering a second groan.

" Here's a label on 'em, surr," remarked Fraser, as he lifted the flowers out of their cotton-wool covering.

" A label!" taking it impatiently—then read " *For the last time. Good bye.*" A moment later the label was burnt to a cinder, and Kerr had turned to the toilette-table.

' Get me dressed—sharp," he repeated.

There were other flowers in the room besides the forget-me-nots—a great Indian enamelled tray filled with the rarest hot-house exotics and ferns, waxen camellias, fragrant tuberoses, gardenias, moss-rose buds, eucharis lilies and many others ; flowers more fit for the bridal bouquet of a princess than for the bare-looking room of a cavalry officer. They had come up from the town but an hour ago, from the handsome widow, whose face, just then, filled his heart, together with a little woe-begone countenance belonging to the sender of the forget-me-nots— Pussey, whose message had been, " *Good bye.*"

" Well, if this here ain't a rum start," mused Fraser to himself, trying to fit the message on the label with the perplexed shadow in his master's grey clouded eyes—the eyes that the men of the Scarlet Lancers were wont to declare could see straight through a stone wall.

He would have thought it a considerable " rummer " start, if, after he had left the officer alone, he could have seen him bending over the dainty blue flowers—irresolution in his heart —a forgotten tenderness on his tongue—and what were almost like tears in his grey eyes.

" Poor little Pussey ! Shall I go back and make friends with you again ? You'll forgive me, I know—nobody'll ever be as fond of me as you, and yet——" He lifted up his eyes to the brilliant hot-house blooms, and in one instant all the old tender pure love had vanished, before a remembrance of the newer, stronger passion, for the rich handsome widow. who had taken his heart captive by one single glance.

"Lord help me! I'm getting more like a drivelling idiot than anything else," he muttered savagely between his white teeth, and with another great groan : " Oh ! but these women do play the very deuce with one. The poor little woman will get over it and marry a curate in next to no time. Anyway, it wouldn't have done to marry her, feeling as I do—it wouldn't have been fairly honest. There's dinner—faugh ! all the sherry and bitters in the mess won't give me an appetite to-night."

Just then the door of the opposite room was opened and a young man came forth, singing gaily to the time of his spurred heels :

> "Over the hills and far away !
> In a village by the sea,
> A small sweet rose of a maiden dwells,
> Who is dear, so dear to me."

Charlie Kerr flung open his door, with a very audible and a very naughty word.

" What's the matter *now?*" laughed a voice behind him.

"Oh, I hate fellows who sing !" Kerr growled, testily. " Always caterwauling about the place like a confounded maid-of-all-work."

> "With loving lips and true grey eyes,
> I call her my Rose Marie !
> Over the hills and far away,
> Dwells my love, my Rose-Marie."

Sang Calvert in front of them.

" You're engaged to some girl down in the West, ain't you ?" Preston laughed.

" No, I'm not," curtly.

" But you were," rejoined Preston, quickly, adding to himself, as Kerr looked stonily at nothing, " Ho, ho ! my friend, so that's where the shoe pinches, is it ?"

Of a certainty the shoe did pinch horribly, though not quite in the place Preston thought.

I wonder, is there any pinch of a moral kind, which is not somewhat alleviated by one's dinner? Under the influence of gravy soup and salmon the discomfort of Kerr's pinch subsided considerably ; an *entrée* of chickens' livers ; and venison, with

French beans, found him at peace (*pro 'tem.*) with himself, the
world, and every one else.　　He had not reached that age when
a mess-dinner becomes a nuisance; when a man listens im
patiently to oft-told stories, and looks to the rising of the senior
officer as a blessed relief.　　He was young and strong, and handsome, if not possessed of any great intellectual powers; he
enjoyed hearing Power tell how he had "spotted" the prettiest
little girl that afternoon he had seen for a twelve-month, "With
eyes like saucers, I give you my word of honour; and the
neatest little pair of steppers in England;" how he had
promptly tackled her, and been met with as prompt a "Who
are you? I don't know you!"　　How he had taken off his hat,
with the utmost politeness, and explained that his name was
Power, of the Scarlet Lancers; how the incognita of the
saucer eyes had looked him up and down, and through and
through, until "By Gad, you know, I felt like some shop-
lifter," finally drawling out "Ah! and a credit you are to the
Scarlet Lancers, I'm sure.　　Have they *all* manners as polished
as yours?"

He enjoyed hearing Garnet, the third up the list of captains,
despite his fifty and odd years and his bald head, groan over the
evil fate which had sent him into the army twenty years too
soon, or had made the abolition of purchase come—so far as he
was concerned—twenty years too late.

"I'd be a major-general now, by gad, if I'd never been
under the confounded purchase-system," he was wont to remark.

And with "poor old Garnet," as they called him, was a
tradition of a pert young sub., who had condoled with him one
day somewhat after the fashion of the comforters of Job—a
tradition which by frequent repetition had passed into a
universal plaster of comfort, for all the ills which can fall to the
lot of a soldier.　"Never you mind, Garnet," this youngster
had called out, on the occasion of a troop being bought over
the then senior sub.'s head; "never you mind, Mr. Garnet, sir
—you'll soon be dead, an' then you'll be as well off as any of
'em!"

Garnet had got his troop, and the pert young sub. had broken his neck at a steeplechase, and his mother's heart at the same moment, but his comfort remained a regimental fixture.

It was not Garnet who entertained them on that particular evening, but the colonel himself, who, when once started on certain subjects, was wont to hold forth until half his listeners were asleep. His most favourite and inexhaustible topic was the end to which those old women—otherwise the War Office —are supposed, amongst a certain class of officers, to be bringing the army.

"Gad, they'll bring it up to something," he went on volubly to those in his immediate neighbourhood. "What is the latest *fad?* Norfolk jackets and gaiters! Nor—folk jac—kets *and* gai—ters. All I can say is, the day that sees my men measured for Norfolk jackets and gaiters sees my papers sent in likewise."

"Well, but, colonel," Kerr advanced mischievously, for the sake of argument, "there are a good many advantages to be urged in defence of the scheme—there's no denying that."

"And what are they?" explosively.

"Ease and freedom, to begin with."

"A good soldier wants neither ease nor freedom," retorted the colonel, fiercely.

"Faith, sir," put in Graves, laughing, "I often feel on a field-day as if I'd be thankful for a little of either."

"Oh! *you*," with unconcealed disdain, "I've no doubt. If ever you come to command a regiment, you'll do without field-days altogether, I daresay."

"Oh, I never shall come to that," laughing again.

"For the good of your regiment *in futuro*, it is sincerely to be hoped not," Colonel Wilson retorted.

"Well, but Colonel," from Kerr, with a kick to arrest the attention of his neighbours, "such a uniform would certainly be cheap."

"Cheap, sir! We don't want cheapness; it would simply open the army to a lot of snivelling vagabonds our present expenses keep out of it. Non-purchase lets 'em in, and the outfits keep 'em out."

"But, I've another plea to urge," Kerr went on, wickedly. "Less conspicuous in the field. There's no getting over that."

"And, bless my soul, why should you try to get over it?" cried the chief, almost bursting with exasperation. "England always has been conspicuous in the field, and, please God, England always will be—not but what she's made a sad hash of it lately. And whose fault is it? Not the generals' fault— nor the officers—nor the men, but those molly-coddling stingy old women, who please to call themselves *the authorities!* Sending out one man where ten are needed. Less conspicuous in the field! Good heavens! what next? Mark my words, the day that sees England's army clad in Norfolk jackets and gaiters will see England's glory go down with a rush that she will never be able to recover."

"But no army is so conspicuously clad as ours."

"What army has ever been as uniformly glorious? Do you think I have forgotten, amongst all these new fads, how a handful of us kept our ground at Inkerman, against ten times our numbers of those infernal grey-clad Russian brutes, that we could hardly distinguish from the grey mist; only 1,400 of us, and we kept our ground six long hours, until the reinforcements came up and saved us? What was good enough to lick the Russians in at Inkerman, ought to be good enough to lick Afghans and African savages."

"But you'd have done just as well in your shooting-jacket or your morning-coat," Kerr maintained.

"I don't know—I don't know at all."

"Well, sir, if poor ——, of the ——, had been in undress during that sortie from Canbool, depend upon it, he would have been spared the agony of carrying a bullet eight months in his stomach before it killed him; his scarlet facings cost him his life." .

"Oh! very likely. An individual case, that. Would you re-organize the whole army because of *one* case? No, no; depend upon it, I know rather more about *practical* soldiering than any of you—or half those duffers up at the War Office for the matter of that."

And, remembering the half-dozen medals and clasps Colonel Wilson displayed on the breast of his tunic, they were all silent. He had got the best of the argument. He rose from the table, with a laugh.

"They'll not carry it in my time; by then they'll have made me a staff officer, with twenty letters after my name— D.A.C.G.—a kind of head-cook to the district, and open to tips from the contractors; eh, Mordaunt?" bringing a heavy friendly hand down on the shoulder of the man nearest to him.

During the whole harangue Mordaunt had been half asleep, but on being distinctly addressed roused himself with a start. "Never you mind, sir," pulling himself together, sleepily; "never you mind, Colonel Wilson, sir; you'll soon be dead, and then you'll be as well off as any of 'em."

Perhaps it was the absence of the usual laugh that warned him he had put his foot in it—perhaps it was the boiled-lobster expression on the chief's astonished face—any way, Mordaunt suddenly became very wide awake indeed, and stumbled to his feet, with a stammering apology.

"Oh, I beg a thousand pardons, colonel! I did not know it was you; at least, I'm afraid I must have been half-asleep; you know, sir, I've been up three nights."

Colonel Wilson cooled down instantly. "By-the-bye, how is Colyon to night?"

"Bad, sir, bad—very. I don't believe he's had an easy moment the last eight-and-forty hours; and really, what with the sitting up, lifting and moving and rubbing—anything to get a moment's ease for him—*and* the field-day—I could pretty nearly go to sleep as I stand. It's a horrible business—rheumatic fever."

"Oh, horrible—horrible! Well, if you are going to do all this nursing, you must be excused field-days and duty."

"Thank you, sir."

"I think Mr. Graves, you are the next for duty?"

"Yes, sir."

"Nice for you, Graves, you lazy beggar; you were going

away on Wednesday, weren't you?" laughed Calvert, as the door closed behind the colonel and Mordaunt.

"Say a swear, Bones," laughed another.

"*Nev*—ar mind, Bones," put in a third.

"Ah, that poor devil's got rheumatic fever," answered Graves. "I couldn't cut up nasty at sparing Mordaunt to him; and oh, by gad! if ever I get rheumatic fever myself, let me have Mordaunt to look after me."

"Why?"

"Never saw anything like it—rub—rub—rub, chafe—chafe —chafe, up and down, just like a woman—only ten times as strong. Poor Colyon yells out if any one else goes near him. I suppose Mordaunt's caught the knack of it."

"Poor old Mordaunt, what a good-natured chap he is," Kerr put in; then beginning to laugh, "oh, but it was good his coming out with 'comfort' to the chief; I thought he was going to burst."

"No wonder Mordaunt went to sleep with that everlasting jaw—jaw—jaw droning in his ears," laughed Preston.

"And Mordaunt wasn't the only one either," added Calvert, "look at old Garnet."

Kerr jumped up from his seat in a moment; "Hus———sh! don't wake him, get the mustard-pot—quickly."

"Where is it?"

"How the deuce should I know? Ask Farrer."

"Stop. I've got a mustard-leaf in my room. I'll get it in a minute. There now, stick it in water for half-a-minute, and clap it on his bald head."

So they did! For full five minutes Garnet slept serenely on, then he awoke with a yell, like the war-whoop of a wild Indian.

"What a dream," he spluttered, rubbing his eyes. But it wasn't altogether a dream—*it* continued. "What the devil!—" he began; then he put his hand up to his head and found them out. "Why, can't you leave a fellow alone?"

"And what was the dream, Garnet?" Kerr asked, when he had recovered his laughter.

"Oh, I dreamed I was like the soldier at Perim," Garnet answered, wiping his head, gingerly.

"And what was he?"

"Don't you know? A black sheep—and died—and didn't go to Paradise, but the other place. Bless you, in two days back he came for his blanket—he said it was cold, *compared to Perim.*"

"Ha—ha—ha! you know then what you'll have to expect," cried Kerr. "Hollo! who's that?—why it's Bootles! Well, Bootles, old man, when did you come, and where do you hail from?"

"London—Antwerp—Amsterdam—Norway, &c.," returned Bootles, concisely. "How are you all?"

"Oh, flourishing!" answered Kerr, for everyone; "except Colyon, who's down with rheumatic fever."

"Colyon!—very bad?"

"Very bad; won't get over it, poor chap, I'm afraid. Well! have you had good sport?"

"Splendid! never better."

"Picked up any extra good stories? Garnet here has just come out with a new one; and oh, such a joke! The chief's been having an extra jaw to-night on those 'damned old women up at the Horse Guards, sir,' and sent Mordaunt off as sound as a church. Mordaunt's been up three nights with Colyon. The chief spoke to him suddenly and he blurted out, 'Never you mind, sir, you'll soon be dead, and——'"

"No," cried Bootles, with an incredulous laugh.

"Fact; the chief's face was a study, and so, by Jove, was Mordaunt's, when he got fairly awake! Well, any news?"

"No; but I came across two splendid ''Arrys' yesterday."

"Go on," cried half-a-dozen voices; Bootles was a favourite story-teller.

"One was at Antwerp—at dinner. I found him in the midst of a group of deferential foreigners, who probably thought him a lord at least, from the flash rings on his fingers and the amount of pomatum on his head. Perhaps they expected to improve their English—heaven knows. I didn't hear the

Z

beginning, for I was looking at a little girl over the other side of the table—the smartest girl I've seen for an age : jolly dark hair and eyes, and a regular English figure ; all said and done, English girls——"

" But, 'Arry—get on," impatiently from Calvert.

" Oh, yes, to be sure. Well, 'Arry, leaning his elbows on the table, with graceful negligence, caught my attention with, " Ah ! the last time I was outside of a 'orse I gort short orf, and the 'orse 'e must 'ave known his way 'ome better than I did, for when I gort 'ome the pore 'orse was standing a-poring at the staible-dore.' My little gal, across the table looked at him for full five minutes, then muttered under her breath, ' Pore 'Arry.' Gad, it was fine !"

Of course a great roar of laughter greeted the story, nor was he permitted to relapse into a reverie on the attractions of the little girl, with the jolly dark hair and eyes.

" Go on," said Kerr, " let's have the other."

" Oh, the other was at Amsterdam : a lanky, loose-limbed, lantern-jawed, yellow-toothed Yankee, with eyes like a dead cod-fish, and a skin like an old parchment deed ; with a wife to match. Charteris and I breakfasted at the Amstel, and these two sat opposite. I never so much as looked at the brute, as you may imagine, but he tackled me, with ' A fine city this, sir.' ' Oh, er—awfully so !' I answered. Then he tried Charteris ; you know Charteris ?"

" I do," answered Preston. " Big — fair — impressive ; speaks at the rate of a word a minute, with a ' haw ' or ' er ' thrown in."

" That's the man. Says my big Yankee to him, ' I kind o' kalkalate these yere *Zoo*—logical Guardens are the best in Eu—*rope*.' Charteris looked up, opened his mouth, then shut it, pulled one arm a little out of his sleeve, then the other, ' I—er—think—*not*.' " Oh, yes ! I kalkalate they're regular tip-top-pers.' ' Reallay,' returned Charteris, with mature deliberation over each word ; " but-haw—I-er—think—if-er — you-er — go— to-haw — the-er — Guar — dens — in-er — Regent's-er — Park—you'll-er—' ' I guess not !' broke in

Jonathan, 'at these yere Guardens they've a real live Hippopotamus and his missus —only ones in the werld.' 'Haw —no!" said Charteris, gravely, 'If-er—you—go-er—to— Regent's-er-er—Park, you-er—will—not-er —onlay —see-er — Mis-taw — Hippopotamus — and - er — Mrs. — Hippo-er - potamus—but-er—Babay— Hippopotamus-er — also.' I can't quite give you the way in which Charteris said 'reallay' and 'onlay' and 'babay,' but I can tell you that not the least little bit of amusement flickered on his good-looking wooden face, not the faintest twinkle came into his steady blue eyes. Gad, he might have been giving evidence on a court martial! it kept me from bursting out laughing in Jonathan's face. The Yankee collapsed; not one word—good, bad, or indifferent— did he utter to anyone at the table; but when a waiter brought him bread instead of beer, didn't he slang him, rather. However, the cream of the joke is to come; and, oddly enough, neither Charteris nor the Yankee heard it. He left me at Antwerp to go on to Paris, and there I picked up some charming people—half Dutch, half Portuguese-Jewish—father, mother, and two pretty daughters. I was telling one of them about it, when she said, ' But, do you not know dat de leetal Ba-bee Hippo was born of de Amsterdamsche parents, and *sold* to de people at Regent's Park ?' Now, did you ever hear of such a sell in all your days?"

" Pooh! you make it all up as you go on," Calvert laughed, struggling with a yawn.

" Not I. Well, I am as tired as a dog, so I'll be off to bed. Good night, you fellows."

" So am I," said Kerr, following him. " I'll come with you."

As Kerr turned and closed the door behind them, Bootles — otherwise Algy Ferrers—slipped his arm into that of his friend.

" What have you been doing, whilst I've been away, Charlie?"

" The usual grind. I had three days in town last week."

" See Mademoiselle Mignon ?" with a laugh, and a squeeze of the arm he held.

z 2

"Yes, I saw her," the shadow leaping into his grey eyes again.

"And did she send me a message? I say, Charlie, old fellow, I'm glad your future wife likes me as well as she does: I should detest a woman who was jealous of me, and somehow nine women out of ten *are* jealous of their husband's friends."

"Pussey will never be jealous of you, Bootles."

"No, I'm sure she won't. Did she tell you I called on her, as I passed through; and, as I had the afternoon to spare, I took her to the Academy?"

"She wrote to me of it."

"Yes! I admire her immensely; such a perfect little lady—a regular Mademoiselle Mignon. After all, Charlie, we poor devils, knocking about from pillar to post, we can appreciate that sort of thing when we meet with it, which is not often. Now, little Mademoiselle Mignon is not only so excessively pretty, but so true and simple with it. She spoke out so nicely about you; never made a bit of sham humbug about what she cared for you. 'If anything were to come between Charlie and me, I should die,' she said. We were looking at a picture, that suggested the idea; and she said it as if she meant it too."

"I hope not," said Kerr, gravely.

"I hope not, too," rejoined Bootles, misunderstanding him. "Not that there is any fear of it. I think, Charlie, when you are married, I shall make up to the younger sister; I just saw her for two minutes."

"Bootles—I'm not going to be married."

"WHAT?"

"At least—that is—it's all off," said Kerr, miserably.

"*All off!*" Bootles echoed, "is it possible? Lord, how these women do take us in. I would have staked my very life and soul on her fidelity." In answer to which Charlie fairly groaned. Somehow, the groan let a light in upon the other's perplexity. "Oh," he remarked, in tones that were decidedly changed, "then it's you, is it? you surprise me."

Kerr looked up. "Don't speak in that tone, Bootles," he began, but Bootles interrupted him.

"My dear fellow," with a laugh—a make-believe sort of laugh. "it's no earthly concern of mine, I've no right to take any 'tone' at all! as I said before—you have surprised me."

"But I want to tell you——"

"I want to go to bed. I'm dead tired," trying hard to make his voice and manner the same; "talking and telling won't do any good, so good night."

"Good night," answered Kerr, wretchedly. Left to himself, he determined that he would ask for two days' leave on the morrow; that he might go back and beg the girl who loved him to forget the cloud which had come between them, and let things be as they had been aforetime. He thought over all Bootles had said about her—"Mademoiselle Mignon—a perfect little lady—so excessively pretty—so true and simple." What a fool he had been to let such charms be thrown into the shade by the face of a woman he barely knew; a widow—*a Mrs. Smith!* Thank heaven, the warm terms in which his best friend had spoken of his first love had opened his eyes, just in time. Not for a week had Kerr felt so happy, as when he got into his bed that night. Calvert came singing to his room, just afterwards:

> "An arm like iron and a muscle like steel,
> A heart for a friend that can always feel.
> A will, once made, no man can repeal,
> This is what an Englishman is made of."

And that time Charlie Kerr did not greet Calvert's singing with an oath, or a growl as to "a caterwauling maid-of-all-work."

CHAPTER II.

IT was a great Frenchman who said, "All things come to him who can afford to wait." Between you and me, that was one of the most wonderful truths ever written; only, there are so many who cannot afford it. Many an artist would make a great name if he could wait, but he cannot; he must daub away at pot-boilers and push through the drudgery of teaching, trusting to some future time of comparative ease of circumstances to be able to work for a name : and, long before that time draws near, his style is fixed, and he has sunk into a slough of mediocrity, from which he will never be able to extricate himself.

How many a writer of talent might make his mark, if he could take time with his work, prune it and pare it, re-write and re-model ! But he cannot do that ! The sordid needs of to-day outweigh the golden promises of to-morrow ; and after awhile he finds himself written out, with no elegance and purity of style to fall back upon, when the freshness of his ideas has gone ; like the artist, his style is fixed, and a bad, jerky, slipshod style it is—the style that must get on—the style that cannot afford to wait.

And how many there are who cannot afford to wait, in a moral sense ; whose good resolutions, if carried out at once, would tide them safely over many a slippery place ; but, put to the test of waiting, fail them altogether, and end by an even greater backsliding.

Charlie Kerr was one of these. Could he have gone straight up to town and renewed his love for the girl he called Pussey.— Mademoiselle Mignon—in reality, Rosa Wendall—it is quite certain that I should have had no further story to tell, save of the orthodox satin and orange blossoms ; but, unfortunately, leave he could not obtain.

" I am sorry to refuse you, Kerr," the colonel said to him ; " but I have just had a letter to say the Duke is coming on Friday, to inspect the regiment—with a foreign personage in the background ; shouldn't wonder if it's the Crown Prince ; and I have had to recall those who are away. You can have leave on Saturday, if you like."

" Thank you sir," he answered, real disappointment gnawing at his heart.

His good resolutions did not fail him that day, for he had not so much as a glimpse of the fascinating widow ; but on the following afternoon, when after a very long field-day and a long parade, he was sauntering down the High Street, he met her, in all the charms of her beautiful womanhood. Of course, he stopped ; ostensibly to thank her for the flowers she had sent him—he had already done so formally on paper—but, in reality to feast his soul on the glorious loveliness of her amber hair and the blue radiance of her large eyes. Once, whilst he was speaking, it occurred to him she was different.

" Does your head ache, Mrs. Smith?" he asked.

" My head—oh, no ! thank you," she replied. " I am going home—will you come in and have a cup of tea ?"

" I shall be delighted," he answered, turning to walk beside her ; and then, alas ! the last of his good resolutions went towards the paving of that famous road, which leads ever downwards and downwards.

They had their cup of tea *tête-à-tête* ; and certainly Mrs. Smith did her utmost to amuse and entertain her visitor. She had only been about a fortnight in Bathingtown, where she had taken a furnished house for three months. She explained to him that she had flowers and fruit and things sent from her own place in Wiltshire every morning; and, by means of the first-named, managed to give her rooms a tolerably home-like appearance.

" Did you not wonder at my sending you the flowers ?" she asked.

" Perhaps a little ; it was very pleasant wonder, though," he told her.

" Yes. I sent them for a reason I will tell you of some day ; to-morrow, I will send you some for a very different one."

" You are quite too kind," he murmured. " Do you know, Mrs. Smith, I am sure you are not well—or you're bothered— or something ?"

" I am—worried," she answered, lifting her great clear limpid eyes to his. " I went up to town yesterday to see my mother ; and there I heard news that has worried me, more than I was ever worried before, in all my eight-and-twenty years."

" I am very sorry to hear it," with a very gentle sigh of commiseration. " I hope Mrs.—er—you see I don't know what your maiden name was—but your mother, I mean ; I hope she is not ill."

"My maiden name was Bolitho," answered Mrs. Smith, watching him through half-closed eyelids. "No; my mother is not ill, thanks."

She chatted on for the best part of an hour; talking fluently and well on many topics, charming him as poor little Rosa Wendall had never been able to do—charming him, as a beautiful, rich, thoroughly cultivated, travelled woman of eight-and-twenty can charm a man of the world; and the result of it all was, that he went away more hopelessly infatuated and entangled than ever.

"Come in to-morrow afternoon," said the fair widow at parting. "Come any day after five; you will always find me in."

Before he dressed for mess, he thought the whole scene over again, with a pipe. In spite of himself, he was a little puzzled. There was something in the background; something behind all the sweet speeches, the coquettish glances, and, for the life of him, he couldn't make out what that something was? He knew very well, that if he were not desperately in love with her, her evident—well, what should he call it?—her—her—preference for him, would fill him with disgust; and yet, behind the coquettish glances was a certain hard glitter that reminded him of cold steel; among all the gay laughter was an artificial ring that jarred upon him; in spite of the downright spooney manner, he had a very fixed idea that if he were to give her a kiss she would slap his face—probably slap it hard! He couldn't make her out! Was she some adventuress, on the prowl for a husband, and did those costly hot-house blooms come from Covent Garden? Who was she? Mrs. Smith might be anybody; and though he had known a dozen different Bolithos, all in good society—yet the name might be but assumed. He couldn't understand it a bit; but, oh, how gloriously lovely she was! and how he longed and looked forward to the days, when she would lay that proud head down upon his breast, and promise to be his own. She might be an adventuress of the most outrageous type—her "place" might be a humbug—her name a sham; her person was what he had fallen in love with, and, as to that, there could be no deception.

The inspection-day came and went; so did the Duke; so did the foreign personage, who wasn't a crown prince at all, but only a Saxe-somebody or other, but Kerr never applied for the leave the colonel had promised him. Day after day found him in Mrs. Smith's drawing-room—the only visitor. If she was, indeed, as he had suspected, an adventuress, she played a very concentrated game—a game that would inevitably land her fish.

And yet, he was more puzzled than ever. The cold steel look, the artificial laughter, and the stand-offishness still remained, though he went in and out of her house like a dog in a fair, and they had become very intimate; nor did she seem in any hurry to get her fish landed. Her three months' term had almost expired, and yet the momentous words had never been uttered; the words he was dying to utter, and those he was dying to hear. Twice, on the days he was on duty, his brother officers, one or other of them, had mentioned the fact that the handsome widow had been up to town; they had seen her at the station, and so forth. Yet, she had not mentioned the circumstance to him on either occasion; though when he had spoken of it, she had answered carelessly enough, "Yes, I was in town yesterday;" in a manner which had not encouraged him to ask for further particulars.

He was not very happy at that time! He did not think she cared anything about him; though he could not shut his eyes to the fact that she encouraged him, as much as a lady could do. At all manner of inconvenient and unexpected hours, too, the remembrance of Mademoiselle Mignon's little wan face recurred to him, in a way that made his ears tingle and his cheeks burn! Not that he ever heard her name mentioned. The only one of his brother officers who knew her name was Bootles, and during the past two months between Bootles and himself a barrier had risen up, which the one could not and the other would not break down. Outwardly, Bootles was the same, but he never entered Kerr's room now; he never called him "Charlie" or by any of the odd terms of endearment soldiers are accustomed to apply to one another; least of all, did he ever mention or allude in any way to the girl, whom he had called "Mademoiselle Mignon—the perfect little lady—so simple and true."

December had set in and half the fellows were on leave. Bathingtown was deserted, and many people wondered that the handsome widow, who made so few friends and seemed so entirely taken up with the tall lancer, stayed. "Charlie's widow," the fellows called her; and Charlie, hearing them, used to smile, wondering if she would ever consent to run the risk of becoming so?

"I say, Charlie," said one of the fellows to him one afternoon, when he was on duty; "I saw your widow this afternoon; she came down from town in the next carriage to me. Bootles was with her, and, 'pon my word, they seemed so awfully thick, I didn't like to get into the same carriage, though I was going to."

"Bootles!" echoed Charlie, blankly.

"Bootles," the other repeated; "and the widow was crying—crying like anything."

It was inexplicable—Bootles and Mrs. Smith?

The idea of the two together seemed as impossible to him as a union of fire and water. Why, he couldn't have said, for he had never heard either mention the other. He was, however, so astonished and so curious, that he went into his old friend's room; a thing he had not done for weeks.

"I say, Bootles," he said, entering.

Bootles, who was lying in a big chair, smoking, looked up. "Oh, is that you, Kerr?" with a sudden politeness, that cut Charlie to the very heart; "have a chair."

"Have you been to town?" Charlie asked.

"Yes, I have. Why?"

"I say, I didn't know you knew Mrs. Smith."

"Didn't you? I've known her some time."

"Really. She was in town to-day also?"

"Yes," looking straight into the fire; "she's a very nice woman, comes of a nice family."

"What was she crying about, to-day?"

" Who told you she was crying?" turning to him sharply.

" Preston told me."

" Oh, Preston; he was in the train, then. It was some family trouble. Ask her yourself, to-morrow. I daresay she'll tell you."

" Oh, I'm sure she will," returned Charlie, stung by the other's tone, and rising; " well, it's time to dress."

Accordingly, about five on the following afternoon, he went down to Mrs. Smith's house. The drawing-room was empty, but she came to him almost immediately. The awful change in her appearance struck Charlie instantly.

" My own darling, what is it ?" he asked.

She drew her hand away from the eager clasp of his, and sank on to a couch, pointing to a chair.

But Charlie did not take it; he flung himself down at her feet; and, now that the flood-gates of his passions were opened, poured out the whole story of his love—his adoration—his abject worship—for her.

" Do you want me to marry you ?" asked Mrs. Smith, in a very low voice.

" My dearest, I have been wishing that ever since the day I first saw you," he cried.

" I have something to tell you "—with an evident effort.

" I don't want to hear it." He thought the confirmation of his suspicions was at hand. " Nothing will make any difference in my love for you ; I will hear nothing."

" You must." She sat upright, and pushed the golden hair off her white forehead, with a weary gesture. " I have told you that my maiden name was Bolitho."

" Yes."

" My mother married again."

" You did not tell me that ?"

" Nevertheless, it is so. She married early. I was but a child—and she had two daughters."

" Yes."

" The eldest of these two, whilst staying in Cornwall a few months ago, met with an officer, who fell in love with her."

"Yes!" He was becoming horribly interested by her story. "Yes! And his name was——"

"Kerr—Charlie Kerr," said Mrs. Smith.

"Oh, God in Heaven!" he gasped.

"I was always very fond of Rosey; and I took this house, solely to give her the pleasure of being with you—in deference to her wishes, I did not mention the relationship between us, when you were introduced to me. The child wished to surprise you by her sudden appearance here."

"And—and——"

"And I ruined her life—all innocently. It never entered my mind you could have a false thought in your head, until I saw Rosey, the week after you jilted her."

"No! no!" he cried out.

"Jilted her," Mrs. Smith repeated. "I couldn't understand it; but when I met you, it suddenly became clear to me. From that moment I set myself to win your love—your heart—and I think I succeeded."

"Yes! you succeeded," he said, growing whiter and whiter each moment.

"And do you think, Mr. Kerr," her eyes all cold steel now, "that I shall be likely to answer 'yes' to your very flattering proposal?"

He did not speak at all, but slowly rose up to his feet, with a face like a statue of marble.

"I have succeeded in punishing you," the widow went on, "but what will give my little sister back—— ?"

"I will! I have been a scoundrel, a cad, a brute, anything you like; but I am not altogether callous. She knows nothing of this; let me go back and make friends with her again; I know she will forgive me. You have dealt out justice to me with a merciless hand, be merciful now, and trust me to give my whole life for her happiness."

"It is too late," she answered, "my sister died at noon, yesterday." Then she broke down altogether, and hid her face among the cushions of the sofa.

For five minutes he stood watching her; then he went out

of her house, like a man in a dream, to carry for his whole life the burden of an upbraiding conscience, which had tried so very very hard in the days that were gone to keep all this misery from coming to pass.

In his room, Calvert was singing—

"With loving lips and true grey eyes,
    I call her my Rose-Marie!
Over the hills and far away,
    Dwells my love, my Rose-Marie!

The stick and gloves Kerr carried slipped from his fingers on to the floor; and the fingers flew to cover the handsome grey eyes that were full of tears!

THE END.

PRINTED BY
KELLY AND CO., GATE STREET, LINCOLN'S INN FIELDS;
AND MIDDLE MILL, KINGSTON-ON-THAMES.

CHATTO & WINDUS'S
LIST OF BOOKS.

* * * * * * * * * * * *

About.—The Fellah : An Egyptian Novel. By EDMOND ABOUT. Translated by Sir RANDAL ROBERTS. Post 8vo, illustrated boards, 2s. ; cloth limp, 2s. 6d.

Adams (W. Davenport), Works by :

A Dictionary of the Drama. Being a comprehensive Guide to the Plays, Playwrights, Players, and Playhouses of the United Kingdom and America, from the Earliest to the Present Times. Crown 8vo, half-bound, 12s. 6d. [*Preparing.*

Latter-Day Lyrics. Edited by W. DAVENPORT ADAMS. Post 8vo, cloth limp, 2s. 6d.

Quips and Quiddities. Selected by W. DAVENPORT ADAMS. Post 8vo, cloth limp, 2s. 6d.

Advertising, A History of, from the Earliest Times. Illustrated by Anecdotes, Curious Specimens, and Notices of Successful Advertisers. By HENRY SAMPSON. Crown 8vo, with Coloured Frontispiece and Illustrations, cloth gilt, 7s. 6d.

Agony Column (The) of "The Times," from 1800 to 1870. Edited, with an Introduction, by ALICE CLAY. Post 8vo, cloth limp, 2s. 6d.

Aide (Hamilton), Works by :

Carr of Carrlyon. Post 8vo, illustrated boards, 2s.

Confidences. Post 8vo, illustrated boards, 2s.

Alexander (Mrs.), Novels by :
Post 8vo, illustrated boards, 2s. each : crown 8vo, cloth extra, 3s 6d. each
Maid, Wife, or Widow ? A Romance.
Valerie's Fate.

Allen (Grant), Works by :
Crown 8vo, cloth extra, 6s. each.
The Evolutionist at Large. Second Edition, revised.
Vignettes from Nature.
Colin Clout's Calendar.
Strange Stories. With a Frontispiece by GEORGE DU MAURIER.

Babylon : A Novel. With 12 Illusts. by P. MACNAB. Three Vols., cr. 8vo.
Philistia : A Novel. New and Cheaper Edit. Crown 8vo, cloth extra, 3s. 6d.

Architectural Styles, A Handbook of. Translated from the German of A. ROSENGARTEN, by W. COLLETT-SANDARS. Crown 8vo, cloth extra, with 639 Illustrations, 7s. 6d.

Artemus Ward :

Artemus Ward's Works : The Works of CHARLES FARRER BROWNE, better known as ARTEMUS WARD. With Portrait and Facsimile. Crown 8vo, cloth extra, 7s. 6d.
Artemus Ward's Lecture on the Mormons. With 32 Illustrations. Edited, with Preface, by EDWARD P. HINGSTON. Crown 8vo, 6d.
The Genial Showman : Life and Adventures of Artemus Ward. By EDWARD P. HINGSTON. With a Frontispiece. Cr. 8vo, cl. extra, 3s. 6d.

Art (The) of Amusing : A Collection of Graceful Arts, Games, Tricks, Puzzles, and Charades. By FRANK BELLEW. With 300 Illustrations. Cr. 8vo, cloth extra, 4s. 6d.

Ashton (John), Works by :

A History of the Chap-Books of the Eighteenth Century. With nearly 400 Illusts., engraved in facsimile of the originals. Cr. 8vo, cl. ex., 7s. 6d.

Social Life in the Reign of Queen Anne. From Original Sources. With nearly 100 Illusts. Cr.8vo,cl.ex.,7s.6d.

Humour, Wit, and Satire of the Seventeenth Century. With nearly 100 Illusts. Cr. 8vo, cl. extra, 7s. 6d.

English Caricature and Satire on Napoleon the First. 120 Illusts. from Originals. Two Vols., demy 8vo, 28s.

Bacteria.—A Synopsis of the Bacteria and Yeast Fungi and Allied Species. By W. B. GROVE, B.A. With 87 Illusts. Crown 8vo, cl. extra, 3s. 6d.

Balzac's "Comedie Humaine" and its Author. With Translations by H. H. WALKER. Post 8vo, cl.limp,2s. 6d.

Bankers, A Handbook of London; together with Lists of Bankers from 1677. By F. G. HILTON PRICE. Crown 8vo, cloth extra, 7s. 6d.

Bardsley (Rev. C.W.), Works by :

English Surnames: Their Sources and Significations. Third Ed., revised. Cr. 8vo, cl. extra, 7s. 6d.

Curiosities of Puritan Nomenclature. Crown 8vo, cloth extra, 7s. 6d.

Bartholomew Fair, Memoirs of. By HENRY MORLEY. With 100 Illusts. Crown 8vo, cloth extra, 7s. 6d.

Basil, Novels by :

Crown 8vo., cloth extra, 3s. 6d. each.

A Drawn Game.

"The Wearing of the Green."

Beaconsfield, Lord : A Biography. By T. P O'CONNOR, M.P. Sixth Edit., New Preface. Cr.8vo, cl.ex.7s.6d.

Beauchamp. — Grantley Grange: A Novel. By SHELSLEY BEAUCHAMP. Post 8vo, illust. bds., 2s.

Beautiful Pictures by British Artists: A Gathering of Favourites from our Picture Galleries. In Two Series. All engraved on Steel in the highest style of Art. Edited, with Notices of the Artists, by SYDNEY ARMYTAGE, M.A. Imperial 4to, cloth extra, gilt and gilt edges, 21s. per Vol.

Bechstein. — As Pretty as Seven, and other German Stories. Collected by LUDWIG BECHSTEIN. With Additional Tales by the Brothers GRIMM, and 100 Illusts. by RICHTER. Small 4to, green and gold, 6s. 6d. ; gilt edges, 7s. 6d.

Beerbohm. — Wanderings in Patagonia ; or, Life among the Ostrich Hunters. By JULIUS BEERBOHM. With Illusts. Crown 8vo, cloth extra, 3s. 6d.

Belgravia for 1885. One Shilling Monthly, Illustrated by P. MACNAB. — A Strange Voyage, by W. CLARK RUSSELL, was begun in the JANUARY Number, and will be continued throughout the year. This Number contained also the Opening Chapters of a New Story by CECIL POWER, Author of "Philistia," entitled Babylon.

* *Now ready, the Volume for JULY to OCTOBER, 1885, cloth extra, gilt edges, 7s. 6d. ; Cases for binding Vols., 2s. each.*

Belgravia Annual. With Stories by F.W. ROBINSON, Mrs.LYNN LINTON, GRANT ALLEN "BASIL," JUSTIN H. McCARTHY, B. MONTGOMERIE RANKING, and others. Demy 8vo, with Illustrations. 1s.

Bennett (W.C.,LL.D.),Works by:

A Ballad History of England. Post 8vo, cloth limp, 2s.

Songs for Sailors. Post 8vo, cloth limp, 2s.

Besant (Walter) and James Rice, Novels by. Post 8vo, illust. boards, 2s. each; cloth limp, 2s. 6d. each; or cr. 8vo, cl. extra,3s. 6d. each.

Ready-Money Mortiboy.

With Harp and Crown.

This Son of Vulcan.

My Little Girl.

The Case of Mr. Lucraft.

The Golden Butterfly.

By Celia's Arbour.

The Monks of Thelema.

'Twas in Trafalgar's Bay.

The Seamy Side.

The Ten Years' Tenant.

The Chaplain of the Fleet.

Besant (Walter), Novels by :

Crown 8vo, cloth extra, 3s. 6d. each; post 8vo, illust. boards, 2s. each; cloth limp, 2s. 6d. each

All Sorts and Conditions of Men: An Impossible Story. With Illustrations by FRED. BARNARD.

The Captains' Room, &c. With Frontispiece by E. J. WHEELER.

All in a Garden Fair. With 6 Illusts. by H. FURNISS.

BESANT (WALTER), *continued—*
Crown 8vo, cloth extra, 3s. 6d. each.
Dorothy Forster. With Frontispiece by CHARLES GREEN.
Uncle Jack, and other Stories.

The Art of Fiction. Demy 8vo, 1s.

Betham-Edwards (M.), Novels

by. Crown 8vo, cloth extra, 3s. 6d. each. ; post 8vo, illust. bds., 2s. each.

Felicia. | Kitty.

Bewick (Thos.) and his Pupils.

By AUSTIN DOBSON. With 95 Illustrations. Square 8vo, cloth extra, 10s. 6d.

Birthday Books:—

The Starry Heavens: A Poetical Birthday Book. Square 8vo, bandsomely bound in cloth, 2s. 6d.
Birthday Flowers: Their Language and Legends. By W. J. GORDON. Beautifully Illustrated in Colours by VIOLA BOUGHTON. In illuminated cover, crown 4to, 6s.
The Lowell Birthday Book. With Illusts., small 8vo, cloth extra, 4s. 6d.

Blackburn's (Henry) Art Handbooks. Demy 8vo, Illustrated, uniform in size for binding.

Academy Notes, separate years, from 1875 to 1884, each 1s.
Academy Notes, 1885. With 142 Illustrations. 1s.
Academy Notes, 1875–79. Complete in One Vol.,with nearly 600 Illusts. in Facsimile. Demy 8vo, cloth limp, 6s.
Academy Notes, 1880–84. Complete in One Volume, with about 700 Facsimile Illustrations. Cloth limp, 6s.
Grosvenor Notes, 1877. 6d.
Grosvenor Notes, separate years, from 1878 to 1884, each 1s.
Grosvenor Notes, 1885. With 75 Illustrations 1s.
Grosvenor Notes, 1877–82. With upwards of 300 Illustrations. Demy 8vo, cloth limp, 6s.
Pictures at South Kensington. With 70 Illustrations. 1s.
The English Pictures at the National Gallery. 114 Illustrations. 1s.
The Old Masters at the National Gallery. 128 Illustrations. 1s. 6d.
A Complete Illustrated Catalogue to the National Gallery. With Notes by H. BLACKBURN, and 242 Illusts. Demy 8vo, cloth limp, 3s.

Illustrated Catalogue of the Luxembourg Gallery. Containing about 250 Reproductions after the Original Drawings of the Artists. Edited by F. G. DUMAS. Demy 8vo, 3s. 6d.

ART HANDBOOKS, *continued—*
The Paris Salon, 1884. With over 300 Illusts. Edited by F. G. DUMAS. Demy 8vo, 3s.
The Paris Salon, 1885. With about 300 Facsimile Sketches. Edited by F. G. DUMAS. Demy 8vo, 3s.
The Art Annual, 1883–4. Edited by F. G. DUMAS. With 300 full-page Illustrations. Demy 8vo, 5s.

Boccaccio's Decameron; or,

Ten Days' Entertainment. Translated into English, with an Introduction by THOMAS WRIGHT, F.S.A. With Portrait, and STOTHARD'S beautiful Copperplates. Cr. 8vo, cloth extra, gilt, 7s. 6d.

Blake (William): Etchings from

his Works. By W. B. SCOTT. With descriptive Text. Folio, half-bound boards, India Proofs, 21s.

Bowers'(G.) Hunting Sketches:

Canters in Crampshire. Oblong 4to, half-bound boards, 21s.
Leaves from a Hunting Journal. Coloured in facsimile of the originals. Oblong 4to, half-bound, 21s.

Boyle (Frederick), Works by:

Camp Notes: Stories of Sport and Adventure in Asia, Africa, and America. Crown 8vo, cloth extra, 3s. 6d. ; post 8vo, illustrated bds., 2s.
Savage Life. Crown 8vo, cloth extra, 3s. 6d. ; post 8vo, illustrated bds., 2s.
Chronicles of No-Man's Land. Crown 8vo, cloth extra, 6s.; post 8vo, illust. boards, 2s.

Brand's Observations on Pop-

ular Antiquities, chiefly Illustrating the Origin of our Vulgar Customs, Ceremonies, and Superstitions. With the Additions of Sir HENRY ELLIS. Crown 8vo, cloth extra, gilt, with numerous Illustrations, 7s. 6d.

Bret Harte, Works by:

Bret Harte's Collected Works. Arranged and Revised by the Author. Complete in Five Vols., crown 8vo, cloth extra, 6s. each.
Vol. I. COMPLETE POETICAL AND DRAMATIC WORKS. With Steel Portrait, and Introduction by Author.
Vol. II. EARLIER PAPERS—LUCK OF ROARING CAMP, and other Sketches —BOHEMIAN PAPERS — SPANISH AND AMERICAN LEGENDS.
Vol. III. TALES OF THE ARGONAUTS —EASTERN SKETCHES.
Vol. IV. GABRIEL CONROY.
Vol. V. STORIES — CONDENSED NOVELS, &c.

Collins (Mortimer), Novels by :

Sweet Anne Page. Post 8vo, illustrated boards, 2s. ; crown 8vo, cloth extra, 3s. 6d.

Transmigration. Post 8vo, illust.bds., 2s. ; crown 8vo, cloth extra, 3s. 6d.

From Midnight to Midnight. Post 8vo, illustrated boards, 2s. ; crown 8vo, cloth extra, 3s. 6d.

A Fight with Fortune. Post 8vo, illustrated boards, 2s.

Collins (Wilkie), Novels by :

Each post 8vo, illustrated boards, 2s.; cloth limp, 2s. 6d.; or crown 8vo, cloth extra, Illustrated, 3s. 6d.

Antonina. Illust. by Sir JOHN GILBERT.

Basil. Illustrated by Sir JOHN GILBERT and J. MAHONEY.

Hide and Seek. Illustrated by Sir JOHN GILBERT and J. MAHONEY.

The Dead Secret. Illustrated by Sir JOHN GILBERT.

Queen of Hearts. Illustrated by Sir JOHN GILBERT.

My Miscellanies. With a Steel-plate Portrait of WILKIE COLLINS.

The Woman in White. With Illustrations by Sir JOHN GILBERT and F. A. FRASER.

The Moonstone. With Illustrations by G. DU MAURIER and F. A. FRASER.

Man and Wife. Illust. by W. SMALL.

Poor Miss Finch. Illustrated by G. DU MAURIER and EDWARD HUGHES.

Miss or Mrs.? With Illustrations by S. L. FILDES and HENRY WOODS.

The New Magdalen. Illustrated by G. DU MAURIER and C. S. RANDS.

The Frozen Deep. Illustrated by G. DU MAURIER and J. MAHONEY.

The Law and the Lady. Illustrated by S. L. FILDES and SYDNEY HALL.

The Two Destinies.

The Haunted Hotel. Illustrated by ARTHUR HOPKINS.

The Fallen Leaves.

Jezebel's Daughter.

The Black Robe.

Heart and Science: A Story of the Present Time.

"**I Say No.**" Crown 8vo, cloth extra, 3s. 6d.

Colman's Humorous Works :

"Broad Grins," "My Nightgown and Slippers," and other Humorous Works, Prose and Poetical, of GEORGE COLMAN. With Life by G. B. BUCKSTONE, and Frontispiece by HOGARTH. Crown 8vo, cloth extra, gilt, 7s. 6d.

Convalescent Cookery: A

Family Handbook. By CATHERINE RYAN. Crown 8vo, 1s. ; cloth, 1s. 6d.

Conway (Moncure D.), Works by :

Demonology and Devil-Lore. Two Vols., royal 8vo. with 65 Illusts., 28s.

A Necklace of Stories. Illustrated by W. J. HENNESSY. Square 8vo, cloth extra, 6s.

The Wandering Jew. Crown 8vo, cloth extra, 6s.

Thomas Carlyle: Letters and Recollections. With Illustrations. Crown 8vo, cloth extra, 6s.

Cook (Dutton), Works by :

Hours with the Players. With a Steel Plate Frontispiece. New and Cheaper Edit., cr. 8vo, cloth extra, 6s.

Nights at the Play: A View of the English Stage. New and Cheaper Edition. Crown 8vo, cloth extra, 6s.

Leo: A Novel. Post 8vo, illustrated boards, 2s.

Paul Foster's Daughter. Post 8vo, illustrated boards, 2s.; crown 8vo, cloth extra, 3s. 6d.

Copyright. — A Handbook of

English and Foreign Copyright in Literary and Dramatic Works. By SIDNEY JERROLD, of the Middle Temple, Esq., Barrister-at-Law. Post 8vo, cloth limp, 2s. 6d.

Cornwall. — Popular Romances

of the West of England; or, The Drolls, Traditions, and Superstitions of Old Cornwall. Collected and Edited by ROBERT HUNT, F.R.S. New and Revised Edition, with Additions, and Two Steel-plate Illustrations by GEORGE CRUIKSHANK. Crown 8vo, cloth extra, 7s. 6d.

Craddock. — The Prophet of

the Great Smoky Mountains. By CHARLES EGBERT CRADDOCK. Post 8vo, illust. bds., 2s. ; cloth limp, 2s. 6d.

Creasy.—Memoirs of Eminent

Etonians : with Notices of the Early History of Eton College. By EDWARD CREASY, Author of " The Fifteen Decisive Battles of the World." Crown 8vo, cloth extra, gilt, with 13 Portraits, 7s. 6d.

Cruikshank (George) :

The Comic Almanack. Complete in TWO SERIES ; The FIRST from 1835 to 1843; the SECOND from 1844 to 1853. A Gathering of the BEST HUMOUR of THACKERAY, HOOD, MAYHEW, ALBERT SMITH, A'BECKETT, ROBERT BROUGH, &c. With 2,000 Woodcuts and Steel Engravings by CRUIKSHANK, HINE, LANDELLS, &c. Crown 8vo, cloth gilt, two very thick volumes, 7s. 6d. each.

CRUIKSHANK (G.), *continued—*

The Life of George Cruikshank. By
BLANCHARD JERROLD, Author of
"The Life of Napoleon III.," &c.
With 84 Illustrations. New and
Cheaper Edition, enlarged, with Additional Plates, and a very carefully
compiled Bibliography. Crown 8vo,
cloth extra, **7s. 6d.**

Robinson Crusoe. A beautiful reproduction of Major's Edition, with
37 Woodcuts and Two Steel Plates
by GEORGE CRUIKSHANK, choicely
printed. Crown 8vo, cloth extra,
7s. 6d. A few Large-Paper copies,
printed on hand-made paper, with
India proofs of the Illustrations, **36s.**

Cussans.—Handbook of Heraldry; with Instructions for Tracing
Pedigrees and Deciphering Ancient
MSS., &c. By JOHN E. CUSSANS.
Entirely New and Revised Edition,
illustrated with over 400 Woodcuts
and Coloured Plates. Crown 8vo,
cloth extra, **7s. 6d.**

Cyples.—Hearts of Gold: A
Novel. By WILLIAM CYPLES. Crown
8vo, cloth extra, **3s. 6d.**; post 8vo,
illustrated boards, **2s.**

Daniel. — Merrie England in
the Olden Time. By GEORGE DANIEL.
With Illustrations by ROBT. CRUIKSHANK. Crown 8vo, cloth extra, **3s. 6d.**

Daudet.—Port Salvation; or,
The Evangelist. By ALPHONSE
DAUDET. Translated by C. HARRY
MELTZER. With Portrait of the
Author. Crown 8vo, cloth extra,
3s. 8d.; post 8vo, illust. boards, **2s.**

Davenant. — What shall my
Son be? Hints for Parents on the
Choice of a Profession or Trade for
their Sons. By FRANCIS DAVENANT,
M.A. Post 8vo, cloth limp, **2s. 6d.**

Davies (Dr. N. E.), Works by:

One Thousand Medical Maxims.
Crown 8vo, **1s.**; cloth, **1s. 6d.**

Nursery Hints: A Mother's Guide.
Crown 8vo, **1s.**; cloth, **1s. 6d.**

Aids to Long Life. Crown 8vo, **2s.**;
cloth limp, **2s. 6d.**

Davies' (Sir John) Complete
Poetical Works, including Psalms I.
to L. in Verse, and other hitherto Unpublished MSS., for the first time
Collected and Edited, with Memorial-Introduction and Notes, by the Rev.
A. B. GROSART, D.D. Two Vols.,
crown 8vo, cloth boards, **12s**

De Maistre.—A Journey Round
My Room. By XAVIER DE MAISTRE.
Translated by HENRY ATTWELL. Post
8vo, cloth limp, **2s. 6d.**

De Mille.—A Castle in Spain.
A Novel. By JAMES DE MILLE. With
a Frontispiece. Crown 8vo, cloth
extra, **3s. 6d.**; post 8vo, illust. bds., **2s.**

Derwent (Leith), Novels by:
Crown 8vo, cloth extra, **3s. 6d.**; post 8vo,
illustrated boards, **2s.**

Our Lady of Tears.

Circe's Lovers.

Dickens (Charles), Novels by:
Post 8vo, illustrated boards, **2s. each.**

Sketches by Boz.	Nicholas Nickleby.
Pickwick Papers.	Oliver Twist.

The Speeches of Charles Dickens.
(*Mayfair Library.*) Post 8vo, cloth
limp, **2s. 6d.**

The Speeches of Charles Dickens,
1841-1870. With a New Bibliography,
revised and enlarged. Edited and
Prefaced by RICHARD HERNE SHEPHERD. Crown 8vo, cloth extra, **6s.**

About England with Dickens. By
ALFRED RIMMER. With 57 Illustrations by C. A. VANDERHOOF, ALFRED
RIMMER, and others. Sq. 8vo, cloth
extra, **10s. 6d.**

Dictionaries:

A Dictionary of Miracles: Imitative,
Realistic, and Dogmatic. By the
Rev. E. C. BREWER, LL.D. Crown
8vo, cloth extra, **7s. 6d.**; hf.-bound, **9s.**

**The Reader's Handbook of Allusions, References, Plots, and
Stories.** By the Rev. E. C. BREWER,
LL.D. Fourth Edition, revised
throughout, with a New Appendix,
containing a Complete English Bibliography. Crown 8vo, 1,400 pages,
cloth extra, **7s. 6d.**

**Authors and their Works, with the
Dates.** Being the Appendices to
"The Reader's Handbook," separately printed. By the Rev. Dr.
BREWER. Crown 8vo, cloth limp, **2s.**

Familiar Allusions: A Handbook
of Miscellaneous Information; including the Names of Celebrated
Statues, Paintings, Palaces, Country
Seats, Ruins, Churches, Ships,
Streets, Clubs, Natural Curiosities,
and the like. By WM. A. WHEELER
and CHARLES G. WHEELER. Demy
8vo, cloth extra, **7s. 6d.**

Short Sayings of Great Men. With
Historical and Explanatory Notes.
By SAMUEL A. BENT. M.A. Demy
8vo, cloth extra, **7s. 6d.**

DICTIONARIES, *continued—*

A Dictionary of the Drama: Being a comprehensive Guide to the Plays, Playwrights, Players, and Playhouses of the United Kingdom and America, from the Earliest to the Present Times. By W. DAVENPORT ADAMS. A thick volume, crown 8vo, half-bound, 12s 6d.   [*In preparation.*

The Slang Dictionary: Etymological, Historical, and Anecdotal. Crown 8vo, cloth extra, 6s. 6d.

Women of the Day: A Biographical Dictionary. By FRANCES HAYS. Cr. 8vo, cloth extra, 5s.

Words, Facts, and Phrases: A Dictionary of Curious, Quaint, and Out-of-the-Way Matters. By ELIEZER EDWARDS. New and Cheaper Issue. Cr. 8vo, cl. ex., 7s. 6d.; hf.-bd., 9s.

Diderot.—The Paradox of Act-ing. Translated, with Annotations, from Diderot's "Le Paradoxe sur le Comédien," by WALTER HERRIES POLLOCK. With a Preface by HENRY IRVING. Cr. 8vo, in parchment, 4s. 6d.

Dobson (W. T.), Works by:
Literary Frivolities, Fancies, Follies, and Frolics. Post 8vo, cloth lp., 2s. 6d.
Poetical Ingenuities and Eccentri-cities. Post 8vo, cloth limp, 2s. 6d.

Doran. — Memories of our Great Towns; with Anecdotic Gleanings concerning their Worthies and their Oddities. By Dr. JOHN DORAN, F.S.A. With 38 Illustrations. New and Cheaper Ed., cr. 8vo, cl. ex., 7s. 6d.

Drama, A Dictionary of the. Being a comprehensive Guide to the Plays, Playwrights, Players, and Playhouses of the United Kingdom and America, from the Earliest to the Present Times. By W. DAVENPORT ADAMS. (Uniform with BREWER'S "Reader's Handbook.") Crown 8vo, half-bound, 12s. 6d.   [*In preparation.*

Dramatists, The Old. Cr. 8vo, cl. ex., Vignette Portraits, 6s. per Vol.
Ben Jonson's Works. With Notes Critical and Explanatory, and a Biographical Memoir by WM. GIFFORD. Edit. by Col. CUNNINGHAM. 3 Vols.
Chapman's Works. Complete in Three Vols. Vol. I. contains the Plays complete, including doubtful ones; Vol. II., Poems and Minor Translations, with Introductory Essay by A. C. SWINBURNE; Vol. III., Translations of the Iliad and Odyssey.
Marlowe's Works. Including his Translations. Edited, with Notes and Introduction, by Col. CUNNINGHAM. One Vol.

DRAMATISTS, THE OLD, *continued—*
Massinger's Plays. From the Text of WILLIAM GIFFORD. Edited by Col. CUNNINGHAM. One Vol.

Dyer. — The Folk Lore of Plants. By Rev. T. F THISELTON DYER, M.A. Crown 8vo, cloth extra, 7s. 6d.   [*In preparation.*

Early English Poets. Edited, with Introductions and Annotations, by Rev. A. B. GROSART, D.D. Crown 8vo, cloth boards, 6s. per Volume.
Fletcher's (Giles, B.D.) Complete Poems. One Vol.
Davies' (Sir John) Complete Poetical Works. Two Vols.
Herrick's (Robert) Complete Collected Poems. Three Vols.
Sidney's (Sir Philip) Complete Poetical Works. Three Vols.

Herbert (Lord) of Cherbury's Poems. Edited, with Introduction, by J. CHURTON COLLINS. Crown 8vo, parchment, 8s.

Edwardes (Mrs. A.), Novels by:
A Point of Honour. Post 8vo, illustrated boards, 2s.
Archie Lovell. Post 8vo, illust. bds., 2s.; crown 8vo, cloth extra, 3s. 6d.

Eggleston.—Roxy: A Novel. By EDWARD EGGLESTON. Post 8vo, illust. boards, 2s.

Emanuel.—On Diamonds and Precious Stones: their History, Value, and Properties; with Simple Tests for ascertaining their Reality. By HARRY EMANUEL, F.R.G.S. With numerous Illustrations, tinted and plain. Crown 8vo, cloth extra, gilt, 6s.

Englishman's House, The: A Practical Guide to all interested in Selecting or Building a House, with full Estimates of Cost, Quantities, &c. By C. J. RICHARDSON. Third Edition. Nearly 600 Illusts. Cr. 8vo, cl. ex., 7s. 6d.

English Merchants: Memoirs in Illustration of the Progress of British Commerce. By H. R. Fox BOURNE. With Illustrations. New and Cheaper Edition, revised. Cr. 8vo, cloth extra, 7s. 6d.   [*Shortly.*

Ewald (Alex. Charles, F.S.A.), Works by:
Stories from the State Papers. With an Autotype Facsimile. Crown 8vo, cloth extra, 6s.
Studies Re-studied: Historical Sketches from Original Sources. Demy 8vo, cloth extra, 12s.

Ewald (Alex. Charles), *continued—*

The Life and Times of Prince Charles Stuart, Count of Albany, commonly called the Young Pretender. From the State Papers and other Sources. New and Cheaper Edition, with a Portrait, crown 8vo, cloth extra, **7s. 6d.**

Eyes, The.—How to Use our Eyes, and How to Preserve Them. By John Browning, F.R.A.S., &c. With 52 Illustrations. **1s.**; cloth, **1s. 6d.**

Fairholt.—Tobacco : Its His- tory and Associations; with an Account of the Plant and its Manufacture, and its Modes of Use in all Ages and Countries. By F. W. Fairholt, F.S.A. With upwards of 100 Illustrations by the Author. Crown 8vo, cloth extra, **6s.**

Familiar Allusions : A Hand- book of Miscellaneous Information; including the Names of Celebrated Statues, Paintings, Palaces, Country Seats, Ruins, Churches, Ships, Streets, Clubs, Natural Curiosities, and the like. By William A. Wheeler, Author of " Noted Names of Fiction ; " and Charles G. Wheeler. Demy 8vo, cloth extra, **7s. 6d.**

Faraday (Michael), Works by :

The Chemical History of a Candle : Lectures delivered before a Juvenile Audience at the Royal Institution. Edited by William Crookes, F.C.S. Post 8vo, cloth extra, with numerous Illustrations, **4s. 6d.**

On the Various Forces of Nature, and their Relations to each other : Lectures delivered before a Juvenile Audience at the Royal Institution. Edited by William Crookes, F.C.S. Post 8vo, cloth extra, with numerous Illustrations. **4s. 6d.**

Farrer. — Military Manners and Customs. By J. A. Farrer, Author of " Primitive Manners and Customs," &c. Cr. 8vo, cloth extra, **6s.**

Fin.Bec. — The Cupboard Papers : Observations on the Art of Living and Dining. By Fin-Bec. Post 8vo, cloth limp, **2s. 6d.**

Fitzgerald (Percy), Works by :

The Recreations of a Literary Man ; or, Does Writing Pay? With Recollections of some Literary Men, and a View of a Literary Man's Working Life. Cr.8vo, cloth extra, **6s.**

The World Behind the Scenes. Crown 8vo, cloth extra, **3s. 6d.**

Fitzgerald (Percy), *continued—*

Little Essays : Passages from the Letters of Charles Lamb. Post 8vo, cloth limp. **2s. 6d.**

Post 8vo, illustrated boards, **2s.** each.
Bella Donna. | Never Forgotten.
The Second Mrs. Tillotson.
Polly.
Seventy-five Brooke Street.
The Lady of Brantome.

Fletcher's (Giles, B.D.) Com- plete Poems : Christ's Victorie in Heaven, Christ's Victorie on Earth, Christ's Triumph over Death, and Minor Poems. With Memorial-Introduction and Notes by the Rev. A. B. Grosart, D.D. Cr. 8vo, cloth bds., **6s.**

Fonblanque.—Filthy Lucre : A Novel. By Albany de Fonblanque. Post 8vo, illustrated boards, **2s.**

Francillon (R. E.), Novels by :
Crown 8vo, cloth extra, **3s. 6d.** each ; post 8vo, illust. boards, **2s** each.
Olympia. | Queen Cophetua.
One by One. | A Real Queen.

Esther's Glove. Fcap. 8vo, **1s.**

French Literature, History of. By Henry Van Laun. Complete in 3 Vols., demy 8vo, cl. bds., **7s. 6d.** each.

Frere.—Pandurang Hari ; or, Memoirs of a Hindoo. With a Preface by Sir H. Bartle Frere, G.C.S.I., &c. Crown 8vo, cloth extra, **3s. 6d.** ; post 8vo, illustrated boards, **2s.**

Friswell.—One of Two: A Novel. By Hain Friswell. Post 8vo, illustrated boards, **2s.**

Frost (Thomas), Works by :
Crown 8vo, cloth extra, **3s. 6d.** each.
Circus Life and Circus Celebrities.
The Lives of the Conjurers.
The Old Showmen and the Old London Fairs.

Fry.—Royal Guide to London Charities, 1885-6. By Herbert Fry. Showing their Name, Date of Foundation, Objects, Income, Officials, &c. Published Annually. Cr. 8vo, cloth, **1s. 6d.**

Gardening Books :
A Year's Work in Garden and Greenhouse : Practical Advice to Amateur Gardeners as to the Management of the Flower, Fruit, and Frame Garden. By George Glenny. Post 8vo, **1s.** : cloth, **1s. 6d.**
Our Kitchen Garden : The Plants we Grow, and How we Cook Them. By Tom Jerrold. Post 8vo, **1s.** cloth limp, **1s. 6d.**

GARDENING BOOKS, *continued—*

Household Horticulture: A Gossip about Flowers. By TOM and JANE JERROLD. Illustrated. Post 8vo, 1s.: cloth limp, 1s. 6d.

The Garden that Paid the Rent. By TOM JERROLD. Fcap. 8vo, illustrated cover, 1s.; cloth limp, 1s. 6d.

My Garden Wild, and What I Grew there. By F. G. HEATH. Crown 8vo, cloth extra, 5s.; gilt edges, 6s.

Garrett.—The Capel Girls: A Novel. By EDWARD GARRETT. Post 8vo, illust.bds., 2s.; cr.8vo, cl.ex., 3s. 6d.

Gentleman's Magazine (The) for 1885. One Shilling Monthly. A New Serial Story, entitled "The Unforeseen," by ALICE O'HANLON, begins in the JANUARY Number. "Science Notes," by W. MATTIEU WILLIAMS, F.R.A.S., and "Table Talk," by SYLVANUS URBAN, are also continued monthly.

*** *Now ready, the Volume for* JANUARY *to* JUNE, 1885, *cloth extra, price* **8s. 6d.**; *Cases for binding,* 2s. *each.*

Gentleman's Annual (The) for Christmas, 1885. Price 1s. Containing a Complete Novel entitled "A Barren Title," by T. W. SPEIGHT, Author of "The Mysteries of Heron Dyke."

German Popular Stories. Collected by the Brothers GRIMM, and Translated by EDGAR TAYLOR. Edited, with an Introduction, by JOHN RUSKIN. With 22 Illustrations on Steel by GEORGE CRUIKSHANK. Square 8vo, cloth extra, 6s. 6d.; gilt edges, 7s. 6d.

Gibbon (Charles), Novels by:
Crown 8vo, cloth extra, 3s. 6d. each; post 8vo, illustrated boards, 2s. each.

Robin Gray.	The Braes of Yarrow.
For Lack of Gold.	
What will the World Say?	The Flower of the Forest.
In Honour Bound.	A Heart's Problem.
In Love and War.	
Queen of the Meadow.	The Golden Shaft.
	Of High Degree.

Post 8vo, illustrated boards, 2s. each.
For the King. | In Pastures Green.
The Dead Heart.

Crown 8vo, cloth extra, 3s. 6d. each.
Fancy Free. | Loving a Dream.

By Mead and Stream. Three Vols., crown 8vo.
A Hard Knot. Three Vols., cr. 8vo.
Heart's Delight. Three Vols., crown 8vo.

Gilbert (William), Novels by:
Post 8vo, illustrated boards, 2s. each.
Dr. Austin's Guests.
The Wizard of the Mountain.
James Duke, Costermonger.

Gilbert (W. S.), Original Plays by: In Two Series, each complete in itself, price 2s. 6d. each.
The FIRST SERIES contains—The Wicked World—Pygmalion and Galatea — Charity — The Princess — The Palace of Truth—Trial by Jury.
The SECOND SERIES contains—Broken Hearts—Engaged—Sweethearts—Gretchen—Dan'l Druce—Tom Cobb—H.M.S. Pinafore—The Sorcerer—The Pirates of Penzance.

Glenny.—A Year's Work in Garden and Greenhouse: Practical Advice to Amateur Gardeners as to the Management of the Flower, Fruit, and Frame Garden. By GEORGE GLENNY. Post 8vo, 1s.; cloth, 1s. 6d.

Godwin.—Lives of the Necromancers. By WILLIAM GODWIN. Post 8vo, cloth limp, 2s.

Golden Library, The:
Square 16mo (Tauchnitz size), cloth limp, 2s. per volume.
Bayard Taylor's Diversions of the Echo Club.
Bennett's (Dr. W. C.) Ballad History of England.
Bennett's (Dr.) Songs for Sailors.
Byron's Don Juan.
Godwin's (William) Lives of the Necromancers.
Holmes's Autocrat of the Breakfast Table. Introduction by SALA.
Holmes's Professor at the Breakfast Table.
Hood's Whims and Oddities. Complete. All the original Illustrations.
Irving's (Washington) Tales of a Traveller.
Irving's (Washington) Tales of the Alhambra.
Jesse's (Edward) Scenes and Occupations of a Country Life.
Lamb's Essays of Elia. Both Series Complete in One Vol.
Leigh Hunt's Essays: A Tale for a Chimney Corner, and other Pieces. With Portrait, and Introduction by EDMUND OLLIER.
Mallory's (Sir Thomas) Mort d'Arthur: The Stories of King Arthur and of the Knights of the Round Table. Edited by B. MONTGOMERIE RANKING.
Pascal's Provincial Letters. A New Translation, with Historical Introduction and Notes, by T. M'CRIE, D.D.
Pope's Poetical Works. Complete.

GOLDEN LIBRARY, THE, *continued—*

Rochefoucauld's Maxims and Moral Reflections. With Notes, and Introductory Essay by SAINTE-BEUVE.

St. Pierre's Paul and Virginia, and The Indian Cottage. Edited, with Life, by the Rev. E. CLARKE.

Shelley's Early Poems, and Queen Mab. With Essay by LEIGH HUNT.

Shelley's Later Poems: Laon and Cythna, &c.

Shelley's Posthumous Poems, the Shelley Papers, &c.

Shelley's Prose Works, including A Refutation of Deism, Zastrozzi, St. Irvyne, &c.

Golden Treasury of Thought,

The: An ENCYCLOPÆDIA OF QUOTATIONS from Writers of all Times and Countries. Selected and Edited by THEODORE TAYLOR. Crown 8vo, cloth gilt and gilt edges, 7s. 6d.

Gordon Cumming (C. F.), Works

by:

In the Hebrides. With Autotype Facsimile and numerous full-page Illustrations. Demy 8vo, cloth extra, 8s. 6d.

In the Himalayas and on the Indian Plains. With numerous Illustrations. Demy 8vo, cloth extra, 8s. 6d.

Via Cornwall to Egypt. With a Photogravure Frontispiece. Demy 8vo, cloth extra, 7s. 6d.

Graham. — The Professor's

Wife: A Story. By LEONARD GRAHAM. Fcap. 8vo, picture cover, 1s.; cloth extra, 2s. 6d.

Greeks and Romans, The Life

of the, Described from Antique Monuments. By ERNST GUHL and W. KONER. Translated from the Third German Edition, and Edited by Dr. F. HUEFFER. With 545 Illustrations. New and Cheaper Edition, demy 8vo, cloth extra, 7s. 6d.

Greenwood (James), Works by:

The Wilds of London. Crown 8vo, cloth extra, 3s. 6d.

Low-Life Deeps: An Account of the Strange Fish to be Found There. Crown 8vo, cloth extra, 3s. 6d.

Dick Temple: A Novel. Post 8vo, illustrated boards, 2s.

Guyot.—The Earth and Man;

or, Physical Geography in its relation to the History of Mankind. By ARNOLD GUYOT. With Additions by Professors AGASSIZ, PIERCE, and GRAY; 12 Maps and Engravings on Steel, some Coloured, and copious Index. Crown 8vo, cloth extra, gilt, 4s. 6d.

Hair (The): Its Treatment in

Health, Weakness, and Disease. Translated from the German of Dr. J. PINCUS. Crown 8vo, 1s; cloth, 1s. 6d.

Hake (Dr. Thomas Gordon),

Poems by:

Maiden Ecstasy. Small 4to, cloth extra, 8s.

New Symbols. Cr. 8vo, cloth extra, 6s.

Legends of the Morrow. Crown 8vo, cloth extra, 6s.

The Serpent Play. Crown 8vo, cloth extra, 6s.

Hall.—Sketches of Irish Cha-

racter. By Mrs. S. C. HALL. With numerous Illustrations on Steel and Wood by MACLISE, GILBERT, HARVEY, and G. CRUIKSHANK. Medium 8vo, cloth extra, gilt, 7s. 6d.

Hall Caine.—The Shadow of a

Crime: A Novel. By HALL CAINE. Cr. 8vo, cloth extra, 3s 6d.

Halliday.—Every-day Papers.

By ANDREW HALLIDAY. Post 8vo, illustrated boards, 2s.

Handwriting, The Philosophy

of. With over 100 Facsimiles and Explanatory Text. By DON FELIX DE SALAMANCA. Post 8vo, cl. limp, 2s. 6d.

Hanky-Panky: A Collection of

Very Easy Tricks, Very Difficult Tricks, White Magic, Sleight of Hand, &c. Edited by W. H. CREMER. With 200 Illusts. Crown 8vo, cloth extra, 4s. 6d.

Hardy (Lady Duffus). — Paul

Wynter's Sacrifice: A Story. By Lady DUFFUS HARDY. Post 8vo, illust. boards, 2s.

Hardy (Thomas).—Under the

Greenwood Tree. By THOMAS HARDY, Author of "Far from the Madding Crowd." Crown 8vo, cloth extra, 3s. 6d.; post 8vo, illustrated bds., 2s.

Haweis (Mrs. H. R.), Works by:

The Art of Dress. With numerous Illustrations. Small 8vo, illustrated cover, 1s.; cloth limp, 1s. 6d.

The Art of Beauty. New and Cheaper Edition. Crown 8vo, cloth extra, with Coloured Frontispiece and Illustrations, 6s.

The Art of Decoration. Square 8vo, handsomely bound and profusely Illustrated, 10s. 6d.

Chaucer for Children: A Golden Key. With Eight Coloured Pictures and numerous Woodcuts. New Edition, small 4to, cloth extra, 6s.

Chaucer for Schools. Demy 8vo, cloth limp, 2s. 6d.

Haweis (Rev. H. R.).—American
Humorists. Including WASHINGTON
IRVING, OLIVER WENDELL HOLMES,
JAMES RUSSELL LOWELL, ARTEMUS
WARD, MARK TWAIN, and BRET HARTE.
By the Rev. H. R. HAWEIS, M.A.
Crown 8vo, cloth extra, 6s.

Hawthorne (Julian), Novels by.
Crown 8vo, cloth extra, 3s. 6d. each;
post 8vo, illustrated boards, 2s. each.

Garth.	Sebastian Strome
Ellice Quentin.	Dust.
Prince Saroni's Wife.	
Fortune's Fool.	
Beatrix Randolph.	

Crown 8vo, cloth extra, 3s. 6d. each.
Miss Cadogna.
Love—or a Name.   [*Shortly*.

Mrs. Gainsborough's Diamonds.
Fcap. 8vo, illustrated cover, 1s. ;
cloth extra, 2s. 6d.

Hays.—Women of the Day: A
Biographical Dictionary of Notable
Contemporaries. By FRANCES HAYS.
Crown 8vo, cloth extra, 5s.

Heath (F. G.). — My Garden
Wild, and What I Grew There. By
FRANCIS GEORGE HEATH, Author of
" The Fern World," &c. Crown 8vo,
cloth extra, 5s. ; cl. gilt, gilt edges, 6s.

Helps (Sir Arthur), Works by :
Animals and their Masters. Post
8vo, cloth limp, 2s. 6d.
Social Pressure. Post 8vo, cloth limp,
2s. 6d.
Ivan de Biron: A Novel. Crown 8vo,
cloth extra, 3s. 6d.; post 8vo, illustrated boards, 2s.

Heptalogia (The); or, The
Seven against Sense. A Cap with
Seven Bells. Cr. 8vo, cloth extra, 6s.

Herbert.—The Poems of Lord
Herbert of Cherbury. Edited, with
Introduction, by J. CHURTON COLLINS.
Crown 8vo, bound in parchment, 8s.

Herrick's (Robert) Hesperides,
Noble Numbers, and Complete Collected Poems. With Memorial-Introduction and Notes by the Rev. A. B.
GROSART, D.D., Steel Portrait, Index
of First Lines, and Glossarial Index,
&c. Three Vols., crown 8vo, cloth, 18s.

Hesse - Wartegg (Chevalier
Ernst von), Works by :
Tunis: The Land and the People.
With 22 Illustrations. Crown 8vo,
cloth extra, 3s. 6d.
The New South-West: Travelling
Sketches from Kansas, New Mexico,
Arizona, and Northern Mexico.
With 100 fine Illustrations and Three
Maps. Demy 8vo, cloth extra,
14s.   [*In preparation*.

Hindley (Charles), Works by :
Crown 8vo, cloth extra, 3s. 6d. each.
Tavern Anecdotes and Sayings: In-
cluding the Origin of Signs, and
Reminiscences connected with
Taverns, Coffee Houses, Clubs, &c.
With Illustrations.
The Life and Adventures of a Cheap
Jack. By One of the Fraternity.
Edited by CHARLES HINDLEY.

Hoey.—The Lover's Creed.
By Mrs. CASHEL HOEY. With Frontis-
piece by P. MACNAB. New and Cheaper
Ed.t. Crown 8vo, cloth extra, 3s. 6d.

Holmes (O. Wendell), Works by :
The Autocrat of the Breakfast-
Table. Illustrated by J. GORDON
THOMSON. Post 8vo, cloth limp,
2s. 6d.; another Edition in smaller
type, with an Introduction by G. A.
SALA. Post 8vo, cloth limp, 2s.
The Professor at the Breakfast-
Table ; with the Story of Iris. Post
8vo, cloth limp, 2s.

Holmes. — The Science of
Voice Production and Voice Preser-
vation: A Popular Manual for the
Use of Speakers and Singers. By
GORDON HOLMES, M.D. With Illus-
trations. Crown 8vo, 1s.; cloth, 1s. 6d.

Hood (Thomas):
Hood's Choice Works, in Prose and
Verse. Including the Cream of the
Comic Annuals. With Life of the
Author, Portrait, and 200 Illustra-
tions. Crown 8vo, cloth extra, 7s. 6d.
Hood's Whims and Oddities. Com-
plete. With all the original Illus-
trations. Post 8vo, cloth limp, 2s.

Hood (Tom), Works by :
From Nowhere to the North Pole:
A Noah's Arkæological Narrative.
With 25 Illustrations by W. BRUN-
TON and E. C. BARNES. Square
crown 8vo, cloth extra, gilt edges, 6s.
A Golden Heart: A Novel. Post 8vo,
illustrated boards, 2s.

Hook's (Theodore) Choice Humorous Works, including his Ludicrous Adventures, Bons Mots, Puns and Hoaxes. With a New Life of the Author, Portraits, Facsimiles. and Illusts. Cr. 8vo, cl. extra, gilt, 7s. 6d.

Hooper.—The House of Raby: A Novel. By Mrs. GEORGE HOOPER. Post 8vo, illustrated boards, 2s.

Horne.—Orion: An Epic Poem, in Three Books. By RICHARD HENGIST HORNE. With Photographic Portrait from a Medallion by SUMMERS. Tenth Edition, crown 8vo, cloth extra, 7s.

Howell.—Conflicts of Capital and Labour, Historically and Economically considered: Being a History and Review of the Trade Unions of Great Britain, showing their Origin, Progress, Constitution, and Objects, in their Political, Social, Economical, and Industrial Aspects. By GEORGE HOWELL. Cr. 8vo, cloth extra, 7s. 6d.

Hugo. — The Hunchback of Notre Dame. By VICTOR HUGO. Post 8vo, illustrated boards, 2s.

Hunt.—Essays by Leigh Hunt. A Tale for a Chimney Corner, and other Pieces. With Portrait and Introduction by EDMUND OLLIER. Post 8vo, cloth limp, 2s.

Hunt (Mrs. Alfred), Novels by: Crown 8vo, cloth extra, 3s. 6d. each; post 8vo, illustrated boards, 2s. each.
Thornicroft's Model.
The Leaden Casket.
Self-Condemned.

Ingelow.—Fated to be Free: A Novel. By JEAN INGELOW. Crown 8vo, cloth extra, 3s. 6d.; post 8vo, illustrated boards, 2s.

Irish Wit and Humour, Songs of. Collected and Edited by A. PERCEVAL GRAVES. Post 8vo, cl. limp, 2s. 6d.

Irving (Washington), Works by: Post 8vo, cloth limp, 2s. each.
Tales of a Traveller.
Tales of the Alhambra.

Janvier.—Practical Keramics for Students. By CATHERINE A. JANVIER. Crown 8vo, cloth extra, 6s.

Jay (Harriett), Novels by:
The Dark Colleen. Post 8vo, illustrated boards, 2s.
The Queen of Connaught. Crown 8vo, cloth extra, 3s. 6d.; post 8vo, illustrated boards, 2s.

Jefferies (Richard), Works by:
Nature near London. Crown 8vo, cloth extra, 6s.
The Life of the Fields. Crown 8vo, cloth extra, 6s.

Jennings (H. J.), Works by:
Curiosities of Criticism. Post 8vo, cloth limp, 2s. 6d.
Lord Tennyson: A Biographical Sketch. With a Photograph-Portrait. Crown 8vo, cloth extra, 6s.

Jennings (Hargrave). — The Rosicrucians: Their Rites and Mysteries. With Chapters on the Ancient Fire and Serpent Worshippers. By HARGRAVE JENNINGS. With Five full-page Plates and upwards of 300 Illustrations. A New Edition, crown 8vo, cloth extra, 7s. 6d.

Jerrold (Tom), Works by:
The Garden that Paid the Rent. By TOM JERROLD. Fcap. 8vo, illustrated cover, 1s.; cloth limp, 1s. 6d.
Household Horticulture: A Gossip about Flowers. By TOM and JANE JERROLD. Illustrated. Post 8vo, 1s.; cloth, 1s. 6d.
Our Kitchen Garden: The Plants we Grow, and How we Cook Them. By TOM JERROLD. Post 8vo, 1s.; cloth limp, 1s. 6d.

Jesse.—Scenes and Occupations of a Country Life. By EDWARD JESSE. Post 8vo, cloth limp, 2s.

Jeux d'Esprit. Collected and Edited by HENRY S. LEIGH. Post 8vo, cloth limp, 2s. 6d.

Jones (Wm., F.S.A.), Works by:
Finger-Ring Lore: Historical, Legendary, and Anecdotal. With over 200 Illusts. Cr. 8vo, cl. extra, 7s. 6d.
Credulities, Past and Present; including the Sea and Seamen, Miners, Talismans, Word and Letter Divination, Exorcising and Blessing of Animals, Birds, Eggs, Luck, &c. With an Etched Frontispiece. Crown 8vo, cloth extra, 7s. 6d.
Crowns and Coronations: A History of Regalia in all Times and Countries. With One Hundred Illustrations. Cr. 8vo, cloth extra, 7s. 6d.

Jonson's (Ben) Works. With Notes Critical and Explanatory, and a Biographical Memoir by WILLIAM GIFFORD. Edited by Colonel CUNNINGHAM. Three Vols., crown 8vo, cloth extra, 18s.; or separately, 6s each.

Josephus,The CompleteWorks
of. Translated by WHISTON. Containing both "The Antiquities of the Jews" and "The Wars of the Jews." Two Vols., 8vo, with 52 Illustrations and Maps, cloth extra, gilt, 14s.

Kempt.—Pencil and Palette:
Chapters on Art and Artists. By ROBERT KEMPT. Post 8vo, cloth limp, 2s. 6d.

Kingsley (Henry), Novels by:
Each crown 8vo, cloth extra, 3s. 6d.; or post 8vo, illustrated boards, 2s.

Oakshott Castle. | Number Seventeen

Knight.—The Patient's Vade
Mecum: How to get most Benefit from Medical Advice. By WILLIAM KNIGHT, M.R.C.S., and EDWARD KNIGHT, L.R.C.P. Crown 8vo, 1s.; cloth, 1s. 6d.

Lamb (Charles):
Mary and Charles Lamb: Their Poems, Letters, and Remains. With Reminiscences and Notes by W. CAREW HAZLITT. With HANCOCK'S Portrait of the Essayist, Facsimiles of the Title-pages of the rare First Editions of Lamb's and Coleridge's Works, and numerous Illustrations. Crown 8vo, cloth extra, 10s. 6d.

Lamb's Complete Works, in Prose and Verse, reprinted from the Original Editions, with many Pieces hitherto unpublished. Edited, with Notes and Introduction, by R. H. SHEPHERD. With Two Portraits and Facsimile of Page of the "Essay on Roast Pig." Cr. 8vo, cloth extra, 7s. 6d.

The Essays of Elia. Complete Edition. Post 8vo, cloth extra, 2s.

Poetry for Children, and Prince Dorus. By CHARLES LAMB. Carefully reprinted from unique copies. Small 8vo, cloth extra, 5s.

Little Essays: Sketches and Characters. By CHARLES LAMB. Selected from his Letters by PERCY FITZGERALD. Post 8vo, cloth limp, 2s. 6d.

Lane's Arabian Nights, &c.:
The Thousand and One Nights: commonly called, in England, "THE ARABIAN NIGHTS' ENTERTAINMENTS." A New Translation from the Arabic, with copious Notes, by EDWARD WILLIAM LANE. Illustrated by many hundred Engravings on Wood, from Original Designs by WM. HARVEY. A New Edition, from a Copy annotated by the Translator, edited by his Nephew, EDWARD STANLEY POOLE. With a Preface by STANLEY LANE-POOLE. Three Vols., demy 8vo, cloth extra, 7s. 6d. each.

LANE'S ARABIAN NIGHTS, *continued—*
Arabian Society in the Middle Ages: Studies from "The Thousand and One Nights." By EDWARD WILLIAM LANE, Author of "The Modern Egyptians," &c. Edited by STANLEY LANE-POOLE. Cr. 8vo, cloth extra, 6s.

Lares and Penates; or, The
Background of Life. By FLORENCE CADDY. Crown 8vo, cloth extra, 6s.

Larwood (Jacob), Works by:
The Story of the London Parks. With Illustrations. Crown 8vo, cloth extra, 3s. 6d.

Forensic Anecdotes. Post 8vo, cloth limp, 2s. 6d.

Theatrical Anecdotes. Post 8vo, cloth limp, 2s. 6d.

Life in London; or, The History
of Jerry Hawthorn and Corinthian Tom. With the whole of CRUIKSHANK's Illustrations, in Colours, after the Originals. Crown 8vo, cloth extra, 7s. 6d.

Linton (E. Lynn), Works by:
Post 8vo, cloth limp, 2s. 6d. each.

Witch Stories.

The True Story of Joshua Davidson.

Ourselves: Essays on Women.

Crown 8vo, cloth extra, 3s. 6d. each; post 8vo, illustrated boards, 2s. each.

Patricia Kemball.

The Atonement of Leam Dundas.

The World Well Lost.

Under which Lord?

With a Silken Thread.

The Rebel of the Family.

"My Love!"

Ione.

Locks and Keys.—On the De-
velopment and Distribution of Primitive Locks and Keys. By Lieut.-Gen. PITT-RIVERS, F.R.S. With numerous Illustrations. Demy 4to, half Roxburghe, 16s.

Longfellow:
Longfellow's Complete Prose Works. Including "Outre Mer," "Hyperion," "Kavanagh," "The Poets and Poetry of Europe," and "Driftwood." With Portrait and Illustrations by VALENTINE BROMLEY. Crown 8vo, cloth extra, 7s. 6d.

Longfellow's Poetical Works. Carefully Reprinted from the Original Editions. With numerous fine Illustrations on Steel and Wood. Crown 8vo, cloth extra, 7s. 6d.

Long Life, Aids to: A Medical, Dietetic, and General Guide in Health and Disease. By N. E. DAVIES, L.R.C.P Crown 8vo, 2s. ; cloth limp, 2s. 6d.

Lucy.—Gideon Fleyce: A Novel. By HENRY W. LUCY. Crown 8vo, cloth extra, 3s. 6d.; post 8vo, illustrated boards, 2s.

Lusiad (The) of Camoens. Translated into English Spenserian Verse by ROBERT FFRENCH DUFF. Demy 8vo, with Fourteen full-page Plates, cloth boards, 18s.

McCarthy (Justin, M.P.),Works by :

A History of Our Own Times, from the Accession of Queen Victoria to the General Election of 1880. Four Vols. demy 8vo, cloth extra, 12s. each.—Also a POPULAR EDITION, in Four Vols. cr. 8vo, cl. extra, 6s. each.

A Short History of Our Own Times. One Vol., crown 8vo, cloth extra, 6s.

History of the Four Georges. Four Vols. demy 8vo, cloth extra, 12s. each. [Vol. I. *now ready.*

Crown 8vo, cloth extra, 3s. 6d. each ; post 8vo, illustrated boards, 2s. each.

 Dear Lady Disdain.
 The Waterdale Neighbours.
 My Enemy's Daughter.
 A Fair Saxon.
 Linley Rochford.
 Miss Misanthrope.
 Donna Quixote.
 The Comet of a Season.
 Maid of Athens.

Camiola: A Girl with a Fortune. Three Vols., crown 8vo. [*Preparing.*

McCarthy (Justin H., M.P.), Works by :

An Outline of the History of Ireland, from the Earliest Times to the Present Day. Cr. 8vo, 1s. ; cloth, 1s. 6d.

England under Gladstone, 1880-85. Second Edition, revised and brought down to the Fall of the Gladstone Administration. Crown 8vo, cloth extra, 6s.

MacDonald (George, LL.D.), Works by :

The Princess and Curdle. With 11 Illustrations by JAMES ALLEN. Small crown 8vo, cloth extra, 5s.

MacDonald (GEORGE), *continued—*

Gutta-Percha Willie, the Working Genius. With 9 Illustrations by ARTHUR HUGHES. Square 8vo, cloth extra, 3s. 6d.

Paul Faber, Surgeon. With a Frontispiece by J. E. MILLAIS. Crown 8vo, cloth extra, 3s. 6d.; post 8vo, illustrated boards, 2s.

Thomas Wingfold, Curate. With a Frontispiece by C. J. STANILAND. Crown 8vo, cloth extra, 3s. 6d.; post 8vo, illustrated boards, 2s.

Macdonell.—Quaker Cousins: A Novel. By AGNES MACDONELL. Crown 8vo, cloth extra, 3s. 6d. ; post 8vo, illustrated boards, 2s.

Macgregor. — Pastimes and Players. Notes on Popular Games. By ROBERT MACGREGOR. Post 8vo, cloth limp, 2s. 6d.

Maclise Portrait-Gallery (The) of Illustrious Literary Characters; with Memoirs—Biographical, Critical, Bibliographical, and Anecdotal—illustrative of the Literature of the former half of the Present Century. By WILLIAM BATES, B.A. With 85 Portraits printed on an India Tint. Crown 8vo, cloth extra, 7s. 6d.

Macquoid (Mrs.), Works by :

In the Ardennes. With 50 fine Illustrations by THOMAS R. MACQUOID. Square 8vo, cloth extra, 10s. 6d.

Pictures and Legends from Normandy and Brittany. With numerous Illustrations by THOMAS R. MACQUOID. Square 8vo, cloth gilt, 10s. 6d.

Through Normandy. With 90 Illustrations by T. R. MACQUOID. Square 8vo, cloth extra, 7s. 6d.

Through Brittany. With numerous Illustrations by T. R. MACQUOID. Square 8vo, cloth extra, 7s. 6d.

About Yorkshire. With 67 Illustrations by T. R. MACQUOID, Engraved by SWAIN. Square 8vo, cloth extra, 10s. 6d.

The Evil Eye, and other Stories. Crown 8vo, cloth extra, 3s. 6d.; post 8vo, illustrated boards, 2s.

Lost Rose, and other Stories. Crown 8vo, cloth extra, 3s. 6d. ; post 8vo, illustrated boards, 2s.

Mackay.—Interludes and Un- dertones: or, Music at Twilight. By CHARLES MACKAY, LL.D. Crown 8vo, cloth extra, 6s.

Magic Lantern (The), and its
Management: including full Practical Directions for producing the Limelight, making Oxygen Gas, and preparing Lantern Slides. By T. C. HEPWORTH. With 10 Illustrations. Crown 8vo, 1s. ; cloth, 1s. 6d.

Magician's Own Book (The):
Performances with Cups and Balls, Eggs, Hats, Handkerchiefs, &c. All from actual Experience. Edited by W. H. CREMER. With 200 Illustrations. Crown 8vo. cloth extra. 4s. 6d.

Magic No Mystery: Tricks with Cards, Dice, Balls. &c., with fully descriptive Directions; the Art of Secret Writing; Training of Performing Animals, &c. With Coloured Frontispiece and many Illustrations. Crown 8vo, cloth extra, 4s. 6d.

Magna Charta. An exact Facsimile of the Original in the British Museum, printed on fine plate paper, 3 feet by 2 feet, with Arms and Seals emblazoned in Gold and Colours. Price 5s.

Mallock (W. H.), Works by:
The New Republic ; or, Culture, Faith and Philosophy in an English Country House. Post 8vo, cloth limp, 2s. 6d. ; Cheap Edition, illustrated boards, 2s.

The New Paul and Virginia ; or, Positivism on an Island. Post 8vo, cloth limp, 2s. 6d.

Poems. Small 4to, bound in parchment, 8s.

Is Life worth Living? Crown 8vo, cloth extra, 6s.

Mallory's (Sir Thomas) Mort
d'Arthur: The Stories of King Arthur and of the Knights of the Round Table. Edited by B. MONTGOMERIE RANKING. Post 8vo, cloth limp, 2s.

Marlowe's Works. Including his Translations. Edited. with Notes and Introduction, by Col. CUNNINGHAM. Crown 8vo, cloth extra, 6s.

Marryat (Florence), Novels by:
Crown 8vo, cloth extra, 3s. 6d. each; or post 8vo, illustrated boards, 2s.

Open! Sesame!
Written in Fire.

Post 8vo, illustrated boards, 2s. each.
A Harvest of Wild Oats.
A Little Stepson.
Fighting the Air.

Masterman.—Half a Dozen
Daughters: A Novel. By J. MASTERMAN. Post 8vo, illustrated boards, 2s.

Mark Twain, Works by:
The Choice Works of Mark Twain. Revised and Corrected throughout by the Author. With Life, Portrait, and numerous Illustrations. Crown 8vo, cloth extra, 7s. 6d.

The Adventures of Tom Sawyer. With 111 Illustrations. Crown 8vo, cloth extra, 7s. 6d.

⁎ Also a Cheap Edition, post 8vo, illustrated boards, 2s.

An Idle Excursion, and other Sketches. Post 8vo, illustrated boards, 2s.

The Prince and the Pauper. With nearly 200 Illustrations. Crown 8vo, cloth extra, 7s. 6d.

The Innocents Abroad ; or, The New Pilgrim's Progress : Being some Account of the Steamship " Quaker City's " Pleasure Excursion to Europe and the Holy Land. With 234 Illustrations. Crown 8vo, cloth extra, 7s. 6d. CHEAP EDITION (under the title of " MARK TWAIN'S PLEASURE TRIP "), post 8vo, illust. boards. 2s.

Roughing It, and The Innocents at Home. With 200 Illustrations by F. A. FRASER. Crown 8vo, cloth extra, 7s. 6d.

The Gilded Age. By MARK TWAIN and CHARLES DUDLEY WARNER. With 212 Illustrations by T. COPPIN. Crown 8vo, cloth extra, 7s. 6d.

A Tramp Abroad. With 314 Illustrations. Crown 8vo, cloth extra, 7s. 6d. ; post 8vo, illustrated boards, 2s.

The Stolen White Elephant, &c. Crown 8vo, cloth extra, 6s.; post 8vo, illustrated boards, 2s.

Life on the Mississippi. With about 300 Original Illustrations. Crown 8vo, cloth extra, 7s. 6d.

The Adventures of Huckleberry Finn. With 174 Illustrations by E. W. KEMBLE. Crown 8vo, cloth extra, 7s. 6d.

Massinger's Plays. From the Text of WILLIAM GIFFORD. Edited by Col. CUNNINGHAM. Crown 8vo, cloth extra, 6s.

Mayhew.—London Characters
and the Humorous Side of London Life. By HENRY MAYHEW. With numerous Illustrations. Crown 8vo, cloth extra, 3s. 6d.

Mayfair Library, The:
Post 8vo, cloth limp, 2s. 6d. per Volume.
A Journey Round My Room. By XAVIER DE MAISTRE. Translated by HENRY ATTWELL.
Latter-Day Lyrics. Edited by W. DAVENPORT ADAMS.

Mayfair Library, *continued—*

Quips and Quiddities. Selected by W. Davenport Adams.

The Agony Column of "The Times," from 1800 to 1870. Edited, with an Introduction, by Alice Clay.

Balzac's "Comedie Humaine" and its Author. With Translations by H. H. Walker.

Melancholy Anatomised: A Popular Abridgment of "Burton's Anatomy of Melancholy."

Gastronomy as a Fine Art. By Brillat-Savarin.

The Speeches of Charles Dickens.

Literary Frivolities, Fancies, Follies, and Frolics. By W. T. Dobson.

Poetical Ingenuities and Eccentricities. Selected and Edited by W. T. Dobson.

The Cupboard Papers. By Fin-Bec.

Original Plays by W. S. Gilbert, First Series. Containing: The Wicked World — Pygmalion and Galatea — Charity — The Princess — The Palace of Truth—Trial by Jury.

Original Plays by W. S. Gilbert, Second Series. Containing: Broken Hearts — Engaged — Sweethearts — Gretchen—Dan'l Druce—Tom Cobb —H.M.S. Pinafore — The Sorcerer —The Pirates of Penzance.

Songs of Irish Wit and Humour. Collected and Edited by A. Perceval Graves.

Animals and their Masters. By Sir Arthur Helps.

Social Pressure. By Sir A. Helps.

Curiosities of Criticism. By Henry J. Jennings.

The Autocrat of the Breakfast Table. By Oliver Wendell Holmes. Illustrated by J. Gordon Thomson.

Pencil and Palette. By Robert Kempt.

Little Essays: Sketches and Characters. By Chas. Lamb. Selected from his Letters by Percy Fitzgerald.

Forensic Anecdotes; or, Humour and Curiosities of the Law and Men of Law. By Jacob Larwood.

Theatrical Anecdotes. By Jacob Larwood.

Jeux d'Esprit. Edited by Henry S. Leigh.

True History of Joshua Davidson. By E. Lynn Linton.

Witch Stories. By E. Lynn Linton.

Ourselves: Essays on Women. By E. Lynn Linton.

Pastimes and Players. By Robert Macgregor.

The New Paul and Virginia. By W. H. Mallock.

Mayfair Library, *continued—*

The New Republic. By Mallock.

Puck on Pegasus. By H. Cholmonde-ley-Pennell.

Pegasus Re-Saddled. By H. Cholmondeley-Pennell. Illustrated by George Du Maurier.

Muses of Mayfair. Edited by H. Cholmondeley-Pennell.

Thoreau: His Life and Aims. By H. A. Page.

Puniana. By the Hon. Hugh Rowley.

More Puniana. By the Hon. Hugh Rowley.

The Philosophy of Handwriting. By Don Felix de Salamanca.

By Stream and Sea. By William Senior. [Thornbury.

Old Stories Re-told. By Walter

Leaves from a Naturalist's Note-Book. By Dr. Andrew Wilson.

Medicine, Family.—One Thousand Medical Maxims and Surgical Hints, for Infancy, Adult Life, Middle Age, and Old Age. By N. E. Davies, L.R.C.P. Lond. Cr. 8vo, 1s.; cl., 1s. 6d.

Merry Circle (The): A Book of New Intellectual Games and Amusements. By Clara Bellew. With numerous Illustrations. Crown 8vo, cloth extra, 4s. 6d.

Mexican Mustang (On a). Through Texas, from the Gulf to the Rio Grande. A New Book of American Humour. By Alex. E. Sweet and J. Armoy Knox, Editors of "Texas Siftings." 265 Illusts. Cr. 8vo, cloth extra, 7s. 6d.

Middlemass (Jean), Novels by:
Touch and Go. Crown 8vo, cloth extra, 3s. 6d.; post 8vo, illust. bds., 2s.
Mr. Dorillion. Post 8vo, illust. bds., 2s.

Miller.—**Physiology for the** Young; or, The House of Life: Human Physiology, with its application to the Preservation of Health. For Classes and Popular Reading. With numerous Illusts. By Mrs. F. Fenwick Miller. Small 8vo, cloth limp, 2s. 6d.

Milton (J. L.), Works by:

The Hygiene of the Skin. A Concise Set of Rules for the Management of the Skin; with Directions for Diet, Wines, Soaps, Baths, &c. Small 8vo, 1s.; cloth extra, 1s. 6d.

The Bath in Diseases of the Skin. Small 8vo, 1s.; cloth extra, 1s. 6d.

The Laws of Life, and their Relation to Diseases of the Skin. Small 8vo, 1s.; cloth extra, 1s. 6d.

Moncrieff. — The Abdication;
or, Time Tries All. An Historical Drama. By W. D. Scott-Moncrieff. With Seven Etchings by John Pettie, R.A., W. Q. Orchardson, R.A., J. MacWhirter, A.R.A., Colin Hunter, R. Macbeth, and Tom Graham. Large 4to, bound in buckram, 21s.

Murray (D. Christie), Novels
by. Crown 8vo, cloth extra, 3s. 6d. each; post 8vo, illustrated boards, 2s. each.

A Life's Atonement.

A Model Father.

Joseph's Coat.

Coals of Fire.

By the Gate of the Sea.

Val Strange.

Hearts.

Crown 8vo, cloth extra, 3s. 6d. each.

The Way of the World.

A Bit of Human Nature.

First Person Singular: A Novel. Three Vols., cr. 8vo. [*Preparing*.

North Italian Folk. By Mrs. Comyns Carr. Illust. by Randolph Caldecott. Square 8vo, cloth extra, 7s. 6d.

Number Nip (Stories about),
the Spirit of the Giant Mountains. Retold for Children by Walter Grahame. With Illustrations by J. Moyr Smith. Post 8vo, cloth extra, 5s.

Nursery Hints: A Mother's
Guide in Health and Disease. By N. E. Davies, L.R.C.P. Crown 8vo, 1s.; cloth, 1s. 6d.

Oliphant. — Whiteladies: A
Novel. With Illustrations by Arthur Hopkins and Henry Woods. Crown 8vo, cloth extra, 3s. 6d.; post 8vo, illustrated boards, 2s.

O'Connor. — Lord Beaconsfield
A Biography. By T. P. O'Connor, M.P. Sixth Edition, with a New Preface, bringing the work down to the Death of Lord Beaconsfield. Crown 8vo, cloth extra, 7s. 6d.

O'Hanlon. — The Unforeseen:
A Novel. By Alice O'Hanlon. Three Vols., crown 8vo.

O'Reilly. — Phœbe's Fortunes:
A Novel. With Illustrations by Henry Tuck. Post 8vo, illustrated boards, 2s.

O'Shaughnessy (Arth.), Works
by:

Songs of a Worker. Fcap. 8vo, cloth extra, 7s. 6d.

Music and Moonlight. Fcap. 8vo, cloth extra, 7s. 6d.

Lays of France. Crown 8vo, cloth extra, 10s. 6d.

Ouida, Novels by. Crown 8vo, cloth extra, 5s. each; post 8vo, illustrated boards, 2s. each.

Held in Bondage.	Pascarel.
Strathmore.	Signa.
Chandos.	In a Winter City.
Under Two Flags.	Ariadne.
Cecil Castlemaine's Gage.	Friendship.
	Moths.
Idalia.	Pipistrello.
Tricotrin.	A Village Commune.
Puck.	
Folle Farine.	Bimbi.
TwoLittleWooden Shoes.	In Maremma.
	Wanda.
A Dog of Flanders.	Frescoes.

Bimbi: Presentation Edition. Sq. 8vo, cloth gilt, cinnamon edges, 7s. 6d.

Princess Napraxine. New and Cheaper Edition. Crown 8vo, cloth extra, 5s.

Othmar: A Novel. (A Sequel to "Princess Napraxine." Three Vols., crown 8vo. [*Preparing*.

Wisdom, Wit, and Pathos. Selected from the Works of Ouida by F. Sydney Morris. Small crown 8vo, cloth extra, 5s.

Page (H. A.), Works by:

Thoreau: His Life and Aims: A Study. With a Portrait. Post 8vo, cloth limp, 2s. 6d.

Lights on the Way: Some Tales within a Tale. By the late J. H. Alexander, B.A. Edited by H. A. Page. Crown 8vo, cloth extra, 6s.

Pascal's Provincial Letters. A New Translation, with Historical Introduction and Notes, by T. M'Crie, D.D. Post 8vo, cloth limp, 2s.

Patient's (The) Vade Mecum:
How to get most Benefit from Medical Advice. By William Knight, M.R.C.S., and Edward Knight, L.R.C.P. Crown 8vo, 1s.; cloth, 1s. 6d.

Paul Ferroll :

Post 8vo, illustrated boards, **2s.** each.

Paul Ferroll : A Novel.

Why Paul Ferroll Killed his Wife.

Paul.—Gentle and Simple. By MARGARET AGNES PAUL. With a Frontispiece by HELEN PATERSON. Cr. 8vo, cloth extra, **3s. 6d.** ; post 8vo, illustrated boards, **2s.**

Payn (James), Novels by. Crown 8vo, cloth extra, **3s. 6d.** each ; post 8vo, illustrated boards, **2s.** each.

Lost Sir Massingberd.

The Best of Husbands.

Walter's Word.

Halves. | Fallen Fortunes.

What He Cost Her.

Less Black than we're Painted.

By Proxy. | High Spirits.

Under One Roof. | Carlyon's Year.

A Confidential Agent.

Some Private Views.

A Grape from a Thorn.

For Cash Only. | From Exile.

Post 8vo, illustrated boards, **2s.** each.

A Perfect Treasure.

Bentinck's Tutor.

Murphy's Master.

A County Family.

At Her Mercy.

A Woman's Vengeance.

Cecil's Tryst.

The Clyffards of Clyffe.

The Family Scapegrace

The Foster Brothers.

Found Dead.

Gwendoline's Harvest.

Humorous Stories.

Like Father, Like Son.

A Marine Residence.

Married Beneath Him.

Mirk Abbey.

Not Wooed, but Won.

Two Hundred Pounds Reward.

Kit : A Memory.

The Canon's Ward.

In Peril and Privation : Stories of Marine Adventure Re-told. A Book for Boys. With numerous Illustrations. Crown 8vo, cloth gilt, **6s.**

Pears.—The Present Depression in Trade : Its Causes and Remedies. Being the " Pears " Prize Essays (of One Hundred Guineas). By EDWIN GOADBY and WILLIAM WATT. With an Introductory Paper by Prof. LEONE LEVI, F.S.A., F.S.S. Demy 8vo, **1s.**

Pennell (H. Cholmondeley), Works by : Post 8vo, cloth limp, **2s. 6d.** each.

Puck on Pegasus. With Illustrations.

The Muses of Mayfair. Vers de Société, Selected and Edited by H. C. PENNELL.

Pegasus Re-Saddled. With Ten full-page Illusts. by G. DU MAURIER.

Phelps.—Beyond the Gates. By ELIZABETH STUART PHELPS, Author of " The Gates Ajar." New and Cheaper Edition. Post 8vo, illust. boards, **1s.** ; cloth limp, **1s. 6d.**

Pirkis (Mrs. C. L.) Novels by :

Trooping with Crows. Fcap. 8vo, picture cover, **1s.**

Lady Lovelace. Three Vols., crown 8vo.

Planché (J. R.), Works by :

The Pursuivant of Arms ; or, Heraldry Founded upon Facts. With Coloured Frontispiece and 200 Illustrations. Cr. 8vo, cloth extra, **7s. 6d.**

Songs and Poems, from 1819 to 1879. Edited, with an Introduction, by his Daughter, Mrs. MACKARNESS. Crown 8vo, cloth extra, **6s.**

Play-time : Sayings and Doings of Baby-land. By E. STANFORD. Large 4to, handsomely printed in Colours, **5s.**

Plutarch's Lives of Illustrious Men. Translated from the Greek, with Notes Critical and Historical, and a Life of Plutarch, by JOHN and WILLIAM LANGHORNE. Two Vols., 8vo, cloth extra, with Portraits, **10s. 6d.**

Poe (Edgar Allan) :—

The Choice Works, in Prose and Poetry, of EDGAR ALLAN POE. With an Introductory Essay by CHARLES BAUDELAIRE, Portrait and Fac-similes. Crown 8vo, cl. extra, **7s. 6d.**

The Mystery of Marie Roget, and other Stories. Post 8vo, illust.bds.,**2s.**

Pope's Poetical Works. Complete in One Vol. Post 8vo, cl. limp, **2s.**

Price (E. C.), Novels by:

Crown 8vo, cloth extra, 3s. 6d.; post 8vo, illustrated boards, 2s.

Valentina. | The Foreigners.
Mrs. Lancaster's Rival.

Gerald. Three Vols., crown 8vo.

Proctor (Richd. A.), Works by:

Flowers of the Sky. With 55 Illusts. Small crown 8vo, cloth extra, 4s. 6d.

Easy Star Lessons. With Star Maps for Every Night in the Year, Drawings of the Constellations, &c. Crown 8vo, cloth extra, 6s.

Familiar Science Studies. Crown 8vo, cloth extra, 7s. 6d.

Rough Ways made Smooth: A Series of Familiar Essays on Scientific Subjects. Cr. 8vo, cloth extra, 6s.

Our Place among Infinities: A Series of Essays contrasting our Little Abode in Space and Time with the Infinities Around us. Crown 8vo, cloth extra, 6s.

The Expanse of Heaven: A Series of Essays on the Wonders of the Firmament. Cr. 8vo, cloth extra, 6s.

Saturn and its System. New and Revised Edition, with 13 Steel Plates. Demy 8vo, cloth extra, 10s. 6d.

The Great Pyramid: Observatory, Tomb, and Temple. With Illustrations. Crown 8vo, cloth extra, 6s.

Mysteries of Time and Space. With Illusts. Cr. 8vo, cloth extra, 7s. 6d.

The Universe of Suns, and other Science Gleanings. With numerous Illusts. Cr. 8vo, cloth extra, 7s. 6d.

Wages and Wants of Science Workers. Crown 8vo, 1s. 6d.

Pyrotechnist's Treasury (The);

or, Complete Art of Making Fireworks. By THOMAS KENTISH. With numerous Illustrations. Cr. 8vo, cl. extra, 4s. 6d.

Rabelais' Works. Faithfully

Translated from the French, with variorum Notes, and numerous characteristic Illustrations by GUSTAVE DORÉ. Crown 8vo, cloth extra, 7s. 6d.

Rambosson.—Popular Astro-

nomy. By J. RAMBOSSON, Laureate of the Institute of France. Translated by C. B. PITMAN. Crown 8vo, cloth gilt, with numerous Illustrations, and a beautifully executed Chart of Spectra, 7s. 6d.

Reader's Handbook (The) of

Allusions, References, Plots, and Stories. By the Rev. Dr. BREWER. Fourth Edition, revised throughout, with a New Appendix, containing a COMPLETE ENGLISH BIBLIOGRAPHY. Cr. 8vo, 1,400 pages, cloth extra, 7s. 6d.

Richardson. — A Ministry of

Health, and other Papers. By BENJAMIN WARD RICHARDSON, M.D., &c. Crown 8vo, cloth extra, 6s.

Reade (Charles, D.C.L.), Novels

by. Post 8vo, illust., bds., 2s. each; or cr. 8vo, cl. ex., illust., 3s. 6d. each.

Peg Woffington. Illustrated by S. L. FILDES, A.R.A.

Christie Johnstone. Illustrated by WILLIAM SMALL.

It is Never Too Late to Mend. Illustrated by G. J. PINWELL.

The Course of True Love Never did run Smooth. Illustrated by HELEN PATERSON.

The Autobiography of a Thief; Jack of all Trades; and James Lambert. Illustrated by MATT STRETCH.

Love me Little, Love me Long. Illustrated by M. ELLEN EDWARDS.

The Double Marriage. Illust. by Sir JOHN GILBERT, R.A., and C. KEENE.

The Cloister and the Hearth. Illustrated by CHARLES KEENE.

Hard Cash. Illust. by F. W. LAWSON.

Griffith Gaunt. Illustrated by S. L. FILDES, A.R.A., and WM. SMALL.

Foul Play. Illust. by DU MAURIER.

Put Yourself in His Place. Illustrated by ROBERT BARNES.

A Terrible Temptation. Illustrated by EDW. HUGHES and A. W. COOPER.

The Wandering Heir. Illustrated by H. PATERSON, S. L. FILDES, A.R.A., C. GREEN, and H. WOODS, A.R.A.

A Simpleton. Illustrated by KATE CRAUFORD.

A Woman-Hater. Illustrated by THOS. COULDERY.

Readiana. With a Steel-plate Portrait of CHARLES READE.

Singleheart and Doubleface: A Matter-of-fact Romance. Illustrated by P. MACNAB.

Good Stories of Men and other Animals. Illustrated by E. A. ABBEY, PERCY MACQUOID, and JOSEPH NASH.

The Jilt, and other Stories. Illustrated by JOSEPH NASH.

Riddell (Mrs. J. H.), Novels by:

Crown 8vo, cloth extra, 3s. 6d. each; post 8vo, illustrated boards, 2s. each.

Her Mother's Darling.
The Prince of Wales's Garden Party.
Weird Stories.
The Uninhabited House.
Fairy Water.

Rimmer (Alfred), Works by :

Our Old Country Towns. With over 50 Illusts. Sq. 8vo, cloth gilt, 10s. 6d.

Rambles Round Eton and Harrow. 50 Illusts. Sq. 8vo, cloth gilt, 10s. 6d.

About England with Dickens. With 58 Illusts. by ALFRED RIMMER and C. A. VANDERHOOF. Sq. 8vo, cl. gilt, 10s. 6d

Robinson (F W.), Novels by :

Crown 8vo, cloth extra. 3s. 6d. ; post 8vo, illustrated boards, 2s.

Women are Strange.
The Hands of Justice.

Robinson (Phil), Works by :

Crown 8vo, cloth extra, 7s. 6d. each.

The Poets' Birds.
The Poets' Beasts.
Poets' Natural History. [*Preparing.*

Robinson Crusoe : A beautiful reproduction of Major's Edition, with 37 Woodcuts and Two Steel Plates by GEORGE CRUIKSHANK, choicely printed. Crown 8vo, cloth extra, 7s. 6d. A few Large-Paper copies, printed on handmade paper, with India proofs of the Illustrations, price 36s.

Rochefoucauld's Maxims and Moral Reflections. With Notes, and an Introductory Essay by SAINTE-BEUVE. Post 8vo, cloth limp, 2s.

Roll of Battle Abbey, The ; or, A List of the Principal Warriors who came over from Normandy with William the Conqueror, and Settled in this Country, A.D. 1066-7. With the principal Arms emblazoned in Gold and Colours. Handsomely printed, 5s.

Rowley (Hon. Hugh), Works by :

Post 8vo, cloth limp, 2s. 6d. each.

Puniana : Riddles and Jokes. With numerous Illustrations.

More Puniana. Profusely Illustrated.

Runciman. — Skippers and Shellbacks : Stories, chiefly of the Sea. By JAMES RUNCIMAN. Post 8vo, illust. boards, 2s. ; cloth limp, 2s 6d

Russell (W. Clark), Works by :

Round the Galley-Fire. Crown 8vo, cloth extra, 6s. ; post 8vo, illustrated boards, 2s.

On the Fo'k'sle Head : A Collection of Yarns and Sea Descriptions. Crown 8vo, cloth extra, 6s.

Sala.—Gaslight and Daylight. By GEORGE AUGUSTUS SALA. Post 8vo, illustrated boards, 2s.

Sanson.—Seven Generations of Executioners : Memoirs of the Sanson Family (1688 to 1847). Edited by HENRY SANSON. Cr. 8vo, cl. ex. 3s. 6d.

Saunders (John), Novels by :

Crown 8vo, cloth extra, 3s. 6d. each ; post 8vo, illustrated boards, 2s. each.

Bound to the Wheel.
One Against the World.
Guy Waterman.
The Lion in the Path.
The Two Dreamers.

Saunders (Katharine), Novels by : Cr. 8vo, cloth extra, 3s. 6d. each ; post 8vo, illustrated boards, 2s. each.

Joan Merryweather.
Margaret and Elizabeth.
The High Mills.

Crown 8vo, cloth extra, 3s. 6d. each.

Heart Salvage. | Sebastian.
Gideon's Rock.

Science Gossip : An Illustrated Medium of Interchange for Students and Lovers of Nature. Edited by J. E. TAYLOR, F.L.S., &c. Devoted to Geology, Botany, Physiology, Chemistry, Zoology, Microscopy, Telescopy, Physiography, &c. Price 4d. Monthly ; or 5s. per year, post free. Each Number contains a Coloured Plate and numerous Woodcuts. Vols. I. to XIV. may be had at 7s. 6d. each ; and Vols. XV. to XX. (1884), at 5s. each. Cases for Binding, 1s. 6d each.

Scott's (Sir Walter) Marmion. A New Edition of this famous Poem, with over 100 new Illustrations by leading Artists. Small 4to, cloth extra, 16s.

"Secret Out" Series, The : Crown 8vo, cloth extra, profusely Illustrated, 4s. 6d. each.

The Secret Out : One Thousand Tricks with Cards, and other Recreations ; with Entertaining Experiments in Drawing-room or "White Magic." By W. H. CREMER. 300 Engravings.

The Pyrotechnist's Treasury ; or, Complete Art of Making Fireworks. By THOMAS KENTISH. With numerous Illustrations.

The Art of Amusing : A Collection of Graceful Arts, Games, Tricks, Puzzles, and Charades. By FRANK BELLEW. With 300 Illustrations.

Hanky-Panky : Very Easy Tricks, Very Difficult Tricks, White Magic, Sleight of Hand. Edited by W. H. CREMER. With 200 Illustrations.

SECRET OUT " SERIES, *continued—*

The Merry Circle: A Book of New Intellectual Games and Amusements. By CLARA BELLEW. With many Illustrations.

Magician's Own Book: Performances with Cups and Balls, Eggs, Hats, Handkerchiefs, &c. All from actual Experience. Edited by W. H. CREMER. 200 Illustrations.

Magic No Mystery: Tricks with Cards, Dice, Balls, &c., with fully descriptive Directions; the Art of Secret Writing; Training of Performing Animals, &c. With Coloured Frontis. and many Illusts.

Senior (William), Works by :
Travel and Trout in the Antipodes. Crown 8vo, cloth extra, 6s.

By Stream and Sea. Post 8vo, cloth limp, 2s. 6d.

Seven Sagas (The) of Prehistoric Man. By JAMES H. STODDART, Author of " The Village Life." Crown 8vo, cloth extra, 6s.

Shakespeare :
The First Folio Shakespeare.—MR. WILLIAM SHAKESPEARE's Comedies, Histories, and Tragedies. Published according to the true Originall Copies. London, Printed by ISAAC IAGGARD and ED. BLOUNT. 1623.—A Reproduction of the extremely rare original, in reduced facsimile, by a photographic process—ensuring the strictest accuracy in every detail. Small 8vo, half-Roxburghe, 7s. 6d.

The Lansdowne Shakespeare. Beautifully printed in red and black, in small but very clear type. With engraved facsimile of DROESHOUT's Portrait. Post 8vo, cloth extra, 7s. 6d.

Shakespeare for Children: Tales from Shakespeare. By CHARLES and MARY LAMB. With numerous Illustrations, coloured and plain, by J. MOYR SMITH. Cr. 4to, cl. gilt, 6s.

The Handbook of Shakespeare Music. Being an Account of 350 Pieces of Music, set to Words taken from the Plays and Poems of Shakespeare, the compositions ranging from the Elizabethan Age to the Present Time. By ALFRED ROFFE. 4to, half-Roxburghe, 7s.

A Study of Shakespeare. By ALGERNON CHARLES SWINBURNE. Crown 8vo, cloth extra, 8s.

The Dramatic Works of Shakespeare: The Text of the First Edition, carefully reprinted. Eight Vols., demy 8vo, cloth boards, 40s.

Shelley's Complete Works, in Four Vols., post 8vo, cloth limp, 8s.; or separately, 2s. each. Vol. I. contains his Early Poems, Queen Mab, &c., with an Introduction by LEIGH HUNT; Vol. II., his Later Poems, Laon and Cythna, &c.; Vol. III., Posthumous Poems, the Shelley Papers, &c.; Vol. IV., his Prose Works, including A Refutation of Deism, Zastrozzi, St. Irvyne, &c.

Sheridan :—
Sheridan's Complete Works, with Life and Anecdotes. Including his Dramatic Writings, printed from the Original Editions, his Works in Prose and Poetry, Translations, Speeches, Jokes, Puns, &c. With a Collection of Sheridaniana. Crown 8vo, cloth extra, gilt, with 10 full-page Tinted Illustrations, 7s. 6d.

Sheridan's Comedies: The Rivals, and The School for Scandal. Edited, with an Introduction and Notes to each Play, and a Biographical Sketch of Sheridan, by BRANDER MATTHEWS. With Decorative Vignettes and 10 full-page Illusts. Demy 8vo, half-parchment, 12s. 6d.

Short Sayings of Great Men. With Historical and Explanatory Notes by SAMUEL A. BENT, M.A. Demy 8vo, cloth extra, 7s. 6d.

Sidney's (Sir Philip) Complete Poetical Works, including all those in " Arcadia." With Portrait, Memorial-Introduction, Notes, &c., by the Rev. A. B. GROSART, D.D. Three Vols., crown 8vo, cloth boards, 18s.

Signboards: Their History. With Anecdotes of Famous Taverns and Remarkable Characters. By JACOB LARWOOD and JOHN CAMDEN HOTTEN. Crown 8vo, cloth extra, with 100 Illustrations, 7s. 6d.

Sims (George R.), Works by :
How the Poor Live. With 60 Illusts. by FRED. BARNARD. Large 4to, 1s.

Rogues and Vagabonds. Post 8vo, illust. boards, 2s.; cloth limp, 2s. 6d.

Sketchley.—A Match in the Dark. By ARTHUR SKETCHLEY. Post 8vo, illustrated boards, 2s.

Slang Dictionary, The: Etymological, Historical, and Anecdotal. Crown 8vo, cloth extra, gilt, 6s. 6d.

Smith (J. Moyr), Works by :
The Prince of Argolis: A Story of the Old Greek Fairy Time. By J. MOYR SMITH. Small 8vo, cloth extra, with 130 Illustrations, 3s. 6d.

SMITH'S (J. MOYR) WORKS, *continued—*
Tales of Old Thule. Collected and Illustrated by J. MOYR SMITH. Cr. 8vo, cloth gilt, profusely Illust., 6s.

The Wooing of the Water Witch: A Northern Oddity. By EVAN DALDORNE. Illustrated by J. MOYR SMITH. Small 8vo, cloth extra, 6s.

Society in London. By a FOREIGN RESIDENT. Eighth Edition. Crown 8vo, cloth extra, 6s.

Spalding.-Elizabethan Demonology: An Essay in Illustration of the Belief in the Existence of Devils, and the Powers possessed by Them. By T. ALFRED SPALDING, LL.B. Crown 8vo, cloth extra, 5s.

Spanish Legendary Tales. By Mrs. S. G. C. MIDDLEMORE, Author of "Round a Posada Fire." Crown 8vo, cloth extra, 6s.

Speight. — The Mysteries of Heron Dyke. By T. W. SPEIGHT. With a Frontispiece by M. ELLEN EDWARDS. Crown 8vo, cloth extra, 3s. 6d ; post 8vo, illustrated boards, 2s.

Spenser for Children. By M. H. TOWRY. With Illustrations by WALTER J MORGAN. Crown 4to, with Coloured Illustrations, cloth gilt, 6s.

Staunton.—Laws and Practice of Chess; Together with an Analysis of the Openings, and a Treatise on End Games. By HOWARD STAUNTON. Edited by ROBERT B. WORMALD. New Edition, small cr. 8vo, cloth extra, 5s.

Sterndale.—The Afghan Knife: A Novel. By ROBERT ARMITAGE STERNDALE. Cr. 8vo, cloth extra, 3s. 6d.; post 8vo, illustrated boards, 2s.

Stevenson (R. Louis), Works by :
Travels with a Donkey in the Cevennes. Frontispiece by WALTER CRANE. Post 8vo, cloth limp, 2s. 6d.
An Inland Voyage. With Front. by W. CRANE. Post 8vo, cl. lp., 2s. 6d.
Virginibus Puerisque, and other Papers. Crown 8vo, cloth extra, 6s.
Familiar Studies of Men and Books. Crown 8vo, cloth extra, 6s.
New Arabian Nights. Crown 8vo, cl. extra, 6s., post 8vo, illust. bds., 2s.
The Silverado Squatters. With Frontispiece. Cr. 8vo, cloth extra, 6s.
Prince Otto: A Romance. Crown 8vo, cloth extra, 6s. [*In preparation.*

St. John.—A Levantine Family. By BAYLE ST. JOHN. Post 8vo, illustrated boards, 2s.

Stoddard.—Summer Cruising in the South Seas. By CHARLES WARREN STODDARD. Illust. by WALLIS MACKAY. Crown 8vo, cl. extra, 3s. 6d.

St. Pierre.—Paul and Virginia, and The Indian Cottage. By BERNARDIN ST. PIERRE. Edited, with Life, by Rev. E. CLARKE. Post 8vo, cl. lp., 2s.

Stories from Foreign Novelists. With Notices of their Lives and Writings. By HELEN and ALICE ZIMMERN; and a Frontispiece. Crown 8vo, cloth extra, 3s. 6d.

Strutt's Sports and Pastimes of the People of England; including the Rural and Domestic Recreations, May Games, Mummeries, Shows, Processions, Pageants, and Pompous Spectacles, from the Earliest Period to the Present Time. With 140 Illustrations. Edited by WILLIAM HONE. Crown 8vo, cloth extra, 7s. 6d.

Suburban Homes (The) of London: A Residential Guide to Favourite London Localities, their Society, Celebrities, and Associations. With Notes on their Rental, Rates, and House Accommodation. With Map of Suburban London. Cr. 8vo cl. ex., 7s. 6d.

Swift's Choice Works, in Prose and Verse. With Memoir, Portrait, and Facsimiles of the Maps in the Original Edition of "Gulliver's Travels." Cr. 8vo, cloth extra, 7s. 6d.

Swinburne (Algernon C.), Works by :
The Queen Mother and Rosamond. Fcap. 8vo, 5s.
Atalanta in Calydon. Crown 8vo, 6s.
Chastelard. A Tragedy. Cr. 8vo, 7s.
Poems and Ballads. FIRST SERIES. Fcap. 8vo, 9s. Cr. 8vo, same price.
Poems and Ballads. SECOND SERIES. Fcap. 8vo, 9s. Cr. 8vo, same price.
Notes on Poems and Reviews. 8vo, 1s.
William Blake: A Critical Essay. With Facsimile Paintings. Demy 8vo, 16s.
Songs before Sunrise. Cr. 8vo, 10s 6d.
Bothwell: A Tragedy. Cr. 8vo, 12s. 6d.
George Chapman: An Essay. Crown 8vo, 7s.
Songs of Two Nations. Cr. 8vo, 6s.
Essays and Studies. Crown 8vo, 12s.
Erechtheus: A Tragedy. Cr. 8vo, 6s.
Note on an English Republican on the Muscovite Crusade. 8vo, 1s.
A Note on Charlotte Bronte. Crown 8vo, 6s.
A Study of Shakespeare. Cr. 8vo, 8s.
Songs of the Springtides. Cr. 8vo, 6s.
Studies in Song. Crown 8vo, 7s.

SWINBURNE'S (A. C.) WORKS, *continued*.
Mary Stuart: A Tragedy. Cr. 8vo, 8s.
Tristram of Lyonesse, and other Poems. Crown 8vo, 9s.
A Century of Roundels. Small 4to, 8s.
A Midsummer Holiday, and other Poems. Crown 8vo, 7s.
Marino Faliero: A Tragedy. Cr. 8vo. 6s.
Victor Hugo: Essays. Crown 8vo, 6s. [*Shortly.*

Symonds.—Wine, Women and Song: Mediæval Latin Students' Songs. Now first translated into English Verse, with Essay by J. ADDINGTON SYMONDS. Small 8vo, parchment, 6s.

Syntax's (Dr.) Three Tours: In Search of the Picturesque, in Search of Consolation, and in Search of a Wife. With the whole of ROWLANDSON's droll page Illustrations in Colours and a Life of the Author by J. C. HOTTEN. Med. 8vo. cloth extra, 7s. 6d.

Taine's History of English Literature. Translated by HENRY VAN LAUN. Four Vols., small 8vo, cloth boards, 30s.—POPULAR EDITION, Two Vols., crown 8vo, cloth extra, 15s.

Taylor (Dr. J. E., F.L.S.), Works by:
The Sagacity and Morality of Plants: A Sketch of the Life and Conduct of the Vegetable Kingdom. With Coloured Frontispiece and 100 Illusts. Crown 8vo, cl. extra, 7s. 6d.
Our Common British Fossils, and Where to Find Them: A Handbook for Students. Numerous Illustrations. Crown 8vo, cloth extra, 7s. 6d.

Taylor's (Bayard) Diversions of the Echo Club: Burlesques of Modern Writers. Post 8vo. cl. limp, 2s.

Taylor's (Tom) Historical Dramas: "Clancarty," "Jeanne Darc," "'Twixt Axe and Crown," "The Fool's Revenge," "Arkwright's Wife," "Anne Boleyn," "Plot and Passion." One Vol., cr. 8vo, cloth extra, 7s. 6d.
. The Plays may also be had separately, at 1s. each.

Tennyson (Lord): A Biographical Sketch. By H. J. JENNINGS. With a Photograph-Portrait. Crown 8vo, cloth extra, 6s.

Thackerayana: Notes and Anecdotes. Illustrated by Hundreds of Sketches by WILLIAM MAKEPEACE THACKERAY, depicting Humorous Incidents in his School-life, and Favourite Characters in the books of his every-day reading. With Coloured Frontispiece. Cr. 8vo, cl. extra, 7s. 6d.

Thomas (Bertha), Novels by.
Crown 8vo, cloth extra, 3s. 6d. each; post 8vo, illustrated boards, 2s. each.
Cressida. | Proud Maisie.
The Violin-Player.

Thomas (M.).—A Fight for Life: A Novel. By W. MOY THOMAS. Post 8vo, illustrated boards, 2s.

Thomson's Seasons and Castle of Indolence. With a Biographical and Critical Introduction by ALLAN CUNNINGHAM, and over 50 fine Illustrations on Steel and Wood. Crown 8vo, cloth extra, gilt edges, 7s. 6d.

Thornbury (Walter), Works by
Haunted London. Edited by EDWARD WALFORD, M.A. With Illustrations by F. W. FAIRHOLT, F.S.A. Crown 8vo, cloth extra, 7s. 6d.
The Life and Correspondence of J. M. W. Turner. Founded upon Letters and Papers furnished by his Friends and fellow Academicians. With numerous Illusts. in Colours, facsimiled from Turner's Original Drawings. Cr. 8vo, cl. extra, 7s. 6d.
Old Stories Re-told. Post 8vo, cloth limp, 2s. 6d.
Tales for the Marines. Post 8vo, illustrated boards, 2s.

Timbs (John), Works by:
The History of Clubs and Club Life in London. With Anecdotes of its Famous Coffee-houses, Hostelries, and Taverns. With numerous Illustrations. Cr. 8vo, cloth extra, 7s. 6d.
English Eccentrics and Eccentricities: Stories of Wealth and Fashion, Delusions, Impostures, and Fanatic Missions, Strange Sights and Sporting Scenes, Eccentric Artists, Theatrical Folks, Men of Letters, &c. With nearly 50 Illusts. Crown 8vo, cloth extra, 7s. 6d.

Torrens. — The Marquess Wellesley, Architect of Empire. An Historic Portrait. By W. M. TORRENS, M.P. Demy 8vo, cloth extra, 14s.

Trollope (Anthony), Novels by:
Crown 8vo, cloth extra, 3s. 6d. each; post 8vo, illustrated boards, 2s. each.
The Way We Live Now.
Kept in the Dark.
Frau Frohmann. | Marion Fay.
Mr. Scarborough's Family.
The Land-Leaguers.

Post 8vo, illustrated boards, 2s. each.
The Golden Lion of Granpere.
John Caldigate.
The American Senator.

Trollope (Frances E.), Novels by
Crown 8vo, cloth extra, 3s. 6d. ; post
8vo, illustrated boards, 2s.
Like Ships upon the Sea.
Mabel's Progress. ' Anne Furness.

Trollope (T. A.).—Diamond Cut
Diamond, and other Stories. By
T. ADOLPHUS TROLLOPE. Cr. 8vo, cl.
ex., 3s. 6d.; post 8vo. illust. boards. 2s.

Trowbridge.—Farnell's Folly :
A Novel. By J. T. TROWBRIDGE. Two
Vols., crown 8vo, 12s.

Turgenieff (Ivan), &c. Stories
from Foreign Novelists. Post 8vo,
illustrated boards, ?s.

Tytler (Sarah), Novels by :
Crown 8vo, cloth extra, 3s. 6d. each ;
post 8vo, illustrated boards, 2s. each.
What She Came Through.
The Bride's Pass.

Crown 8vo, cloth extra, 3s. 6d. each.
Saint Mungo's City.
Beauty and the Beast. With a
Frontispiece by P. MACNAB.

Buried Diamonds : A Novel. Three
Vols., crown 8vo. [Preparing.

Tytler (C. C. Fraser-). — Mis-
tress Judith : A Novel. By C. C.
FRASER-TYTLER. Cr. 8vo, cloth extra,
3s. 6d : post 8vo. illust boards, 2s.

Van Laun.— History of French
Literature. By H. VAN LAUN. Three
Vols., demy 8vo, cl. bds., 7s. 6d. each.

Villari.— A Double Bond : A
Story. By LINDA VILLARI. Fcap.
8vo, picture cover, 1s.

Walcott.— Church Work and
Life in English Minsters ; and the
English Student's Monasticon. By the
Rev. MACKENZIE E. C. WALCOTT, B.D.
Two Vols., crown 8vo, cloth extra,
with Map and Ground-Plans, 14s.

Walford (Edw., M.A.), Works by :
The County Families of the United
Kingdom. Containing Notices of
the Descent, Birth, Marriage, Educa-
tion, &c., of more than 12,000 dis-
tinguished Heads of Families, their
Heirs Apparent or Presumptive, the
Offices they hold or have held, their
Town and Country Addresses, Clubs,
&c. Twenty-fifth Annual Edition,
for 1885, cloth, full gilt, 50s.
The Shilling Peerage (1885). Con-
taining an Alphabetical List of the
House of Lords, Dates of Creation,
Lists of Scotch and Irish Peers,
Addresses, &c. 32mo, cloth, 1s.
Published annually.

WALFORD'S (EDW.) WORKS, continued—
The Shilling Baronetage (1885).
Containing an Alphabetical List of
the Baronets of the United Kingdom,
short Biographical Notices, Dates
of Creation, Addresses, &c. 32mo,
cloth, 1s. Published annually.
The Shilling Knightage (1885). Containing an Alphabetical List of the
Knights of the United Kingdom,
short Biographical Notices, Dates
of Creation, Addresses, &c. 32mo,
cloth, 1s. Published annually.
The Shilling House of Commons
(1885). Containing a List of all the
Members of Parliament, their Town
and Country Addresses, &c. 32mo,
cloth, 1s. Published annually.
The Complete Peerage, Baronetage, Knightage, and House of
Commons (1885). In One Volume,
royal 32mo, cloth extra, gilt edges,
5s. Published annually.
Haunted London. By WALTER
THORNBURY. Edited by EDWARD
WALFORD, M.A. With Illustrations
by F. W. FAIRHOLT, F.S.A. Crown
8vo, cloth extra, 7s. 6d.

Walton and Cotton's Complete
Angler ; or, The Contemplative Man's
Recreation ; being a Discourse of
Rivers, Fishponds, Fish and Fishing,
written by IZAAK WALTON ; and In-
structions how to Angle for a Trout or
Grayling in a clear Stream, by CHARLES
COTTON. With Original Memoirs and
Notes by Sir HARRIS NICOLAS, and
61 Copperplate Illustrations. Large
crown 8vo, cloth antique, 7s. 6d.

Wanderer's Library, The :
Crown 8vo, cloth extra, 3s. 6d. each.
Wanderings in Patagonia ; or, Life
among the Ostrich Hunters. By
JULIUS LEENHOLD. Illustrated.
Camp Notes : Stories of Sport and
Adventure in Asia, Africa, and
America. By FREDERICK BOYLE.
Savage Life. By FREDERICK BOYLE.
Merrie England in the Olden Time.
By GEORGE DANIEL. With Illustra-
tions by ROBT. CRUIKSHANK.
Circus Life and Circus Celebrities.
By THOMAS FROST.
The Lives of the Conjurers. By
THOMAS FROST.
The Old Showmen and the Old
London Fairs. By THOMAS FROST.
Low-Life Deeps. An Account of the
Strange Fish to be found there. By
JAMES GREENWOOD.
The Wilds of London. By JAMES
GREENWOOD.

WANDERER'S LIBRARY, THE, *continued*—

Tunis: The Land and the People. By the Chevalier de HESSE-WARTEGG. With 22 Illustrations.

The Life and Adventures of a Cheap Jack. By One of the Fraternity. Edited by CHARLES HINDLEY.

The World Behind the Scenes. By PERCY FITZGERALD.

Tavern Anecdotes and Sayings: Including the Origin of Signs, and Reminiscences connected with Taverns, Coffee Houses, Clubs, &c. By CHARLES HINDLEY. With Illusts.

The Genial Showman: Life and Adventures of Artemus Ward. By E. P HINGSTON. With a Frontispiece.

The Story of the London Parks. By JACOB LARWOOD. With Illusts.

London Characters. By HENRY MAYHEW. Illustrated.

Seven Generations of Executioners: Memoirs of the Sanson Family (1688 to 1847). Edited by HENRY SANSON.

Summer Cruising in the South Seas. By C. WARREN STODDARD. Illustrated by WALLIS MACKAY.

Warner.—A Roundabout Journey. By CHARLES DUDLEY WARNER, Author of "My Summer in a Garden." Crown 8vo, cloth extra, 6s.

Warrants, &c. :—

Warrant to Execute Charles I. An exact Facsimile, with the Fifty-nine Signatures, and corresponding Seals. Carefully printed on paper to imitate the Original, 22 in. by 14 in. Price 2s.

Warrant to Execute Mary Queen of Scots. An exact Facsimile, including the Signature of Queen Elizabeth, and a Facsimile of the Great Seal. Beautifully printed on paper to imitate the Original MS. Price 2s.

Magna Charta. An exact Facsimile of the Original Document in the British Museum, printed on fine plate paper, nearly 3 feet long by 2 feet wide, with the Arms and Seals emblazoned in Gold and Colours. Price 5s.

The Roll of Battle Abbey; or, A List of the Principal Warriors who came over from Normandy with William the Conqueror, and Settled in this Country, A.D. 1066-7. With the principal Arms emblazoned in Gold and Colours. Price 5s.

Weather, How to Foretell the, with the Pocket Spectroscope. By F. W. CORY, M.R.C.S. Eng., F.R.Met. Soc., &c. With 10 Illustrations. Crown 8vo. 1s ; cloth, 1s. 6d.

Westropp.—Handbook of Pottery and Porcelain ; or, History of those Arts from the Earliest Period. By HODDER M. WESTROPP. With numerous Illustrations, and a List of Marks. Crown 8vo cloth limp, 4s. 6d.

Williams (W. Mattieu, F.R.A.S.), Works by :

Science Notes. See the GENTLEMAN'S MAGAZINE. 1s. Monthly.

Science in Short Chapters. Crown 8vo, cloth extra, 7s. 6d.

A Simple Treatise on Heat. Crown 8vo, cloth limp, with Illusts., 2s. 6d.

The Chemistry of Cookery. Crown 8vo, cloth extra, 6s.

Wilson (Dr. Andrew, F.R.S.E.), Works by :

Chapters on Evolution: A Popular History of the Darwinian and Allied Theories of Development. Second Edition. Crown 8vo, cloth extra, with 259 Illustrations, 7s. 6d.

Leaves from a Naturalist's Notebook. Post 8vo, cloth limp, 2s. 6d.

Leisure-Time Studies, chiefly Biological. Third Edition, with a New Preface. Crown 8vo, cloth extra, with Illustrations, 6s.

Winter (J. S.), Stories by : Crown 8vo, cloth extra, 3s. 6d. each. post 8vo, illustrated boards, 2s. each.

Cavalry Life. | Regimental Legends.

Women of the Day : A Biographical Dictionary of Notable Contemporaries. By FRANCES HAYS. Crown 8vo, cloth extra, 5s.

Wood.—Sabina: A Novel. By Lady WOOD. Post 8vo, illust. bds., 2s.

Words, Facts, and Phrases: A Dictionary of Curious, Quaint, and Out-of-the-Way Matters. By ELIEZER EDWARDS. New and cheaper issue, cr. 8vo, cl. ex., 7s. 6d. ; half-bound, 9s.

Wright (Thomas), Works by :

Caricature History of the Georges. (The House of Hanover.) With 400 Pictures, Caricatures, Squibs, Broadsides, Window Pictures, &c. Crown 8vo, cloth extra, 7s. 6d.

History of Caricature and of the Grotesque in Art, Literature, Sculpture, and Painting. Profusely Illustrated by F. W. FAIRHOLT, F.S.A. Large post 8vo, cl. ex., 7s. 6d.

Yates (Edmund), Novels by : Post 8vo, illustrated boards, 2s. each.

Castaway. | The Forlorn Hope. Land at Last.

NEW THREE-VOLUME NOVELS IN THE PRESS.

OUIDA'S NEW NOVEL.
Othmar: A Novel. (A Sequel to "Princess Napraxine.") By OUIDA. Three Vols., crown 8vo.

CHRISTIE MURRAY'S NEW NOVEL
First Person Singular: A Novel. By D. CHRISTIE MURRAY, Author of "Joseph's Coat," &c. Three Vols., crown 8vo.

JUSTIN McCARTHY'S NEW NOVEL
Camiola: A Novel. By JUSTIN McCARTHY, Author of "Dear Lady Disdain," &c. Three Vols., crown 8vo.

GRANT ALLEN'S NEW NOVEL.
Babylon: A Novel. By GRANT ALLEN, Author of "Philistia," "Strange Stories," &c. With 12 Illustrations by P. MACNAB. Three Vols., crown 8vo.

SARAH TYTLER'S NEW NOVEL.
Buried Diamonds: A Novel. By SARAH TYTLER, Author of "Saint Mungo's City," &c. Three Vols., crown 8vo.

MISS O'HANLON'S NEW NOVEL.
The Unforeseen: A Novel. By ALICE O'HANLON. Three Vols., crown 8vo.

THE PICCADILLY NOVELS.

Popular Stories by the Best Authors. LIBRARY EDITIONS, many Illustrated, crown 8vo, cloth extra, 3s. 6d. each.

BY MRS. ALEXANDER.
Maid, Wife, or Widow?

BY GRANT ALLEN.
Philistia.

BY BASIL.
A Drawn Game.
"The Wearing of the Green."

BY W. BESANT & JAMES RICE.
Ready-Money Mortiboy.
My Little Girl.
The Case of Mr. Lucraft.
This Son of Vulcan.
With Harp and Crown.
The Golden Butterfly.
By Celia's Arbour.
The Monks of Thelema.
'Twas in Trafalgar's Bay.
The Seamy Side.
The Ten Years' Tenant.
The Chaplain of the Fleet.
Dorothy Forster.

BY WALTER BESANT.
All Sorts and Conditions of Men.
The Captains' Room.
All in a Garden Fair.
Dorothy Forster.
Uncle Jack.

BY ROBERT BUCHANAN.
A Child of Nature.
God and the Man.
The Shadow of the Sword.
The Martyrdom of Madeline.
Love Me for Ever.
Annan Water. | The New Abelard.
Matt. | Foxglove Manor.

BY MRS. H. LOVETT CAMERON.
Deceivers Ever. | Juliet's Guardian.

BY MORTIMER COLLINS.
Sweet Anne Page.
Transmigration.
From Midnight to Midnight.

MORTIMER & FRANCES COLLINS.
Blacksmith and Scholar.
The Village Comedy.
You Play me False.

BY WILKIE COLLINS.
Antonina.
Basil.
Hide and Seek.
The Dead Secret.
Queen of Hearts.
My Miscellanies.
Woman in White.
The Moonstone.
Man and Wife.
Poor Miss Finch.
Miss or Mrs. ?
New Magdalen.
The Frozen Deep.
The Law and the Lady.
The Two Destinies.
Haunted Hotel.
The Fallen Leaves.
Jezebel's Daughter.
The Black Robe.
Heart and Science.
I Say No.

BY DUTTON COOK.
Paul Foster's Daughter.

BY WILLIAM CYPLES.
Hearts of Gold.

BY ALPHONSE DAUDET.
Port Salvation.

BY JAMES DE MILLE.
A Castle in Spain.

BY J. LEITH DERWENT.
Our Lady of Tears. | Circe's Lovers.

PICCADILLY NOVELS, *continued—*

BY M. BETHAM-EDWARDS.
Felicia. | Kitty.

BY MRS. ANNIE EDWARDES.
Archie Lovell.

BY R. E. FRANCILLON.
Olympia. | One by One.
Queen Cophetua. | A Real Queen.

Prefaced by Sir BARTLE FRERE.
Pandurang Hari.

BY EDWARD GARRETT.
The Capel Girls.

BY CHARLES GIBBON.
Robin Gray. | For Lack of Gold.
In Love and War.
What will the World Say?
In Honour Bound.
Queen of the Meadow.
The Flower of the Forest.
A Heart's Problem.
The Braes of Yarrow.
The Golden Shaft. | Of High Degree.
Fancy Free. | Loving a Dream.

BY HALL CAINE.
The Shadow of a Crime.

BY THOMAS HARDY.
Under the Greenwood Tree.

BY JULIAN HAWTHORNE.
Garth. | Ellice Quentin.
Sebastian Strome.
Prince Saroni's Wife.
Dust. | Fortune's Fool.
Beatrix Randolph.
Miss Cadogna.
Love—or a Name.

BY SIR A. HELPS.
Ivan de Biron.

BY MRS. CASHEL HOEY.
The Lover's Creed.

BY MRS. ALFRED HUNT.
Thornicroft's Model.
The Leaden Casket.
Self-Condemned.

BY JEAN INGELOW.
Fated to be Free.

BY HARRIETT JAY.
The Queen of Connaught

BY HENRY KINGSLEY.
Number Seventeen.
Oakshott Castle.

PICCADILLY NOVELS, *continued—*

BY E. LYNN LINTON.
Patricia Kemball.
Atonement of Leam Dundas.
The World Well Lost.
Under which Lord?
With a Silken Thread.
The Rebel of the Family
"My Love!" | Ione.

BY HENRY W. LUCY.
Gideon Fleyce.

BY JUSTIN McCARTHY, M.P.
The Waterdale Neighbours.
My Enemy's Daughter.
Linley Rochford. | A Fair Saxon.
Dear Lady Disdain.
Miss Misanthrope. | Donna Quixote.
The Comet of a Season.
Maid of Athens.

BY GEORGE MACDONALD.
Paul Faber, Surgeon.
Thomas Wingfold, Curate.

BY MRS. MACDONELL.
Quaker Cousins.

BY KATHARINE S. MACQUOID.
Lost Rose | The Evil Eye.

BY FLORENCE MARRYAT.
Open! Sesame! | Written in Fire.

BY JEAN MIDDLEMASS.
Touch and Go.

BY D. CHRISTIE MURRAY
Life's Atonement. | Coals of Fire.
Joseph's Coat. | Val Strange.
A Model Father. | Hearts.
By the Gate of the Sea
The Way of the World.
A Bit of Human Nature.

BY MRS. OLIPHANT.
Whiteladies.

BY MARGARET A. PAUL.
Gentle and Simple.

BY JAMES PAYN.
Lost Sir Massing- | Carlyon's Year.
berd. | A Confidential
Best of Husbands | Agent.
Fallen Fortunes. | From Exile.
Halves. | A Grape from a
Walter's Word. | Thorn.
What He Cost Her | For Cash Only.
Less Black than | Some Private
We're Painted. | Views.
By Proxy. | Kit: A Memory.
High Spirits. | The   Canon's
Under One Roof. | Ward.

PICCADILLY NOVELS, *continued—*

BY E. C. PRICE.
Valentina. | The Foreigners.
Mrs. Lancaster's Rival.

BY CHARLES READE, D.C.L.
It Is Never Too Late to Mend.
Hard Cash.
Peg Woffington.
Christie Johnstone.
Griffith Gaunt. | Foul Play.
The Double Marriage.
Love Me Little, Love Me Long.
The Cloister and the Hearth.
The Course of True Love.
The Autobiography of a Thief.
Put Yourself in His Place.
A Terrible Temptation.
The Wandering Heir. | A Simpleton.
A Woman-Hater. | Readiana.
Singleheart and Doubleface.
The Jilt.
Good Stories of Men and other
  Animals.

BY MRS. J. H. RIDDELL.
Her Mother's Darling.
Prince of Wales's Garden-Party.
Weird Stories.

BY F. W. ROBINSON.
Women are Strange.
The Hands of Justice.

BY JOHN SAUNDERS.
Bound to the Wheel.
Guy Waterman.
Two Dreamers.
One Against the World.
The Lion in the Path.

PICCADILLY NOVELS, *continued—*

BY KATHARINE SAUNDERS.
Joan Merryweather.
Margaret and Elizabeth.
Gideon's Rock. | Heart Salvage.
The High Mills. | Sebastian.

BY T. W. SPEIGHT.
The Mysteries of Heron Dyke.

BY R. A. STERNDALE.
The Afghan Knife.

BY BERTHA THOMAS.
Proud Maisie. | Cressida.
The Violin-Player.

BY ANTHONY TROLLOPE.
The Way we Live Now.
Frau Frohmann. | Marion Fay.
Kept in the Dark.
Mr. Scarborough's Family.
The Land-Leaguers.

BY FRANCES E. TROLLOPE.
Like Ships upon the Sea.
Anne Furness.
Mabel's Progress.

BY T. A. TROLLOPE.
Diamond Cut Diamond.

By IVAN TURGENIEFF and Others.
Stories from Foreign Novelists.

BY SARAH TYTLER.
What She Came Through.
The Bride's Pass.
Saint Mungo's City.
Beauty and the Beast.

BY C. C. FRASER-TYTLER.
Mistress Judith.

BY J. S. WINTER.
Cavalry Life.
Regimental Legends.

CHEAP EDITIONS OF POPULAR NOVELS.
Post 8vo, illustrated boards, 2s. each.

BY EDMOND ABOUT.
The Fellah.

BY HAMILTON AÏDÉ.
Carr of Carrlyon. | Confidences.

BY MRS. ALEXANDER.
Maid, Wife, or Widow?
Valerie's Fate.

BY SHELSLEY BEAUCHAMP.
Grantley Grange.

BY W. BESANT & JAMES RICE.
Ready-Money Mortiboy.
With Harp and Crown.
This Son of Vulcan. | My Little Girl.
The Case of Mr. Lucraft.

BY BESANT AND RICE, *continued—*
The Golden Butterfly.
By Celia's Arbour.
The Monks of Thelema.
'Twas in Trafalgar's Bay.
The Seamy Side.
The Ten Years' Tenant.
The Chaplain of the Fleet.

BY WALTER BESANT.
All Sorts and Conditions of Men.
The Captains' Room.
All in a Garden Fair.

BY FREDERICK BOYLE.
Camp Notes. | Savage Life.
Chronicles of No-man's Land.

CHEAP POPULAR NOVELS, *continued*—

BY BRET HARTE.

An Heiress of Red Dog.
The Luck of Roaring Camp.
Californian Stories.
Gabriel Conroy. | Flip.
Maruja.

BY ROBERT BUCHANAN.

The Shadow of the Sword.	The Martyrdom of Madeline.
A Child of Nature.	Annan Water.
God and the Man.	The New Abelard.
Love Me for Ever.	

BY MRS. BURNETT.

Surly Tim.

BY MRS. LOVETT CAMERON.

Deceivers Ever. | Juliet's Guardian.

BY MACLAREN COBBAN.

The Cure of Souls.

BY C. ALLSTON COLLINS.

The Bar Sinister.

BY WILKIE COLLINS.

Antonina.	Miss or Mrs.?
Basil.	New Magdalen.
Hide and Seek.	The Frozen Deep.
The Dead Secret.	Law and the Lady.
Queen of Hearts.	The Two Destinies
My Miscellanies.	Haunted Hotel.
Woman in White.	The Fallen Leaves.
The Moonstone.	Jezebel's Daughter
Man and Wife.	The Black Robe.
Poor Miss Finch.	Heart and Science

BY MORTIMER COLLINS.

Sweet Anne Page. | From Midnight to
Transmigration. | Midnight.
A Fight with Fortune.

MORTIMER & FRANCES COLLINS.

Sweet and Twenty. | Frances.
Blacksmith and Scholar.
The Village Comedy.
You Play me False.

BY DUTTON COOK.

Leo. | Paul Foster's Daughter.

BY C. EGBERT CRADDOCK.

The Prophet of the Great Smoky Mountains.

BY WILLIAM CYPLES.

Hearts of Gold.

BY ALPHONSE DAUDET.

The Evangelist; or, Port Salvation.

BY DE MILLE.

A Castle in Spain.

BY J. LEITH DERWENT.

Our Lady of Tears. | Circe's Lovers.

BY CHARLES DICKENS.

Sketches by Boz. | Oliver Twist.
Pickwick Papers. | Nicholas Nickleby

CHEAP POPULAR NOVELS, *continued*—

BY MRS. ANNIE EDWARDES.

A Point of Honour. | Archie Lovell.

BY M. BETHAM-EDWARDS.

Felicia. | Kitty.

BY EDWARD EGGLESTON.

Roxy.

BY PERCY FITZGERALD.

Bella Donna. | Never Forgotten.
The Second Mrs. Tillotson.
Polly.
Seventy-five Brooke Street.
The Lady of Brantome.

BY ALBANY DE FONBLANQUE.

Filthy Lucre.

BY R. E. FRANCILLON.

Olympia. | Queen Cophetua.
One by One. | A Real Queen.

Prefaced by Sir H. BARTLE FRERE.
Pandurang Hari.

BY HAIN FRISWELL.

One of Two.

BY EDWARD GARRETT.

The Capel Girls.

BY CHARLES GIBBON.

Robin Gray.	Queen of the Meadow.
For Lack of Gold.	
What will the World Say?	The Flower of the Forest.
In Honour Bound.	A Heart's Problem
The Dead Heart.	The Braes of Yarrow.
In Love and War.	
For the King.	The Golden Shaft.
In Pastures Green	Of High Degree.

BY WILLIAM GILBERT.

Dr. Austin's Guests.
The Wizard of the Mountain.
James Duke.

BY JAMES GREENWOOD.

Dick Temple.

BY ANDREW HALLIDAY.

Every-Day Papers.

BY LADY DUFFUS HARDY.

Paul Wynter's Sacrifice.

BY THOMAS HARDY.

Under the Greenwood Tree.

BY JULIAN HAWTHORNE.

Garth. | Sebastian Strome
Ellice Quentin. | Dust.
Prince Saroni's Wife.
Fortune's Fool. | Beatrix Randolph.

BY SIR ARTHUR HELPS.

Ivan de Biron.

BY TOM HOOD.

A Golden Heart.

BY MRS. GEORGE HOOPER.

The House of Raby.

CHEAP POPULAR NOVELS, *continued—*

BY VICTOR HUGO.
The Hunchback of Notre Dame.

BY MRS. ALFRED HUNT.
Thornicroft's Model.
The Leaden Casket.
Self-Condemned.

BY JEAN INGELOW.
Fated to be Free.

BY HARRIETT JAY.
The Dark Colleen.
The Queen of Connaught.

BY HENRY KINGSLEY.
Oakshott Castle. | Number Seventeen

BY E. LYNN LINTON.
Patricia Kemball.
The Atonement of Leam Dundas.
The World Well Lost.
Under which Lord?
With a Silken Thread.
The Rebel of the Family.
"My Love!" | Ione.

BY HENRY W. LUCY.
Gideon Fleyce.

BY JUSTIN McCARTHY, M.P.
Dear LadyDisdain | Linley Rochford.
The Waterdale | MissMisanthrope
Neighbours. | Donna Quixote.
My Enemy's | The Comet of a
Daughter. | Season.
A Fair Saxon. | Maid of Athens.

BY GEORGE MACDONALD.
Paul Faber, Surgeon.
Thomas Wingfold, Curate.

BY MRS. MACDONELL.
Quaker Cousins.

BY KATHARINE S. MACQUOID.
The Evil Eye. | Lost Rose.

BY W. H. MALLOCK.
The New Republic.

BY FLORENCE MARRYAT.
Open! Sesame! | A Little Stepson.
A Harvest of Wild | Fighting the Air.
Oats. | Written in Fire.

BY J. MASTERMAN.
Half-a-dozen Daughters.

BY JEAN MIDDLEMASS.
Touch and Go. | Mr. Dorillion.

BY D. CHRISTIE MURRAY.
ALife'sAtonement | By the Gate of the
A Model Father, | Sea.
Joseph's Coat. | Val Strange.
Coals of Fire. | Hearts.

BY MRS. OLIPHANT.
Whiteladies.

BY MRS. ROBERT O'REILLY.
Phœbe's Fortunes.

CHEAP POPULAR NOVELS, *continued—*

BY OUIDA.
Held in Bondage. | TwoLittleWooden
Strathmore. | Shoes.
Chandos. | In a Winter City.
Under Two Flags. | Ariadne.
Idalia. | Friendship.
Cecil Castle- | Moths.
maine. | Pipistrello.
Tricotrin. | A Village Com-
Puck. | mune.
Folle Farine. | Bimbi.
A Dog of Flanders. | In Maremma.
Pascarel. | Wanda.
Signa. | Frescoes.

BY MARGARET AGNES PAUL.
Gentle and Simple.

BY JAMES PAYN.
Lost Sir Massing- | Like Father, Like
berd. | Son.
A Perfect Trea- | A Marine Resi-
sure. | dence.
Bentinck's Tutor. | Married Beneath
Murphy's Master. | Him.
A County Family. | Mirk Abbey.
At Her Mercy. | Not Wooed, but
A Woman's Ven- | Won.
geance. | Less Black than
Cecil's Tryst. | We're Painted.
Clyffards of Clyffe | By Proxy.
The FamilyScape- | Under One Roof.
grace. | High Spirits.
Foster Brothers. | Carlyon's Year.
Found Dead. | A Confidential
Best of Husbands. | Agent.
Walter's Word. | Some Private
Halves. | Views.
Fallen Fortunes. | From Exile.
What He Cost Her | A Grape from a
HumorousStories | Thorn.
Gwendoline's Har- | For Cash Only.
vest. | Kit: A Memory.
£200 Reward. | The Canons Ward

BY EDGAR A. POE.
The Mystery of Marie Roget.

BY E. C. PRICE.
Valentina. | The Foreigners.
Mrs. Lancaster's Rival.

BY CHARLES READE.
It is Never Too Late to Mend
Hard Cash. | Peg Woffington.
Christie Johnstone.
Griffith Gaunt.
Put Yourself in His Place.
The Double Marriage.
Love Me Little, Love Me Long.
Foul Play.
The Cloister and the Hearth.
The Course of True Love.
Autobiography of a Thief.
A Terrible Temptation.
The Wandering Heir.

CHEAP POPULAR NOVELS, *continued—*
By CHARLES READE, *continued.*
A Simpleton. | A Woman-Hater.
Readiana. | The Jilt.
Singleheart and Doubleface.
Good Stories of Men and other Animals.

BY MRS. J. H. RIDDELL.
Her Mother's Darling.
Prince of Wales's Garden Party.
Weird Stories.
The Uninhabited House.
Fairy Water.

BY F. W. ROBINSON.
Women are Strange.
The Hands of Justice.

BY JAMES RUNCIMAN.
Skippers and Shellbacks.

BY W. CLARK RUSSELL.
Round the Galley Fire.

BY BAYLE ST. JOHN.
A Levantine Family.

BY GEORGE AUGUSTUS SALA.
Gaslight and Daylight.

BY JOHN SAUNDERS.
Bound to the Wheel.
One Against the World.
Guy Waterman.
The Lion in the Path.
Two Dreamers.

BY KATHARINE SAUNDERS.
Joan Merryweather.
Margaret and Elizabeth.
The High Mills.

BY GEORGE R. SIMS.
Rogues and Vagabonds.

BY ARTHUR SKETCHLEY.
A Match in the Dark.

BY T. W. SPEIGHT.
The Mysteries of Heron Dyke.

BY R. A. STERNDALE.
The Afghan Knife.

BY R. LOUIS STEVENSON.
New Arabian Nights.

BY BERTHA THOMAS.
Cressida. | Proud Maisie.
The Violin-Player.

BY W. MOY THOMAS.
A Fight for Life.

BY WALTER THORNBURY.
Tales for the Marines.

BY T. ADOLPHUS TROLLOPE.
Diamond Cut Diamond.

BY ANTHONY TROLLOPE.
The Way We Live Now.
The American Senator.
Frau Frohmann.

CHEAP POPULAR NOVELS, *continued—*
By ANTHONY TROLLOPE, *continued.*
Marion Fay.
Kept in the Dark.
Mr. Scarborough's Family.
The Land-Leaguers.
The Golden Lion of Granpere.
John Caldigate.

By FRANCES ELEANOR TROLLOPE
Like Ships upon the Sea.
Anne Furness.
Mabel's Progress.

BY IVAN TURGENIEFF, &c.
Stories from Foreign Novelists.

BY MARK TWAIN.
Tom Sawyer.
An Idle Excursion.
A Pleasure Trip on the Continent of Europe.
A Tramp Abroad.
The Stolen White Elephant.

BY C. C. FRASER-TYTLER.
Mistress Judith.

BY SARAH TYTLER.
What She Came Through.
The Bride's Pass.

BY J. S. WINTER.
Cavalry Life. | Regimental Legends.

BY LADY WOOD.
Sabina.

BY EDMUND YATES.
Castaway. | The Forlorn Hope.
Land at Last.

ANONYMOUS.
Paul Ferroll.
Why Paul Ferroll Killed his Wife.

Fcap. 8vo, picture covers, 1s. each.
Jeff Briggs's Love Story. By BRET HARTE.
The Twins of Table Mountain. By BRET HARTE.
Mrs. Gainsborough's Diamonds. By JULIAN HAWTHORNE.
Kathleen Mavourneen. By Author of "That Lass o' Lowrie's."
Lindsay's Luck. By the Author of "That Lass o' Lowrie's."
Pretty Polly Pemberton. By the Author of "That Lass o' Lowrie's."
Trooping with Crows. By Mrs. PIRKIS.
The Professor's Wife. By LEONARD GRAHAM.
A Double Bond. By LINDA VILLARI.
Esther's Glove. By R. E. FRANCILLON.
The Garden that Paid the Rent. By TOM JERROLD.
Curly. By JOHN COLEMAN. Illustrated by J. C. DOLLMAN.
Beyond the Gates. By E. S. PHELPS.

THE BEST REMEDY FOR INDIGESTION.

DR. J. COLLIS BROWNE'S
Original & Only Genuine. CHLORODYNE

Coughs,

Colds,

Asthma,

Bronchitis,

Diarrhœa

Cholera,

ETC.

COUGHS,
COLDS,
ASTHMA,
BRONCHITIS.

IS THE
GREAT SPECIFIC FOR
CHOLERA, DYSENTERY
DIARRHŒA.

We have never used any other form of this medicine than Collis Browne's, from a firm conviction that it is decidedly the best, and also from a sense of duty we owe to the profession and the public, as we are of opinion that the substitution of any other than Collis Browne's is a deliberate breach of faith on the part of the chemist to prescriber and patient alike.—We are, Sir, faithfully yours, SYMES & CO., Members of the Pharm. Society of Great Britain, His Excellency the Viceroy's Chemists.

Dr. J. COLLIS BROWNE'S CHLORODYNE is the TRUE PALLIATIVE in NEURALGIA, GOUT, CANCER, TOOTHACHE, RHEUMATISM.

Dr. J. COLLIS BROWNE'S CHLORODYNE rapidly cuts short all attacks of EPILEPSY, SPASMS, COLIC, PALPITATION, HYSTERIA.

IMPORTANT CAUTION.—The IMMENSE SALE of this REMEDY has given rise to many UNSCRUPULOUS IMITATIONS. N.B.—EVERY BOTTLE OF GENUINE CHLORODYNE BEARS on the GOVERNMENT STAMP the NAME of the INVENTOR.

Dr. J. COLLIS BROWNE. SOLD IN BOTTLES, 1s. 1½d., 2s. 9d., & 4s. 6d. by all Chemists. SOLE MANUFACTURER, J. T. DAVENPORT, 33, GREAT RUSSELL STREET, W.C

Dr. J. COLLIS BROWNE'S CHLORODYNE.—Dr. J. C. BROWNE (late Army Medical Staff) DISCOVERED a REMEDY to denote which he coined the word CHLORODYNE. Dr. Browne is the SOLE INVENTOR, and, as the composition of Chlorodyne cannot possibly be discovered by Analysis (organic substances defying elimination), and since the formula has never been published, it is evident that any statement to the effect that a compound is identical with Dr. Browne's Chlorodyne must be false.

This Caution is necessary, as many persons deceive purchasers by false representations.

The GENERAL BOARD of HEALTH, London, REPORT that it ACTS as a CHARM, one dose generally sufficient. Dr. GIBBON, Army Medical Staff, Calcutta, states: "2 DOSES COMPLETELY CURED ME of DIARRHŒA."

From Symes & Co., Pharmaceutical Chemists, Medical Hall, Simla.—
January 5, 1880.

To J. T. Davenport, 33, Great Russell Street, Bloomsbury, London.

DEAR SIR,—We embrace this opportunity of congratulating you upon the widespread reputation this justly-esteemed medicine has earned for itself, not only in Hindostan, but all over the East. As a remedy of general utility, we much question whether a better is imported into the country, and we shall be glad to hear of its finding a place in every Anglo-Indian home. The other brands, we are happy to say, are now relegated to the native bazaars, & judging from their sale, we fancy their sojourn there will be but evanescent. We could multiply instances *ad infinitum* of the extraordinary efficacy of Dr. COLLIS BROWNE'S CHLORODYNE in Diarrhœa and Dysentery, Spasms, Cramps, and the Vomiting of Pregnancy, &c.

Dr. J. COLLIS BROWNE'S CHLORODYNE.—Vice Chancellor Sir W. PAGE WOOD stated publicly in Court that Dr. J. COLLIS BROWNE was UNDOUBTEDLY the INVENTOR of CHLORODYNE, that the whole story of the defendant Freeman was deliberately untrue, and he regretted to say it had been sworn to. See *The Times*, July 13th, 1864.

Dr. J. COLLIS BROWNE'S CHLORODYNE is a liquid medicine which assuages PAIN of EVERY KIND, affords a calm, refreshing sleep, WITHOUT HEADACHE, and INVIGORATES the nervous system when exhausted of cured under our personal observation in Choleraic Diarrhœa, and even in the more terrible forms of Cholera itself, we have witnessed its surprisingly controlling power.

PEARS'
SOAP

A SPECIALTY FOR THE COMPLEXION

Recommended by SIR ERASMUS WILSON, F.R.S., *late President of the Royal College of Surgeons of England, as*

"The most refreshing and agreeable of balms for the skin."

MDME. ADELINA PATTI writes :—" I have found PEARS' SOAP *matchless for the hands and complexion.*"

MRS. LANGTRY writes :—" Since using PEARS' SOAP for the hands and complexion, *I have discarded all others.*"

MDME. MARIE ROZE (*Prima Donna, Her Majesty's Theatre*) writes :—" For preserving the complexion, keeping the skin soft, free from redness and roughness, and the hands in nice condition, PEARS' SOAP *is the finest preparation in the world.*"

MISS MARY ANDERSON writes :—" I have used PEARS' SOAP for two years with the greatest satisfaction, for *I find it the very best*"

PEARS' SOAP—SOLD EVERYWHERE